Liturgy, O
and the Law

C000184395

RUPERT D. H. BURSELL

QC, LLB, MA, D Phil, Of Lincoln's Inn
Clerk in Holy Orders
Chancellor of the Dioceses of Durham and St Albans
Deputy Chancellor of the Diocese of York
One time Chancellor of the Diocese of Bath and Wells

CLARENDON PRESS • OXFORD
1996

Oxford University Press, Walton Street, Oxford OX2 6DP
Oxford New York
Athens Auckland Bangkok Bombay
Calcutta Cape Town Dar es Salaam Delhi
Florence Hong Kong Istanbul Karachi
Kuala Lumpur Madras Madrid Melbourne
Mexico City Nairobi Paris Singapore
Taipei Tokyo Toronto
and associated companies in
Berlin Ibadan

Oxford is a trade mark of Oxford University Press

Published in the United States
by Oxford University Press Inc., New York

British Library Cataloguing in Publication Data
Data available

Library of Congress Cataloging in Publication Data
Bursell, Rupert.
Liturgy, order and the Law / Rupert D.H. Bursell.
p. cm.
1. Ecclesiastical law—Great Britain. 2. Liturgies (Canon law)
I. Title.
KD8642.B87 1996
262.9'0941—dc20 95-26852
ISBN 0–19–826250–7.—ISBN 0–19–826249–3 (pbk.)

1 3 5 7 9 10 8 6 4 2

Typeset by Graphicraft Typesetters Ltd. Hong Kong
Printed in Great Britain
on acid-free paper by
Bookcraft Ltd., Midsomer Norton, Avon

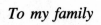

To my family

PREFACE

At the present time there is a renewed interest in, and appreciation of the need for, ecclesiastical law which has been particularly fostered by the Ecclesiastical Law Society. When a working party on the law relating to liturgy was suggested within the Society it seemed to me that the complications were such that it was necessary at first for one person alone to grapple with the subject. I also felt that as a priest and lawyer I should perhaps myself make the attempt. This is the result.

I have tried throughout to remember that liturgy is concerned with the worship of God. Yet in spite of that – some might say *because* of that – it is necessary to have rules. Indeed, as liturgical law is also concerned with the legal status of persons within the civil society, it is essential that those rules are understood by those involved. I have therefore tried to make what I have written intelligible not only to clergy and lawyers but to anyone involved with taking services. Indeed, in these days when the clergy may once again be faced with the possibility of being sued in the civil courts for a delay in celebrating a wedding or taking a funeral, the advisability of understanding the law becomes even more apparent. I hope in some measure that this book will assist in that understanding.

I am most grateful to Lord Habgood for agreeing to write a Foreword and to Peter Moore for all his hard work on Tables and Index.

Finally, I wish to acknowledge the debts that I owe to Professor Parker and Professor Lasok QC at Exeter University, to the Rt Rev Eric Kemp, Bishop of Chichester, and the late Rev Dr E Garth Moore and to His Honour Judge Peter Fallon QC, Recorder of Bristol. Without them my knowledge of the law would have been much diminished. My debt to my wife I cannot adequately express: without her this book would never have been written.

Rupert Bursell

FOREWORD

This is a timely book. As the Church of England embarks on a further round of liturgical revision, it is important for those involved to understand the current state of liturgical law. This is not easy to discover or interpret, and Chancellor Bursell has done a first rate job in bringing together an enormous range of material in an accessible form.

There are those who question the need for any such laws, and there are parishes where little attention is in practice paid to them. The growth of informal worship, intended mainly for the unchurched, has put a further strain on the notion of legality in worship, despite attempts by the House of Bishops to bring it under control by authorising flexible guidelines. There is also plenty of evidence from the past hundred years about the perils of trying to impose the law in matters which deeply affect peoples' consciences.

Nevertheless the Church of England remains committed to lawfully ordered worship, and rightly so. Worship uniquely expresses the mind of the church and encapsulates its doctrine. The Book of Common Prayer and its supplements provide the clearest indication of what the Church of England is, and to undermine the legal basis of these would be to erode its identity. Furthermore as a national church it has a responsibility to protect worshippers against the idiosyncrasies of individual clergy and parishes by prescribing forms and standards which are common to all.

If the law is to be obeyed, it needs to be known, understood and presented in ways which make sense in today's circumstances. Dr Bursell has brought to this task experience both as an ecclesiastical lawyer and as a clergyman, and has provided an indispensable resource. He is to be congratulated on this very thorough survey of a complex field.

John Habgood

CONTENTS

TABLE OF CASES

TABLE OF STATUTES AND MEASURES

TABLE OF CANONS

1

AUTHORISED SERVICES

Forms of service are now primarily governed by the Church of England (Worship and Doctrine) Measure 1974, and Canons made thereunder. Only the Book of Common Prayer and other forms of service authorised under Canon B 1 may lawfully be used. Forms of service may in particular circumstances be authorised by the General Synod, Convocations, archbishops, diocesan bishops and ministers having the cure of souls.

The rigorist interpretation of the rubrics no longer applies and, unless it is itself a statement of doctrine or indicative of Church order, a rubric is now to be treated as a mere directive.

Only those duly authorised may take services or preach, although in particular instances these may include members of the laity and members of other denominations. In certain circumstances Anglican ministers may participate in services of other denominations.

The object of the Act of Uniformity in 1662 had been to produce 'an universal agreement in the public worship of Almighty God'[1]. Nonetheless, over the years the provisions of the Book of Common Prayer came to be seen as 'far too rigid, and in certain cases completely inapplicable to modern conditions'[2]. The first attempt at revision, the Deposited Book, was rejected by Parliament in 1928[3]. However, the matter was ultimately[4] addressed in 1974 by the Church of England

---

[1] Section 2. See *Martin* v. *Mackonochie* (1868) LR 2 PC 365 at p. 383 *per* Lord Cairns.

[2] Stephen Neill, *Anglicanism* (Penguin) (3rd ed., 1965) at p. 394. See, too, *Wylde* v. *Attorney-General for New South Wales ex rel. Ashelford* (1948) 78 CLR 224 at p. 256 *per* Latham CJ: 'The Church of England is not a congregational church. The members of the congregation worshipping in a particular church building are not at liberty to adopt any doctrine or ritual which commends itself to them and still to describe themselves as members of the Church of England. On the other hand, there are members of the Church of England who regard some changes as desirable, though others may consider them to involve an abandonment or repudiation of vital and binding principles. This case illustrates the difficulties of a Church being what is called a "living church" and at the same time being a Church the doctrine and ritual of which have been fixed by statutes which it has proved impossible to amend.' On the other hand, as Lord Hatherley LC said in *Sheppard* v. *Bennett* (1871) LR 4 PC 371 at p. 404 in relation to the service of Holy Communion in the Book of Common Prayer: ' . . . the service . . . was meant to be, common ground on which all Church people may meet, though they differ about doctrines . . . . [T]he Church of England has wisely left a certain latitude of opinion in matters of belief, and has not insisted on a rigorous uniformity of thought which might reduce her communion to a narrow compass.' Cp. *Wylde* v. *Attorney-General for New South Wales ex rel. Ashelford per* Dixon J at p. 290.

[3] Neill (**footnote 2,** *supra*) comments at p. 398: 'The most humiliating thing of all is that Parliament seems to have judged more correctly than the Church.'. For the legal position in relation to the Deposited Book see **p. 273 et seq. infra**.

[4] For the history of previous developments see 14 Halsbury's Laws of England (Butterworths, 1975) (4th ed.) at para. 958.

(Worship and Doctrine) Measure[5]. This was passed in order to enable the General Synod[6]:

> (a)   to make provision by Canon with respect to worship in the Church of England, including provision for empowering the General Synod to approve[7], amend, continue or discontinue forms of service;
>
> (b)   to make provision by Canon or regulations made thereunder for any matter, except in the publication of banns of matrimony, to which any of the rubrics[8] contained in the Book of Common Prayer[9] relate[10] . . . .

It was nonetheless made plain[11] that these powers should be 'so exercised as to ensure that the forms of service contained in the Book of Common Prayer continue to be available for use in the Church of England'. The powers are to be exercised by or under the authority of Canons made by the General Synod[12],

[5]   The Measure is set out in **Appendix 1**. It extends to the whole of the provinces of Canterbury and York except the Channel Islands, but may be applied to the Channel Islands as defined in the Channel Islands (Church Legislation) Measures 1931 and 1957 or either of them in accordance with those Measures: s. 7(3). A canon under sections 1 or 2 of the Measure requires a two-thirds majority of those present and voting: s. 3; see *Brown* v. *Runcie*, *The Times*, 20 February 1991; see also *R* v. *Ecclesiastical Committee of the Houses of Parliament, ex parte The Church Society* [1994] COD 319, *The Times*, 4 November 1993; *Ex parte Williamson*, *The Times*, 9 March 1994. For full transcripts of these cases see Hill, *Ecclesiastical Law* (Butterworths, 1995) at pp. 68, 72 and 77 respectively.

[6]   Section 1. The powers are extremely far-reaching: see s. 6(1). In *Ex parte Williamson*, *The Times*, 9 March 1994, the question was left open whether the effect of ss. 1 and 5(2) was that no alteration to the Book of Common Prayer or the Ordinal could be made save in accordance with the Measure: see Hill, *Ecclesiastical Law* at pp. 80–81.

[7]   This is not affected by the Burial Laws Amendment Act 1880, s. 13: see **p. 219** *et seq. infra*.

[8]   For the purposes of the Church of England (Worship and Doctrine) Measure 1974, section 5(2) enacts that '"rubrics" of the Book of Common Prayer include all directions and instructions contained in the said Book, and all tables, prefaces, rules, calendars and other contents thereof.'.

[9]   For the purposes of the 1974 Measure '"Book of Common Prayer" means the Book annexed to the Act of Uniformity 1662 and entitled 'The Book of Common Prayer and Administration of the Sacraments and other Rites and Ceremonies of the Church according to the use of the Church of England together with the Psalter or Psalms of David appointed as they are to be sung or said in Churches and the Form and Manner of Making, Ordaining and Consecrating Bishops, Priests and Deacons', as altered or amended by any Act or Measure or in accordance with section 1(7) of this Measure': s. 5(2).

[10]   The words are not so wide that any canon concerning impediments to ordination falls within s. 1(1) (b): *Brown* v. *Runcie*, *The Times*, 20 February 1991; see Hill, *Ecclesiastical Law* at pp. 71–72.

[11]   Church of England (Worship and Doctrine) Measure 1974, s. 1. The note headed Affirmations of Faith in *A Service of the Word and Affirmations of Faith* (Church House Publishing, 1994) at p. 23 speaks of 'non-statutory services' which it contrasts with an 'authorized' service (that is, 'approved by General Synod in accordance with the provisions of Canon B2': see the note headed A Service of the Word at p. 7). The former seem to be any services authorised under Canon B 1, para. 1: *In re St John the Evangelist, Chopwell* (1995) in **Appendix 6** at **p. 297** *infra*. The only services specifically authorised by statute are those in The Book of Common Prayer, the shortened forms of Morning and Evening Prayer set out in the Act of Uniformity Amendment Act 1872, and those permitted under the Universities Tests Act 1871 (see **p. 3 footnote 14** *infra*).

[12]   Canons are binding on the clergy in ecclesiastical matters (*Matthew* v. *Burdett* (1703) 2 Salk. 412; 14 Halsbury's Laws of England (4th ed.) at para. 308) and a clergyman is liable to prosecution in the ecclesiastical courts for failure to adhere to them: 14 Halsbury's Laws of England (4th ed.) at para. 1352. As to the position of deaconesses, readers and the laity, see 14 Halsbury's Laws of

although those Canons must themselves be within the scope permitted by the Measure.

A   Authorised Services

(i)   Generally

Canon B 1, para. 2, specifies that every minister[13] 'shall use only[14] the forms of service authorised by this Canon, except[15] so far as he[16] may exercise the discretion permitted by Canon B 5'[17]. The authorised services[18] are:

(a)   the forms of service[19] contained in the Book of Common Prayer[20];

(b)   the shortened forms of Morning and Evening Prayer which were

England (4th ed.) at para. 308, especially notes 10 and 11; Church of England (Worship and Doctrine) Measure 1974, s. 2: see, too, **p. 65, footnote 59** *infra*. Canons B 1–5A are set out in **Appendix 2**.

[13]   As to the force of Canons see previous footnote.

[14]   In spite of this wording the use of any abridgement or adaptation of the services of Morning and Evening Prayer according to the Book of Common Prayer in certain university colleges, if authorised in writing by the official visitor, remains legal as the Canon does not override other statutory authority, especially as that authority is in effect confirmed by the 1974 Measure. For this reason such abridgements or adaptations are best seen as falling within Canon B 1, para. 1(a): Universities Tests Act 1871, as amended by the Church of England (Worship and Doctrine) Measure 1974, s. 6(3), Sch. 2; see, too, the Church of England (Worship and Doctrine) Measure 1974, s. 5(2), 'Book of Common Prayer'. See, too, Canon B 36, para. 1, and Canon B 43 and **pp. 26, 192 and 273** *infra*.   [15]   See, too, **Appendices 3 and 4**.

[16]   In so far as the minister is a deacon 'the masculine gender include(s) the feminine': Deacons (Ordination of Women) Measure 1986, s. 4; Canon C 4A, Sch.. Similarly, 'In any Canon, order, rule or regulation relating to priests, words importing the masculine gender include the feminine, unless the contrary intention appears': Priests (Ordination of Women) Measure 1993, s. 9. See, too, Canon C 4B, para. 2: 'In the forms of service contained in the Book of Common Prayer or in the Ordinal words importing the masculine gender in relation to the priesthood shall be construed as including the feminine, except where the context otherwise requires.' See *Brown* v. *Runcie, The Times*, 20 February 1991; *Ex parte Williamson, The Times*, 9 March 1994 (for full transcripts see Hill, *Ecclesiastical Law* at pp. 68 and 77 respectively).

[17]   For the meaning of this exception see **p. 47** *et seq. infra*.

[18]   Canon B 1, para. 1; see, too, Canon C 3, para. 4A, and Canon C 4A, para. 4.

[19]   '. . . [T]he expression 'form of service' shall be construed as including (i) the prayers known as Collects; (ii) the lessons designated in any Table of Lessons; (iii) any other matter to be used as part of a service; (iv) any Table of rules for regulating a service; (v) any Table of Holy days which expression includes 'A Table of all the Feasts' in the Book of Common Prayer and such other Days as shall be included in any Table approved by the General Synod': Canon B 1, para. 3. Section 5 of the Act of Uniformity Amendment Act 1872, specifically regarded the litany as a separate form of service within the Book of Common Prayer; presumably this position remains in spite of the section's repeal: see **p. 126** *infra*. A sermon preached by itself, even with a bidding prayer, does not amount to a service: see **p. 69, footnote 105,** *infra* and the Act of Uniformity Amendment Act 1872, ss. 5 and 6 (now repealed). It is possible that some things may be permitted in forms of service approved in accordance with Canon B 4 or Canon B 5, para. 2, that would not be permissible in other forms of service: see **p. 25, footnote 189,** *infra*.

[20]   It is important to remember that this does not mean the Book of Common Prayer precisely as appended to the Act of Uniformity 1662, but as amended thereafter by statutory authority: see

set out in the Schedule to the Act of Uniformity Amendment Act 1872[21];

(c)　the form of service authorised by Royal Warrant for use upon the anniversary of the day of accession of the reigning sovereign[22];

(d)　any form of service approved under Canon B 2 subject to any amendments so approved, to the extent permitted by such approval[23];

(e)　any form of service approved under Canon B 4 subject to any amendments so approved, to the extent permitted by such approval[24]; and

(f)　any form of service authorised by the Archbishops under Canon B 5A, to the extent permitted by such authorisation.

No other services may lawfully[25] be used. Even if it existed prior to 1974, no episcopal *jus liturgicum* can now be exercised[26] save in so far as it may still survive in a limited form in the discretion given to bishops to settle questions of doubt arising within the Book of Common Prayer[27]. Custom can no longer legalise other forms of service[28].

p. 2, footnote 9, *supra*. It also includes the use in certain university colleges of any abridgement or adaptation of the services of Morning and Evening Prayer according to the Book of Common Prayer, if authorised in writing by the official visitor: see **p. 3, footnote 14, *supra***.

[21]　See the Church of England (Worship and Doctrine) Measure 1974, s. 6(3) and Sch. 3, para. 3.

[22]　Interestingly this is narrower than the law as enacted by the Prayer Book (Alternative and other Services) Measure 1965, ss. 8 and 10: see **p. 282, footnote 14** *infra*. Alterations to 'the prayers for or referring to the Sovereign or other members of the Royal Family' may be made by Royal Warrant: Church of England (Worship and Doctrine) Measure 1974, s. 1(7). See, too, **p. 36, footnote 33, *supra***.　　　　　[23] That is, by the General Synod; see **p. 5** *infra*.

[24]　That is, by the Convocations, archbishops or diocesan bishops: see **pp. 5 and 216** *et seq. infra*.

[25]　This is why it is necessary to regard any form of service authorised under Canon C 4A, para. 4, as embraced within Canon B 4, para. 2: see **pp. 5 and 232** *infra*. See, too, **Appendix 4**.

[26]　See **Appendix 3**.　　　[27] See **p. 31** *et seq. infra*.

[28]　Reference to contrary custom is made in the Sacrament Act 1547, s. 8: '. . . any law, statute, ordinance, or custom contrary thereunto in any wise notwithstanding.'. See *What is the Place of Custom in English Canon Law?* (1989) 1 Ecc LJ (4) 16, especially at p. 22 *et seq.*. (Although a different view is expressed in so far as the Church in Wales is concerned by Gainer, The Jus Liturgicum of the Bishop and the Church in Wales in *Essays in Canon Law* at p. 131, no satisfactory legal reason is given; indeed, it is far from clear that the examples given are in fact examples of the force of custom. What is said in *The Archbishops on the Lawfulness of the Use of Incense and the Carrying of Lights in Procession* (MacMillan & Co., 1899) at p. 8 as to 'long-continued custom' supports the view that custom cannot legalise the otherwise illegal but is nevertheless relevant when deciding whether to prosecute.) This cannot be affected by Note 4 to The Ordinal of the Alternative Service Book at p. 338, which is merely a *directive*: 'Questions concerning the form of service to be used, and other matters concerning the conduct of the service, are to be determined by the bishop who presides at it, in accordance with the rubrics of the service *and having regard to tradition and local custom*'; the only *rule* is that laid down in Canon B 3, para. 5. Similarly, Note 3 to Rite A in the Alternative Service Book at p. 115 reads: 'When a certain posture is particularly appropriate, it is indicated in the margin. For the rest of the service *local custom* may be *established* and followed'. (Emphasis supplied in both examples.) The words 'local custom' must be read as referring to any local usage or practice in spite of the word 'established'; see, too, the Marriages Confirmation Act 1825, s. 2. A rubric cannot resurrect a rule of law which (at the very least in relation to liturgy) did not survive the Reformation and the Acts of Uniformity. As to the words 'as hath been accustomed' in the Churching of Women, see **p. 222** *infra*. See, too, *Lent, Holy Week, Easter* at pp. 196–197 and *Ministry at the Time of Death*, note 2(c) at p. 3. Similarly Canon B 9 seems to be a directive: '. . . When the Prayers are read and the Psalms and Canticles are said or

Canon B 2 deals with the approval by the General Synod[29], with or without time limit, of forms of service for use in the Church of England and with their subsequent amendment, extension and discontinuance[30]. Canon B 4[31] provides for the approval[32] by the Convocations of Canterbury and York, the archbishops[33] and the bishops[34] within their respective jurisdictions of:

> ... forms of service for use in any cathedral or church or elsewhere on occasions for which no provision is made in the Book of Common Prayer or

sung, have regard (*sic*) to the rubrics of the service and locally established custom in the matter of posture, whether of standing kneeling or sitting': cp. Canon B 42. At the very least, a canonical custom (in the strict legal meaning of that word) takes twenty years to establish; indeed, if it could be established it would not require a rubric or canon to give it legal effect: see Canon B 13, para. 1, which may well in the particular context refer to pre-Reformation custom. In fact, the Alternative Service Book seems to refer to a practice which may be set up shortly after its own promulgation, rather than waiting twenty years: as to deviation from a prevailing practice, see *Howell* v. *Holdroyd* [1897] P 198; *Marson* v. *Unmack* [1923] P 163 at p. 168 ('the sanction of long standing custom'). As to Canon B 8, para. 3, and B 42 see **pp. 66 and 93 *infra***; see, too, Note 7 at p. 338 of the Alternative Service Book ('customary vesture'). Continued user over several centuries may nonetheless render something legal: see *Ridsdale* v. *Clifton* (1877) 2 PD 276 at 331; *In re Robinson. Wright* v. *Tugwell* [1897] 1 Ch 85 (preaching gown); *Read* v. *Bishop of Lincoln* [1892] AC 644 at p. 660 (hymns); 14 Halsbury's Laws of England (4th ed.) at para. 303, note 5.

[29] A majority of two-thirds of those present and voting is required in each House: see Canon B 2, para. 2.

[30] 'Every Canon or regulation making any such provision as is mentioned in section 1(1) of this Measure, every form of service or amendment thereof approved by the General Synod under any such Canon and every Canon making any such provision as is mentioned in section 2(1) of this Measure shall be such as in the opinion of the General Synod is neither contrary to, nor indicative of any departure from, the doctrine of the Church of England in any essential matter': Church of England (Worship and Doctrine) Measure 1974, s. 4(1). 'The final approval by the General Synod of any such ... form of service or amendment thereof shall conclusively determine that the Synod is of such opinion as aforesaid with respect to the matter so approved: s. 4(2). See, further, s. 5(1), and **p. 216, footnote 10**. See, too, *R* v. *Ecclesiastical Committee of the Houses of Parliament, ex parte The Church Society* [1994] COD 319, *The Times*, 4 November 1993; *Ex parte Williamson*, *The Times*, 9 March 1994 (for full transcripts see Hill, *Ecclesiastical Law* at pp. 72 and 77 respectively). For the forms of service so authorised see *Public Worship in the Church of England. A guide to the law governing worship and doctrine in the Church of England* (General Synod, 1986) (5th ed.), although this currently requires updating.

[31] Made pursuant to the Church of England (Worship and Doctrine) Measure 1974, ss. 1(5)(a) and 4.

[32] Until the diocesan bishop gives specific directions the approval cannot be inferred from a general commendation by the House of Bishops: see the preface to *Lent, Holy Week, Easter, The Promise of His Glory* and *Services of Prayer and Dedication after Civil Marriage*: see, too, **p. 59 *infra***. It may possibly be inferred from the approval of the General Synod: see **p. 128 *infra***.

[33] Canon C 4A, para. 4, specifies that 'the archbishops may *jointly* authorise forms of service for deaconesses to be ordained deacon'. (Emphasis supplied.) As such forms of service are not individually specified by Canon B 1 this must be seen as a specific application of the power given by Canon B 4, para. 2. Another problem, however, arises: Canon B 4, para. 2, seems only to empower the archbishops to act jointly (contrast the use of the words 'respective provinces' in para. 1 and the omission of the word 'respective' in para. 2) but, if so, why was it necessary to use the word 'jointly' in Canon C 4A? This might suggest that the archbishops may, other than in relation to forms of service for deaconesses to be ordained deacon, act alone in relation to their own provinces. See, too, **p. 217 *infra***.

[34] Canon B 4, para. 3, refers to the 'Ordinary'. Although the word 'Ordinary' often has a wider meaning (see **p. 22, footnote 155 *infra***) it is clear from section 1(5)(a) of the Church of England (Worship and Doctrine) Measure 1974, that it must here refer only to the bishop. Contrast this, however, with Canons B 15A, para. 3, and C 8, para. 2.

by the General Synod under Canon B 2 ... being forms of service which in both words and order are [in their opinion][35] reverent and seemly and neither contrary to, nor indicative of any departure from, the doctrine of the Church of England in any essential matter.

The parts of The Alternative Service Book 1980[36] duly authorised[37] under Canon B 2 are 'The services ... , together with the Calendar, Rules to Order the Service, and the Lectionary ... '[38]. Versions of the Psalter authorised for use in conjunction with the Alternative Service Book 1980 are 'the Prayer Book Psalter, The Revised Psalter, the Liturgical Psalter, and the Grail Psalter.'[39]

(ii) Collects, Calendars and Lectionaries

The 1973 code of rules to order the service in the Book of Common Prayer are technically still without authority; however, on particular occasions they may be used pursuant to Canon B 5, para. 1.

The Prayer Book (Alternative and other Services) Measure 1965[40], gave the National Assembly power to approve forms of sevice for experimental use differing from those provided by the Book of Common Prayer but did not permit the alteration of Prayer Book services[41]. In 1973, however, the General Synod purported to authorise a code of 'rules to order the service' for inclusion in the Book of Common Prayer, although it was recognised that such rules really required statutory authority[42].

It has been suggested that even by 1981 no such statutory authority had been taken[43], although this view seems to be incorrect. By section 1 of the Church of England (Worship and Doctrine) Measure 1974, the General Synod was given power[44] *inter alia*:

to make provision by Canon or regulations made thereunder for any matter, except the publication of banns of matrimony, to which any of the rubrics contained in the Book of Common Prayer relate ...

[35] These words only appear in Canon B 4, para. 2.
[36] (Clowes: SPCK: Cambridge University Press: Hodder & Stoughton: Oxford University Press: A R Mowbray & Co Ltd, 1980). Page 71 has been amended so as to include A Service of the Word: *A Service of the Word and Affirmations of Faith* at p. 10.
[37] From the date of publication until 31 December 2000.
[38] The Alternative Service Book 1980 at p. 8. Unfortunately this is omitted in some editions of the service book.   [39] See previous footnote.
[40] Now repealed.   [41] Section 1 of the 1965 Measure.
[42] See the *Further Alternative Rules to Order the Service together with an Additional Alternative Lectionary* (Church House Publishing), Introduction, at p. 1. Nevertheless, it is possible that its use may now be justified by other arguments: see **p. 128** *infra*.
[43] See the *Further Alternative Rules to Order the Service together with an Additional Alternative Lectionary*.   [44] See s. 1(1)(b).

Although 'the forms of service[45] in the Book of Common Prayer' must 'continue to be available for use in the Church of England'[46] power may possibly have been given by this section to alter the calendar and lectionary[47]. All depends upon the ambit of the word 'rubric'[48] and the matters to which the rubrics 'relate'. Indeed, in this particular context the word 'rubric' has a very wide meaning under the 1974 Measure, section 5(2), which specifically includes:

... all directions and instructions contained in the [Book of Common Prayer], and all tables, prefaces, rules, calendars and other contents thereof.

Pursuant to these powers Canon B 4A[49] did at one time give the General Synod power to approve:

(a) new collects for use in any form of service approved under Canons B 2 and 4;
(b) tables of lessons for use in any service approved under Canon B 2; and
(c) a table of rules for regulating the service when two Holy Days fall on the same day, or their proper services otherwise fall together, or when necessary for any other reason.

Thus the power was indeed taken to approve any variation from the calendar and lectionary in the Book of Common Prayer as set out at (c) *supra*. This provision has, however, now been repealed without the position having been regularized. Moreover, Canon B 6, para. 5, only gave power to the General Synod:

to approve Holy Days which may be observed generally or provincially, and, subject to any directions of the Convocation of the province, for the Ordinary to approve Holy Days which may be observed locally.

In addition to this limited power under Canon B 6, Canon B 2 has now been amended to include a different definition[50] of 'form of service'. This definition

---

[45] These words have a particular meaning under the Church of England (Worship and Doctrine) Measure 1974, s. 5: see **p. 263** *infra*.

[46] Church of England (Worship and Doctrine) Measure 1974, s. 1(1) proviso.

[47] For an apparently similar view see paragraph 4 of *Public Worship in the Church of England* (General Synod) (5th ed., 1986). Even if the view expressed here is incorrect, the use of tables, etc. authorised by the General Synod falls on any particular occasion within the ambit of Canon B 5, para. 1, in so far as any minister is concerned.

[48] Somewhat questionably in *Martin* v. *Mackonochie* (1868) LR 2 A & E 116 at pp. 190–195, Sir Robert Phillimore even treated the provision as to the discretion of the Ordinary in the Preface to the Book of Common Prayer as a rubric. This would now be correct at least for the purposes of the Church of England (Worship and Doctrine) Measure 1974: see s. 5(2).

[49] Promulgated on 25 February 1976.

[50] See **p. 5** *supra*. This definition can only apply to the individual Canon (or any other canon containing a similar definition: Canons B 1–5A); it cannot supersede the definition in section 5(2) of the Church of England (Worship and Doctrine) Measure 1974, which governs the ambit of all canons made pursuant to the 1974 Measure and thus also the ambit of Canon B 2 itself. The use of the same form of words to mean different things, especially within the same scope of the legislation, can only lead to confusion.

now specifically embraces the 'Table of all the Feasts' in the Book of Common Prayer[51]. However, this latter provision would not permit the amendment of the Table as Canon B 2, para. 1(a), only authorises the amendment of 'any form of service approved by the General Synod' under that particular Canon.

Nevertheless, because the new definition of "form of service" has also been included in Canon B 1, para. 3, different collects, tables and lectionaries may in future be authorised pursuant to those powers[52], even in substitution for any within the Book of Common Prayer[53].

(iii)   In a particular parish

As has been seen, a minister may only use the authorised services, 'except so far as he may exercise the discretion permitted by Canon B 5'. This provides[54] *inter alia* that:

> The minister having the cure of souls may on occasions for which no provision is made in the Book of Common Prayer or by the General Synod under Canon B 2 or by the Convocations, archbishops, or Ordinary[55] under Canon B 4 use forms of service considered suitable by him for those occasions and may permit another minister to use the said forms of service.

Thus, a minister may himself make and use (and sanction other ministers to use) a service within his own parish as long as no other authorised service is already provided for that occasion. On the other hand he cannot, for example, sanction the use (either by himself or others) of a service otherwise following the authorised form of a service of Holy Communion at which there is no consecration but at which the reserved sacrament is distributed instead; this is because provision is already made for services at which the sacrament is to be received[56].

Nevertheless, any service[57] used by a minister under Canon B 5 must be 'reverent and seemly' and

---

[51] Canon B 1, para. 3(v). See **p. 3, footnote 19** *supra*.

[52] This oddity is due to the drafting.

[53] Note 5 Readings in *A Service of the Word and Affirmations of Faith* at p. 8 states: 'Readings shall come from an authorized lectionary during the periods from Advent 3 to Epiphany 1 and from Palm Sunday to Trinity Sunday and whenever the service is combined with the Eucharist'. Thus the readings from non-authorised lectionaries are given limited authorisation. However, this does not apply in relation to Holy Communion according to the Book of Common Prayer, as it is only the Alternative Service Book which is amended so as to include the Service of the Word: see *ibid* at p. 10.

[54] Canon B 5, para. 2; Church of England (Worship and Doctrine) Measure 1974, s. 1(5)(b). As to the 'non-statutory' services referred to in the note headed Affirmations of Faith in *A Service of the Word and Affirmations of Faith* at p. 11, see **p. 2, footnote 11** *supra*.

[55] See **p. 5, footnote 34** *supra*.

[56] See **p. 221** *infra*. See, too, Canon B 12, para. 1. This is not to say that the reserved sacrament may not be distributed *simpliciter* by a lay person duly authorised by the bishop: see **p. 110** *infra*.

[57] Canon B 5, para. 3; Church of England (Worship and Doctrine) Measure 1974, s. 4.

shall be neither contrary to, nor indicative of any departure from, the doctrine of the Church of England in any essential matter[58].

In addition, the archbishops may authorise[59] services prepared with a view to its submission to the General Synod for approval under Canon B 2 to be conducted by a minister prior to that submission 'on such terms and in such places or parishes as they may designate'. Such draft services, therefore, may only be used on those terms and in those places or parishes.

Strictly speaking, without the bishop's licence a public service may only be conducted in a consecrated building, although it seems that this does not prevent an occasional open air service[60]. However, by Canon B 40[61]:

No minister shall celebrate the Holy Communion elsewhere than in a consecrated building within his cure or other building licensed for the purpose, except he have permission so to do from the bishop of the diocese: Provided that at all times he may celebrate the Holy Communion as provided by Canon B 37 in any private house wherein there is any person sick, or dying, or so impotent that he cannot go to church.

B   Forms of Service

(i)   Generally

The words 'form of service' are defined by the Church of England (Worship and Doctrine) Measure 1974, as meaning[62]:

any order, service, prayer, rite or ceremony whatsoever, including the services for the ordination of priests and deacons and the consecration of bishops and the catechism or form of instruction before confirmation.

On the face of it these words are very wide indeed (embracing as they do 'any ... prayer ... whatsoever'), as also are the words of the preamble which make it clear that the Measure was passed "to enable provision to be made ... with respect to worship'[63]; moreover, any Canons made pursuant to the Measure must

---

[58] See **p. 48** *et seq.* and **p. 55** *et seq. infra.*

[59] After consultation with the House of Bishops and subject to the provisions of Canon B 3: see Canon B 5A, paras 1 and 2; Church of England (Worship and Doctrine) Measure 1974, s. 1(6).

[60] 14 Halsbury's Laws of England (4th ed.) at para. 691. In *Finch* v. *Harris* (1702) 12 Mod. Rep. 640 at p. 641 Holt CJ said: 'It is against the law to preach in a place not consecrated; and it would be to set up a conventicle. Indeed one may pray in his own house for his family, but he cannot preach there.'. Equally the law prevented the taking of any service by a layman other than in his own home. Although the Liberty of Religious Worship Act 1855, s. 1, has now been repealed, the matter is now regulated primarily by Canon: see Canons B 14 and 40.

[61] See, too, Canon B 41.   [62] Section 5(2).

[63] Although no doubt these words refer primarily to public worship, they must also embrace some private devotions, as is made clear by Canon C 26, para. 1, which imposes a duty on the clergy 'to say daily the Morning and Evening Prayer, either privately or openly ... '.

be interpreted in the light of them[64]. In fact, they are so wide that they are not restricted to merely public worship[65]; this being so, any auricular confession such as is enjoined by the Exhortation in the Holy Communion service in the Book of Common Prayer must now be governed by Canon B 5, para. 2[66].

Indeed, Canon C 26, para. 1, reasserts[67] an obligation upon the clergy 'to be diligent in daily prayer and intercession' in addition to saying daily 'the Morning and Evening Prayer, either privately or openly'. This obligation clearly refers to Morning and Evening Prayer as authorised by statute or canon; moreover, Canon B 1, para. 2, states that:

Every minister shall use only the forms of service[68] authorised by this Canon, except so far as he may exercise the discretion permitted under Canon B 5 . . .

Therefore, even in private[69], a minister must use only duly authorised services of Morning and Evening Prayer, although other devotions may be made in addition.

However, this raises the question: what is private prayer? To some extent this question depends on the circumstances of any particular case[70]. However, in *Freeland* v. *Neale*[71] it was pointed out that although:

Undoubtedly a clergyman may read prayers to his own private family and household, without committing an ecclesiastical offence, . . . where two or three are gathered together, who do not strictly form a part of a family, there is a congregation, and the reading to them the service of the Church is a reading in public.

It would seem that a meditation or Bible study would not be within the ambit of 'reading to them the service of the Church', even if the latter were to be

[64] This is so although Canon B 1 now also gives its own partial definition of the words 'form of service' which applies also within Canons B 2–5: see *infra* and **p. 3, footnote 19** *supra*.

[65] This is so in spite of Canon B 1, para. 2, which states that the minister 'shall endeavour to ensure that the worship offered glorifies God and edifies the people.' This provision, of course, assumes that others are in fact present.

[66] That is not to say that in an emergency a priest may not use some other proper form of service, as was the position whilst the canons made no specific provision for confession.

[67] The Book of Common Prayer, *Concerning the Service of the Church*, made it clear that the forms of service there prescribed were to be used even when the clergy said Morning and Evening Prayer 'privately' (save that they may do so 'in any language that they themselves do understand'). This mirrored the pre-Reformation canon law (see Stephens, *The Book of Common Prayer* (London, 1849), vol. I, at p. 134), although it might be argued that the particular obligation is new if only because the services to be said daily are different.

[68] However, it is the definition referred to in **footnote 62** *supra* that applies to this Canon, even though that definition must itself be read subject to the statutory definition.

[69] It is true that the Declarations of Assent under the Clerical Subscription Act 1865, and now under Canon C 15, para. 1(1), only relate to what is done 'in public prayer and administration of the sacraments' but the canonical obligation nevertheless remains.

[70] Cripps, *The Law relating to the Church and Clergy* (Sweet and Maxwell, 1937) (8th ed.) at p. 512, note (x).

[71] (1848) 1 Rob. Eccl. 643 at pp. 649 & 651. See, too, *Barnes* v. *Shore* (1846) 1 Rob. Eccl. 382 and *Nesbitt* v. *Wallace* [1901] P 163.

ended with prayer. On the other hand, anything resembling a service would be[72].
A house church would certainly fall within the definition of public prayer[73].

(ii) Under the Canons

Under Canon B 1, para. 2, it is a 'minister's responsibility to have a good understanding of the forms of service used' and, as has been seen, he may only use the
forms of service authorised by that Canon. Those forms of service are as defined
by the Church of England (Worship and Doctrine) Measure 1974[74], but for the
purposes of the first five Canons the words 'shall be construed as including':

(i)   the prayers known as Collects;
(ii) the lessons designated in any Table of Lessons;
(iii) any other matter to be used as part of a service;
(iv) any Table of rules for regulating a service;
(v)   any Table of Holy Days which expression includes 'A Table of all the
Feasts' in the Book of Common Prayer and such other Days as shall be
included in any Table approved by the General Synod[75].

C Interpretation

The rigorist interpretation of the rubrics no longer applies and, unless it is a statement of
doctrine or indicative of Church order, a rubric is now to be treated as a mere directive.

Problems of interpretation have already been noted but even greater problems
arise when considering how the forms of services should themselves be interpreted. In *Martin* v. *Mackonochie*[76] the Judicial Committee of the Privy Council
stated that:

---

[72] This is important as only a minister having a cure of souls may use or permit forms of service
not otherwise authorised: see Canon B 5, para. 2. The Act of Uniformity 1662, spoke of services
being 'openly' and 'publicly' read (see s. 3) whereas the Act of Uniformity 1558 spoke of 'open
prayer', which it defined as 'that prayer which is for others to come unto, or hear, either in common
churches, or private chapels or oratories, commonly called the service of the church': see s. 4.

[73] The provisions of Canon B 14A relate to *which* services shall be held and do not permit the
bishop to authorise otherwise unlawful services. Any other interpretation would be contrary to the
provisions of the Church of England (Worship and Doctrine) Measure 1974, under which the Canon
was made.   [74] Section 5(2). See **p. 6** *supra* and **p. 263** *infra*.

[75] Canon B 1, para. 3, and Canons B 2–5.

[76] (1868) LR 2 PC 365 at pp. 382–3. The question of interpretation of the rubrics was also
considered when the case came before the Court of the Arches in *Martin* v. *Mackonochie* (1868) LR
2 A & E 116 at pp. 190–198. Sir Robert Phillimore said at p. 196: 'It is often said that a rubric
should be construed on the same principles as an Act of Parliament; but admitting this to be so, it
is obvious that there are peculiar difficulties incident to the construction of a rubric which seldom,
or in a much less degree, beset the construction of an ordinary statute. And it will appear from what
has already been said, that the right understanding of the rules supplied by the rubric for the
regulation of the services may often require a reference to the sources not only of historical, but to
a certain extent theological knowledge.'. See, too, *Sheppard* v. *Bennett* (1872) LR 4 PC 371 *per*
Lord Hatherley LC at pp. 404 and 414.

... it is not open to a Minister of the Church ... to draw a distinction, in acts which are a departure from or violation of the Rubric, between those which are important and those which appear trivial. The object of a *Statute of Uniformity* is, as its preamble expresses, to produce 'an universal agreement in the public worship of Almighty God,' an object which would be wholly frustrated if each Minister, on his own view of the relative importance of the details of the service, were to be at liberty to omit, to add to, or to alter any details of those details. The rule upon this subject has been already laid down by the Judicial Committee in *Westerton* v. *Liddell*[77], and their Lordships are disposed entirely to adhere to it: 'In the performance of the services, rites, and ceremonies ordered by the Prayer Book, the directions contained in it must be strictly observed; no omission and no addition can be permitted.'

This statement of the law was in fact also in accordance with Canon 14 of the 1603 Canons, which enjoined all ministers to:

... observe the Orders, Rites, and Ceremonies prescribed in the Book of Common Prayer, as well in reading the holy Scriptures, and saying of Prayers, as in the administration of the Sacraments, without either diminishing in regard of preaching, or in any other respect, or adding any thing in the matter or form thereof.

Canon 14 clearly left little leeway. As Lord Penzance said in *Combe* v. *De la Bere*[78]:

Exact observance of the Prayer Book is enjoined by the Act of Uniformity, and to fail to observe it is an offence not only against that statute, but against the Queen's ecclesiastical laws.

Then, having set out the terms of the Canon, he continued:

In this unmistakeable manner have the canons of the Church added their sanction and authority to that of the Legislature for the strict observance of the forms prescribed by the Prayer Book, to the exclusion of all other forms not so prescribed.

Indeed, in 1811 Sir John Nicholl had already stated in *Newbery* v. *Goodwin*[79]:

The law directs that a clergyman is not to diminish in any respect, or to add to the prescribed form of worship; uniformity in this respect is one of the leading and distinguishing principles of the Church of England – nothing

---

[77] (1857) Moore's Special Report 1 at p. 188.   [78] (1881) 6 PD 157 at p. 173.
[79] (1811) 1 Phillim. 282 at pp. 282–3. In *Kemp* v. *Wickes* (1809) 3 Phillim. 264 Sir John Nicholl, having summarised the legislative history of the Book of Common Prayer, said at p. 269: 'The rubric then, or the directions of the Book of Common Prayer, form a part of the statute law of the land. Now that law in the rubric forbids the burial service for persons who die unbaptized. It is not matter of option; it is not matter of expediency or benevolence (as seems to have been represented in

is left to the discretion or fancy of the individual. If every minister were to alter, omit, or add according to his own taste, this uniformity would soon be destroyed, and though the alteration might begin with little things, yet it would soon extend itself to more important changes in the public worship of the Established Church, and even in the Scriptures themselves; the most important passages might be materially altered, under the notion of giving a more correct version, or omitted altogether, as unauthorised interpolations.

Of course, this passage reads somewhat uneasily in the light of the versions of the Bible and rites now authorised by the General Synod and, indeed, the view has been expressed[80] that:

... when dealing with the Book of Common Prayer it must be remembered that, although it has statutory authority, it is not itself an Act of Parliament and should not be construed as such. Its rubrics, though binding, are clerical directives, written in the seventeenth century by clerics for the guidance largely of clerics, and unless they are interpreted as such and in the context of the seventeenth century they will not make sense. They must be interpreted with the elasticity which directives usually require.

What is more, the Book of Common Prayer had itself recognized the problem[81]:

And forasmuch as nothing can be so plainly set forth, but doubts may arise in use and practice of the same; to appease all such diversity (if any arise) and for the resolution of all doubts, concerning the manner how to understand, do, and execute, the things contained in this Book; the parties that so doubt, or diversity take anything, shall always resort to the Bishop of the Diocese, who by his discretion shall take order for the quieting and appeasing of the same; so that the same order be not contrary to anything contained in this Book. And if the Bishop of the Diocese be in doubt, then he may send for the resolution of the same to the Archbishop.

Unfortunately – perhaps in part due to the wording of Canon 14 of 1603 – the rubrics were in the past often interpreted without such elasticity[82].

---

argument), whether a clergyman shall administer the burial service, or shall refuse it; for the rubric, thus confirmed by statute, expressly enjoins him to perform the office in the specified cases ... '

[80] Briden & Hanson, *Moore's Introduction to English Canon Law* (Mowbray) (3rd ed.) at p. 50. This view of the law is, of course, contrary to the law as expressed in the cases just cited in the text; the cases themselves are not discussed in detail and no indication is given as to why this interpretation should now be applied.

[81] *Concerning the Service of the Church.* See, too, Canon 55 of the 1603 Canons, although the emphasis is different.

[82] See, for example, *Clifton v. Ridsdale* (1876) 1 PD 316 at pp. 343–349 on the question of celebration of Holy Communion when only one member of the congregation received communion with the incumbent; see, too, **p. 103 *et seq. infra*.** If a rigorist interpretation were to prevail, a bishop merely 'present' in the congregation at a celebration of Holy Communion would have to pronounce the absolution and blessing: see **p. 18 footnote 120 *infra*.**

However, Canon 14 has now been repealed[83], as also have the relevant parts of the Act of Uniformity[84]. Yet, in spite of this fact the statement of the law by the Privy Council in the cases set out above had until recently never been reconsidered[85]. The question now arises whether in strict law it still provides a definitive statement of the law, either in so far as the proper approach to the Book of Common Prayer is concerned or in relation to the Alternative Service Book[86].

In fact, because of the disquiet that a number of the Judicial Committee's decisions in the realm of liturgy have caused[87], neither the Court of Ecclesiastical Causes Reserved nor a Commission of Review are now ' . . . bound by any decision of the Judicial Committee of the Privy Council in relation to matter of doctrine, ritual or ceremonial.'[88]. Nevertheless, none of the actual decisions has yet been overruled even though, if at all possible, a minister is entitled to know how the law stands from day to day. Indeed, the consistory court would have first to consider how the question of interpretation should now be approached before the matter could ever be considered on appeal by either of those two superior courts.

It has now been decided in *In re St Thomas, Pennywell*[89] that in fact the previous rigorist approach should no longer be followed in relation to either prayer book[90]

---

[83] See the Introduction to *The Canons of the Church of England* (SPCK, 1969) at pp. xi–xii.

[84] Church of England (Worship and Doctrine) Measure 1974, s. 6(3), Sch. 2. Some rubrics were inserted by the Prayer Book (Further Provisions) Measure 1968. This Measure has been repealed with savings but these savings do not affect the arguments as to the proper interpretation of the rubrics: see the Church of England (Worship and Doctrine) Measure 1974, s. 6(3), (4), Schs. 2 and 3.

[85] In *Escott* v. *Mastin* (1842) 4 Moo. PCC 104 at p. 130 the Privy Council held that the rubrics were 'given force and effect' by the Act of Uniformity, 1662. See, too, *In re Perry Almshouses* [1898] 1 Ch 391 at p. 400 *per* Stirling J: 'The rubrics are incorporated in the Act of Uniformity (13 & 14 Car. 2, c. 4): see *Escott* v. *Mastin*, and, so far as that statute remains unrepealed, must, I conceive, be duly regarded by a court of law'; *Gore-Booth* v. *Bishop of Manchester* [1920] 2 KB 412 at p. 421 *per* Lord Coleridge J: 'We have it in the rubric, which has a statutory force . . . '. Logically, however, just because the rubrics were given force and effect by an Act of Parliament, it did not necessarily mean that they should be interpreted according to the same rules as an Act of Parliament. Moreover, as has been seen, the relevant parts of the 1662 Act have now been repealed.

[86] See *In re St Thomas, Pennywell* [1995] 2 WLR 154 at pp. 166G–168G. It must be borne in mind that the earlier cases may still be binding on matters of doctrine: *ibid* at pp. 168C and 172F.

[87] As to what are known as 'the worship and doctrine cases' in both the Judicial Committee of the Privy Council and the lower courts, see the excellent account in Rodes, *Law and Modernization in the Church of England: Charles II to the Welfare State* (University of Notre Dame Press, 1991) at pp. 250 *et seq.*

[88] Ecclesiastical Jurisdiction Measure, 1963 ss. 45(3) and 48(5). This is expressed to be 'In the exercise of [their] jurisdiction under this Measure' but it is inconceivable that different law should apply in different jurisdictions.

[89] [1995] 2 WLR 154 at pp. 166G–168G. See, too, *In re St John the Evangelist, Chopwell* (1995) in **Appendix 6** at **p. 285** *infra.*

[90] In *Re St Peter and St Paul, Leckhampton* [1968] P 495 Chancellor Garth Moore said at p. 499C–D that a rubric in The Alternative Services (second series) ' . . . now has as much . . . force of law as the Rubric in the 1662 Book of Common Prayer'. If this is right, the same must be true of the rubrics in the Alternative Service Book. Certainly, there is now no reason why a rubric in the Book of Common Prayer should have greater force than any other rubric merely because the Book of Common Prayer must remain available for use: see **p. 2** *supra.* Contrast, however, the views of the Legal Advisory Commission referred to at **pp. 52** *et seq. infra.*

and the rubrics are now to be given the elasticity that in practice they require[91]. As has been seen, the law as previously interpreted depended upon the wording both of the Act of Uniformity 1662, and Canon 14 of 1603. Not only have the relevant parts of the former and the whole of the latter been repealed but the heading to Canon B 1 speaks now of 'conformity' rather than of 'uniformity'. In addition, the preface to the Alternative Service Book[92] describes the reasons for its creation in the following way[93]:

> Rapid social and intellectual changes ..., together with a world-wide re-awakening of interest in liturgy, have made it desirable that new understandings of worship should find expression in new forms and styles. Christians have become readier to accept that, even within a single church, unity need no longer be seen to entail strict uniformity of practice.

Not only has there been repeal of the relevant Act and Canon upon which rigorist interpretation was based but the whole spirit is manifestly different. Moreover, although the powers of the General Synod to make provision for worship must be so exercised as to 'ensure that the forms of service contained in the Book of Common Prayer continue to be available for use'[94], the Canons by which they have done so draw no distinction in approach between any particular rite. All this being so, the rubrics in all forms of service should in general be interpreted as directives rather than regulations[95]. Indeed, if this is right, the emphasis in so many of the old liturgy cases on what were lawful or unlawful ceremonies is now entirely obsolete[96], although that does not mean that they can therefore be entirely ignored. Rather, they must now be approached in the light of the subsequent alterations to the liturgy that have themselves been sanctioned by statutory authority.

However, not all rubrics are mere directives[97]. The rubric in the Book of

---

[91] See 14 Halsbury's Laws of England (4th ed.) at para. 955, note 2. In fact some elasticity has always been essential: for example, the word 'priest' in the marriage service must be interpreted so as to include 'deacon', otherwise the deacon's exercise of his or her lawful right to solemnize a marriage would still be illegal: see **p. 176 et seq. infra**.

[92] The preface is not itself part of what is actually authorised (see *Authorization* at p. 8) but it is clearly persuasive in relation to what approach should now be adopted.

[93] See *Preface* at p. 9.

[94] Church of England (Worship and Doctrine) Measure 1974, s. 1(1); and see **p. 2 supra**. This argument is unaffected by the provision in s. 1(1)(b) excepting the matter of 'the publication of banns of matrimony' from the powers of the General Synod as this provision is to keep that matter, which is already governed by the Marriage Act 1949, within the sole purview of Parliament.

[95] *In re St Thomas, Pennywell* [1995] 2 WLR 154 at p. 168C-E.

[96] See, for example, **p. 72 et seq. infra** and 14 Halsbury's Laws of England (4th ed.) at para. 959. If this is so, the 'ceremonial' use of incense is now legal, as is the 'ceremonial' use of candles: *ibid*; see now *In re St Thomas, Pennywell* [1995] 2 WLR 154 at p. 171B-G; *In re St John the Evangelist, Chopwell* (1995) in Appendix 6 at **p. 287 infra**. Nevertheless, a problem would still arise in relation to the ornaments rubric in the Book of Common Prayer, unless that is now a mere directive: see **p. 73 infra**.

[97] See *In re St Thomas, Pennywell* [1995] 2 WLR 154 at pp. 168H–169A.

Common Prayer at the end of the Order of Confirmation[98], for instance, is not only a directive but also a statement of both Church order and dogma[99]:

> And there shall none be admitted to the holy Communion, until such time as he be confirmed, or be ready and desirous to be confirmed.

Another example is the direction in the service of Holy Communion in the Alternative Service Book[100] that the President must receive the sacrament 'on every occasion'[101]. Another is in the rubric concerning Emergency Baptism in the Alternative Service Book[102] that states that parents should be assured:

> that [the] question of ultimate salvation . . . [does] not depend upon whether or not [a child] ha[s] been baptised.

Moreover, although only appearing once, some rubrics are clearly intended to apply throughout the Prayer Book, for example, the note as to how lessons ought to be announced[103]. So, too, those rubrics that seem to deal with questions of Church order generally[104] are likely to be indicative[105] of the position in relation to other rites as well[106]. However, if there is doubt[107], it should be resolved by

---

[98] Reflected now in Canon B 15A, para. 1(a).

[99] See, too, **p. 21, footnote 150**, and **p. 100** *et seq. infra*.   [100] Note 2 at p. 115.

[101] Canon B 12, para. 2, also states that 'Every minister, as often as he shall celebrate the Holy Communion, shall receive that sacrament himself.'   [102] See Note 106 at p. 280.

[103] See the note before the Te Deum Laudamus in Morning Prayer according to the Book of Common Prayer.

[104] *In re St Thomas, Pennywell* [1995] 2 WLR 154 at p. 169B-F. Canon B 15, para. 2, specifically envisages that 'such preparation as is required by the Book of Common Prayer' should be used before anyone comes to the sacrament of the Holy Communion, whichever rite is used.

[105] They cannot, however, overrule a rubric in another rite: see the Church of England (Worship and Doctrine) Measure, 1974 s. 1(2).

[106] A clear example is in relation to the occasions when the Litany is to be said: see **p. 126** *infra*. Another example is Note 107 preceding the service for Emergency Baptism in the Alternative Service Book: it is inconceivable that an emergency baptism might legally be administered by a layman according to one rite but not according to the other: see, further, **p. 17, footnote 112**, and **p. 144** *et seq. infra*. What if in the emergency only the Book of Common Prayer could be found? There are problems in the application of this view, however. For example, Notes 24 and 14 at pp. 118 and 178 respectively in Rites A and B in the Alternative Service Book permit a lay person to conduct a service of Ante-Communion but, when so doing, the word 'us' is to be substituted for the word 'you' in the Absolution: see **p. 100** *infra*. A similar provision is made in Note 4 before Morning and Evening Prayer at p. 46 but the substituted rubric in Morning and Evening Prayer in the Book of Common Prayer states: 'If no priest be present the person saying the Service shall read the collect for the Twenty-first Sunday after Trinity . . . ' If that is the position at mattins and evensong, does that mean (i) that the collect should be used when the Ante-Communion is said according to the Book of Common Prayer? (ii) that the absolution should be used but with the substitution of the words indicated? or (iii) that, because provision is specifically made as to the Absolution in mattins and evensong but not in the Communion Service, no lay person may say the Ante-Communion according to the Rite in Book of Common Prayer? Each argument is tenable but it is thought that on balance (ii) is correct. Indeed, (ii) can probably now be justified under Canon B5, para. 1, particularly in the light of the Appendix to *A Service of the Word and Affirmations of Faith* at p. 11, although this provision does not directly authorise such a substitution in a service according to the Book of Common Prayer: see *ibid* at pp. 7 and 10. Nevertheless, as there is some doubt, it should be resolved by the diocesan bishop. For a contrasting position concerning baptism see **p. 18, footnote 122** *infra*.

[107] See, for example, **p. 240** *et seq. infra*. The rubric after the service of Confirmation in the Book

the diocesan bishop[108]. In addition, it must always be borne in mind that the new canons are made under the Church of England (Worship and Doctrine) Measure 1974, which specifically safeguards the continued availability of the forms of service contained in the Book of Common Prayer[109]. Moreover, both the Measure[110] and Canon B 5, para. 1, specify the amount to which variations are permitted within authorised services.

D Ministers

(i) Generally

Nobody, unless duly authorised[111], may take any form of service[112] on consecrated ground[113] and, generally speaking[114], no clergyman[115] may take services in

---

of Common Prayer states that 'And there shall none be admitted to the holy Communion, until such time as he be confirmed, or be ready and desirous of being confirmed.'. This rubric must surely have governed the position under the predecessors to the Alternative Service Book even before Canon B 15A, para. 1(a), became law; the Canon was only promulgated in 1972 under the Admission to Holy Communion Measure 1972, s. 1. For an example of a rubric that does not govern the position in the Alternative Service Book, see the rubric concerning alms before the Prayer for the Church Militant and **p. 248** *infra*.

[108] See **p. 31** *et seq. infra*.   [109] Section 1(1).   [110] See s. 1(5)(b).

[111] 'By the ecclesiastical law, no person, unless he be duly authorised, can be permitted to perform a service on consecrated ground': *Johnson* v. *Friend* (1860) 6 Jur. NS 280 *per* Dr Lushington. As to persons from other denominations see Canon B 43 and **p. 26** *et seq. infra*. As to local ecumenical projects see Canon B 44 and *The Opinions of the Legal Advisory Commission* (General Synod, 1994) (7th ed.) at p. 172. Where any priest or deacon of the Church of South India, the Church of North India, the Church of Pakistan or the Church of Bangladesh is granted permission under the Overseas and Other Clergy (Ministry and Ordination) Measure 1967, to officiate for a limited period as a priest or deacon in the province of Canterbury or York, he is not inhibited from exercising his ministry in an other Church to which the Church of England (Ecumenical Relations) Measure 1988, applies: Church of England (Ecumenical Relations) Measure 1988, s. 4.

[112] However, in cases of necessity baptism may be administered by a layman: Phillimore, *The Ecclesiastical Law of the Church of England* (Sweet and Maxwell, 1895) (2nd ed.) at p. 491. This is recognised in the Book of Common Prayer by the rubrics before the Ministration of Private Baptism in Private Houses: *Escott* v. *Mastin* (1842) 4 Moo. PCC 104 *passim* (although the rubrics before that service, coupled with the words 'Minister of the same Parish' in the rubric in relation to the certification of the form of baptism, seem on their face to demand that an ordained minister be procured; see, too, *Kemp* v. *Wickes* (1808) 3 Phillim. 264 at p. 284 *et seq. per* Sir John Nicholl and Gibson, *Codex Iuris Ecclesiastici Anglicani* (2nd ed., Oxford, 1761), vol. I, at p. 369, note). It is certainly recognised by Note 107 in the service of Emergency Baptism according to the Alternative Service Book at p. 280; see, too, Canon B 22, para. 8, and 14 Halsbury's Laws of England (4th ed.) at para. 990. In *Cope* v. *Barber* (1872) LR 7 CP 393 Willes J said at p. 402: 'The ministering of the sacrament of the Lord's Supper necessarily requires the presence of a priest. So also the rite of baptism properly, though not necessarily, for in certain cases it may be performed by a layman or a woman.'

[113] *Johnson* v. *Friend* (1860) 6 Jur. NS 280.

[114] See the provisions of Canon C 8 set out in **Appendix 2** at **p. 269** *et seq. infra*; see also **p. 24, footnote 175**, and **p. 200** *et seq. infra*.

[115] An overseas clergyman may be given written permission to officiate as a priest or deacon by the Archbishop of Canterbury or York: Overseas and Other Clergy (Ministry and Ordination) Measure 1967 S1(1). It is lawful for a clergyman of the Scottish Episcopal Church to officiate in England

the parish of another clergyman[116] without the consent of the incumbent[117]. Only an episcopally ordained priest may consecrate and administer[118] the holy sacrament of the Lord's Supper[119]. If present[120] at a celebration of Holy Communion according to a rite contained in the Alternative Service Book 1980, a bishop should act as president[121]. Baptism is normally to be administered by the incumbent, although it may be delegated[122]. Confirmation can only, of course, be administered by a bishop[123]; however, in the rite according to the Alternative

in a church or chapel belonging to the Church of England, if invited to do so by the minister having the cure of souls, without notifying the diocesan bishop for the same period and subject to the same conditions as would be applicable to him if he had been admitted into Holy Orders by a diocesan bishop in the Church of England: Episcopal Church (Scotland) Act 1964, s. 1(1); see, too, *Legal Opinions concerning the Church of England* at pp. 173–174. As the greater includes the less it would seem that the diocesan bishop could in any event authorise such an act (other, possibly, than the solemnisation of marriage) if the cure is vacant. The position as to clergymen of the Church of Ireland without permission under the 1967 Measure is unclear (see *op. cit.* at p. 174) but it would seem that at the least they require the permission of the diocesan bishop in addition to any other consents. See, further, **p. 177, footnote 216,** *infra*.

[116] See, too, **pp. 22 and 24** *infra*.

[117] *Wood* v. *Headingley-cum-Burley Burial Board* [1892] 1 QB 713 at p. 729. But see also Canon B 29, para. 4, and **p. 226** *infra*, concerning the ministry of absolution.

[118] See **p. 98, footnote 5,** *infra*.

[119] Canon B 12, para. 1. This is so even in an emergency: see *Escott* v. *Mastin* (1842) 4 Moo. PC 104 at p. 128 and **p. 43, footnote 96,** *infra*.

[120] It is most likely that the words are intended to mean 'present and taking part in his capacity as a bishop': contrast Canon C 26, para. 1; if this were not so, a suffragan bishop attending a cathedral as a canon would always have to preside at the eucharist unless the diocesan bishop were there. In The Ordering of Priests in the Book of Prayer the rubric before the laying on of hands speaks of 'the priests present'. Presumably this has the same meaning (namely, taking an active part and not merely being in the congregation), in spite of the rubric before the Veni Creator which speaks of 'the Priests, and others that are present'; fortunately a strict statutory interpretation is no longer necessary and the latter rubric only emphasises the participation of the whole congregation. This is confirmed by the rubrics in The Ordination of Priests in the Alternative Service Book at pp. 378–379 which make it clear that the reference to those laying on hands is, in fact, to the priests who are assisting the bishop: see, too, Canon C 3, para. 4. Contrast the clearer wording of Canon C 2, para. 1: 'present together and joining in the act of consecration'.

[121] Although he would no doubt ordinarily do so at a service celebrated according to the rite in the Book of Common Prayer, this rubric cannot be seen as laying down a rule of Church order as the rubrics in the Book of Common Prayer specify the necessary role of a bishop who is present: see **p. 98** *et seq. supra*.

[122] See Note 1 to the Baptism of Children in the Alternative Service Book at p. 241. The rubrics before the Ministration of Private Baptism to be Used in the Church according to the Book of Common Prayer (see particularly the penultimate rubric) seem to assume that the minister will normally be the minister having the cure of souls; this is the more evident when looking at the second rubric before the Ministration of Private Baptism in Houses in the same prayer book. Indeed, this seems also to be reflected in the original Canon B 21 which stated that 'It is desirable that every minister having a cure of souls shall from time to time administer the sacrament of Holy Baptism upon Sundays or other Holy Days . . .'. However, the new Canon B 21 has been amended (on 20 February 1979) so that the word 'normally' is substituted for the words 'from time to time'. Even this more naturally refers to timing than to who is to be the minister. Note 1, however, states that 'Holy Baptism is normally administered by the parish priest in the course of public worship on Sunday; but it may be administered at other times, and he may delegate its administration to other lawful ministers . . .'. This seems to be a rubric dealing with Church order and therefore applicable whichever rite is being used.   [123] Canon B 27.

Service Book the bishop may delegate to other ministers anything (other that the actual confirmation) that is prescribed to be said or done by him[124]. Although marriage should canonically be solemnized by a priest[125], it may in law also be solemnised by a deacon[126]. Ordination must be by a bishop[127], although the priests taking part shall 'together with the bishop lay their hands upon the head of every person who receives the order of priesthood.'

Consecration of a bishop requires at least three other bishops 'present and joining in the act of consecration'; one of these must be the archbishop of the province or a bishop appointed to act on his behalf[128].

In certain instances provision is made by canon or rubric for services, or parts of services, to be conducted by those who are not ordained[129]. Thus Canon E 4, para 2A[130], permits the bishop[131] to authorise a reader:

> to bury the dead or read the burial service before, at or after a cremation but only, in each case, with the goodwill[132] of the persons responsible and at the invitation of the minister of a parish or extra-parochial parish ...

Canon B 11, para, 1, also provides[133]:

> Readers, such other lay persons as may be authorised by the bishop of the diocese[134], or some other suitable lay person, may, at the invitation of the minister of the parish or, where the cure is vacant or the minister is incapacitated, at the invitation of the churchwardens, say or sing Morning or Evening Prayer (save for the Absolution).

Strangely, no such provision has been made in the Canons in relation to Ante-Communion[135] although the notes to both Rites A and B in the Alternative Service Book contain the provision[136]:

---

[124] Note 3 at p. 252.

[125] See the rubrics to the marriage service in both the Book of Common Prayer and the Alternative Service Book.

[126] 14 Halsbury's Laws of England (4th ed.) at paras 664 and 1030. A clergyman may not solemnize his own marriage: *Beamish* v. *Beamish* (1861) 9 HL Cas. 274.

[127] See the Ordinal in both the Book of Common Prayer and the Alternative Service Book.

[128] Canon C 2, para. 1.   [129] As to ecumenical projects see **p. 28** *infra*.

[130] As to deaconesses and lay workers see Canon D 1, para. 4(b), (c), and Canon E 7, para. 5(b), (c) respectively.   [131] This must refer to the diocesan bishop.

[132] This does not seem to require actual consent but permits the reader to proceed as long as there appears to be no opposition.

[133] See, too, the rubric inserted into the Book of Common Prayer by the Prayer Book (Further Provisions) Measure 1968, s. 1(1). Although this Measure is now repealed, the insertion remains unchanged: Church of England (Worship and Doctrine) Measure 1974, s. 6(4), Sch. 3, para. 4; Interpretation Act 1978, s. 16(1)(b).

[134] See also Canons D 1, para. 3(a), and E 4, para. 2(b).

[135] As to Ante-Communion see **p. 118** *infra*.

[136] See Notes 24 and 14 at pp. 118 and 178 respectively.

When there is no communion, the minister reads the service as far as the Absolution . . . , and then adds the Lord's Prayer, the General Thanksgiving, and/or other prayers . . . at his discretion, ending with the Grace. When such service is led by a deacon or lay person, 'us' is said instead of 'you' in the Absolution.

Clearly such lay ministration is permitted in relation to those two rites but it is far from clear whether, in the absence of specific regulation by canon, it is permissible in relation to the rite in the Book of Common Prayer. It is, however, likely that it is indeed permissible by reason of the fact that the notes in the Alternative Service Book must be regarded as indicative of proper Church order[137]. In addition, a baptised and confirmed person may be authorised by the bishop[138], subject to specified circumstances or conditions, to distribute the Holy Sacrament in a particular parish[139].

Subject to the general directions of the bishop, the Epistle, the Gospel and the Prayer of Intercession may at the invitation of the minister be read by a lay person at the celebration of Holy Communion[140]. In the rite according to the Alternative Service Book[141] a deacon or lay person may also preside[142] over the Ministry of the Word 'when necessity dictates'[143]. No mention is made of the lessons in Morning and Evening Prayer and it could be argued from this, and from the fact that Canon E 4 provides *inter alia* that it is lawful for those admitted to the office of reader 'to read the word of God'[144], that other lay persons may not in fact read those lessons. However this argument must be fallacious. Not only has it long been the practice for such lessons to be read by the laity[145] but, as has been seen, the whole of mattins and evensong may in

---

[137] Being a matter of doubt it is for the diocesan bishop to resolve: see **p. 31** *et seq. infra*. See, further, **p. 100** *infra*.

[138] On written application by the incumbent or priest-in-charge and supported by the churchwardens, specifying the name and relevant particulars of the person to whom the application relates. See, too, Canons D 1, para. 3(a), and E 4, para. 2(c).

[139] See Canon B 12, para. 3; *Ministry to the Sick*, at p. 3, note 6; and the Regulations made by the Church Assembly in November 1969. See, too, **p. 110** *et seq. infra*.

[140] Canon B 12, para. 4; see, further, Canon E 7, para. 4(b) (lay workers). There is, of course, no specific 'Prayer of Intercession' in the Holy Communion according to the rite contained in the Book of Common Prayer, unless Canon B 12 refers to the Prayer for the Church Militant; on the other hand, the reading of the latter prayer by a lay person would seem now to fall within the ambit of Canon B5, para. 1: see **p. 47** *et seq. infra*.

[141] As to the position in the Book of Common Prayer see **p. 99** *infra*.

[142] It is unclear precisely what this means but it would not permit a lay person to preach without the licence or specific permission of the diocesan bishop: see Canon B 18, para. 2, and **p. 24** *infra*.

[143] See Note 2 at p. 115 of the Alternative Service Book. No guidance is given as to what such a 'necessity' may be. It would probably encompass pastoral considerations as well, for example, as a situation where the priest is struggling with loss of voice. See, too, **p. 46, footnote 103** *infra*.

[144] This was, of course, the duty of the Reader in the ancient Church: Phillimore, *Ecclesiastical Law*, (2nd ed.) vol. I at p. 450.

[145] This would not in any event seem to be contrary to the rubric after the Creed in the Book of Common Prayer: see **p. 85** *infra*.

certain circumstances be said by a lay person. Moreover, the rubric in the Book of Common Prayer (although it could refer to another clergyman) speaks of 'He that readeth' and thus of a person not necessarily the minister[146]. At the very least the reading of the lessons by a lay person would be regarded as *de minimis*[147] and therefore not contrary to the law[148]. Moreover, if it is permissible for a lay person to read the Epistle and Gospel, it is inconceivable that it is not equally permissible at Morning and Evening Prayer.

Save in the instance noted above[149], only one minister is required in order to take a service. However, that does not necessarily mean that other ministers may not participate. Indeed, if a bishop is present[150] at Holy Communion, he should pronounce the absolution and the blessing; as a directive dealing with Church order this should also be followed in other services as well, whether or not the form of service is contained in the Book of Common Prayer. Similarly, the note[151] to the Order of Holy Communion in the Alternative Service Book provides that:

> The president ... presides over the whole service. He says the opening Greeting, the Collect, the Absolution, the Peace, and the Blessing; he himself must take the bread and the cup before replacing them on the holy table, say the Eucharistic Prayer, break the consecrated bread, and receive the sacrament on every occasion. The remaining parts of the service he may delegate to others. When necessity dictates, a deacon or lay person may preside[152] over the Ministry of the Word.

The question of concelebration is nowhere addressed. It would certainly not have been permitted under the rigorist interpretation of the Book of Common

---

[146] This may perhaps be borne out by the note immediately before the Te Deum Laudamus: 'Note, that before every Lesson the Minister shall say, Here beginneth such a Chapter, or Verse of such a Chapter, of such a Book: and after every Lesson, Here endeth the First Lesson, or the Second Lesson.'. This note, which applies whoever reads the lessons, is possibly the most ignored of all the rubrics; it probably underlines, however, that the precise words are *de minimis*.

[147] The reading of the lessons by members of the laity was permitted by the Prayer Book (Further Provisions) Measure 1968, s. 1(5). This provision has been repealed by the Church of England (Worship and Doctrine) Measure 1974, s. 6(2), Sch. 2, and it might be argued that it was intended that lay persons should no longer read the lessons. However, in the light of the long standing practice that has remained unchanged and uncommented upon after the repeal, it is best to regard the matter as *de minimis* and thus as not requiring further legislation.

[148] That it is now legal is confirmed by Canon B 43, para 1(1) (b): see **p. 26 infra**. If it is legal for a lay person from another denomination 'to read the Holy Scriptures at *any* service' (emphasis supplied), it must similarly be legal for an Anglican lay person.   [149] See **p. 19 supra**.

[150] As this is at the least a directive as to how the service is to be taken, it must refer to a bishop in an officiating capacity; it is also a rubric dealing, if not with dogma, with Church order. For the situation of a bishop who is robed and part of the liturgical procession but not otherwise taking an active part in the service, for example, in a cathedral: see **p. 18, footnote 120, supra**.

[151] See Note 2 at p. 115.

[152] It is unclear precisely what this means, although its ambit is presumably wider than Canon B 12, para. 4. This provision cannot give lay persons generally the authority to preach: see Canon B 18, para. 2, and **p. 25 infra**.

Prayer already discussed but the position may be regarded as doubtful now that a more elastic approach to the rubrics is called for. This being so, it would seem to be a question for the diocesan bishop to decide pursuant to his discretion as provided in the Book of Common Prayer, *Concerning the Service of the Church*. This would seem also to be the position in relation to any rite under the Alternative Service Book[153]. Even if permitted, however, concelebration can only be lawful if those speaking the relevant words do so audibly and distinctly and if all those participating do so in such a manner that the celebration itself is reverent[154].

(ii)   Women priests

Canon C 8, para. 2(a), makes provision for ministers of good life and standing to minister in a church or chapel for a period of not more than seven days within three months without reference to the diocesan bishop or other Ordinary[155]. This provision applies even within a diocese where the bishop has made a declaration[156] that a woman is not to be given a licence or permission to officiate as a priest within his diocese[157]. Nonetheless, the Code of Practice issued in the light of the Measure states[158] that the House of Bishops would regard it as an abuse to use the above provisions: 'to further a policy of a regular ministry of women priests in the parish or parishes of his benefice'.

However, where a parochial church council has passed a resolution under the Measure that it will not accept a woman as a minister who presides[159] at or celebrates the Holy Communion or pronounces the Absolution[160] in the parish, Canon C 8, para. 2(a), does not permit any act in contravention of the resolution[161].

---

[153] See **p. 33** *infra*.

[154] Canon B 13, para. 1, and Canon B 14, para. 1. Each minister must also 'endeavour to ensure that the worship offered glorifies God and edifies the people': Canon B 1, para. 2. See, generally, **p. 237** *infra*.

[155] The provisions of Canon C 8 are set out in **Appendix** 2 at **p. 269** *infra*. 'The word [Ordinary] doth chiefly take place in a Bishop, and other Superiours, who alone are Universal in their Jurisdictions; yet under this word are comprized also other Ordinaries, viz. such as to whom Ordinary Jurisdiction doth of right belong whether by Privilege or by Custome': Godolphin, *Reportorium Canonicum* (London, 1680) (2nd ed.) at p. 23; see, too, 14 Halsbury's Laws of England (4th ed.) at para. 458, note 3.

[156] Under the Priests (Ordination of Women) Measure 1993, s. 2(1)(c).

[157] Priests (Ordination of Women) Measure 1993, s. 2(7).

[158] Paragraph 11(iii). The Code of Practice cannot create more than a moral obligation.

[159] See **p. 99** *et seq. infra*.

[160] In so far as this may apply to women deacons see **p.** 124 *et seq. infra*.

[161] Priests (Ordination of Women) Measure 1993, s. 3(6); Canon C 8, para. 2(a) (i). For similar provisions in relation to cathedrals see Priests (Ordination of Women) Measure 1993, s. 4(5) and Canon C 8, para. 2(a)(ii).

(iii)   Extra-parochial ministry

(a)   Non-resident parishioners

The minister of a parish[162] may perform offices and services at the home[163] of any person whose name is on the electoral roll of the parish but who is not resident[164] in the parish to the like extent and in the like circumstances as he performs offices and services at the homes of his parishioners resident in the parish; any such office or service may only be attended by persons who are the members of the family and household of the person whose name is on the church electoral roll[165].

(b)   Institutions

The bishop of a diocese in which any university, college, school, hospital or public or charitable institution[166] is situated may license[167] a clergyman of the Church of England to perform such offices and services as may be specified in the licence on any premises forming part of, or belonging to, that institution[168]. The performance of such offices and services[169] do not require the consent, nor are they subject to the control, of the minister of the parish in which they are performed[170].

---

[162] 'Minister of a parish' includes a curate licensed under seal by the Bishop to the charge of a parish, and the powers exercisable by the Minister of a parish shall be exercisable by an assistant curate or other clergyman assisting the Minister: Extra-Parochial Ministry Measure 1967, s. 3. 'Parish' means an ecclesiastical parish or district the minister of which has a separate cure of souls and includes a conventional district to the charge of which a separate curate is licensed: *ibid.*

[163] 'Home' in relation to any person means the house, flat or other place where he is living, whether permanently or temporarily: Extra-Parochial Ministry Measure 1967, s. 3.

[164] See **pp. 88** *et seq.* and **165** *infra.*   [165] Extra-Parochial Ministry Measure 1967, s. 1.

[166] Whether or not it possesses a chapel: Extra-Parochial Ministry Measure 1967, s. 2(1).

[167] The licence may be revoked by the diocesan bishop at any time: Extra-Parochial Ministry Measure 1967, s. 2(4). It may not extend to the solemnization of marriage, save for a marriage of a person who is house bound or is a detained person within the meaning of those terms in the Marriage Act 1949; the marriage must be at the institution in question and according to the rites of the Church of England: Extra-Parochial Ministry Measure, 1967, s. 2(1A); Canon B 41, para. 2. See, too, **p. 178** *infra.*

[168] Extra-Parochial Ministry Measure 1967, s. 2(1); Canon B 41, para. 2. This includes any residential premises managed by the institution and occupied by the members of staff of the institution: *ibid.* On balance it would seem that the bishop may license a woman priest under s. 2(1), even though the institution is within a parish that has passed a resolution under the Priests (Ordination of Women) Measure 1993, s. 3(1). The Public Schools Act 1868, s. 31 (see *infra*), is unaffected by s. 2 of the 1967 Measure: Extra-Parochial Ministry Measure 1967, s. 2(5).

[169] The alms collected in the course of, or in connection with, the performance of such offices and services must be disposed of in such manner as the officiating minister may determine; however, this is subject to the direction of the diocesan bishop: Extra-Parochial Ministry Measure 1967, s. 2(3).

[170] Extra-Parochial Ministry Measure 1967, s. 2(2); Canon B 41, para. 3. Technically, any visiting clergy require the consent, and are subject to the control, of the incumbent in which the institution falls.

(c)   Public schools

In certain schools[171] the chapel is deemed to be a chapel dedicated and allowed by the ecclesiastical law for the performance of public worship and the administration of the liturgy of the Church of England and, also, to be free from the jurisdiction or control of the incumbent of the parish in which it is situated[172].

E Preachers and Lecturers[173]

Sermons may only be preached by the incumbent[174] or by those having the permission or licence of the bishop to preach[175]. Even with episcopal permission, sermons may generally only be preached in a parish with the incumbent's permission[176]. According to Canon B 18, para. 2:

> The sermon shall be preached by a minister[177], deaconess[178], reader[179] or lay worker[180] duly authorised in accordance with Canon Law[181]. At the invitation of the minister having the cure of souls another person may preach with the permission of the bishop of the diocese[182] given either in relation to the particular occasion or in accordance with diocesan directions[183].

---

[171] Namely, Eton, Winchester, Westminster, Charterhouse, Harrow, Rugby and Shrewsbury: see the Public Schools Act 1868, s. 3.   [172] Public Schools Act 1868, s. 31.

[173] See, too, **p. 69** *et seq. infra*.   [174] Canon C 24, para. 3.

[175] 'And ... no person shall be or be received as a lecturer or permitted suffered or allowed to preach as a lecturer or to preach or read any sermon or lecture in any church chapel or other place of public worship within this realm of England or the dominion of Wales and town of Berwick upon Tweed unless he be first approved and thereunto licensed by the archbishop of the province or the bishop of the diocese or (in case the see be void) by the guardian of the spiritualites under his seal ....': Act of Uniformity 1662, s. 15. It is likely that preaching is embraced within the ministration permitted by Canon C 8, para. 2(a). See, too, Canon C 8, para. 2(c), Canon C 12, para. 1(a), Canon D 1, para. 4(a), and Canon E 4, para. 2 (b). A priest (unless the incumbent) or deacon nevertheless requires a licence to preach: *Finch* v. *Harris* (1702) 12 Mod. Rep. 640; Canon C 8, para. 3; and the charge by the bishop in The Ordering of Deacons in the Book of Common Prayer (' ... and to preach, if he be admitted thereto by the Bishop.') As to visiting Anglican ministers, see Canon C 8, para. 2(a).

[176] 14 Halsbury's Laws of England (4th ed.) at paras. 666, 690 and 691.

[177] See *Finch* v. *Harris* (1702) 12 Mod. Rep. 640.   [178] See also Canon D 1, para. 4(a).

[179] See also Canon E 4, para. 2(b).   [180] See also Canon E 7, para. 5(a).

[181] By Canon B 43, para. 1(1), 'A minister or lay person who is a member in good standing of a Church to which [the] Canon applies and is a baptised person may, subject to the provisions of this Canon, be invited ... (c) to preach at any service ... if the minister or lay person is authorised to perform a similar duty in his or her own Church.' The approval of the parochial church council must be obtained and, if the preaching is to be on a regular basis, the bishop's approval in writing must also be obtained: Canon B 43, paras 1(2)(a)(ii), (3) and 11. See **p. 26** *et seq. infra*.

[182] See, too, the Act of Uniformity 1662, s. 15, at footnote 175 *supra*.

[183] There is, however, no obligation upon a diocesan bishop to give such diocesan directions.

Unless so authorised by the bishop[184], a lay person[185] may not preach even though he or she is duly reading Morning or Evening Prayer[186] or presiding at the Ministry of the Word at Holy Communion[187]. A person who has been duly authorised as a lecturer by the archbishop of the province or the diocesan bishop may also preach[188].

A 'sermon' has never been legally defined[189] but according to the Oxford Dictionary it is a 'discourse[190], usually delivered from a pulpit and based upon a text of Scripture, for the purpose of giving religious instruction or exhortation'[191]. Bearing in mind that the only form of address, other than a sermon, that is permitted by the Book of Common Prayer is 'one of the Homilies[192] already set forth, or hereafter to be set forth, by authority'[193], no other type of address[194]

---

[184] The reason for this is 'to prevent heresies and schisms': *per curiam Finch* v. *Harris* (1702) 12 Mod. Rep. 640 at p. 641. There seems to be no reason why permission should not be given in relation to a particular occasion or by general diocesan directions. See Article xxiii of the Articles of Religion and Canon 49 of the 1603 Canons (although Bullard, *Constitutions and Canons Ecclesiastical 1604* at p. 192 is clearly wrong in seeking to widen the ambit of this Canon, as it is specifically aimed at a minister 'in his own Cure').

[185] See, however, Canon B 43, para. 1(1)(c) and **footnote 181 *supra***.

[186] 14 Halsbury's Laws of England (4th ed.) at para. 946.

[187] In these circumstances it might be suggested that the lay person could lawfully read one of the homilies; the Act of Uniformity 1662, s. 15, does not refer to homilies and homilies are 'regarded as authoritative statements of doctrine' (see 14 Halsbury's Laws of England (4th ed.) at para. 946, note 2). This is highly unlikely to arise in practice, however.

[188] Act of Uniformity 1662, s. 15; Halsbury's Laws of England (4th ed.) at para. 724.

[189] Note 7 in *A Service of the Word and Affirmations of Faith* at p. 8 gives the first partial definition although it is restricted to services of Morning and Evening Prayer according to the Alternative Service Book or a Service of the Word with Holy Communion Rite A: *ibid* at p. 10. Note 7 reads: 'The term sermon may include less formal exposition, the use of drama, interviews, discussion, and audio-visuals. Hymns or other sections of the service may be inserted between parts of the sermon. The sermon may come after one of the readings, or before or after the prayers.' In relation to the Agape with the Holy Communion in *Lent, Holy Week, Easter* the introduction at p. 98 says: 'There could be discussion instead of a sermon . . . It is necessary for the president to steer, order, and guide the congregation so that all is done without uncertainty and with dignity.' see, too, *Patterns for Worship* (Church House Publishing, 1995) at p. 211, and **p. 69 *et seq. infra.***

[190] A 'sermon' includes a eulogy at a funeral, if the eulogy includes a Christian content such as the deceased having led a good Christian life: see **p. 210 *infra***. Save in the limited circumstances where Note 7 of *A Service of the Word and Affirmations of Faith* applies (see **the previous footnote**) the use of this word may exclude, for example, a dialogue between two authorised persons from different pulpits. It is unclear whether a sermon is an integral part of the ministration of a service (see **p. 70, footnote 116 *infra***); if it is, a dialogue would seem to fall within the ambit of the minister's discretion under Canon B 5, para. 1. In any event (and even when Note 7 applies) care would have to be taken that the presentation of such a dialogue did not become disputatious, as it would then be in breach of good order: see **p. 237 *infra***; see, too, Canon 53 of the 1603 Canons (now repealed). In any event, such a dialogue, or a question and answer session, is permissible within a form of service approved by the Ordinary under Canon B 4, para. 3, for example for use at an archdeacon's visitation, or by the minister having the cure of souls under Canon B 5, para. 2.

[191] This excludes, for example, a presentation on proposed building alterations. This must be done after the service is concluded.　　　　　　　　[192] See Article XXXV of the Articles of Religion.

[193] See the rubrics after the Creed in the Holy Communion.

[194] This also precludes theological introductions to lessons: see Article XXV of the Articles of Religion and Canon 67 of the 1603 Canons; however, this is probably now permissible in the

is lawful. A testimony made by any person (whether ordained or lay) would in any event be regarded in law as a form of sermon[195] and would certainly require the permission of the bishop[196]; such permission would, of course, be encompassed by a general licence to preach[197].

Similarly, lectures may only be given by someone who is duly licensed by the bishop or the archbishop of the province[198].

F   Ecumenical[199]

(i)   Anglican services

As has been seen, no unauthorised person may in normal circumstances take a ministerial part in an Anglican service. However, Canon B 43 makes provision for certain persons from other denominations so to participate. Canon B 43, para. 1(1), states:

> A minister or lay person who is a member in good standing of a church to which this Canon applies[200] and is a baptised person may, subject to the provisions of this Canon, be invited to perform all or any of the following duties:
>
> (a)   to say or sing Morning or Evening Prayer or the Litany;
> (b)   to read the Holy Scriptures at any service;
> (c)   to preach at any service;
> (d)   to lead the Intercessions at the Holy Communion and to lead prayers at other services;
> (e)   to assist[201] at Baptism or the Solemnisation of Matrimony or conduct a Funeral Service;

exercise of the minister's discretion under Canon B 5, para. 1 (see, too, Note 7 in *A Service of the Word and Affirmations of Faith* at p. 8). See, also, **footnote 196** *infra* and **p. 37** *infra*. A preacher may, of course, use visual aids.

[195] A testimony is, after all, a discourse for the purpose of religious exhortation.

[196] This is also reflected in the rubric after the Creed in the Holy Communion service in the Book of Common Prayer: 'And nothing shall be proclaimed or published in the Church, during the time of Divine Service, but by the Minister.'. See, too, *Williams* v. *Glenister* (1824) 2 B & C 699 and **p. 82** *et seq. infra*.

[197] Similarly, the addition of a theological introduction, however short, before the reading of a lesson could only be justified if made by someone similarly having the bishop's permission: see *Finch* v. *Harris* (*supra*). If that introduction were prepared (or previously vetted) by the minister, the subsequent reading might well then be regarded as *de minimis*.

[198] Act of Uniformity 1662, s. 15; 14 Halsbury's Laws of England (4th ed.) at para. 724.

[199] For ecumenical projects see Canon B 44, especially Canon B 44, para. 4(1)(b).

[200] That is, every Church to which the Church of England (Ecumenical Relations) Measure 1988, applies: Canon B 43, para. 12(1).

[201] This means that they cannot take the essential parts of the service: see **p. 178** *infra*.

(f)   to assist in the distribution of the holy sacrament of the Lord's Supper to the people at the Holy Communion;

if the minister or lay person is authorised to perform a similar duty in his or her own Church.

Such an invitation in relation to a parish church or other place of worship[202] in the parish[203], other than duties in connection with a service of ordination or confirmation[204], may only be given by the incumbent[205]. In relation to a duty mentioned in subparagraph (1)(f), or any duty mentioned in subparagraphs (1)(a), (c) or (e) which is to be performed on a regular basis, an invitation may only be given if the approval of the bishop[206] has first been obtained[207]. In the case of a duty mentioned in subparagraph (1)(e) the invitation may only be given if the persons concerned have requested the incumbent to give the invitation[208] and in the case of any duty mentioned in subparagraphs (1)(a), (c) or (f) if the approval of the parochial church council has been obtained[209].

In addition an incumbent may, with the approval of the parochial church council[210] and the bishop of the diocese[211], invite members of another Church to which the Canon applies[212] to take part in joint worship with the Church of

[202] 'Place of worship' means a building or part of a building licensed for public worship: Canon B 43, para. 12(2)(c).

[203] Similar invitations may be given in relation to a cathedral but with the same qualifications as appear in Canon B 43, para. 1(2), (3), subject to certain modifications: (a) for any reference to the incumbent there is substituted (i) in the case of a dean and cathedral cathedral, the dean and chapter, and (ii) in the case of a parish church cathedral, the cathedral chapter; and (b) the provisions relating to the approval of the parochial church council do not apply: Canon B 43, para. 1(4).

[204] An invitation to perform any duty in connection with a service of ordination or confirmation in a parish church or other place of worship in the parish may be given only by the bishop and may only be given if the approval of the incumbent and the parochial church council has been obtained: Canon B 43, para. 3.

[205] Canon B 43, para. 2. In this context 'the incumbent' includes (a) in a case where the benefice concerned is vacant (and paragraph (b) does not apply), the rural dean; (b) in a case where a suspension period (within the meaning of the Pastoral Measure 1983) applies to the benefice concerned, the priest-in-charge; and (c) in the case where a special cure of souls in respect of the parish has been assigned to a vicar in a team ministry under the Pastoral Measure 1983 or by his licence from the bishop, that vicar: Canon B 43, para. 12(2).

[206] This must be in writing and must be given in accordance with such directions as may from time to time be given by the House of Bishops of the General Synod: Canon B 43, para. 11. Although the 'bishop of the diocese' is only particularly specified in Canon B 43, para. 9, 'the bishop' referred to throughout this Canon must nonetheless be a diocesan bishop because *inter alia* of the wording of para. 12(2)(c).   [207] Canon B 43, para. 1(2)(a).

[208] Canon B 43, para. 1(2)(b).

[209] Canon B 43, para. 1(2)(c). Where the approval of the parochial church council is required, it may be given in respect of the performance of such duties as may be specified in the approval by such persons or persons, or such class of persons, as may be so specified and may be given generally for an unlimited period or given subject to such limitations, whether as to duration or occasion, as may be so specified: Canon B 43, para. 8.   [210] See **preceding footnote**.

[211] See **footnote 206 *supra***.   [212] See *supra*.

England[213]. Joint worship[214] is not defined[215] but any minister in the Church of England nevertheless remains under a duty only to use the forms of service authorised by Canon B 5[216]. Similar provision is made in relation to cathedrals, although no approval is then required from any parochial church council[217].

Where there is a local ecumenical project[218] the diocesan bishop may in an instrument in writing made after consultation[219] with the parochial church council of each parish or part of a parish in the area of the project authorise ministers[220] of any other participating Church[221] with the goodwill of the persons concerned[222] to baptise in a place of worship of the Church of England in that area in accordance with a rite authorised by any participating Church[223]. Similar provision may be made for the holding of joint services, including services of baptism and confirmation[224], as well as the holding of services of Holy Communion presided over by a minister of any other participating Church[225].

(ii)   Non-Anglican services

A priest or deacon who receives from a person authorised by a Church to which Canon B 43 applies[226] an invitation to take part in a non-Anglican service may in the course of that service perform any duty assigned to him if the duty assigned to him is, or is similar to, a duty which he is authorised to perform in the Church of England[227]. Before accepting the invitation he must first obtain the

---

[213] Canon B 43, para. 9. Such an invitation may also be given to use a church in the parish for worship in accordance with the forms of service and practice of that other Church on such occasions as may be specified in the approval given by the bishop: *ibid.* In this provision 'form of service' must mean 'rite'.

[214] As to joint services under Canon B 44, para. 4(1)(f), see **p. 228** *et seq. infra.*

[215] However, it includes the blessing of a memorial in an Anglican churchyard by a Roman Catholic bishop in the presence of Anglicans: *In re St Edmund's Churchyard, Gateshead* [1995] 3 WLR 253 at pp. 258H–259B.

[216] As to this and the meaning of incumbent in these particular circumstances, see **p. 228, footnote 132** *infra.*   [217] Canon B 43, para. 10.

[218] See Canon B 44.   [219] See **p. 122, footnote 17** *infra.*

[220] Namely, any person ordained to the ministry of the Word and Sacraments: Canon B 44, para. 9.   [221] That is, a Church participating in the project: Canon B 44, para. 9.

[222] Presumably this means those bringing the child for baptism. It seems that their prior consent is not strictly necessary but it would clearly be sensible to consider this question before the service is arranged so as to prevent a situation in which the lack of goodwill only manifests itself immediately before, or even during, the service.   [223] Canon B 44, para. 4(1)(c).

[224] Canon B 44, para. 4(1)(e), and **p. 228** *infra.*

[225] Canon B 44, para. 4(1)(f). In such circumstances there is special provision for the giving of notice (see **p. 82** *infra*) as well as in relation to the conveying of consecrated elements in Sick Communion pursuant to Canon B 37, para. 2 (see **p. 117, footnote 173** *infra*): Canon B 44, para. 4(3)(a),(c). No such service is to be regarded as a celebration of the Holy Communion according to the use of the Church of England: Canon B 44, para. 4(3)(b). The bishop must be satisfied that the rite and elements to be used are not contrary to, nor indicative of any departure from, the doctrine of the Church of England in any essential matter: Canon B 44, para. 4(2).   [226] See *supra.*

[227] Canon B 43, para. 3(a).

approval of the incumbent[228] of the parish in which the service is to take place and, if he is to participate on a regular basis, the approval of both the bishop of the diocese[229] and the parochial church council[230] of the parish in which the service is to take place[231]. A similar provision applies when a bishop has received such an invitation, save that he must first obtain the approval of the incumbent of the parish in which the service is to take place and, in the case of an invitation to take part in a service in another diocese, the approval of the bishop of that diocese[232].

In the case of an invitation to a priest or deacon to take part in the ordination of a minister of a Church to which the Canon applies or to preside at the Holy Communion[233], the written approval of the bishop of the diocese in which the service is to take place must first be obtained in addition to the other approvals[234]. Similarly, a bishop who has received such an invitation must first obtain the approval of the archbishop of the province rather than that of the bishop of the diocese where the service is to take place[235]. In the case of an invitation to preside at the Holy Communion, the bishop or archbishop may not give his approval unless he is satisfied that there are special circumstances which justify acceptance of the invitation and that the rite and the elements to be used are not contrary to, nor indicative of any departure from, the doctrine of the Church of England[236]. A bishop or priest who has accepted an invitation to take part in the ordination or consecration of a minister of a Church to which Canon B 43

---

[228] In this context 'the incumbent' includes (a) in a case where the benefice concerned is vacant (and paragraph (b) does not apply), the rural dean; (b) in a case where a suspension period (within the meaning of the Pastoral Measure 1983) applies to the benefice concerned, the priest-in-charge; and (c) in the case where a special cure of souls in respect of the parish has been assigned to a vicar in a team ministry under the Pastoral Measure 1983 or by his licence from the bishop, that vicar: Canon B 43, para. 12(2). If the approval of the incumbent is withheld, the applicant may appeal to the bishop of the diocese in which the service is to take place and if, after considering the views of the applicant and the incumbent, the bishop determines that approval has been unreasonably withheld, the bishop may authorise the applicant to take part in the service in question. Where the bishop so determines he must inform the incumbent in writing of the reasons for that determination: Canon B 43, para. 7.

[229] This must be in writing and given in accordance with such directions as may from time to time be given by the House of Bishops of the General Synod: Canon B 43, para. 11.

[230] Where the approval of the parochial church council is required, it may be given in respect of the performance of such duties as may be specified in the approval by such persons or persons, or such class of persons, as may be so specified and may be given generally for an unlimited period or given subject to such limitations, whether as to duration or occasion, as may be so specified: Canon B 43, para. 8.   [231] Canon B 43, para. 3(b)(i), (iii).

[232] Canon B 43, para. 2(a), (b)(i), (ii). The bishop's approval must be in writing and may only be given in accordance with any directions that may from time to time have been given by the House of Bishops of the General Synod: Canon B 43, para. 11.

[233] Different considerations apply in relation to local ecumenical projects: see Canon B 44, paras 4(1)(d), (2) and 5.   [234] Canon B 43, para. 3(b)(ii).

[235] Canon B 43, para. 2(b)(iii). By analogy with para. 3(b)(iii) presumably this means the archbishop of the province where the service is to take place. The archbishop's approval must be in writing and may only be given in accordance with any directions that may from time to time have been given by the House of Bishops of the General Synod: Canon B 43, para. 11.

[236] Canon B 43, para. 4.

applies may not, by the laying on of hands or otherwise, do any act which is a sign of the conferring of Holy Orders, unless that Church is an episcopal Church with which the Church of England has established intercommunion[237].

A deaconess, lay worker or reader who receives from a person authorised by a Church to which Canon B 43 applies an invitation to take part in a service may in the course of that service perform any duty assigned to him or her if the duty so assigned is, or is similar to, a duty which he or she is authorised to perform in the Church of England[238]. Before accepting the invitation the approval of the incumbent of the parish[239] in which the service is to take place must be obtained and also, in the case of an invitation to take part in a service on a regular basis, the approval of both the bishop of the diocese and the parochial church council of that parish[240].

---

[237] Canon B 43, para. 5.   [238] Canon B 43, para. 6(a).

[239] For a right of appeal, see Canon B 43, para. 7, and *supra*.

[240] Canon B 43, para. 6(b). The bishop's approval must be in writing and may only be given in accordance with any directions that may from time to time have been given by the House of Bishops of the General Synod: Canon B 43, para. 11. As to the form of the approval of the parochial church council, see Canon B 43, para. 8.

2

RESOLUTION, ALTERATION
AND VARIATION

A bishop cannot release from the application of the rubrics but he may resolve questions of doubt within the ambit of the law. Few alterations, additions or omissions are permitted to forms of service, although in rare circumstances reliance may be placed on the doctrine of necessity.

Trifling deviations from the forms of service are disregarded by the law. In addition Canon B 1, para. 1, permits the minister conducting a service to use variations which are not of substantial importance according to particular circumstances; such variations must be reverent and seemly and may not be contrary to the doctrine of the Church of England in any essential matter.

A Resolution

The Book of Common Prayer itself recognized that, however much care was taken in its writing, it would be impossible to eliminate all doubtful questions[1]:

> And forasmuch as nothing can be so plainly set forth, but doubts may arise in the use and practice of the same; to appease all such diversity (if any arise) and for the resolution of all doubts, concerning the manner how to understand, do, and execute, the things contained in this Book; the parties that so doubt, or diversly take any thing, shall always resort to the Bishop of the Diocese, who by his discretion shall take order for the quieting and appeasing of the same; so that the same order be not contrary to any thing contained in this Book[2]. And if the Bishop of the Diocese be in doubt, then he may send for the resolution thereof to the Archbishop.

This provision has been described as 'a faint echo' of the *jus liturgicum*[3] and still stands in relation to the Book of Common Prayer[4]. There is, however, no

---

[1] *Concerning the Service of the Church.*

[2] 'But the bishop is subordinate to the statute law, and where the rubrics are express, he has no authority to release any minister from obedience to them, or to determine anything "that is contrary to what is contained in the service book"': Stephens, *The Book of Common Prayer* (Ecclesiastical History Society, 1849) vol. I, at p. 123. This remains so even though a rubric is now usually only a directive: see, further, **p. 11 *et seq. supra.*** Nevertheless, when rubrics are to be treated as directives, the scope for resolution by the bishop would seem to be enhanced.

[3] Briden & Hanson, *Moore's Introduction to English Canon Law* (3rd ed.) at p. 57.

[4] See *Faulkner* v. *Litchfield* (1845) 1 Rob. Eccl. 184 at p. 255; *Westerton* v. *Liddell* (1857) Moore's Special Report 1 at p. 188; *Martin* v. *Mackonochie* (1868) LR 2 A & E 116 at pp. 191–194. In the last case Sir Robert Phillimore considered this provision at some length and concluded (at p. 193) that it relates only to 'things neither ordered nor prohibited expressly or by implication' by the rubrics.

similar provision in relation to the Alternative Service Book, although there is once again a faint echo in the discretion of the bishop to decide upon which occasional office (other than confirmation) should be used in the case of any failure to agree between the minister and the person concerned[5].

It must be stressed, however, that the bishop may only resolve doubts between two otherwise lawful actions; he cannot permit actions which are unlawful. As Sir Robert Phillimore said in *Martin* v. *Maconochie*[6]:

> Was there any limitation to this authority? Only one, it appears; that his order 'shall not be *contrary* to anything contained in this book;' leaving therefore, in my judgment, within the domain of his authority that third category to which I have referred, namely, 'things neither ordered nor prohibited expressly or by implication'.

It follows, therefore, that the final arbiter of what is legal is always the court[7]; this is so whichever rite the resolution of doubt refers to.

(i) Book of Common Prayer

It is clear[8] that once a doubt arises it must be decided by the diocesan bishop; if the bishop is in doubt, the decision must be by the archbishop[9]. The person who is in doubt is not entitled himself to opt for one view rather than another; to do so would be an ecclesiastical offence[10]. In addition, not to follow the decision of the bishop once communicated (at least if the decision is accompanied by an order to comply[11]) would be a breach of the canonical oath of obedience, if such an oath has been taken[12].

---

[5] Canon B 3, para. 4; Church of England (Worship and Doctrine) Measure, 1974, s. 1(4). See **p. 62** *infra*. [6] (1868) LR 2 A & E 116 at p. 193.
   [7] See, too, *Kemp* v. *Wickes* (1809) 3 Phillim. 264 at p. 283 *per* Sir John Nicholl and the proviso to Canon B 5, para. 4. See, also, *The Archbishop of York on Reservation of Sacrament* (MacMillan & Co., 1899) at p. 15: 'Speaking as I do to-day as a father in God than as an ecclesiastical judge . . . '.
   [8] See also **pp. 31** *supra* and **48** *infra*.
   [9] Although the Prayer Book does not say so, this must mean the archbishop of the relevant province.
   [10] Presumably a bishop's direction remains valid until he revokes it, at least while he is in office; once another bishop is appointed, that new bishop may give another ruling. Nevertheless, once a direction has been given a minister cannot ignore it, even when the bishop giving it has left office; rather, he is under a duty either to obey the direction given or to seek a further direction.
   [11] In *Martin* v. *Mackonochie* (1868) LR 2 A & E 116 Sir Robert Phillimore expressed the view (at pp. 193–194) that 'The mode of resolution is not stated, but the language is such as to render it improbable that any formal proceedings in a court were contemplated . . . It may be said that the bishop, when he had taken order for appeasing the doubt, would have no legal means of enforcing that order, and that for the purpose of such enforcement he must have recourse to his court. But it appears to me that, on the supposition that the matter was one on which he could exercise his discretion, he could clothe his order with the character of a monition, and that a disobedience to such monition would subject the person disobeying to the penalties of contumacy.'. It is interesting to note that Canon B 5, para. 4, has been amended to make it clear that the bishop may give 'directions' as well as pastoral advice and guidance.
   [12] Canon C 14, para. 3; 14 Halsbury's Laws of England (4th ed.) at para. 660; *Bishop of St Albans* v. *Fillingham* [1906] P 163.

(ii) Alternative Service Book

As has already been noted there is no specific provision in the Alternative Service Book 1980 which is the equivalent of that in the Book of Common Prayer. Nevertheless, being a question of good Church order, it would be strange if there were not the same power in relation to every rite[13]. In fact, the situation is covered by Canon C 18, para. 4, which states:

> Every bishop is, within his diocese[14], the principal minister and to him belongs the right, save in places and over persons exempt by law or custom[15], of ... ordering, controlling, and authorising[16] all services in churches, chapels, churchyards and consecrated burial grounds ...

The bishop cannot be empowered by the Canon to do anything not otherwise authorised by the Church of England (Worship and Doctrine) Measure 1974, but the words are apt to cover the resolution of any doubt[17]. It is likely, too, that the

---

[13] Indeed, if the bishop's discretion under the Book of Common Prayer is the vestige of the *jus liturgicum*, then that discretion within the same parameters also applies to other legally authorised rites as well, even if not specifically expressed. In *Martin* v. *Mackonochie* (1868) LR A & E 116 at p. 192 Sir Robert Phillimore said of the provision for resolution in the Book of Common Prayer: 'It is important to notice the nature and character of the remedy proposed. It is one in perfect accordance with the principle upon which order and discipline of the Church had, in obedience to the will of Christ, been founded by his apostles; a principle which recognized the apostolical order of bishops as necessary for the due constitution of the Church; and in perfect accordance with the great principle of the Reformation of the Church of England, that a duly consecrated bishop had a divine authority, perfect and complete in itself, and wholly independent of the previous consent or subsequent ratification of that authority of the Pope.' A similar comment could be made about the view expressed in the text.

[14] The discretion can only therefore be exercised by the diocesan bishop. This general authority of the bishop in such matters seems to have been recognised in *Westerton* v. *Liddell* (1857) Moore's Special Report 1 at p. 188 (quoted in *Martin* v. *Mackonochie* (1868) LR 2 A & E 116 at p. 194) where the Privy Council, having decided that altar frontals are legal, observed: 'Whether the cloths so used are suitable or not, is a matter to be left to the discretion of the ordinary.' Although in *Martin* v. *Mackonochie* Sir Robert Phillimore seems to have treated this as part of the discretion given by the Book of Common Prayer to resolve questions of doubt, it is not clear that this was in fact so. Questions as to altar frontals are now recognized as falling within the faculty jurisdiction.

[15] See, for example, Canons B 15A, para. 3, and C 8, para. 2. See, too, **p. 22, footnote 155** *supra*.

[16] As to this see **p. 218** *et seq. infra.*

[17] See, however, Canon B 5, para. 4, which only permits the bishop to give 'pastoral guidance, advice or directions' in relation to variations which are not of substantial importance and to the use of services on occasions for which no other provisions are made: see **pp. 48 and 220** *infra*. However, this Canon applies equally to variations made to services according to the Book of Common Prayer and it is unlikely that the bishop's discretion expressed in *Concerning the Service of the Church* (see above) has been impliedly taken away. Either (i) the resolution of doubt is restricted to matters already appearing in any services expressly authorised, or (ii) the bishop's discretion is in fact always 'pastoral guidance, advice or direction(s)' subject to the adjudication of the ecclesiastical courts. On the latter view Canon B 5, para. 4, is only a reflection of the bishop's wider discretion. Nonetheless, if (ii) is correct, why is paragraph 4 only expressly applied to those matters falling within Canon B 5? What is more, as no bishop is likely to permit the prosecution of a

provincial archbishop has the discretion to resolve any doubts that a diocesan bishop may have as he is 'within his province, the principal minister'[18]. It follows, again, that any doubts must be referred to higher authority and any resulting directions must be obeyed[19].

(iii)   Canons

Canon B 5, para. 4, and Canon B 38, para. 6, each give specific power to the diocesan bishop to resolve matters of doubt. These will be considered in relation to variation[20] and burials[21] but the difference in their wording should be noted, particularly as under the latter the minister must refer any doubt to the bishop whereas under the former he does not have to do so.

B   Alteration

As has been seen, Canon 14 of the 1603 Canons (now repealed) enjoined that:

> All Ministers . . . shall observe the Orders, Rites and Ceremonies prescribed in the Book of Common Prayer . . . without either diminishing . . . in any respect, or adding any thing in the matter of form thereof.

In spite of this and the rigorist interpretation usually placed upon the rubrics, some flexibility[22] was still allowed[23].

---

minister who abides by his resolution of a particular doubt (see the Ecclesiastical Jurisdiction Measure 1963, s. 23(1)), it is thought that (i) is the correct interpretation. Nevertheless, as a bishop is also unlikely to allow the prosecution of anyone who follows his pastoral guidance, advice or direction on any matter, the whole position is perhaps best regarded as unclear. Fortunately, if the bishop's direction is followed, the question is most unlikely to matter in practice.

[18] Canon C 17, para. 4. The Guidelines issued jointly by the Archbishops of Canterbury and York on *Solemnisation of Marriage by Deacons* (see *The Canons of the Church of England* at p. 187) would seem to be issued under this authority, even if it is not necessarily to be regarded as an example of the resolution of doubt arising in a service.   [19] See *supra*.

[20] See **p. 48** *infra*.   [21] See **p. 213, footnote 134** *infra*.   [22] See **p. 13** *supra*.

[23] This is in spite of the words of the Judicial Committee in *Martin* v. *Mackonochie* (1868) LR 2 PC 365 at pp. 382–383: 'Their Lordships are of opinion, that it is not open to a Minister of the Church, or even to their Lordships in advising Her Majesty as the highest Ecclesiastical Tribunal of appeal, to draw a distinction, in acts which are a departure from or violation of the Rubric, between those which are important and those which appear to be trivial.' Nonetheless, even if these words are to be read within the context of the arguments then being put forward (see *op. cit.* at p. 382), they emphasise that the *de minimis* rule could only (at that time at least) have had very limited application. That they are so to be read is confirmed by the words of the same judge in *Julius* v. *Bishop of Oxford* (1880) 5 App. Cas. 214 at p. 226. The words in the rubric before the Absolution in the Order for the Visitation of the Sick in the Book of Common Prayer to the effect that 'the Priest shall absolve him . . . after this sort' should not be seen as permitting variation from the words thereafter set out: see, further, **p. 225** *infra*.

This, however, was limited[24] and it was necessary for the Act of Uniformity Amendment Act 1872, to resolve various doubts that had by then arisen[25]. In particular it was made clear that Morning Prayer, the Litany and Holy Communion according to the Book of Common Prayer might be used separately or together[26]. With the repeal of that Act[27] those doubts technically return but the fact that they are separate services in the Alternative Service Book is sufficient either to resolve them[28] or to permit the separate use of those services by analogy[29]. Any flexibility permitted by statute in 1872 is likely also to be permitted now by reason of Canon B 5[30], not only in relation to the Book of Common Prayer but in relation to all rites.

(i) De minimis[31]

The law has always recognised[32] that a matter '... may be of so trifling and insignificant a nature that no one, having any discretion in the matter, ought to

---

[24] See, too, the Universities Tests Act 1871, s. 6 (now amended by the Church of England (Worship and Doctrine) Measure 1974, s. 6(3), Sch. 2) and **p. 123** *infra*.

[25] See also **pp. 70 and 121** *infra*.

[26] 'Whereas doubts have arisen as to whether the following services, that is to say, the order for morning service, the litany, and the order for the administration of the Lord's Supper or holy communion, may be used as separate services, and it is expedient to remove such doubts: be it therefore enacted and declared that any form of such services may be used together or in varying order as separate services, or that the litany may be said after the third collect in the order for evening prayer, either in lieu of or in addition to the use of the litany in the order of morning prayer, without prejudice nevertheless to any legal powers vested in the ordinary; and any of the said forms of service may be used with or without the preaching of a sermon or lecture, or the reading of a homily': Act of Uniformity Amendment Act 1872, s. 5.

[27] By the Church of England (Worship and Doctrine) Measure, 1974, s. 6, Sch. 2.

[28] The rubrics in the Alternative Service Book may be seen as ones concerning Church order and therefore of general application.

[29] That is, by reason of Canon B 5, para. 1. Morning prayer, the litany and Holy Communion should then be seen as different parts of the same service. Thus any argument that Canon B 5 can only allow variations actually *within* a service does not arise.

[30] See **p. 48** *et seq. infra*.

[31] This also overlaps with Additions: see **p. 38** *infra* and *Marson* v. *Unmack* [1923] P 163 at pp. 168–169.

[32] See *In re St Mary, Tyne Dock* [1954] P 369 at p. 382 *per* Hylton-Foster Ch; *In re St John the Evangelist, Chopwell* (1995) in **Appendix 6 at p. 296**; *Patterson* v. *Helling* [1960] Crim LR 562 and commentary. See, too, the Care of Churches and Ecclesiastical Jurisdiction Measure 1991, s. 11(8), which is based upon this rule of law. The question of *de minimis* does not seem to have been considered in *The Archbishops on the Lawfulness of the Liturgical Use of Incense and the Carrying of Lights in Procession* (MacMillan & Co., 1899) at p. 8: 'These practices are probably in strictness all illegal; but no Bishop would be wise in allowing a prosecution for such unimportant deviations from the strict letter of the law.' Nor does it seem to have been considered in *Elphinstone* v. *Purchas* (1870) LR 3 A & E 66 at p. 111 *per* Sir Robert Phillimore: 'It appears to me that the epithet "high" [to describe a celebration of the eucharist in a notice given during divine service] has no sanction from the rubric, and, though perhaps in itself not very material, cannot legally be used.' If, which is doubtful, the case of *Re St Mary's, West Fordington* (1956) (briefly reported in *Opinions of the Legal Advisory Commission* (6th ed.) at p. 143) can legally be supported, it can only be on the basis of *de minimis*.

allow it to be the subject of litigation'[33]. An example of this was given by Sir John Nicholl in *Bennett* v. *Bonaker*[34]:

> The articles charge various departures from the rule, and various neglects without any just cause. It neither is likely, nor would it be proper, that the parishioners should complain of occasional accidental omissions, but here the number of times shew that the vicar's neglect was habitual . . .

There is clearly a distinction between accident and negligence, although in practice it may be difficult to decide which is which. Similarly, the omission of words from a lesson, although not legally justified, may be greatly extenuated if done through feelings of delicacy[35]. No doubt the omission of those portions of the psalms as were enclosed within brackets in the 1928 Deposited Book[36] would fall under this head.

So, too, the addition of the invitation 'Let us pray' in places not otherwise specified would seem (unless it were to become intrusive) to fall within the *de minimis* rule[37]. The same may be said of the use of a short prefatory prayer by a preacher, such as one based on Psalm 19 verse 14[38], or the conclusion of the sermon with the Grace. To announce the objects to which the offertory is to be

---

[33] *Julius* v. *Bishop of Oxford* (1880) 5 App. Cas. 214 at p. 226 *per* Earl Cairns; *Parham* v. *Templar* (1821) 3 Phillim. 515 at p. 527 *per* Sir John Nicholl. An Admonition to all Ministers Ecclesiastical in *Certain Sermons or Homilies appointed to be read in Churches* (Oxford, 1683) reads at p. 2: 'And where it may so chance some one or other Chapter of the Old Testament to fall in order to be read upon the Sunday or Holy-days, which were better to be changed with some other of the New Testament of more edification, it shall be well done to spend your time to consider well of such Chapters before-hand, whereby your prudence and diligence in your office may appear, so that your people may have cause to glorifie God for you, and be the readier to embrace your labours, to your commendation, to the discharge of your Consciences and their own.'. In so far as this has any legal authority it is likely to be an example of *de minimis* rather than an amendment 'by lawful authority', as the Act of Uniformity 1662, s. 25, only provided for very limited amendments: 'Provided always . . . that in all those prayers, litanies, and collects, which do any way relate to the king, queen, or royal progeny, the names be altered and changed from time to time, and fitted to the present occasion, according to the direction of lawful authority': see, too, **p. 4, footnote 22,** *supra* and **p. 280** *et seq., infra*. However, the homilies were also 'to be set forth, by authority': see **p. 25,** *supra*.   [34] (1828) 2 Hag. Ecc. 25 at p. 28.

[35] See *Newbery* v. *Goodwin* (1811) 1 Phillim. 282 at p. 284 *per* Sir John Nicholl. If the omission is more than *de minimis* in the circumstances, motive would be relevant in mitigation of the censure to be passed. Contrast, however, *Re Todd* (1842) 3 Notes of Cases, Supp. li, and **p. 41** *et seq. infra*.

[36] For example, Psalm 137 verses 7–9: see the note at the commencement of The Psalms of David.

[37] Note 9 of the Alternative Service Book states at p. 116: '**The Collect** (section 11) The Collect may be introduced by the words "Let us pray" and a brief bidding, after which silence may be kept.' This should not be seen as excluding the use of the words 'Let us pray' on other unspecified occasions.

[38] This must in any event be so as, in addition to the long bidding prayer provided for by Canon B 19, the Canon specifically permits a prayer 'in this form or to this effect, as briefly as is convenient'. On the other hand it may well not be *de minimis* to omit the Lord's Prayer at the end of a bidding prayer, as the Canon specifically enjoins that it should always so conclude. Of course, Canon B 5 cannot be relied upon as the bidding prayer is not part of the 'any form of service authorised by Canon B 1'; it is an addition permitted to that form of service by canon. Perhaps there is a difference between an actual bidding prayer and a private devotion by the preacher, although the difficulty about such an argument is that private devotions are not usually declaimed.

put is *de minimis*[39]. Therefore, to announce the hymn or psalm about to be sung, to indicate the place in the service book, to give a short factual[40] introduction to a lesson, or to give a verbal translation of an anthem[41], must also be *de minimis*. Similarly it would be lawful to make a short announcement at a place in the service not specified for that purpose as long as it were at a time when it did not interrupt the flow of the service, for example, an invitation to coffee at the end of the service made prior[42] to the dismissal in rite A or B[43].

Interjections by the congregation, or by a non-presiding minister, such as 'Halleluja' or 'Amen', for example during a sermon, would be regarded as acts of personal devotions[44] unless they were to become intrusive; if they were to become intrusive it would be for the churchwardens to restore order[45]. On the other hand, if such interjections were encouraged by the presiding minister, they would become part of the service and would need to be justified under Canon B 5.

Arguments based on *de minimis* always depend upon the particular circumstances. What may be acceptable on one occasion may not be acceptable on another; similarly, what may be acceptable once may not be acceptable if regularly repeated on the same or similar occasions. For example, the Book of Common Prayer uses language which many regard as extremely beautiful while others regard it as archaic. The habitual alteration of 'thee' and 'thou' to 'you' would be regarded by many who treasure its language as desecrating the whole Book of Common Prayer and would probably not be *de minimis*; however, to alter those words in the Lord's Prayer, when said in a parish that habitually uses the alternative version in its other services, might well be permissible. On the other hand, to do so in a service taken especially for The Prayer Book Society[46] might not be *de minimis*, unless done accidentally. The alteration at the end of the lessons of 'Here endeth the . . . lesson'[47] to 'Here ends the . . . lesson', although apparently irritating to some, can surely never be other than *de minimis*.

The line is not easy to draw and in some circumstances may even be governed by history. As will be seen, the singing of hymns even during a service according

---

[39] *Marson* v. *Unmack* [1923] P 163 at pp. 168–169.

[40] There is the world of difference between a *factual* introduction (for example, 'The story of the three wise men') and a *theological* introduction (for example, 'The story of the three wise men may be seen as purely symbolic'). As to the legality of such a theological introduction see **p. 25, footnote 197 supra**.

[41] This is especially so as the anthem may very well not be an actual part of the service: see **p. 67 infra**. In any event to give such a translation would be likely to assist in the edification of the people: see Canon B 1, para. 2.

[42] See *A Service of the Word and Affirmations of Faith* at p. 8.

[43] See 14 Halsbury's Laws of England (4th ed.) at para. 948.

[44] See, too, *Patterns for Worship* at pp. 104–105 and 211, and **p. 40, footnote 65 infra**.

[45] See *Hutchins* v. *Denziloe and Loveland* (1792) 1 Hag. Con. 170 at pp. 173–174 *per* Sir William Scott; and see *infra*.

[46] The Prayer Book Society itself publishes guidance as to what it regards as permissible in the use of Collects, Epistles and Gospels: updated and re-issued in May 1990. This guidance has no legal authority in itself.   [47] See the note before the Te Deum Laudamus.

to the Book of Common Prayer is legal[48]. The singing in English of the Agnus Dei at the reception of the elements at Holy Communion was therefore also held to be legal[49]. It is, therefore, entirely arguable that to say the Agnus Dei in English immediately before the reception of the elements during the rite of Holy Communion according to the Book of Common Prayer would be *de minimis*[50]. On the other hand, some things can never be regarded as *de minimis*, such as knowingly consecrating water instead of wine[51].

(ii)   Alterations

Very few alterations were, or are now, permissible. Canon B 2, para. 2, itself states that:

> Any ... amendment ... of any form of service shall not have effect unless the ... amendment ... is finally approved by the General Synod ...

What is more, section 1(7) of the Church of England (Worship and Doctrine) Measure 1974 makes specific provision for limited alteration:

> In the prayers for or referring to the Sovereign or other members of the Royal Family contained in any form of service authorised for use in the Church of England, the names may be altered, and any other necessary alterations made, from time to time as the circumstances require by Royal Warrant, and those prayers so altered shall be used thereafter[52].

(iii)   Additions[53]

In *Hutchins* v. *Denziloe and Loveland*[54] it was decided that, because of liturgical practice (both ancient and at the Reformation) and in spite of the preclusion

---

[48] See, too, Note 3 in *A Service of the Word and Affirmations of Faith* at p. 8
[49] *Read* v. *Bishop of Lincoln* [1892] AC 644 at pp. 659–661 in effect overruling *Elphinstone* v. *Purchas* (1870) LR 3 A & E 66 and *Martin* v. *Mackonochie (No.2)* (1874) LR 4 A & E 279 on this question.
[50] A contrary argument could be based upon the cases forbidding interpolations and the words of Lord Halsbury in *Read* v. *Bishop of Lincoln* [1892] AC 644 at p. 660: 'But the archbishop did not understand [the pleadings] as alleging that the celebrant waited till the end of the hymn before he and others received the elements. No evidence was given on this point, and the archbishop's construction was not questioned before their Lordships. No case of "letting" any part of the service, therefore, was made out against the Respondent.' Nevertheless, by reason of Canon B 5, para. 1, its interpolation now would almost certainly be justified against this historical background and its inclusion in both Rites A and B.
[51] *Beddoe* v. *Hawkes* (1888) 4 TLR 315. But see **p. 43** *infra* as to arguments from necessity.
[52] See, too, Canon B 1, para. 1(c).
[53] This section is concerned with additions other than those stipulated by the service books themselves. For example, in the Book of Common Prayer the rubric after the Creed is the only such rubric to deal with notices but it nevertheless specifically deals with all notices 'during the time of Divine Service': see **p. 84** *infra*. Similarly, *A Service of the Word and Affirmations of Faith* caters for what it describes as 'suitable' additions: see Note 2 at p. 8 and also pp. 12 and 23. 'Suitable' is defined at *ibid*, p. 7.
[54] (1792) I Hag. Con. 170 at pp. 175–180; see, too, *Read* v. *Bishop of Lincoln* [1892] AC 644 at pp. 659–661.

of other additions to the Book of Common Prayer[55], the singing of psalms and hymns during a service was legal even when not specifically authorised by the Prayer Book itself[56]. The Alternative Service Book reflects this position in its General Notes[57]:

> Various points are indicated for the singing of hymns; but, if occasion requires, they may be sung at other points also.

That is not to say, however, that it would be *de minimis* to interrupt the Prayer of Consecration with a hymn. On the other hand periods of silence have never been illegal if they add to the reverence of the service[58].

Moreover, in *Marson* v. *Unmack*[59] the Dean of the Arches said:

> A collection during Mattins or Evensong – I exclude an offertory during the Communion service because that is expressly provided for by rubric, and may therefore perhaps be regarded as part of the service – is not provided for in the Prayer Book. It is an incident occurring during a service or interposed between different portions of it, but it is no more part of the service than a voluntary played on the organ or the action of a verger closing windows or lighting the gas while the service is in progress. Though varying greatly in degree of importance, they are all alike in being matters, not in themselves irreverent or unseemly, but outside the rites and ceremonies of public worship. Such a collection is an interlude entirely at the option of the minister, and has its sole justification in the sanction of long custom.

[55] See *The Archbishops on the Lawfulness of the Liturgical Use of Incense and the Carrying of Lights* (MacMillan & Co. 1899) at p. 6. One exception to this rule was the changing of a name at confirmation, although the use of the candidate's name was not enjoined in the rite according to the Book of Common Prayer: *In re Parrott. Cox* v. *Parrott* [1946] Ch 183 at p. 186 *per* Vaisey J: see **p. 156** *infra*.

[56] See, too, *Read* v. *Bishop of Lincoln* [1892] AC 644 at pp. 659–661. 14 Halsbury's Laws of England (4th ed.) at para. 948 suggests that by analogy with *Read* v. *Bishop of Lincoln* the rubric after the Creed in the Holy Communion according to the Book of Common Prayer does not preclude the giving of additional notices as long as they are concerned with the congregation or ordinary church business. Even if this is right, a better ground would seem now to be a reliance upon Canon B 5, para. 1: see **p. 79** *infra*.

[57] Note 9 at p. 32. See also, for example, Note 8 at p. 242 in relation to The Baptism of Children and also Note 3 in *A Service of the Word and Affirmations of Faith* at p. 8.

[58] This is because silence could not in itself amount to a ceremony. The provision of a period of silence in The Ordering of Priests in the Ordinal annexed to the Book of Common Prayer immediately prior to the *Veni, Creator Spiritus* is not a ceremony as it is only to provide the opportunity for the private prayers enjoined of the congregation; strangely, however, there is no such provision in The Ordering of Deacons, although it is most unlikely that the keeping of such a silence would have been illegal even before the changes in the law of liturgy: see, too, **p. 234** *infra*. On the other hand silence might give significance to something that might otherwise be without it. The Alternative Service Book specifically provides for periods of silence in particular places in the service of Holy Communion (see Notes 21 and 13 at pp. 117 and 178 respectively) but it is most unlikely that this prevents the addition of periods of silence elsewhere as long as the 'worship offered glorifies God and edifies the people': see Canon B 1, para. 2. See, too, Note 4 in *A Service of the Word and Affirmations of Faith* at p. 8 and *Patterns for Worship* at p. 211.

[59] [1923] P. 163 at pp. 167–168. This overlaps with both *de minimis* and long practice: see **p. 4, footnote 28,** and **p. 35** *et seq. infra*.

Equally, it is thought that no objection could nowadays[60] be made to the longstanding practices[61] of bowing towards the altar[62], turning to the east in the Creed[63] or Gloria, or making the sign of the Cross. It is true that in *Read* v. *Bishop of Lincoln*[64] the Court of the Archbishop of Canterbury held[65] that it was illegal for the priest to make the sign of the Cross at either the Absolution or the Blessing, as these were regarded as illegal ceremonies[66]. So, too, making the sign of the Cross when about to consecrate the elements was held to be an illegal ceremony in *Elphinstone* v. *Purchas*[67]. Nonetheless, in the light of the new spirit of 'conformity' rather than of 'uniformity'[68] the court's emphasis upon unlawful ceremonies is almost certainly obsolete and these actions, too, are probably now perfectly legal by reason of Canon B 5, para. 1[69].

Canon B 19 provides for the addition of a bidding prayer 'in this form or to this effect, as briefly as is convenient, always concluding with the Lord's Prayer'[70]. Moreover, although technically not an addition, the Book of Common Prayer provides[71] for notice to be given 'of any thing . . . enjoined by the Queen, or by the Ordinary of the place'.

---

[60] See *Read* v. *Bishop of Lincoln* [1892] AC 644 at pp. 659–661.

[61] See Nigel Yates, *Buildings, Faith and Worship* (Clarendon Press, Oxford, 1991) at p. 63. Such actions are often (although not necessarily) examples of private devotion: cp. *In re St John the Evangelist, Bierley* [1989] Fam 60 at pp. 72G-H, 73G and 76C-D (reverencing the sacrament); see, too, **footnote 65 *infra***.

[62] This action is ambiguous and depends upon the individual's intention. There may be a great difference between bowing to the altar itself and bowing in the direction of the altar where a cross is positioned. It is thought that to reverence the altar by kissing it during High Mass would certainly be a ceremony. Whether this can be legally justified either as *de minimis* or under Canon B 5, para. 1, must depend both on the circumstances and on the theology thereby being expressed: cp. *Bishop of Oxford* v. *Henly* [1909] P 319 at pp. 327–328. The resolution of any doubt on the latter head should be referred to the bishop.

[63] Canon B 9, para. 2, only enjoins that the congregation should stand.   [64] [1891] P 9.

[65] At pp. 88–94. 'The definition of a ceremony includes this action. It is a formal symbolic gesture of religious meaning publicly made by the minister in his character of minister, rendering the delivery of language more solemn, and not expressing his personal devotion': *ibid* at p. 89. See, too, *Martin* v. *Mackonochie* (1868) LR 2 A & E. 116 at p. 133 *per* Sir Robert Phillimore; and see the evidence of Canon Mortimer (as he then was) in *Wylde* v. *Attorney-General for New South Wales ex rel. Ashelford* (1948) 78 CLR 224 at p. 278. On the other hand, it is not illegal to make the sign of the Cross if it is merely an act of private devotion: see *In re St John the Evangelist, Chopwell* (1995) in **Appendix 6 at p. 294 *infra***. Indeed, A Service for the Feast of the Baptism of the Lord in *The Promise of His Glory*, at p. 221, Note 30, provides: 'The water may be . . . placed in vessels by the door for them to make the Sign of the Cross as they leave . . .'. In *In re St Mary's, Tyne Dock* [1954] P 369 at p. 382 Chancellor Hylton-Foster regarded a holy water stoup as *de minimis* when it was located in the vestry but cp. 14 Halsbury's Laws of England (4th ed.) at para. 969; see **p. 77 *et seq. infra***.

[66] It was not an illegal ceremony to make the sign of the cross upon the forehead of the person being baptised, as this is specifically enjoined by the baptismal rites in the Book of Common Prayer. See, too, the rubric at the end of The Ministration of Publick Baptism of Infants and Canon 30 of the 1603 Canons.   [67] (1870) LR 3 A & E 66 at pp. 108–109 *per* Sir Robert Phillimore.

[68] See **p. 15 *supra***.

[69] See *In re St John the Evangelist, Chopwell* (1995) in **Appendix 6 at pp. 296–297 *infra***.

[70] As to whether the Lord's Prayer may be omitted see **p. 36, footnote 38 *supra***.

[71] See the rubric after the Creed.

(iv)   Omissions

Although Canon 14 of 1603 has been repealed, omissions from the authorised services are now dealt with by Canon B 1, para. 2[72]:

> Every minister shall use only the forms of service authorised by this Canon, except so far as he may exercise the discretion permitted by Canon B 5[73].

As has been seen, an occasional accidental omission is regarded as *de minimis*[74] and the omission of words from a lesson for reasons of delicacy is greatly extenuated[75]. However, that is where the matter ends. For example, the omission of the Gloria from the Holy Communion service according to the Book of Common Prayer because it is a penitential season such as Lent would not be permissible, unless justified under Canon B 5, para. 1[76]. It is therefore likely that the omission of the Gloria at the end of the psalms for the same theologcal reason would have to be similarly justified. On the other hand, the Alternative Service Book provides for the omission of certain Jewish doxologies in the psalms, if the Christian doxology is used[77]. It also provides for the doxology to be used in Morning and Evening Prayer either at the end of each psalm or only at the end of a group of psalms[78]. This being so, it may be argued that a similar omission in the Book of Common Prayer may indeed be justified under Canon B 5, para. 1.

The care that must be taken before any omission is made is underlined by the case of *Re Todd*[79] in which it was held to be an offence to omit the words 'As our hope is this our brother doth' during the burial service. The clergyman omitted them because he erroneously believed that the deceased had died in a state of intoxication. Although this case was decided before any flexibility was permitted in the performance of services, the same decision would almost certainly be reached today. As the Bishop of Exeter said when delivering sentence[80]:

> It is plain and undeniable, that they were omitted, because the minister did not choose to give expression to the pious and charitable hope of the Church, that the deceased Christian brother resteth in Our Lord Jesus Christ, who is the Resurrection and the Life . . . Even if the deceased had died in a state of intox- ication, however his minister may have lamented it, however it may have impaired the hope of his being admitted to rest in Christ, yet it ought not, on just consideration of the terms of the Christian covenant, to have extinguished

---

[72] The Marriage Act 1949, ss. 9(2), 78(1), envisage portions only of morning and evening prayer being read by a lay person under the authority of the bishop: see **p. 90** *infra*.

[73] See **p. 3** *supra*.   [74] *Bennett* v. *Bonaker* (1828) 2 Hag. Ecc. 25 at p. 28.

[75] *Newbery* v. *Goodwin* (1811) 1 Phillim. 182 at p. 284.   [76] See **p. 48** *et seq. infra*.

[77] Psalms 41, 72, 89 and 106. See *General Note* (g) at p. 10.

[78] See the rubric before *The Psalms* at pp. 51, 64, 75 and 83.

[79] (1842) 3 Notes of Cases, Supp. li.   [80] *op. cit.* at pp. lii–liii.

that hope, much less to have induced him to have proclaimed, or even to suggest, the extinction of it . . . To hold the contrary – to assert for the priesthood a right to judge in every case of the final condition of the deceased – would be to claim a power of the Keys, above that to which Papal Rome ever dared to aspire, and which this reformed Church, while it maintains the just authority of its priest for edification, not for destruction, hath always most strongly repudiated.

(v)   Necessity

Although the pre-Reformation canon law recognized a doctrine of necessity[81], not surprisingly it is rarely referred to in legal cases[82]. Indeed, although the doctrine of necessity was relied upon by Chancellor Garth Moore in *Rector and Churchwardens of Bishopwearmouth* v. *Adey*[83] and referred to in both *Re St Nicholas, Plumstead*[84] and *In re St Peter and St Paul, Leckhampton*[85], it has been questioned what position this doctrine now holds in the ecclesiastical law[86].

In *Rector and Churchwardens of Bishopwearmouth* v. *Adey*[87] Chancellor Garth Moore drew attention to:

---

[81] This was wider in scope than that under the English common law: see *Dictionnaire de Droit Canonique*, 'Necessité'. It must always be borne in mind that a court may refer to a 'necessity' without intending to invoke this particular doctrine: see, for example, *per* the Dean of the Arches in *In re St Mary's, Banbury* [1987] Fam 136 at p. 145C.

[82] See, however, *R* v. *Stewart* (1840) 12 Ad & E 773 at p. 777 *per* Lord Denman CJ: 'We limit the rule thus purposely: for, in passing on to the ground of necessity, we wish to be understood as distinctly recognising its existence, while we deny its application in the way now contended for.' See, also, *Archbishop of York on Reservation of Sacrament* (MacMillan & Co., 1900) at pp. 9–10: 'One such instance was alleged to have occurred in the time of my predecessor, Archbishop Longley. It was stated that during a visitation of cholera in Leeds at the time when he was Bishop of Ripon, he gave permission for the reservation of the consecrated bread and wine, that the Holy Communion might be administered to the sick in this form. The facts are not very clearly ascertained as regards the conditions and limitations under which this permission was given, but he is alleged to have accompanied the permission with the words, *Necessitas non habet leges.*' The Archbishop, however, goes on to point out at p. 14: 'We find in the Prayer Book a special Rubric relaxing the Church's requirements as regards the Communion of the Sick in the time of plague or such other like contagious diseases.' By the Sacrament Act 1547, s. 8, the reception of the sacrament in both kinds is enjoined 'excepte necessitie otherwise require'.

[83] [1958] 3 All ER 441 at pp. 446–447. In *Rector and Churchwardens of Capel St Mary, Suffolk* v. *Packard* [1927] P 289 counsel had argued for an 'aumbry of necessity' (see p. 295).

[84] [1961] 1 All ER 298 at p. 299F.   [85] [1968] P 495 at p. 500F–G.

[86] 14 Halsbury's Laws of England (4th ed.) at para. 934, note 10; but contrast the Sacrament Act 1547, s. 8, and *Legal Opinions concerning the Church of England* at p. 141. As to the general common law see *R* v. *Martin* [1989] 1 All ER 652 (CA). Simon Brown J at p. 653h-j stated: 'English law does, in extreme cases, recognise a defence of necessity. Most commonly the defence arises as duress, that is pressure on the accused's will from the wrongful threats or violence of another. Equally however it can arise from other objective dangers threatening the accused or others. Arising thus it is conveniently called "duress of circumstances" . . . [T]he defence is available only if, from an objective standpoint, the accused can be said to be acting reasonably and proportionately in order to avoid a threat of death or serious danger . . . ' However, it may be argued that a less stringent test applies in the field of ecclesiastical law as a survival from the pre-Reformation canon law. In *Blake* v. *D.P.P.* [1993] Crim. LR 586 a vicar who damaged a pillar by writing a biblical quotation upon it in response to 'the instructions of God' could not rely on necessity or duress to excuse his criminal act. See, too, *R* v. *Pommell* [1995] 2 Ct. App. R. 607.

[87] [1958] 3 All ER 441 at pp. 446–447.

the doctrine of necessity, a doctrine which has its place in the common law of England, though its limits have never been exactly defined. It has an even older place in the jus commune of the church and is, if anything, there more firmly entrenched.

Then, having set out various demographic figures, he went on[88]:

> ... I am satisfied that, if the sick are to receive the Holy Communion, reservation is a necessity, not as striking as in many cases that I have known, but, nevertheless, it is a real necessity. That, in my judgment, would be sufficient reason in law to sanction facilities for reservation in an aumbry ...

This reasoning seems not to have been intended by the Chancellor as a mere *obiter dictum*[89] but in any event there are difficulties in relying upon a general necessity[90] rather than upon one that arises in a particular emergency[91]; this is especially so when provision is being made in advance for what would (on the premise of legal necessity) be otherwise illegal. Nevertheless, Chancellor Garth Moore would again have been prepared to rely upon the same doctrine of necessity in *Re St Nicholas, Plumstead*[92], and also in *In re St Peter and St Paul, Leckhampton*[93] if there had not in the mean time been a change in the relevant rubric and thus a change in the law.

There are, however, two much earlier cases which seem to recognize the doctrine of necessity, one by implication[94] and the other quite specifically. In *Beddoe v. Hawkes*[95] Lord Penzance, the Dean of the Arches, was concerned with the case of a priest[96] who had administered water instead of wine to the communicants on Whit Sunday. The report states[97] that:

---

[88] At p. 447.

[89] See, however, *Re St Nicholas, Plumstead* [1961] 1 All ER 298 at p. 299F.

[90] *In re St Thomas, Pennywell* [1995] 2 WLR 154 at p. 162H. Contrast the wording of the bishops' resolution after the refusal of Parliament to sanction the Deposited Book: see **p. 274 *infra***. See, too, *Blake v. D.P.P.* [1993] Crim. LR 586 referred to in **footnote 86 *supra***.

[91] See *Re St Matthew's, Wimbledon* [1985] 3 All ER 670 at p. 672f *per* Chancellor Garth Moore.

[92] [1961] 1 All ER 298 at p. 299F.   [93] [1968] P 495 at p. 500F–G.

[94] See, too, *Harrod v. Harrod* (1854) 1 K & J 4; see, further, **p. 67 *infra***.

[95] (1888) 4 TLR 315. See, too, *St Luke's, Southport, The Times*, 1 October 1926, referred to at **p. 275, footnote 28 *infra***.

[96] A clergyman is always necessary for a valid eucharist. 'If the rite can only be administered by clerical hands, – if it be wholly void when administerd by a layman, – no necessity can give it validity. The consecration of the elements, for the purpose of giving the eucharist to a dying person, may be as much a matter of urgent necessity, as the baptism of an infant in extremeties; but, neither in the Roman Catholic, nor in the Reformed Church, was it ever supposed, that any extremity could dispense with the interposition of a priest, and enable laymen to administer the sacrament of the Lord's Supper': *Escott v. Mastin* (1842) 4 Moo. PCC 104 at p. 128; see, too, *Cope v. Barber* (1872) LR 7 CP 393 at p. 402. Contrast, ' . . . in the case of Necessity, in the absence of a Priest or Bishop, a Deacon may, suo Jure, baptise and administer the Eucharist unto persons sick and weak; but if a Priest be present in the Church, he cannot do it, tho' Necessity should require it, unless he be commanded thereunto by the Priest, as when there are many Persons to be baptiz'd, or to receive the Eucharist, and one Presbyter is not sufficient for them all': Ayliffe, *Parergon Juris Canonici Anglicani* (London, 1726) at p. 104. The latter part of this quotation, at least, is questionable as it seems to refer to more than distributing the sacrament; if so, in what circumstances will one priest be insufficient? See, too, Canon B 12, paras 1 and 3, and **p. 110 *infra***.   [97] At p. 316.

The defendant explained his conduct as the result of an ill-formed judgment, acted upon by him in a moment of hesitation, induced by the position in which, without warning, he found himself. He (Lord Penzance) thought that there could be little doubt that it was a great error of judgment[98], because when he saw that he had no wine and there was to be Communion it was obvious that the correct course to have pursued would have been to make some short statement to the congregation; or, at any rate, to dismiss the congregation, the circumstances for the moment not permitting the celebration of Holy Communion to take place.

It is unclear at what precise point the priest became aware that he was to consecrate water rather than wine, there being a conflict between the witnesses. The Dean of the Arches dealt with the priest upon the basis that he appreciated the true position 'when . . . there was to be Communion'. If this is so, it is difficult to see why he did not suggest as another possibility that the priest should

---

[98] This does not mean that this would always be the case. Each case depends upon its own facts and the exigencies of war, for example, would be very relevant. According to *Thank you, Padre Memories of World War II*, ed. by Joan Clifford (Fount Paperbacks, London, 1989), at pp. 54–55: 'The holding of Communion or saying Mass often presented practical difficulties, particularly in remote areas or within the P.O.W. camps. In these circumstances, various substances were utilized for the elements, and it was a case of this or nothing. Bill Story says: 'In the later stages of the retreat to Alamein, supplies became difficult and I had to use army biscuits in place of bread and cold tea for wine.' Raymond Bowers in Germany used 'black bread and some scrounged wine'. Herbert Davies in Shamshuipo used 'wafers made from rice flour and for wine, water in which raisins were soaked'. Christopher Ross, in Siam, used 'for bread, inferior canteen biscuits or thin rice-flour cake. For wine, boiled water, weak tea, coffee, coconut milk, brown sugar water, lime juice . . . ' Australian padre 'Happy Harry' Thorpe, on the Burma-Siam railway, used rice bread and pomelo juice.

Neville Metcalfe speaks of the Communion service held on Whit Sunday in the vicinity of Imphal, in the evacuation of Burma. 'We had army biscuits as wafers and some local whisky procured from a friendly Naga "head hunter" tribe and used in lieu of the usual communion wine. Despite the fact that it had been much watered down, it took the silver lining off the silver sports trophy cup which had been pressed into service as a chalice. Stomachs already weakened by attacks of dysentery were alas further aggravated.'

Two padres did startling things about which they had no qualms. W.H. Miller, with Wingate in Burma, left a record of a time when the men were 'very thirsty, they had not found the stream they had been led to believe existed. All went thirsty for two days and nights. I decided to share out the sacramental wine and wafer – it was a mere taste. It seemed the Christian thing to do. I would do it again. The men were pathetically grateful . . . '

According to Steel & Hart, *Defeat at Gallipoli* (Macmillan, 1994) at p. 330 during the Gallipoli Campaign in the First World War a Methodist service was held at which an Anglican clergyman gave the Absolution and Blessing. ' . . . [T]he "elements" consisted of pieces of army biscuit on a paten which half an hour earlier had been the bottom of a tobacco tin; the wine was water seasoned with a lemonade cube – the reason for the insertion of the lemonade cube was I remember a mystery to me at the time – perhaps it was intended to make a difference from ordinary water. Anyway no better substitutes could be devised and we received the distribution in faith and were not a little comforted.' It is unclear to what extent the ecclesiastical law binds the clergy when outside England as 'no laws can be made binding and compulsory beyond the country over which the authority making the laws extends': *per* Sir John Nicholl in *Kemp* v. *Wickes* (1808) 3 Phillim. 264 at p. 272. Nonetheless, it is thought that the ecclesiastical law still binds them when abroad (for example, as to any act of adultery), although they would be entitled to use any liturgy duly authorised by an Anglican Church when within the jurisdiction of that particular Church.

merely have proceeded to the end of the Ante-Communion; this implies that the Dean may have found that the Ante-Communion was completed and the Communion proper begun. Be that as it may, the making of a short statement to the congregation at either point of the service was forbidden (unless it should be treated as *de minimis*); moreover, the further suggestion by the Dean that the congregation should merely have been 'dismissed' in the middle of a service would have been a clear breach of Canon 14 of 1603, unless the doctrine of necessity could be invoked. The doctrine therefore has the very persuasive authority of an *obiter dictum* of Lord Penzance.

It also has the clear support of an *obiter dictum* by Sir William Scott in *Hutchins v. Denziloe and Loveland*[99]:

> ... if the minister introduces any irregularity into the service, [the churchwardens] have no authority to interfere, but they must complain to the ordinary of his conduct. I do not say there may not be cases where they may be bound to interpose; in such cases they may repress, and ought to repress, all indecent interruptions of the service by others, and are the most proper persons to repress them, and they desert their duty if they do not. And if a case could be imagined in which even a preacher himself was guilty of any act grossly offensive, either from natural infirmity or from disorderly habits, I will not say that the churchwardens, and even private persons, might not interpose to preserve the decorum of public worship. But that is a case of instant and overbearing necessity that supersedes all ordinary rules. In cases which fall short of such a singular pressure, and can await the remedy of a proper legal complaint[100], that is the only proper mode to be pursued by a churchwarden – if private and decent application to the minister himself shall have failed in preventing what he deems the repetition of an irregularity. At the same time, it is at his own peril if he makes a public complaint, or even a private complaint, in an offensive manner, of what is no irregularity at all, and is in truth nothing more than a misinterpretation of his own.

In *Moore's Introduction to English Canon Law*[101] the legal position is summarised in this way:

> There is yet one further legal doctrine which may at times be prayed in aid to justify departures from the Book of Common Prayer. It is the doctrine of necessity, known to all branches of the law of England, though about which there is singularly little authority ... It is submitted that the doctrine applies equally to matters ecclesiastical. It is the only doctrine which, for example,

---

[99] (1792) 1 Hag. Con. 170 at pp. 173–174.
[100] See, for example, *Bishop of St Albans v. Fillingham* [1906] P 163 at p. 176 (a case where an incumbent purported to 'ordain' a layman 'to oppose certain ritual practices' (see *ibid*, p. 175) of a neighbouring incumbent).   [101] Briden & Hanson, *op. cit.* (3rd ed.) at pp. 58–59.

would justify a priest in administering the Holy Communion to a person who by reason of infirmity was unable to kneel as directed by the rubric[102]. There would seem to be other instances when the doctrine of necessity may be invoked to justify a departure from the strict letter of the Book of Common Prayer. But great caution is required in the application of the doctrine. Before anyone can avail himself of it, he must show the act, *prima facie* illegal, which he has committed, was the lesser of two evils and the only reasonable way of averting the greater evil. The evil averted must be greater than the evil committed, and no more may be done contrary to the legal prohibition or injunction than is at once necessary and reasonable to avert the greater evil.

It is certainly true that the doctrine is only applicable in very exceptional cases[103] but, for example, it might be relied upon to excuse a priest who stops taking a service in the middle because of illness (whether of himself or a member of the congregation) or because of an urgent call to somebody's deathbed[104]. It is all a matter of degree[105].

Moreover, certain liturgical matters are specifically dealt with in the context of necessity. Canon B 22, para. 6, specifies that:

No minister being informed of the weakness or danger of death of any infant within his cure and therefore desired to go to baptise the same shall either refuse or delay to do so.

Thus the minister would be under a legal obligation to go even if in the middle of a service[106]. The Book of Common Prayer itself provided for The Ministration of Private Baptism of Children in Houses to be used 'when need shall compel'[107]. Indeed, in the Alternative Service Book a note preceding the service for Emergency Baptism specifically states:

In an emergency a lay person may be the minister of baptism, and should subsequently inform those who have pastoral responsibility for the person so baptized.[108]

---

[102] In a footnote it is noted that 'This and similar difficulties may now be overcome by relying on Canon B5.' In the light of the rubric at the end of Holy Communion service in the Book of Common Prayer it may be doubted whether any departure, even in such circumstances, would have been regarded as *de minimis*.

[103] A lay person may preside over the Ministry of the Word in the rite according to the Alternative Service Book 'when necessity dictates' (see **p. 20** *supra*). However, this is unlikely to be an example of necessity in law as the provision would otherwise have a very restricted application.

[104] See, too, Canon 68 of the 1603 Canons and **p. 132** *infra*.

[105] For another example see **p. 140** *infra*.   [106] See **p. 138** *et seq. infra*.

[107] See the first rubric. This and the succeeding rubric do not seem specifically to cater for lay baptism as the latter refers to 'the Minister of the parish (or, in his absence, any other lawful Minister *that can be procured*)' (emphasis supplied). These latter words seem to envisage that no lay person already in the house may in the circumstances be a 'lawful Minister'. Lay baptism in an emergency is, however, legal: Phillimore, *Ecclesiastical Law*, (2nd ed.) vol. I at p. 491. See now the position under the Alternative Service Book and **p. 141** *et seq. infra*.

[108] Note 107 at p. 280. This must be a rubric dealing with Church order and therefore apply also to the situation where the Book of Common Prayer is used.

A further example[109] may be Canon B 15A, para. 1(d), which provides for the admission to Holy Communion of 'any baptised person in immediate danger of death'. At the least this provision, being mandatory, gives a complete defence to any minister in such circumstances who might thereafter be accused of admitting to Communion a person not already confirmed or otherwise falling within Canon B 15A, para. 1(a)[110].

C   Variation

(i)   Generally

The minister conducting the service may use variations that are not of substantial importance; such variations may only be made according to particular circumstances. It is likely that variations from the Book of Common Prayer are more difficult to justify.

Guidance may be gleaned from other rites, although special care must be exercised when appealing to a rite that has only been commended (rather than authorised) for use. Church and liturgical history must be borne in mind. No variation is permitted that is contrary to, or indicative of any departure from, the doctrine of the Church of England in any essential matter. A variation made for doctrinal reasons must in any event necessarily fall outside the scope of the provision.

Both the Book of Common Prayer and the Alternative Service Book provide specific variants that may be used in particular services and *A Service of the Word and Affirmations of Faith* gives even greater flexibility coupled with regulated, but undefined, choice. However, because of the rigorist interpretation applied to the rubrics in the ecclesiastical courts, the Prayer Book (Alternative and other Services) Measure 1965, enacted[111]:

> Subject to the provisions of this Measure[112] the Minister may in his discretion make and use variations which are not of substantial importance in any form of service prescribed by the Book of Common Prayer or authorised for use under this Measure according to particular circumstances.

The 1965 Measure was repealed by the Church of England (Worship and Doctrine) Measure 1974[113], which in turn enacted by section 1(5) that:

---

[109] In contrast see Canon C 2, para. 2 (consecration of a bishop 'upon some Sunday or Holy Day, unless the archbishop, for urgent and weighty cause, shall appoint some other day'), and Canon C 3, para. 1 (ordination 'upon such other day . . . as the bishop of the diocese on urgent occasion shall appoint').

[110] This would seem to be the case even if the person were not in fact in immediate danger of death. The priest should use his Christian judgment but, no doubt, err on the side of administering the sacrament.

[111] Section 5. The section is headed 'Minor variations in the conduct of public prayer'.

[112] See, in particular, s. 7.   [113] See s. 6(3), Sch. 2.

Without prejudice to the generality of subsection (1) of this section, the General Synod may make provision by Canon . . . .

(b) for empowering any minister to make and use minor variations in the form of service contained in the [Book of Common Prayer] or approved by the General Synod, Convocation, archbishops or bishop under Canon . . . .

By section 4(3):

Where provision is made by Canon by virtue of section 1(5) of this Measure, the Canon shall provide for requiring the forms of service approved, made or used thereunder to be neither contrary to, nor indicative of any departure from, the doctrine of the Church of England[114] in any essential matter.

As a result Canon B 5 was promulgated. This Canon is headed 'Of the Discretion of the Minister in Conduct of Public Prayer[115]' and provides:

1. The minister who is to conduct the service[116] may in his discretion make and use variations which are not of substantial importance in any form of service authorised by Canon B 1 according to particular circumstances . . . .
3. All variations in forms of service . . . shall be reverent and seemly and shall be neither contrary to, nor indicative of any departure from, the doctrine of the Church of England in any essential matter.
4. If any question is raised concerning the observance of the provisions of this Canon it may be referred to the bishop[117] in order that he may give such pastoral guidance, advice or directions as he thinks fit, but such reference shall be without prejudice to the matter in question being made the subject matter of proceedings under the Ecclesiastical Jurisdiction Measure 1963[118].
5. In this Canon the expression 'form of service' has the same meaning as in Canon B 1.

---

[114] By section 5(1) 'References in this Measure to the doctrine of the Church of England shall be construed in accordance with the statement concerning doctrine contained in the Canons of the Church of England, which statement is in the following terms: "The doctrine of the Church of England is grounded in the holy Scriptures, and in such teachings of the ancient Fathers and Councils of the Church as are agreeable to the said Scriptures. In particular such doctrine is to be found in the Thirty-nine Articles of Religion, the Book of Common Prayer, and the Ordinal." ' See Canon A 5. [115] See **p. 66, footnote 68** *infra*.
[116] A service may be conducted by more than one minister. Presumably the discretion then lies in the minister conducting the relevant part of the service. If that part of the service has been delegated to him, for example, by the president in a Holy Communion Service according to the Alternative Service Book or by the incumbent, the delegation may be withdrawn as long as disorder is not thereby caused: see **p. 237** *infra*.
[117] This is a reference to the diocesan bishop, in spite of the use of the word 'Ordinary' in para. 2: *In re St John the Evangelist, Chopwell* (1995) in **Appendix 6 at p. 285** *infra*; see also **p. 32** *et seq. supra*.
[118] The final arbiter is the ecclesiastical court: *In re St John the Evangelist, Chopwell* (1995) in **Appendix 6 at p. 285** *infra*.

Unfortunately, it seems that paragraph 4 is narrower in its ambit than the bishop's discretion to resolve other doubts, although this is unlikely to matter in practice[119]. What, however, is the ambit of the minister's discretion[120]?

As has been seen, the 1965 Measure speaks of 'variations which are not of substantial importance'[121] and the 1974 Measure in section 1(5)(b) equates this with 'minor variations', whereas Canon B 5, para. 1, again speaks of 'variations which are not of substantial importance'. The meaning of the two terms is therefore synonymous. Section 4(3), in addition, forbids any variation that is contrary to, or indicative of any departure from, the doctrine of the Church of England 'in any essential matter'. Normally, if a piece of legislation uses different expressions, it is taken to mean different things but what is inessential would seem also not to be of substantial importance. Thus the expressions again seem to mean the same[122]. Nevertheless, these minor variations must amount to more than that which is already allowed under the *de minimis* rule[123]; otherwise, Canon B 5 would be otiose. A liturgical variation that is irreverent or unseemly can never be minor[124].

Until recently[125] no guidance on the interpretation of the Canon had been given by the courts[126], although in a case concerning reservation of the sacrament[127] Chancellor Garth Moore said:

My understanding of Rubric 40[128], which now has as much the force of law as the Rubric in the 1662 Book of Common Prayer, is that the last remaining legal obstacle to what again and again was said to be theologically permissible, namely, reservation, has now been removed, at any rate in respect of reservation

---

[119] See **p. 33, footnote 17** *supra*.

[120] *A Service of the Word and Affirmations of Faith* at p. 10 specifically directs that 'The shorter form of Evening Prayer is not suitable for combination with Holy Communion.'

[121] See **p. 47** *supra*.   [122] See, too, **p. 38** *et seq. supra*.

[123] In spite of the wording of Canon B 1, para. 2 (see **p. 41** *supra*), it is likely that the matters dealt with in this chapter at heading B: Alteration, (iii) *Additions* and (iv) *Omissions* would in any event still apply; even if this is not so, the same additions and omissions would be permissible under Canon B 5, para. 1. The matters dealt with at (i) *De Minimis* and (v) *Necessity* are certainly unaffected.   [124] Canon B 5, para. 3; see, too, Canon B 1, para. 2.

[125] See now *In re St Thomas, Pennywell* [1995] 2 WLR 154 at p. 170C-E and *In re St John the Evangelist, Chopwell* (1995) in **Appendix 6** at **p. 285** *infra*.

[126] As to textbook writers see 14 Halsbury's Laws of England (4th ed.) at para. 941, note 1, and Briden & Hanson, *Moore's Introduction to English Canon Law* (3rd ed.) at pp. 58–59. If proceedings were instituted under section 14(1)(a) of the Ecclesiastical Jurisdiction Measure 1963 in relation to Canon B 5, para. 1, it is thought that (a) it would be for the chancellor (i) to decide whether in law the alleged variation could in the circumstances be regarded as 'not of substantial importance' and (ii) if it could, to direct the assessors as to what in law are the proper paramaters to apply in deciding whether the particular variation were indeed 'not of substantial importance', but (b) it would be for the assessors to decide, not only what facts had been established by the evidence, but also whether any variation from the authorised services thus proved was in fact 'of substantial importance' (in accordance with the directions under (a)(ii) *supra*).

[127] *Re St Peter and St Paul, Leckhampton* [1968] P 495 at p. 499C-E.

[128] This was a reference to The Alternative Services (second series) but the argument in law remains the same.

which takes place during a Communion Service as authorised by the Alternative Services (second series). I hesitate to say whether this permission extends to cover reservation taking place after or during a service in the Book of 1662. But for services within the scope of the Alternative Services (second series), by Rubric 40 it seems to me that reservation is permitted, provided that the reservation takes place for the purposes of Communion, not necessarily at that service, but for Communion.

The Chancellor expressed hesitation about the effect of a rubric in one rite upon the rubric in another. However, if under one rite[129] the unused elements do not have to be immediately consumed, it would hardly seem to be a variation of substantial importance for the minister to refrain from their immediate consumption when celebrating according to a different rite (even though enjoined to do so by a rubric in that rite) so that they might be reserved for Sick Communion[130].

It is here that the distinction as to the purpose of a particular rubric[131] becomes important, whether that purpose is to clarify general Church order or to set out dogma[132]. If it is right that some canons are indeed concerned with dogma[133], then they must be followed whichever rite is used. For example, the rubric in the Book of Common Prayer at the end of the Order of Confirmation states:

And there shall none be admitted to the holy Communion, until such time as he be confirmed, or be ready and desirous to be confirmed.

This was not incorporated into a canon until 1972[134]; however, it is inconceivable that any minister who before 1972 admitted to Communion according to one of the alternative rites a person not yet confirmed, but ready and desirous of being confirmed, was committing an ecclesiastical offence[135].

This being so, what is the effect of a rubric concerned with Church order? The rubric after the Consecration in the Book of Common Prayer directs that the sacrament shall be received 'all meekly kneeling'[136]. In the Alternative Service Book[137] the rubric states:

---

[129] In that case the Alternative Services (second series).
[130] *In re St Thomas, Pennywell* [1995] 2 WLR 154 at p. 170C–F.
[131] This word is used to include a note in the Alternative Service Book.
[132] *In re St Thomas, Pennywell* [1995] 2 WLR 154 at pp. 168H–169G. It is not suggested that each rubric is necessarily concerned with either of these matters.
[133] See **p. 16 *et seq. supra.*** However, this must be read subject to Canon B 15A, para. 1(d). Another example is the final rubric at the end of The Ministration of Publick Baptism of Infants in the Book of Common Prayer.
[134] Promulgated on 9 July 1972 under the Admission to Holy Communion Measure 1972, s. 1. See now Canon B 15A.   [135] *In re St Thomas, Pennywell* [1995] 2 WLR 154 at p. 168H.
[136] A direction explained by the last rubric at end of the Communion service (the so-called 'black rubric'). Canon B 9, para. 2, does not deal with these circumstances as it only states: 'They shall reverently kneel or stand when the prayers are read . . . giving due reverence to the name of Jesus.'
[137] See Note 3 at p. 115. Because of this note it cannot be argued that the 'black rubric' should also apply in the alternative rites.

Posture When a certain posture is particularly appropriate, it is indicated in the margin. For the rest of the service local custom may be established and followed ...

However, neither Rite A nor Rite B indicates any appropriate posture at the time of the reception of the sacrament; therefore, as local custom may be 'established and followed', kneeling is not essential in those rites. Moreover, a minister celebrating according to the Book of Common Prayer would be justified by the doctrine of necessity in distributing the sacrament to someone incapable of kneeling due to infirmity, at the very least upon an occasion (such as Easter) when the reception of Communion is enjoined[138]. Technically, on the other hand, he would in the past have been guilty of aiding and abetting an ecclesiastiacal offence if the recipient were not infirm, at least whilst lay persons fell within the jurisdiction of the ecclesiastical courts[139]. Now the minister could rely upon Canon B 5, para. 1[140]: if kneeling is no longer regarded as essential in one rite it can hardly be essential in another[141].

Equally, if a rubric is concerned with good order and is of substantial importance, it is likely to be of importance elsewhere. For example, the rubric after the Creed in Holy Communion service according to the Book of Common Prayer concerning notices is of application 'during the time of Divine Service', at least .if that service is one in the Book of Common Prayer. Moreover, if the rubric reflects the general canon law, the same law is applicable in services according to the Alternative Service Book even if it is not spelt out in those rubrics[142].

The words of the Canon, and the subsection under which it is promulgated, must always be borne strictly in mind; moreover, the final decision remains that of the courts[143]. In any event the only variations that are permitted are ones that

[138] Rubric after Holy Communion in the Book of Common Prayer.

[139] See 14 Halsbury's Laws of England (4th ed.) at para. 308, note 10. This is probably still the case, even if such behaviour did not amount in itself to a primary offence by the minister. Technically it seems that the Ecclesiastical Jurisdiction Measure 1963, did not abolish the ecclesiastical law in so far as it applies to the laity (see ss. 6 and 82), even though there is no court presently in existence to enforce it: see s. 69.

[140] Section 1(2) of the Church of England (Worship and Doctrine) Measure 1974 enacts that: 'Any Canon making any provision as is mentioned in subsection (1) of this section, and any regulations made under any such Canon, shall have effect notwithstanding anything inconsistent therewith contained in any of the rubrics in the Book of Common Prayer.' However, as Canon B 5 is promulgated in pursuance of s. 1(5)(b), it is not subject to subs.(2) even if, which is unlikely, the latter is intended to be restrictive rather than merely for the avoidance of doubt. It cannot be argued that subs.(5)(b) does not embrace the Book of Common Prayer as subs.(5) begins with the words 'Without prejudice to the generality of subsection (1) of this section ... '

[141] In this regard it may be noted that Canon B 9, para. 2, does not enjoin kneeling at the moment of reception. Briden & Hanson, *Moore's Introduction to English Canon Law* (3rd ed.) at pp. 58–59 uses an argument based on Canon B 5 in relation to those too infirm to kneel.

[142] For example, see Canon B 35, para. 2, and **pp. 87–88 and 186** *infra*.

[143] See Canon B 5, para. 4 proviso. Any doubt may be referred by the minister to the diocesan bishop 'in order that he may give such pastoral guidance, advice or directions as he may think fit': Canon B 5, para. 4. If any such direction were to be ignored, it would be an ecclesiastical offence: see **p. 32** *supra* and **pp. 213** *infra*. This is particularly emphasised by the fact that, as originally

are minor or 'not of substantial importance'[144]. Clearly any alteration that amounts to an amalgamation of more than one rite would not be permissible under this Canon[145].

The Legal Advisory Commission of The General Synod has expressed the opinion[146] that in the rite according to the Book of Common Prayer the substitution of The Summary of the Law for the Ten Commandments[147], the omission of an Exhortation[148], the reading of an Old Testament lesson[149] and, perhaps, the use of a revised Prayer for the Church may fall within variations permitted by Canon B 5. It pointed out that variations not otherwise authorised[150] would be less easy

---

promulgated, the Canon only spoke of the bishop's giving 'pastoral guidance or advice'. See, too, Canon C 14, para. 3. In *Re St Oswald's, Durham* (1988) (unreported) Chancellor Garth Moore said: '. . . I remind myself that *subject to law* liturgical practices are primarily for the incumbent and the P.C.C. and not for me.' (emphasis supplied). To this must now be added a reference to any guidance, etc. given by the bishop.

[144] Once the ordination of women as deacons was declared lawful by section 1(1) of the Deacons (Ordination of Women) Measure 1986, it is difficult to see why it was necessary to promulgate a canon empowering a bishop to substitute the words 'she' or 'her' for any relevant reference to 'he' or 'him' in the Order for Making Deacons in the Ordinal attached to the Book of Common Prayer: see Canon C 4A, para. 3 and Schedule. See, too, the Priests (Ordination of Women) Measure 1993, ss. 1 and 9. Surely this would either be *de minimis* or, at least, fall within the minister's discretion under Canon B 5? No doubt this was added merely *ex abundante cautela* (otherwise there would be no power to use inclusive language when both men and women are being ordained – a ridiculous conclusion) but it must also be seen as underlining that there is less discretion to make variations in the Book of Common Prayer than in other authorised services; after all, it was not felt necessary to make a similar provision in relation to the form of service for the Ordination of Deacons according to the Alternative Service Book. That there is less discretion in relation to the Book of Common Prayer is borne out by *A Service of the Word and Affirmations of Faith* at pp. 7–11, as it is concerned specifically with the services there set out: *ibid* at p. 10. This is emphasised in relation to the Nicene Creed: *ibid* at p. 23.

[145] In principle, each of the forms of service authorised by Canon B 1 must be regarded as separate and distinct from the others. As a general rule, an incumbent is not entitled to use – albeit with the approval of the PCC – a form of service which is in effect an amalgam of two or more of them': *Legal Opinions concerning the Church of England* (Church House Publishing, 1994) at p. 234. No doubt it was for this reason that it was felt necessary to specify in Canon C 3, para. 4A, that 'Any form of service of Holy Communion which is authorised by Canon B 1 may be used at an ordination.' See, too, **p. 227** *infra*. The Alternative Service Book, of course, itself makes provision for borrowing of material from the Book of Common Prayer. That particular borrowing is therefore permissible.

[146] *Legal Opinions concerning the Church of England* at pp. 234–235. See, too, **p. 218, footnote 33** *infra*.   [147] Cp. *Matthews* v. *King* [1934] 1 KB 505.

[148] Prior to the alteration of the law even the shortening of this Exhortation was regarded as 'probably in strictness . . . illegal': see *The Archbishops on the Lawfulness of the Liturgical Use of Incense and the Carrying of Lights in Procession* at p. 8.

[149] Since this opinion was given, however, Canon B 5 has been amended by the addition of a definition of 'form of service' (see **p. 3, footnote 19** *supra*). It would now seem that Canon B 5, para. 5, and Canon B 1, para. 3, would permit such a variation: see **p. 128** *infra*.

[150] By the Further Alternative Rules to Order the Service together with an Additional Alternative Lectionary. The Alternative Service Book itself provides in General Notes 7 and 8 at p. 32: '**Collects** On any occasion when more than one collect is provided (pp. 398ff), only one need be used' and '**Collect Endings** In the case of any collect ending with the words "Christ our Lord", the Minister may at his discretion add the longer ending: "who is alive and reigns with you and the Holy Spirit, one God, now and for ever".' That special provision was thought to be necessary in this regard may give weight to the argument that other variations are unlikely to be of minor importance. On the other hand, the preface to THE COLLECTS *Traditional Language For use with Holy Communion*

to justify in the case of collects[151]. This is because the Book of Common Prayer has a specially entrenched position in the law of litugy[152]; what is more, the previous rigorist approach to the Book of Common Prayer, although now gone[153], possibly[154] has a legacy in the expectation that variations should not lightly be made[155]. The Legal Advisory Commission has also given its opinion that the use of passages of Scripture different from those appointed[156] (for example, for the Epistle or Gospel) or the reading of different prayers[157] may be justified in particular circumstances[158] but in cases of doubt guidance and advice should be sought from the bishop under Canon B 5[159].

Church and liturgical history must also have a bearing upon the matter. For

Rite B (Church House Publishing, 1987) sees the use of the 'thou' form as coming 'easily within the discretion canonically allowed to the minister under Canon B 5.' See now the wide discretion granted because of the addition of a definition of 'form of service' in Canon B 5, para. 5, and *Patterns for Worship* at pp. 63, 217–8 and 240.

[151] But see **p. 8** *supra*. Such variations are now permitted because of the new definition of 'form of service' provided by Canon B 5, para. 5. The Prayer Book (Tables of Lessons) Act 1871, s. 2, Schedule, Second Part, enacts that ' . . . the Collect, Epistle, and Gospel appointed for the Sunday shall serve all the week after' where it is not otherwise ordered in the Book of Common Prayer; see, too, the Rules to Order the Service in the Alternative Service Book at pp. 26–27, especially rule 1(b).

[152] See the Church of England (Worship and Doctrine) Measure 1974, s. 1, and the hesitancy shown in 14 Halsbury's Laws of England (4th ed.) at para.955, note 5 and the text thereto. Liturgical history is no doubt of importance.

[153] *In re St Thomas, Pennywell* [1995] 2 WLR 154 at p. 168B-C.

[154] See especially **p. 14, footnote 90** *supra*.

[155] See the circular produced by the Prayer Book Society updated and reissued in May 1990.

[156] In the light of the definition of 'form of service' now included in Canon B 5, paras 1 and 5, it is now clear that the use of alternative readings is indeed permissible in some circumstances: see, too, **p. 234** *infra*. Because of this definition it is also clear that there may be a number of forms of service within one complete 'form of service'. The choices of version for the set passages of Scripture as printed in the Alternative Service Book (see pp. 398 *et seq.*) are apparently not themselves authorised but were the choice of one individual: see further, **pp. 6** *supra* and **59** *infra*. It is the passages themselves that should not be altered. Indeed, General Note 4 at p. 32 of the Alternative Service Book states: '**Biblical Passages** The sentences, psalms, and readings may be read in any duly authorized version.' See **p. 63** *et seq. infra*.   [157] This would seem to include collects.

[158] The circumstances must be out of the ordinary run of events as is indirectly borne out by rule 1(b) of the Rules to Order the Service in the Alternative Service Book: 'At Baptisms, Confirmations, Ordinations, and Marriages, on days for which provision is made in this rule, unless the Bishop directs otherwise, the readings of the day are used, and the collect of the day is used.' This is so although special readings are otherwise provided.

[159] See, particularly, **p. 36, footnote 33,** *supra*. A different view was expressed in the previous edition of *The Opinions of the Legal Advisory Commission* (see the 6th ed. at p. 140), a view that gained some support from the apparent necessity for Note 4 to The Confirmation of those already baptized at p. 252 of the Alternative Service Book: '**Readings** The Bishop may direct readings to be used other than those appointed in this order, subject to the provisions of Rule 1b in the *Rules to the Order of Service*.' It also gained support from the fact that it was felt necessary to empower a bishop by Canon C 4A, para. 3 and Schedule, to omit the post-communion collect and to use other specified Epistles and Gospel when ordaining a woman according to the Order for Making Deacons in the Ordinal attached to the Book of Common Prayer. The opposing view seems to be expressed, however, in *The Promise of His Glory*: see the notes at pp. ix and 369. The latter states in relation to A Suggested Calendar and Lectionaries: 'Such a Calendar and Lectionary are provided in this Appendix. Because they cover *significant parts* of the Church's year, they require full Synodical authorization.' (emphasis supplied). This implies that such authorisation may be unnecessary in relation to individual occasions. This underlines that a minister would be well advised to seek the guidance of his diocesan bishop under Canon B 5, para, 4, before using this Calendar or Lectionary.

example, unless such a variation is specifically authorised, it is not of minor importance to use the Apostles' Creed instead of the Nicene Creed (or vice versa) where the one is specified in any particular form of service, as the creeds have a historical position within the liturgy[160]. Indeed, the fact that alternatives are provided for within a particular rite tends to suggest that other alternatives should not be used when following that rite. Alternative canticles, for example, are provided for in the Orders for both Morning and Evening Prayer according to the Book of Common Prayer but the use of such other alternatives as are provided by the Alternative Service Book would be more difficult to justify when using the Book of Common Prayer[161].

On the other hand Canon B 5 envisages that the answer to the question whether a variation is of substantial importance depends upon 'the particular circumstances'. It follows that a stricter approach should be adopted, for example, at a celebration at a meeting of the Prayer Book Society; on such an occasion it may well be that the use of the Summary of the Law would not be permissible. The question should, however, be approached from a pastoral point of view rather than from the expectations of particular individuals.

The use of inclusive language[162] throughout a service, although to some people at least not 'contrary to ... the doctrine of the Church of England in any essential matter'[163], would probably at the present time be regarded as 'of substantial importance'[164] in many instances[165], if only because of the heated debate that the question of inclusive language has generated. That is not to say that it may not at some future time become a minor variation nor that it cannot be argued that it is permissible, for example, during a retreat for women deacons[166]. Similarly, the alteration of the invitation to the General Confession in Rite A of

---

[160] For example, at Baptism. See *A Service of the Word and Affirmations of Faith* at p. 23, *Patterns for Worship* at p. 24 and *In re St John the Evangelist, Chopwell* (1995) in **Appendix 6** at **p. 285** *infra*; see, too, **p. 57** *infra*.

[161] Indeed, such a use might well come close to creating an amalgamation of two rites.

[162] That is, language that embraces both genders. The problems that can arise are underlined by the reported problem caused within the Roman Catholic Church in relation to its proposed revision of the catechism. According to *The Times*, 7 January 1994, the Vatican was reluctant to describe Our Lord as becoming incarnate as 'human' rather than as 'man'.   [163] See Canon B 5, para. 3.

[164] It must, however, be permissible when ordaining both men and women as deacons or priests at the same service. See, too, **p. 3, footnote 16** *supra*.

[165] However, the preface to *THE COLLECTS Traditional Language For use with Holy Communion Rite B* expresses the view that 'The adaption to the "thou" form, the use of the BCP Collects and the use of "inclusive" language all come easily within the discretion canonically allowed to the minister under Canon B 5.'

[166] A different Eucharist Prayer for ordinary use in rite A such as in Morley, *All Desires Known* (SPCK, 1994) (2nd ed.) at pp. 46–47 would be difficult to justify pursuant to Canon B 1, para. 1, not only as three choices are already given for ordinary use but also because it is difficult to see how the variation would be 'according to particular circumstances'. These arguments apart, the alteration of the Eucharistic Prayer is likely always to be 'of substantial importance'. For the latter reason special Eucharistic Prayers for use when only women, theological students or members of a Community are present (see *ibid* at pp. 48–57) would be equally difficult to justify under Canon B 5, para. 1, although in such cases it might well be argued that they might be authorised within a form of service falling within the ambit of Canon B 5, para. 2: see **p. 220** *et seq. infra*.

the Alternative Service Book from 'to live in love and peace with all men' to 'with all people' must surely be permissible, whatever the state of the general debate, as the variation merely reflects pastoral sensitivity. If this is so, to alter the General Confession itself to 'we have sinned against you and against our neighbours', rather than 'against our fellow men', would be permissible as long as the congregation is given due warning so that the variation is brought into effect in a 'reverent and seemly' manner[167].

The 'particular circumstances' may also arise due to the Church's own seasons, as well as from locality, time or occasion. Throughout Lent, for example, the much loved collect for Ash Wednesday might be used in services according to the Alternative Service Book, although only appointed for such continued use in the Book of Common Prayer[168]. Equally, the omission of the Gloria, including that at the end of the Psalms, in any penitential period would fall within the ambit of the Canon. Indeed, it may be argued that joint worship[169] in ecumenical circumstances may permit a greater variation than might otherwise be the case[170].

On the other hand special circumstances are not required for the Canon to have application. If not otherwise now permitted[171], making the sign of the Cross at the Absolution or Blessing would surely now be justified by Canon B 5[172]. Alternatively, but less significantly, the Canon would permit the use of the Sentences (or Comfortable Words) prior to the invitation to the General Thanksgiving in rite A when the Prayers of Penitence are said before the Gloria, although they are only set out for use after the Intercession[173].

A far more difficult situation arises, however, when questions of variations involving possible questions of doctrine occur[174]. It seems that in the Book of Common Prayer the words 'militant here in earth' may have been added to limit the prayer to the living[175], although the prayer continues:

---

[167] See Canon B 5, para. 3. See, too, **p. 71** *infra*.

[168] Rubric after the collect. Similarly, it may be easier to justify the use of a collect, for example, for St Athanasius (from *The Cloud of Witnesses* (published for the Alcuin Club by Collins, 1982) at p. 77) within a service according to the Alternative Service Book than according to the Book of Common Prayer: see **p. 52** *infra*. The use of different collects throughout the whole year could not be justified as this would not fall within the meaning of the words 'according to particular circumstances'; on the other hand the use of a different collect on one Sunday might be justified (for example, from Morley, *All Desires Known* at pp. 3–29). See, too, **p. 57** , **footnote 183** *infra*, and *Patterns for Worship* at pp. 217–218 and 240. [169] See **p. 228** *et seq. infra*.

[170] See **p. 228** *infra*. [171] See **p. 40** *supra* and Canon B 25.

[172] Indeed, Canon B 37, para. 3, states that the anointing of a sick person with oil is to be 'on the forehead with the sign of the Cross'. It may perhaps also be underlined by the note at p. 37 of *Ministry at the Time of Death* before *A Commendation at Time of Death*: 'The commendation may be accompanied by the sign of the cross by those present on the forehead of the dying person, recalling his baptism into Christ.'

[173] Contrast pp. 120 and 126 of the Alternative Service Book. This is the more so in the light of *A Service of the Word and Affirmations of Faith*: see Note 2 at p. 8.

[174] *In re St Thomas, Pennywell* [1995] 2 WLR 154 at pp. 168C, 170D and 172F; see, too, *In re St John the Evangelist, Chopwell* (1995) in **Appendix 6** at **p. 285** *infra*.

[175] Daniel, *The Prayer Book, Its History, Language and Contents* (Wells Gardner Darton & Co) (20th ed., 191) at p. 359.

And we also bless thy holy Name for all thy servants departed this life in thy faith and fear.

In Rite A reference to the Church militant is omitted and the Intercession reads[176]:

Hear us as we remember those who have died in the faith of Christ . . . ; according to your promises, grant us with them a share in your eternal kingdom.

In spite of the words 'grant us with them', this still may be seen merely as a thanksgiving for the departed coupled with a prayer for our future salvation. In Rite B[177], however, the First Intercession[178] is quite explicitly a prayer actually for the faithful departed:

And we commend to thy gracious keeping, O Lord, all thy servants departed this life in thy faith and fear, beseeching thee, according to thy promises, to grant them refreshment, light and peace.

If the prayer in Rite A is for all the departed (whether faithful or not), there would therefore seem to be nothing objectionable in law to the variation of the wording[179] in that rite to make the prayer more explicitly a prayer for the dead[180]. Even if Rite A is not already to be read in that way, it may thus be argued that such a variation would not contravene Canon B 5; this, however, would also

---

[176] Alternative Service Book at p. 125; see, too, the Second Intercession in Rite B at p. 186.

[177] See, too, *The Promise of His Glory* at pp. 62 *et seq.* which provides a 'Eucharist for the Commemoration of the Faithful Departed' and a 'Service of Prayers and Readings in Commemoration of the Faithful Departed'.

[178] The Alternative Service Book at p. 184. See, too, the Versicles and Responses in Series 1 Burial Services (Cambridge University Press, Oxford University Press, SPCK) at pp. 16 and 27: '*Minister.* Grant unto him eternal rest; *Answer.* And let perpetual light shine upon him.'

[179] The precise wording of any prayer is, of course, always of the greatest of importance as the words necessarily contain a theological significance. See, for example, the judgment of Chancellor Ellison in *In re Parish of South Creake* [1959] 1 WLR 427 at p. 437 when dealing with the wording proposed for a stained glass window: 'All these authorities clearly show that prayers for the departed are not contrary to law unless they necessarily involve the doctrine of purgatory, which doctrine is expressly prohibited by the Church of England. Such prayers may therefore have one of two objects. On the one hand their purpose may be to relieve the souls of the departed from the pains of purgatory according to Romish teaching, in which event they are to be forbidden. On the other hand, they may comprise prayers that the souls of the departed may rest in peace until the time of the resurrection, following the teaching of the early Church and primitive Christians. Which is the object in any case is a question of fact to be determined from the nature of the particular words themselves, and the inferences to be drawn from all the surrounding circumstances relating to their proposed user.'

[180] As long as the prayer does not embrace the Roman doctrine of purgatory: see 14 Halsbury's Laws of England (4th ed.) at para. 1044. Contrast *Dupuis* v. *Parishioners of Ogbourne St. George* [1941] P 119 and *In re Parish of South Creake* [1959] 1 WLR 427; see, too, Newsom & Newsom, *The Faculty Jurisdiction of the Church of England* (2nd ed.) at p. 145.

entail consideration of the theology relating to prayers for others than those who died actually confessing the faith of Christ[181].

On the other hand, for example, to omit the *filioque*[182] from the Nicene Creed would certainly be contrary to Canon B 5, para. 3, and therefore not permissible[183]. Indeed, any variation deliberately made for doctrinal purposes would be very difficult to justify, for example, the alteration from 'Jesus is the Lamb of God' to 'This is the Lamb of God' in the Additional Words of Invitation to Communion in Rite A[184]. This is because the perceived need for the alteration itself suggests that it is of substantial importance[185]; nevertheless, this would seem not to apply if it can be demonstrated that a similar doctrinal position is taken in another authorised form of service[186].

Clearly any change reflecting doctrine should only be made with great care. The test in Canon B 5, para. 3, as to whether a variation is 'neither contrary to, nor indicative of any departure from, the doctrine of the Church of England in any essential matter' is without doubt an objective one and not left to the subjective views of the minister concerned[187].

It has been suggested[188] that:

In determining whether or not a variation is of substantial importance some guidance may perhaps be derived from a comparison of the rubrics in the Book of Common Prayer with those of other authorised forms of service; thus it might be argued that matters in respect of which mandatory directions are given in the former but not in the latter should not be regarded as of substantial importance.

Indeed, in *In re St Thomas, Pennywell*[189] it was said:

It is clear that if immediate consumption [of the sacrament] is not required in particular circumstances in one rite, it cannot be a matter of 'substantial importance' in another.

---

[181] See Canon B 5, para. 3. See *In re St John the Evangelist, Chopwell* (1995) in **Appendix 6** at **p. 285** *infra*.

[182] That is, the words affirming the procession of the Holy Spirit from the Son as well as from the Father.

[183] See the *Report by the House of Bishops: The Filioque Clause* (General Synod, GS 1119); see, too, *Patterns for Worship* at p. 241. Nevertheless, it is understood that at an enthronement of at least one archbishop the *filioque* was omitted out of sensibility for the views of the Patriarch of the Greek Orthodox Church who was present. Even if this were done in purported reliance upon Canon B 5, the final arbiter is not the archbishop but the court: see the proviso to para. 4. Motive would, of course, be relevant to mitigation.   [184] See p. 172 of the Alternative Service Book.

[185] For example, the variation of the Lord's Prayer so as to begin 'Our Father-Mother, who art in heaven'. Care must, however, be taken. The collect for 8 May (Julian of Norwich) in Morley, *All Desires Known* at p. 27 would seem to be a permissible variation: 'Christ our true mother, you have carried us within you, laboured with us, and brought us forth to bliss . . . '. See, too, **p. 54, footnote 166.**   [186] See the discussion concerning prayers for the dead at **p. 55** *et seq. supra*.

[187] See, for example, *Bishop of St Albans* v. *Fillingham* [1906] P 163.

[188] 14 Halsbury's Laws of England (4th ed.) at para. 941, note 1.

[189] [1995] 2 WLR 154 at p. 170C–D.

However, it is right that any such argument should be used with care and sensit-ivity[190]. An example is likely to be found in relation to the giving of a warning as to the next celebration of Holy Communion, which is enjoined by the Book of Common Prayer[191] but not by the Alternative Service Book[192].

Particular difficulties arise when considering variations from authorised con-fessions and absolutions, as well as in relation to adaptations of historic creeds and other affirmations of faith[193]. Because of the provisions of *A Service of the Word and Affirmations of Faith*[194] there seem to be wider restrictions (as might be expected) in relation to variations from historic affirmations of faith than confessions and absolutions[195].

Even greater care must be exercised in this regard if the form of service with which comparison is being made is not authorised by the General Synod. For example, if a service in draft form has been authorised by the archbishops to be used 'in the presence of a congregation consisting of such persons only as the archbishops may designate'[196], it would be difficult to justify incorporation of part or parts of that draft into a service in the presence of a congregation not so designated.

A further complication arises from such publications[197] as *Lent, Holy Week, Easter*[198] and *The Promise of His Glory*[199]. In a note to the former it is stated:

These Services and Prayers have been commended by the House of Bishops of the General Synod and are published with the agreement of the House.

Under Canon B 4 it is open to each Bishop to authorize, if he sees fit, the form of service to be used within his diocese. He may specify that the services shall be those commended by the House, or that a diocesan form of them shall

---

[190] See *In re St John the Evangelist, Chopwell* (1995) in **Appendix 6** at **pp. 295–296** *infra* for a consideration of some of the problems that may occur.

[191] On Sundays and Holy Days: see the rubric after the Prayer for the Church Militant.

[192] This may well be due to the increased literacy of congregations and the widespread use of parish magazines. Even if it is not, these factors would provide a good argument to substantiate the application of Canon B 5. On the other hand the rubric in the Book of Common Prayer may be one dealing with Church order and therefore applicable to all rites.

[193] See *Patterns for Worship* at p. 241. *A Service of the Word and Affirmations of Faith* at p. 23 states: 'The following adaptations of the historic creeds and other Affirmations of Faith may only be used in non-statutory services or in an authorized Service of the Word. On any occasion, suitable words of introduction or conclusion (such as those indicated) to the Creed or Affirmation of Faith may be used.'. The meaning of the expression 'non-statutory services' is unclear but seems to refer to any form of service authorised under Canon B 1, para. 1: *In re St John the Evangelist, Chopwell* (1995) in **Appendix 6** at **p. 297** *infra*.   [194] *Op. cit.* at p. 23; see the **previous footnote**.

[195] See *In re St John the Evangelist, Chopwell* (1995) in **Appendix 6** at **p. 297** *infra*. Restrictions on variations from confessions and absolutions are not expressed to apply beyond Morning Service or Evening Prayer of a Service of the Word with Holy Communion Rite A: *ibid.* Cp. *Patterns for Worship* at p. 240.   [196] See Canon B 5A.

[197] For other such services see **p. 224** *et seq. infra*.

[198] (Church House Publishing, Cambridge University Press and SPCK, 1986.)

[199] (Church House Publishing and Mowbrays, 1991.)

be used. If the Bishop gives no directions in this matter[200] the priest remains free, subject to the terms of Canon B 5[201], to make use of the Services as commended by the House.

Save for certain exceptions there stated, the note to the latter publication is to a like effect. As these publications have the authoritative weight of the House of Bishops, a comparison with these publications may also be made[202] when considering what variations 'are not of substantial importance'[203]. For example, the use of the Intercession in the Prayers for Use in Eastertide[204] is probably justified during Easter instead of the Intercession in Rite A[205]. Nevertheless, care must always be taken to ensure that only a minor variation is taking place rather than an amalgamation of different forms of service. Moreover, if a diocesan bishop has given general directions in relation to a particular publication or form of service, to act contrary to that direction (even in part) would almost certainly be 'of substantial importance' and thus not permitted by Canon B 5, para. 1[206].

(ii) Alternative Service Book

The Alternative Service Book itself provides for particular variations within that book[207] and these may, of course, be followed as directed. In particular, the general notes[208] provide for the use of any authorised version when reading the sentences, psalms and readings; the use of certain traditional settings; the use of the Lord's Prayer in its traditional, modified or modern form; the use of only one collect although more than one is provided; a different collect ending in the case of any collect ending with the words 'Christ our Lord'[209]; and the use of a Christian doxology instead of the Jewish doxologies in certain psalms[210].

---

[200] That is, pursuant to Canon B 5, para. 4. The bishop's approval under Canon B 4, para. 3, cannot be implied from the general commendation by the House of Bishops: see **pp. 5** *supra* and **221** *infra*. See, too, Canon C 18, para. 4.

[201] This is a reference to Canon B 5, paras 2 and 3: see **p. 220** *et seq. infra*.

[202] Nevertheless, that great care must be taken is underlined by the fact that only the Service for Remembrance Sunday has received a wider authorisation, namely, by the archbishops under Canon B 4: see *The Promise of His Glory* at p. ix.

[203] At the least the commendation by the House of Bishops must be a strong indication that their contents are not contrary to the doctrine of the Church of England: see *In re St John the Evangelist, Chopwell* (1995) in **Appendix 6** at **p. 287** *infra*. A comparison with these publications cannot be used in an argument as to general Church order as they are not authorised under Canon B 1.

[204] *Lent, Holy Week, Easter* at pp. 278–279.

[205] See The Alternative Service Book at pp. 124–125. This is probably so in spite of the fact that Alternative Forms of Intercession are provided at pp. 166–169.

[206] See **p. 51, footnote 143** *supra*.

[207] See also the amendment to that Book made by *A Service of the Word and Affirmations of Faith*: see *ibid* at p. 10. This amendment gives even greater flexibility coupled with regulated, but non-defined, choice within the Alternative Service Book. See, too, *Patterns for Worship passim*.

[208] See General Notes 4–10 at pp. 32–33.

[209] Namely, 'who is alive and reigns with you and the Holy Spirit, one God, now and for ever'.

[210] See psalms 41, 72, 89 and 106 and the words enclosed in brackets.

3

SERVICES IN GENERAL

Other than in relation to occasional services, the choice of service and lectionary is primarily one for the minister of the parish and the parochial church council. The choice of occasional office is for the officiating minister, save that appeal may be made to the diocesan bishop. Particular versions of the Bible are authorised for use.

The diocesan bishop may give directions in relation to what services are to be celebrated.

All worship must glorify God and edify the congregation; the congregation must participate reverently. Many ceremonies that were illegal are now lawful, such as processions, anointing with oil, the ceremonial use of candles, incense and holy water and the ceremonial ringing of bells.

Ministers having a cure of souls must give general notice of feasts and fasts. The additional duties in relation to notices in services may on occasion now be dispensed with; notices may also be given by members of the laity. However, the rules as to the calling of banns must be strictly adhered to.

Special provision is made as to collections.

The vesture to be worn by ministers is specified by canon and regulation. The vesture normally worn in a church or chapel may not be changed without consultation with the parochial church council; disagreements are to be decided by the diocesan bishop. Provision is made for offical lay robes.

A Choices

(i) Services

In accordance with the Church of England (Worship and Doctrine) Measure 1974[1], Canon B 3 deals with the choice of forms of service[2] and the situation where there is a disagreement over which forms of service should be used:

1. Decisions as to which of the forms of service[3] authorised by Canon B 1[4], other than the services known as occasional offices, are to be used in any

---

[1] Section 1(3), (4).

[2] These words have the same meaning as in Canon B 1: Canon B 3, para. 6; and see **p. 9** *supra*. In *Re St Oswald's, Durham* (1988) (unreported) Chancellor Garth Moore said: ' . . . I remind myself that *subject to law* liturgical practices are primarily for the incumbent and the P.C.C. and not for me.' (emphasis supplied).

[3] See, for example, the Note in *A Service of the Word and Affirmations of Faith* at p. 2. The decision as to which form of confession or absolution (*ibid* at p. 11) is to be used is one for the minister taking the service: see **p. 64** *infra*.

[4] This Canon also applies to experimental services authorised under Canon B 5A: Canon B 5A, para. 2. See, too, Canon B 43, para. 9, and **pp. 28** *supra* and **228** *infra*.

church[5] in a parish or in any guild church[6] shall be taken jointly by the minister[7] and the parochial church council or, as the case may be, by the vicar of the guild church and the guild church council.

2. If there is disagreement as to which of the said forms of service are to be used in any such church, then, so long as the disagreement continues the forms of service to be used shall be those contained in the Book of Common Prayer unless other forms of service authorised by Canon B 1 were in regular use therein during at least two of the four years immediately preceding the date when the disagreement arose and the parochial church council or guild church council, as the case may be, resolves that those other forms of service shall be used either to the exclusion of, or in addition to, the forms of service contained in the said Book.

These provisions are slightly strange in that the minister is himself a member of the parochial church council[8]. In the absence of any contrary provision, therefore, it would seem that he is entitled to vote as part of the council in order to obtain its agreement with his wishes. If he and the council nevertheless disagree but other forms of service authorised by Canon B 1 were 'in regular use[9]' in the church 'during at least two of the four years immediately preceding the date when the disagreement arose', it is then a straight vote within the council itself (but including the minister[10]) as to whether those forms of service are to be used exclusively or in addition to those in the Book of Common Prayer. Otherwise, the forms of service contained in the Book of Common Prayer must be used.

It is not entirely clear what services are known as the 'occasional offices[11]' but *The Oxford Dictionary of the Christian Church*[12] gives the following definition:

OCCASIONAL OFFICES. In the [Book of Common Prayer], the services which in distinction from the constant offices of the Church (viz. Mattins and Evensong and the Holy Communion), are used only as occasion demand.

---

[5] 'In this Canon "church" includes any building or part of a building licensed by the bishop for public worship according to the rites and ceremonies of the Church of England': Canon B 3, para. 1.

[6] The Canon does not apply 'in relation to a cathedral which is a parish church nor to any part of a cathedral which is a parish church': see Canon B 3, para. 3.

[7] That is, the incumbent: see Church of England (Worship and Doctrine) Measure 1976, s. 1(3)(a). The word '"incumbent" includes – (a) a curate licensed to the charge of a parish or a minister acting as priest-in-charge of a parish in respect of which rights of presentation are suspended; and (b) a vicar in a team ministry to the extent that the duties of an incumbent are assigned to him by a scheme under the Pastoral Measure 1968 or his licence from the bishop': *ibid* at s. 5(2).   [8] Church Representation Rules, r. 12 (1)(a).

[9] This expression is not further defined and the words must therefore be given their ordinary and natural meaning.

[10] Indeed as chairman he has the casting vote: Church Representation Rules, r.13, App. II, paras 1(a) and 11.   [11] See 14 Halsbury's Laws of England (4th ed.) at para. 936, note 6.

[12] (2nd ed., 1974) at p. 989.

They include Baptism, Confirmation, Matrimony, Visitation of the Sick, Communion of the Sick, Burial of the Dead, and the Commination.

As regards these services (other than the Order of Confirmation[13]), the choice lies initially with the officiating minister. Canon B 3, para. 4, states:

> Where more than one form of any of the services known as occasional offices, other than the Order of Confirmation[14], is authorised by Canon B 1 for use on any occasion the decision as to which form of service to be used shall be made by the minister who is to conduct the service[15], but if any of the persons concerned objects beforehand to the use of the service selected by the minister and he[16] and the minister cannot agree as to which form is to be used, the matter shall be referred to the bishop of the diocese for his decision.

Clearly, the earlier such objection is communicated the better. Presumably, for example, if one of those to be married objected to the form of service selected by the minister[17] so late that a decision could not be obtained from the bishop, the minister would then have a just cause to refuse to conduct the service until such decision had been obtained[18]; that is not to say, however, that he might not be open to ecclesiatical discipline, if he were responsible for the parties not having an earlier opportunity to object[19].

The choice as to which form of service of ordination or consecration is to be used must be made by the bishop or archbishop who is to conduct the service[20].

(ii)   Lectionary

In 1922 an alternative Table of Lessons was authorised[21] to be followed at the discretion of the minister[22]; however, once adopted that particular Table must be continuously followed at least until the end of the ecclesiastical year[23]. Any new

---

[13] See Canon B 3, para. 5; see, also, **p. 155** *infra*.   [14] See **p. 155** *infra*.

[15] There may be more than one minister conducting the service but, if part of the service is to be delegated to him, for example, by the incumbent, the delegation may always be withdrawn. The final arbiter between ministers is the bishop: see **p. 31** *et seq. supra*.

[16] This expression must be taken to include the feminine.

[17] Once the rite according to the Alternative Service Book has been chosen, the choice of vows is up to the couple: *op. cit.* at p. 285, Note 6.

[18] See 14 Halsbury's Laws of England (4th ed.) at para. 1005.

[19] See 14 Halsbury's Laws of England (4th ed.) at para. 1357. On the other hand, as ignorance of the law is no excuse, it is doubtful whether the minister is under any duty to tell the parties of their right to object; cp. the position as to choice of vows: see, too, **p. 186** *et seq. infra*.

[20] See Canon B 3, para. 5; see, also, **p. 232** *infra*. Ordination and consecration are 'occasional offices' within the meaning of the Church of England (Worship and Doctrine) Measure 1974, s. 1(4).   [21] Revised Tables of Lessons Measure, 1922, s. 1, Schedule.

[22] The expression 'minister' is defined as 'the rector vicar or perpetual curate of a parish or the curate in charge of a parish': s. 2.   [23] Revised Tables of Lessons Measure, 1922, s. 1.

lectionary authorised under Canon B1 is a 'form of service'[24] and any choice is therefore governed by the rules already considered concerning services[25].

(iii) Versions of the Bible

(a) Book of Common Prayer

Wherever in the Book of Common Prayer a portion of Scripture is 'set out and appointed to be read, said or sung' the corresponding portion contained in any version of the Bible, or part of the Bible, for the time being authorised for the purpose by the General Synod[26] may be used at the discretion of the minister[27] in place of that set out in the Book of Common Prayer; however, this may not be done without the prior agreement of the parochial, or guild, church council[28]. In the case of occasional offices the set portions must be used if any of the persons concerned objects beforehand to the use of another version[29].

These provisions refer to those portions of the Scriptures 'set out and appointed' and, therefore, only apply where a passage is set out in full[30]. Where a passage is appointed to be read but not actually 'set out'[31], any version of the Bible may be used, subject to the diocesan bishop's direction under Canon C 18, para. 4[32].

(b) Alternative Service Book

In the rites according to the Alternative Service Book the sentences, psalms and readings may be read in 'any duly authorized version'[33]. The choices of version for the set passages of Scripture as printed in that service book[34] were technically never themselves authorised under Canon B 2 in any event[35]. Nevertheless, it is unclear as to who may so authorise the use of a particular version of a passage of Scripture or psalm although presumably it may be either the General Synod[36] or, in relation to a particular diocese, the diocesan bishop[37].

---

[24] See Canon B 1, para. 3, and **p. 3, footnote 19** *supra*.   [25] See **p. 60 *et seq. supra*.**

[26] See *Public Worship in the Church of England* (General Synod) (5th ed., 1986). See, too, Halsbury's Laws of England (4th ed.) at para. 945, note 5.

[27] On balance, because of the provisions as to agreements, this seems to refer to the incumbent rather than to the minister conducting the service.

[28] Prayer Book (Versions of the Bible) Measure 1965, s. 1(1).   [29] *Ibid.*

[30] For example, in the Epistles and Gospels to be used throughout the year.

[31] For example, in the Table of Lessons.

[32] See **p. 33 *supra*** and cp. 14 Halsbury's Laws of England (4th ed.) at para. 945, note 4.

[33] See the General Note 4 at p. 32 of the Alternative Service Book.

[34] See the Alternative Service Book 1980 at pp. 398 *et seq.*.

[35] The parts duly authorised were 'The services . . . , together with the Calendar, Rules to Order of Service, and the Lectionary . . . ': the Alternative Service Book 1980 at p. 8. Unfortunately this note is omitted in some editions of the service book.

[36] See *Public Worship in the Church of England* at p. 13. The authorised versions are not identical as between the Book of Common Prayer and the Alternative Service Book.

[37] See the position in relation to the Book of Common Prayer *supra*.

The choice of which version to use in a particular service is that of the officiating minister or, presumably, of the president if there is more than one.

B   Direction and Dispensation

(i)   Direction

The diocesan bishop may order that there shall be two full[38] services[39] on every Sunday throughout the year, or part of the year, in any church or chapel of every or any benefice in his diocese[40].

(ii)   Dispensation[41]

Canon B 14A[42] provides for the dispensation from certain services. The reading[43] of Morning and Evening Prayer[44] in any parish church[45] as required by Canon B 11[46], or the celebration of Holy Communion in any parish church as required by Canon B 14[47], may be dispensed with:

(a)   on an occasional basis, as authorised by the minister and the parochial church council acting jointly[48];

(b)   on a regular basis, as authorised by the bishop[49] on the request of the minister and the parochial parish council acting jointly . . .

When reaching such a decision they must each be satisfied that there is good reason for so dispensing with the reading of the services. They must also:

(i)   have regard to the frequency of services of Morning and Evening Prayer or the celebration of the Holy Communion (as the case may be) in other parish churches or places of worship[50] in the benefice; and

(ii)   ensure that no church ceases altogether to be used for public worship.

---

[38] The shortened forms of Morning and Evening Prayer may, therefore, not be used.

[39] Including, if he so directs, a sermon or lecture.   [40] Pluralities Act 1838, s. 80.

[41] See also Canon B 44, para. 5, in relation to local ecumenical projects.

[42] See, too, Canon B 44, para. 4(1)(b).

[43] This clearly includes both saying and singing: see Canon B 11A, para. 3.

[44] Although expressed conjunctively, it is likely that either one or both of the services may be dispensed with.

[45] The powers extend to any parish centre of worship under section 29(2) of the Pastoral Measure 1983: Canon B 14A, para. 3.   [46] See **p. 122** *infra*.

[47] See **p. 101** *infra*.

[48] See **p. 60** *et seq. supra*. Although the Church of England (Worship and Doctrine) Measure 1974, s. 1(3)(a), may not be directly applicable, Canon B 14A is nevertheless clearly also referring to the minister of the parish: see, too, Canon B 11, para. 2.

[49] This must on principle refer to the diocesan bishop, as did Canon B 11A (which Canon B 14A replaces).

[50] The phrase 'places of worship' is not defined but must refer to other Anglican places of worship. This interpretation is borne out by Canon B 14A, para. 2.

Where there is more than one parish church or place of worship[51] in a benefice[52] the minister and parochial church council acting jointly must make proposals to the bishop as to what services of Morning and Evening Prayer, or the celebration of Holy Communion, are to be held in each of the parish churches or places of worship. If the bishop is satisfied with the proposals, he must authorise them accordingly. If no satisfactory proposals are put before him, the bishop must make such direction as he considers appropriate. In exercising his powers the bishop must ensure that no church ceases altogether to be used for public worship[53].

C Presentation

(i) Ministers

According to Canon B 1, para. 2:

It is the minister's responsibility to have a good understanding of the forms of the service used and he shall endeavour to ensure that the worship offered glorifies God and edifies the people.

Although only recently incorporated into the Revised Canons[54] this provision only reflects the general canon law[55]. The canons also prescribe that Holy Communion is to be celebrated 'distinctly, reverently and in an audible voice'[56] and that Morning and Evening Prayer is to be said or sung in a similar manner[57]. These provisions, however, are only a particularisation of Canon B 1, para. 2, and there is clearly a duty to celebrate all services in the same way[58]. The duty lies on any person, clerical or lay[59], who is taking part in a service other than as a member of the congregation[60].

---

[51] See **the previous footnote**.

[52] Or where a minister holds benefices in plurality with more than one parish church or place of worship: Canon B 14A, para. 2.   [53] Canon B 14A, para. 2.

[54] 22 February 1994.

[55] See Lyndwood, *Provinciale Angliae* (Oxford, 1679) at p. 226 (it should be borne in mind that Bullard and Bell's book, *Lyndwood's Provinciale* (Faith Press, 1929) omits the all important glosses); Canons 14 and 18 of the 1603 Canons; Canon C 21, para. 4; Canons F 4, F 5, F 15 and F 16, para. 1. The provision in Canon B 35, para. 5, to the effect that it is the incumbent's duty to decide in relation to a wedding 'what furnishings or flowers should be placed in or about the church for the occasion' seems to be a similar reflection. In addition the Burial Laws Amendment Act 1880, s. 7 states: 'All burials under this Act, whether with or without a religious service, shall be conducted in a decent and orderly manner ...'.   [56] Canons B 13, para. 1, and B 14, para. 1.

[57] Canons B 10 and 11, para. 1.   [58] See, too, Canon B 9 and *Music* at **p. 79** *et seq. infra*.

[59] As to the question of enforcement against the laity, see 14 Halsbury's Laws of England (4th ed.) at para. 308, footnotes 10 and 11. Canons do not of their own force bind the laity (*Matthew* v. *Burdett* (1703) 2 Salk. 412) but the provisions as to good order reflect pre-Reformation canon law and thus bind any officiating person: see *supra*.

[60] This is because all the relevant canons and rubrics are dealing with good order within church services.

It is also the duty of the minister[61]:

> to ensure that only such chants, hymns, anthems, and other settings are chosen as are appropriate, both the words and the music, to the solemn act of worship and prayer in the House of God as well as to the congregation assembled for that purpose; and to banish all irreverence in the practice[62] and in the performance of the same.

Indeed, any forms of service authorised by the archbishops or ordinary, and any variation to any form of service, must be 'reverent and seemly'[63]. Moreover, a preacher must also endeavour 'with care and sincerity to minister the word of truth, to the glory of God and to the edification of the people'[64]. None of this should be seen, however, as precluding the proper use of silence within a service[65].

Indeed, embraced within the duty to ensure that 'the worship offered glorifies God' is an obligation to be properly vested[66] and to ensure that communion linen and vestments are clean and in good repair[67].

Canon B 42[68] provides that:

> The Morning and Evening Prayer, and all other prayers and services prescribed in and by the Book of Common Prayer, shall be said or sung in the vulgar tongue[69], save that they may lawfully be said or sung in the Latin tongue in the Convocation of the province, in the chapels or other public places of the several colleges and halls in the universities, or in the university churches in the same, in the colleges of Westminster, Winchester, and Eton, and in such other places of religious and sound learning as custom allows or the bishop or other Ordinary may permit.

---

[61] Canon B 20, para. 3. This does not mean that the choice cannot be delegated but, rather, that the ultimate responsibility rests on the minister.

[62] This presumably refers to practices both during and outside an act of worship.

[63] Canons B 4, paras 2 and 3, and B 5, para. 3. See *In re St John the Evangelist, Chopwell* (1995) in **Appendix 6** at **p. 285** *infra*.   [64] Canon B 18, para. 2.

[65] See, for example, Notes 21 and 13 at pp. 117 and 178 respectively of the Alternative Service Book and Note 4 in *A Service of the Word and Affirmation of Faith* at p. 8.

[66] This is underlined by Canon B 10: ' . . . the officiating ministers and others of the clergy present being duly habited.'. See, too, **p. 93** *et seq. infra*.

[67] This is also reflected in Canons F 4 and 5.

[68] The Canon reflects the provision at the end of *Concerning the Service of the Church* in the preface to the Book of Common Prayer, although the latter also provides 'yet it is not meant that, but when men say Morning and Evening Prayer privately, they may not say the same in any language that they themselves understand'. This proviso nevertheless still has force and the Canon should be read as referring solely to the saying of those two services in public. The provision in the preface is underlined by the rubric before the Te Deum Laudamus in the service of Morning Prayer which states that after the first lesson 'shall be said or sung, in English, the Hymn called Te Deum Laudamus, daily throughout the Year'.

[69] See, too, the final exhortation in The Ministration of Publick Baptism of Infants in the Book of Common Prayer.

There is no similar provision in relation to the Alternative Service Book but, once again, this Canon would seem to be no more than a reflection of the general canon law[70]; in addition, in order to edify the people[71], the service must be comprehensible to those present. This is important as the question arises as to the use of signing where deaf people are in the congregation[72]. If such signing is in addition to the spoken word, it would most certainly be legal[73]. This being so, if only deaf persons make up the congregation to sign alone would be *de minimis*[74] and therefore not unlawful. What is essential is that the service is intelligible to those present[75].

Indeed, in relation to the marriage of a foreigner the Legal Advisory Commission point out that the whole service[76] must be conducted in English and that the officiating minister is obliged to ensure that the persons to be married can understand the service. The essential parts[77] must be translated[78] into a language that the relevant party understands[79]; nevertheless, those parts must still be said in English.

There is, however, the question of anthems sung otherwise than in English[80]. In this regard the anthem may well be seen as not being an integral part of the ministration of the service[81]; if this is so, the provisions of Canon B 42 may not

---

[70] In spite of the Canon the Kyrie Eleison may be used in English or Greek: see Note 7 at p. 116 and Note 4 at p. 179 of the Alternative Service Book. Although this might be seen as indicating that Canon B 42 does not apply to that service book at all, the better view seems to be that the provisions just cited are special exceptions to the norm. If that were not so, the provisions would be superfluous.

[71] See Canon B 1, para. 2, and Article xxiv of the Articles of Religion.

[72] See Chubb, *Lifting up of Hands A Dictionary of Signs used in Church Services* (ABM Publications, 1994: Paper No. 7).

[73] In no sense could it be regarded as a ceremony. The deaf and dumb may signify their consent to marriage by signs: *Harrod* v. *Harrod* (1854) 1 K & J 4; Phillimore, *Ecclesiastical Law* (2nd ed.), vol. I at p. 554.

[74] In *Harrod* v. *Harrod* (1854) 1 K & J 4 at p. 16 Sir W. Page Wood VC, said: 'Swinburne says that any sign of assent is sufficient. When the hands of the parties are joined together, and the clergyman pronounces them to be man and wife, they are married, if they understand that by that act they have agreed to cohabit together and with no other person.' Alternatively, this may be seen as an example of necessity: see **p. 43** *infra*.

[75] For example, even at the time of the rigorist interpretation of the Book of Common Prayer, those who were deaf and dumb might be married: *Harrod* v. *Harrod* (1854) 1 K & J 4.

[76] Where Welsh is commonly spoken in England the vows may be taken in Welsh; in Wales the marriage service may be taken in either Welsh or English: see *Anglican Marriages in England and Wales: A Guide to the Law for the Clergy* (Faculty Office of the Archbishop of Canterbury, 1992) at para. 13.

[77] These include the charge, promises and vows: *Legal Opinions concerning the Church of England* at p. 171. See, too, **p. 185** *infra*.

[78] It is advisable that the interpreter is independent and also that he signs the register book as a witness: *Legal Opinions concerning the Church of England* at p. 171.   [79] *Ibid*.

[80] In the cathedral service of farewell to David Jenkins, the Bishop of Durham, on 3 July 1994, there was a presentation of religious songs yodelled by three Swiss musicians. An English introduction was, however, given to each song.

[81] Compare sermons: see *In re Robinson. Wright* v. *Tugwell* [1897] 1 Ch 85 at p. 96 *per* A.L.Smith LJ; Cripps, *The Law relating to Church and Clergy* at p. 507, footnote (q); contrast Briden & Hanson, *Moore's Introduction to English Canon Law* at p. 80. See, too, **p. 69, footnote 105** *infra*.

apply[82]. However, provision is made in Rites A and B according to the Alternative Service Book for the Kyrie Eleison to be sung in Greek[83]; however, even if in some circumstances at least the Kyrie Eleison is an addition permitted by Canon B 5, para. 1, within the rite of Holy Communion according to the Book of Common Prayer, such an addition would be more difficult to justify if sung in Greek[84].

Canon B 42 specifically applies to singing and the rubric before the Te Deum Laudamus, describing it as a 'hymn[85]', specifically states that it must be sung in English. It seems, therefore, that strictly speaking a carol such as In Dulci Iubilo should not be sung other than in English. However, as its meaning is nowadays so well known, it is likely that to do so would be regarded as *de minimis*. The same is probably true in relation to a less well known carol or hymn if a translation is provided. The glorification of God and the edification of the people is all important[86]; on occasions, this may best be accomplished through musical sounds alone.

This leads on to the question of glossolalia during a service. If this were substantially to disrupt the service, it could not edify the people[87] and it would be for the minister and churchwardens to control it. Nonetheless, whilst any such glossolalia does in fact 'glorify God and edifies the people'[88], it is thought that it is not illegal to permit it to continue. Nonetheless, its encouragement as part of a service is only legal if it falls within the provisions of Canon B 5.

It is, of course, the minister's duty to prevent anything, such as intrusiveness by a photographer during a wedding or baptism, that detracts from the worship offered or the people's edification[89].

(ii)   Congregation

Canon B 9 provides that:

1. All persons present in time of divine service[90] shall audibly with the minister make the answers appointed and in due place join in such parts of the service as are appointed to be said or sung by all present.

2. They shall give reverent attention in the time of divine service, give due

---

[82] If this argument is incorrect, no appeal can be made to Canon B 5, para. 1, as that only permits variations in forms of service and not from the provisions of other Canons. On the other hand, bearing in mind the present almost universal literacy, singing such an anthem is likely to be *de minimis* if a translation were provided: see **p. 37** *supra*.

[83] See Note 7 at p. 116 and paragraph 4 at p. 179.

[84] This is because of the directions as to the use of the vulgar tongue both in Canon B 42 and in *Concerning the Service of the Church* in the preface to the Book of Common Prayer. The Agnus Dei was sung in English in *Read* v. *Bishop of Lincoln* [1892] AC 644 at p. 659: see **p. 47** *et seq. supra*.

[85] In *Read* v. *Bishop of Lincoln* [1892] AC 644 at p. 660 reference is made to both 'hymns and anthems' as lawful additions; this is clearly a reference to a motet being sung.

[86] See Canon B 1, para. 2.   [87] See I Corinthians, chapter 14, verses 13–19.

[88] See Canon B 1, para. 2.   [89] Canon B 1, para. 2.

[90] This must mean any service: see also **p. 84, footnote 243** *infra*.

reverence to the name of the Lord Jesus, stand at the creed and the reading of the Holy Gospel at the Holy Communion. When the Prayers are read and the Psalms and Canticles are said or sung, they shall have regard to the rubrics of the service and locally established custom[91] in the matter of posture, whether of standing or kneeling.

This provision[92], of course, straddles questions both of presentation and good order[93]. Nonetheless, although ordinary members of the congregation are not amenable to prosecution in the ecclesiastical courts[94], they may be asked to leave[95] the church if they continue to breach the Canon[96]. Moreover, if a clergyman is taking the service, he may himself be liable for a breach of Canon B 1, para. 2, if he proceeds with the service in spite of the behaviour in the congregation[97]. This might, for example, arise if some of the congregation were to sing bawdy words to the tune of the hymn being sung[98].

D   Sermons[99]

A sermon must be preached at least every Sunday in every parish church, except for some reasonable cause approved by the bishop of the diocese[100]. If the bishop has ordered that there should be two full services every Sunday in the church or chapel[101], he may also direct that each such service should include a sermon or lecture. Except for some reasonable cause approved by the bishop of the diocese[102], it is the duty of every priest having a cure of souls to preach, or cause to be preached, a sermon in his church at least once each Sunday[103].

The Book of Common Prayer provides that either a sermon or one of the homilies[104] must follow the Creed in the Holy Communion service[105]. Doubts,

[91] See **p. 4, footnote 28** *infra*.   [92] See, too, Canon F 15.

[93] See **p. 237** *et seq. infra*.

[94] See 14 Halsbury's Laws of England (4th ed.) at para. 308, notes 10 and 11.

[95] See Canon F 16; *Cole* v. *Police Constable 443A* [1937] 1 KB 316 (non-parishioner) and **p. 252** *infra*.

[96] It must, of course, be remembered that questions of *de minimis* and necessity may arise: see **pp. 35** *et seq.* and **42** *et seq. supra*.

[97] It is possible that he would also be liable for aiding and abetting the lay person's own breach of duty.   [98] See **p. 79** *infra*.

[99] See also **p. 24** *et seq. supra* for the definition of a 'sermon' and as to who may preach.

[100] Canon B 18, para. 1. Necessity induced by illness (for example, loss of voice) would excuse a failure so to preach, if no-one else were available.

[101] Under the Pluralities Act 1838, s. 80. Such an order may apply to 'every or any benefice within his diocese': *ibid*.

[102] Necessity induced by illness (for example, loss of voice) would excuse such a failure.

[103] Canon C 24, para. 3.   [104] See **footnote 99** *supra*.

[105] Although good order must be preserved during the sermon, it seems that it may not be an integral part of the ministration of the service: *In re Robinson. Wright* v. *Tugwell* [1897] 1 Ch 85 at p. 96 *per* A.L.Smith LJ; Cripps, *The Law relating to Church and Clergy* at p. 507, footnote (q); contrast Briden & Hanson, *Moore's Introduction to English Canon Law* at p. 80. A sermon is probably not a form of service in itself, even when preached with a bidding prayer, collect or the

however, arose and the Act of Uniformity Amendment Act 1872, provided[106] that a sermon, lecture or homily was in fact unnecessary; this Act has now been repealed[107] but the fact that it was unnecessary for so long must suggest that it is not of substantial importance on all occasions now. The doubts that then existed may, therefore, now be answered by reference to Canon B 5, para 1. Although the Alternative Service Book similarly provides that a sermon is to be preached during Holy Communion[108], it must similarly be unnecessary[109], if only by reason of Canon B 5. The provisions as to the number of sermons to be preached on Sundays must nonetheless be observed.

The services of Morning and Evening Prayer in the Book of Common Prayer may conclude prior to the preaching of any sermon[110]. There had been some doubt as to whether a sermon might be preached thereafter[111] but this doubt was also removed by the the Act of Uniformity Amendment Act 1872[112]. Moreover, section 6 of that Act provided that:

> ... a sermon or lecture may be preached without the common prayers or services appointed by the book of common prayer being read before it is preached, so that such sermon or lecture be preceded by any service authorized by this act, or by the bidding prayer[113], or by a collect taken from the book of common prayer, with or without the Lord's Prayer.

In spite of the repeal of that Act[114] the law probably remains the same. The preaching of a sermon at any service is likely[115] sufficiently to fall within the ambit of Canon B 5. Even if the sermon is not an integral part of the service itself[116], a sermon alone with a bidding prayer does not amount to a service either[117].

Lord's Prayer: see the Act of Uniformity Amendment Act 1872, s. 6 (now repealed). Even if it is a form of service, it would fall within the provisions of Canon B 5, para. 2: see **p. 220 *et seq. infra*.**

[106] Section 5. This is set out at **p. 121, footnote 1** *infra*.

[107] By the Church of England (Worship and Doctrine) Measure 1974, s. 6(3), Sch. 2.

[108] The section number is printed in black (see sections 18 and 13 at pp. 123 and 181 respectively): see General Note 1 *Distinctions in the Text* at p. 32. Contrast, however, Note 12 at p. 116: 'The sermon is an integral part of the Ministry of the Word. A sermon should *normally* be preached at all celebrations on Sundays and Holy Days' (emphasis supplied). See, too, p. 239 and Note 1 at p. 252. See, too, *A Service of the Word and Affirmations of Faith* at p. 9.

[109] See, too, **p. 25 *supra*.**

[110] See the concluding rubrics, the Act of Uniformity Amendment Act 1872, s. 5 (now repealed) and **p. 121, footnote 1** *infra*.   [111] See the Act of Uniformity Amendment Act 1872, s. 5.

[112] '... any of the ... forms of service may be used with or without the preaching of a sermon or lecture, or the reading of a homily': *ibid*.   [113] See Canon B 19 and **p. 36, footnote 38** *supra*.

[114] By the Church of England (Worship and Doctrine) Measure 1974, s. 6(3) and Sch. 2.

[115] Depending upon the circumstances.

[116] See *In re Robinson. Wright* v. *Tugwell* [1897] 1 Ch 85 at p. 96 *per* A.L.Smith LJ; Cripps, *The Law relating to Church and Clergy* at p. 507, footnote (q). Contrast Briden & Hanson, *Moore's Introduction to English Canon Law* at p. 80 which suggests that a sermon with prayers after the grace at Morning or Evening Prayer, or a sermon preached alone, is a separate service.

[117] See Canon B 19. A sermon alone, even with bidding prayer, does not fall within the services authorised by Canon B 1; it follows that, if the view expressed on the text is wrong, to preach such a sermon would be illegal.

Although in the Alternative Service Book a sermon is regarded as part of Morning and Evening Prayer, it is nonetheless only optional[118].

The preacher must endeavour with care and sincerity to minister the word of truth to the glory of God and to the edification of the people[119]. A specific bidding prayer is permitted by Canon B 19 before any sermon, lecture or homily; the Canon specifies that the prayer may be used 'in this form or to this effect, as briefly as is convenient, always concluding with the Lord's Prayer'[120]. There is no privilege attaching to words spoken in a sermon[121] and the laws of defamation apply to them[122].

E Ceremonies

As Sir Robert Phillimore stated in *Martin* v. *Mackonochie*[123],

... [T]here is a distinction between a rite and a ceremony[124]; the former consisting in services expressed in words[125], the latter in gestures or acts preceding, accompanying, or following the utterance of these words[126].

Nonetheless, as both were equally covered by the rubrics of the Book of Common Prayer, each was embraced by the rigorist interpretion already considered[127]. As Lord Cairns said in *Martin* v. *Mackonochie*[128]:

If the use of lighted Candles in the manner complained of be a ceremony[129] or a ceremonial act, it might be sufficient to say that it is not – nor is any ceremony in which it forms a part – among those retained in the Prayer Book,

---

[118] See Notes 23 and 46 at pp. 60 and 70 respectively. If the Renewal of Baptismal Vows is used the sermon may be either after the second reading or at the end of the service. In either case it should precede the Renewal: Note 3 at p. 275.　　　　　　　　　　　　　[119] Canon B 18, para. 2.

[120] Canon B 5, of course, does not apply so as to permit the omission of the Lord's Prayer but see **p. 36, footnote 38** *supra*.

[121] As to exclusion from Holy Communion see **p. 239** *et seq. infra*.

[122] It may be the duty of a clergyman to warn a parishioner about the character of a person with whom his child is associating (see *Gilbert* v. *Waldy, The Times*, 19 November 1909) but this should be done privately. See, further, *Gatley on Libel and Slander* (Sweet & Maxwell) (8th ed.) at paras 496 and 507.　　　　　　　　　　　　[123] (1868) LR 2 A & E 116 at pp. 135–136.

[124] It has also recognised that some matters are purely ones of private devotion: see **p. 40, footnote 65** *supra*.

[125] However, in *In re Robinson. Wright* v. *Dugwell* [1897] 1 Ch 85 at p. 96 A.L.Smith LJ stated: 'What the exact meaning of the word "rite" is has not been decided ...'.

[126] 'The very meaning of an ornament is that it is a thing to be used for the fitting performance of a ceremony, and if no ceremony be prescribed the so-called ornament has no place': *per The Archbishops on the Lawfulness of the Liturgical Use of Incense and the Carrying of Lights in Procession* at p. 13.　　　　　　　　　　　　　[127] See **p. 11** *et seq. supra*.

[128] (1868) LR 2 PC 365 at p. 388.

[129] 'As to the argument that the use complained of is at most only part of a ceremony, their Lordships are of opinion that when a part of a ceremony is changed, the integrity of the ceremony is broken, and it ceases to be the same ceremony': *ibid*.

and it must therefore be included among those that are abolished; for the Prayer Book, in the Preface, divides all ceremonies into these two classes: those which are retained are specified, whereas none are abolished specifically or by name; but it is assumed that all are abolished which are not expressly retained.

In other words which ceremonies were retained depended upon the rubrics of the Book of Common Prayer. However, just as the rigorist interpretation is likely no longer to apply in relation to rites, the same may also be said as to ceremonies[130]. What is more, the Preface itself recognized that ceremonies are not immutable[131]. The imposition of ashes during the eucharist on Ash Wednesday was found to be an illegal ceremony in *Elphinstone* v. *Purchas*[132] but is now specifically included in An Order for the Beginning of Lent in *Lent, Holy Week, Easter*[133]. In the light of the arguments outlined below it seems inconceivable that this would now be regarded as an illegal ceremony.

Nonetheless, it should be borne in mind throughout that, even if a ceremony is now legal, problems may still arise by reason of the 'ornaments' rubric in the Book of Common Prayer. This rubric before the Order for Morning and Evening Prayer states:

And here is to be noted, that such Ornaments of the Church, and of the Ministers thereof, at all Times of their Ministration, shall be retained, and be in use, as were in this Church of *England*, by the Authority of Parliament, in the Second Year of the Reign of King *Edward* the Sixth.

The rubric, of course, covers both ornaments and vesture.

In relation to it the Judicial Committee of the Privy Council in *Westerton* v. *Liddell*[134] stated:

Their lordships, after much consideration are satisfied that the construction of this rubric which they suggested at the hearing of the case is its true meaning, and that the word 'ornaments' applies, and in the rubric is confined to those articles the use of which in the services and ministrations of the church is prescribed by the Prayer Book of Edward the Sixth.

---

[130] See, for example, *Elphinstone* v. *Purchas* (1870) LR 3 A & E 66 at pp. 108–109 (kissing the Gospel book and making the sign of the Cross when about to consecrate the elements). See, too, 14 Halsbury's Laws of England (4th ed.) at paras 958–959.

[131] 'And although the keeping or omitting of a Ceremony, in itself considered, is but a small thing; yet the wilful and contemptuous transgression and breaking of a common order and discipline is no small offence before God, *Let all things be done among you*, saith Saint Paul, *in a seemly and due* order: The appointment of the which order pertaineth not to private men; therefore no man ought to take in hand, nor presume to appoint or alter any publick or common Order in Christ's Church, except he be lawfully called and authorized thereunto.' See, too, *The Archbishops on the Lawfulness of the Liturgical Use of Incense and the Carrying of Lights in Procession* at pp. 12–13.

[132] (1870) LR 3 A & E 66 at pp. 97–99.

[133] *Op. cit.* at pp. 26–26 and Note 6 *The Ash* at p. 13.

[134] (1857) Moore's Special Rep. 1 at p. 156.

The word 'ornaments' in ecclesiastical law is not confined, as it is by modern usage, to articles of decoration or embellishment, but is used in the larger sense of the word 'ornamentum,' which, according to the interpretion of Forcellini's Dictionary, is used 'pro quocumque apparatu, seu instrumento'. All the several articles used in the performance of the services and rites of the church are 'ornaments'; vestments, books, cloths, chalices, and patens, are amongst church ornaments . . . In modern times organs and bells are held to be under this denomination.

What effect has the repeal of the relevant parts of the Act of Uniformity 1662 had upon this rubric?

In fact a number of articles that at one time were regarded as 'ornaments' are no longer so regarded; an obvious example is that of organs[135]. Moreover, just as the architectural layout of our churches has changed over the last three hundred years[136], and may well continue to change, so also has the liturgy. It is, therefore, not surprising if the 'ornaments' used in that worship also change. Indeed, once the rigorist intepretation of the Book of Common Prayer disappeared, the ornaments rubric is to be seen as a general guide to the 'ornaments' required whilst that book alone (and in its restrictively interpreted form) governed Anglican worship[137].

It may, of course, be argued that the ornaments rubric deals with a matter of Church order and is therefore more than a mere directive; however, the fact that clerical vestments were also governed by the rubric but are now chiefly governed by Canon B 8 militates against such an argument. For example the use of an alb was held to be illegal in *Hebbert* v. *Purchas*[138] but is now permitted by Canon B 8, para. 3.

It follows that all ornaments now come to be regarded in exactly the same way[139]. Thus in *Martin* v. *Mackonochie*[140] it was pointed out that articles are not to be restrained 'which are consistent with, and subsidiary to, the services.' However, this must also embrace articles consistent with, and subsidiary to, any lawful activity within the Church's ministry. To adopt the words of the Judicial Committee of the Privy Council in *Westerton* v. *Liddell* it must embrace those articles the use of which is required in the services and ministrations of the Church[141]. For example, in *In re St Mary's, Tyne Dock*[142] the Chancellor allowed the retention of a cruet of holy oil as he was 'not satisfied that any

---

[135] See *Westerton* v. *Liddell* (1857) Moore's Special Report 1 at p. 187 and *Martin* v. *Mackonochie* (1868) LR 2 PC 365 at p. 390.
[136] See Addleshaw & Etchells, *The Architectural Setting of Anglican Worship* (Faber & Faber, 1956) and Yates, *Buildings, Faith and Worship* (Clarendon Press, 1991).
[137] *In re St Thomas, Pennywell* [1995] 2 WLR 154 at pp. 170F–171G.
[138] (1871) LR 3 PC 605.
[139] See *In re St John the Evangelist, Chopwell* (1995) in **Appendix 6 at p. 292** *infra*.
[140] (1868) LR 2 PC 365 at p. 390.
[141] *In re St Thomas, Pennywell* [1995] 2 WLR 154 at p. 171E–F.
[142] [1954] P 369 at p. 382.

illegality' attached to it. Such a cruet would, of course, certainly nowadays be legal, as a receptacle is necessary for the use of holy oil pursuant to Canon B 37, para. 3.

(i) Candles

In *Martin* v. *Mackonochie*[143] it was decided that the ceremonial use of lighted candles was illegal as they were not:

> subsidiary to the service, for they do not aid or facilitate – much less are they necessary to – the service[144].

It was, however, only the ceremonial use of candles that was illegal. Each case depended upon its own particular circumstances[145]; the mere presence of lit candles did not of itself amount to an illegal ceremony[146]. Equally, the provision of a stand for votive candles should be seen as an aid to private devotion and not in itself illegal[147].

Now, not only is the giving of a lighted candle a ceremony permitted by the Alternative Service Book in the service of baptism[148], but it is also provided that:

> A lighted candle, which may be the paschal candle[149], may be ready so that other candles may be lighted from it[150].

Moreover, in *Lent, Holy Week, Easter*[151] the Easter Liturgy has a specific section called 'the service of light'[152] in which provision is made for the lighting of the

---

[143] (1868) LR 2 PC 365 at pp. 387–392. See, too, *Sumner* v. *Wix* (1870) LR 3 A & E 58 at p. 64; *Elphinstone* v. *Purchas* (1870) LR 3 A & E 66 at pp. 96–97; *Read* v. *Bishop of Lincoln* [1892] AC 644 at p. 666; *Rector and Churchwardens of Capel St. Mary, Suffolk* v. *Packard* [1927] P 289 at p. 305; *In re St. Mary, Tyne Dock* [1954] P 369 at p. 380.

[144] (1868) LR 2 PC 365 at p. 391.

[145] See, particularly, *In re St. Mary, Tyne Dock* [1954] P 369 at pp. 379–380.

[146] *Read* v. *Bishop of Lincoln* [1891] P 9, on appeal [1892] AC 644 at pp. 666–668; *The Archbishops on the Lawfulness of the Liturgical Use of Incense and the Carrying of Lights in Procession* at p. 15. Previously even the presence of such candles had been regarded as illegal: see 14 Halsbury's Laws of England (4th ed.) at para. 959, note 3.

[147] See **p. 40, footnote 65 supra**; see, too, *Re St Edward, Castle Donnington* (1994) 3 ELJ 349; *In re St John the Evangelist, Chopwell* (1995) in **Appendix 6** at **pp. 288–289 infra**. It is possible, however, as in *In re St John the Evangelist, Chopwell*, that a faculty will only be granted 'until further order' and subject to an undertaking against superstitious use: *ibid* **at p. 289**; cp. Newsom and Newsom, *Faculty Jurisdiction of the Church of England* (2nd ed.) at p. 125. 'Symbolism kept within strict limits helps the understanding. But symbolism may easily be pushed to lengths which divert the attention from what the symbolism is intended to teach, to the symbolism itself': *per The Archbishops on the Liturgical Use of Incense and the Carrying of Lights in Procession* at p. 11.

[148] See the Alternative Service Book at p. 248.

[149] Previously the legality of a Paschal Candleholder depended upon whether its use was ceremonial: see *In re St Mary, Tyne Dock* [1954] P 369 at p. 379.

[150] Note 4 before The Baptism of Children at p. 241.

[151] For the relevance of this book see **p. 58 et seq. supra**.

[152] *Lent, Holy Week, Easter* at pp. 228–234.

Easter Candle[153], a procession with lighted candles[154] and the lighting of further candles held by members of the congregation[155]. It is even suggested that the light for the Easter Candle may be taken from a bonfire outside the church[156]. Similarly, *The Promise of His Glory*[157] not only provides for a Candlemas procession with lighted candles[158] but there is also a service entitled 'The Service of Light' which may be used throughout the year[159]. This suggests that a large candle or a cluster of candles (set near the lectern or the candles on the altar) should be used; on certain occasions it may even be appropriate for the congregation to hold candles[160]. In both the ceremonial use of candles is quite specific. In these circumstances it seems inconceivable that the ceremonial use of lighted candles is now illegal[161]; their ceremonial use, therefore, may be permitted in other rites at the discretion of the minister under Canon B 5[162]. Nonetheless, their use must always be reverent and seemly[163].

(ii) Processions

Not only processions with lighted candles[164] but any procession (at least of a ceremonial nature[165]) was at one time regarded as illegal[166]. As has been seen

[153] The introduction to the Easter Liturgy makes it clear that it is intended that the preparation of the candle 'by marking it with traditional symbolic signs' may take place at sections 7 and 8: see *op. cit. B The Service of Light* at p. 224.

[154] *Op. cit.* at pp. 226–227, Note 4 *The Lighting of the Taper* and Note 5 *The Easter Candle*, together with Notes 10–15 at pp. 229–230.

[155] See *op. cit.* at p. 226, Note 3 *Lighting*, and p. 230, para. 15.

[156] *Op. cit.* at p. 226, Note 4 *The Lighting of the Taper*; see, too, the Note The Easter Candle at p. 275.   [157] For the relevance of this book see **p. 58 et seq. supra.**

[158] *Op. cit.*, at p. 272, Note 1; p. 280, Note 32; p. 283, Appendix.

[159] It is suggested to be 'particularly appropriate in Advent and Epiphanytide, and on the vigils of major festivals, such as All Saints and Candlemas, or for some other specific cause': see the Introduction, *op. cit.*, at p. 10. See, too, *Patterns for Worship* at p. 321.

[160] See Note 2 *The Light* at p. 11.

[161] *In re St John the Evangelist, Chopwell* (1995) in **Appendix 6** at **pp. 286–288 infra**; *In re St Thomas, Pennywell* [1995] 2 WLR 154 at p. 169G-H.

[162] In the Introduction to the service in *The Promise of His Glory* it is suggested that 'The Word Service may take a variety of forms, and a number of outlines are suggested here': see p. 10. This implies that other such services are envisaged although they would have to comply with the provisions of Canon B 5.   [163] See Canon B 5, para. 3, and also Canon B 9.

[164] *Elphinstone* v. *Purchas* (1870) LR 3 A & E 66 at pp. 96–97; *In re St Mary, Tyne Dock* [1954] P 369 at p. 379; *Archbishops on the Lawfulness of the Liturgical Use of Incense and on the Carrying of Lights in Procession* at p. 14.

[165] The line, however, is hard to draw. Everything in church should be done in a reverent and seemly manner. It may, therefore, be argued that for two or more clergy to enter the body of the church together would not be a ceremonial act. Would it make any difference if they did so preceded by the choir? If the clergy and choir were preceded by a crucifer, the procession thus formed would certainly seem to be a ceremonial start to the service rather than a seemly way for people to take their places in church: see *Elphinstone* v. *Purchas* (1870) LR 3 A & E 66 at pp. 96–97; see, too, the monition by Lord Penzance that led to *Enraght's Case* (1881) 6 QBD 376, affd *sub. nom. Enraght* v. *Lord Penzance* (1882) 7 App. Cas. 240. Fortunately such arcane arguments are no longer relevant.

[166] See *Sumner* v. *Wix* (1870) LR 3 A & E 58 at pp. 64–65; 14 Halsbury's Laws of England (4th ed.) at para. 959.

Lent, Holy Week, Easter specifically provides for a procession with candles[167] and a procession with palms[168]. So, too, *The Promise of His Glory* provides for a Candlemas procession[169]; in the Eucharist of Christmas Night it also provides for the president and other ministers to 'go to the Crib'[170] and in the Service of Light for the minister to bring in a light and for other candles to be lit from it[171]. Therefore, not only are processions enjoined in certain circumstances, but these may even include the ceremonial use of candles. Even if a procession to the font is not implied by the possibility of the incorporation of Baptism into Holy Communion, Morning or Evening Prayer[172], a ceremonial procession is now legal in the exercise of the minister's discretion under Canon B 5 as long as it is reverent and seemly[173].

(iii)   Incense

The ceremonial use of incense has in the past been held to be illegal[174]:

> To bring in incense at the beginning or during the celebration, and remove it at the close of the celebration of the eucharist, appears to me a distinct ceremony, additional and not even indirectly incident to the ceremonies ordered by the Book of Common Prayer.[175]

There was nothing, however, to prevent the merely fumigatory use of incense in church as long as it was not done ceremoniously[176]. Nonetheless, as the archbishops pointed out in their opinion on *The Lawfulness of the Liturgical Use of Incense and the Carrying of Lights in Procession*[177]:

> Yet it is right to observe that even now the liturgical use of incense is not by law permanently excluded from the Church's Ritual. The Section in Elizabeth's Act which allows the Crown, with the consent of the Archbishop of Canterbury, to order new ceremonies does not forbid the inclusion of the use of incense in such new ceremonies if such are ordered . . . Many things might

---

[167] *Op. cit.* at pp. 229–230.   [168] *Op. cit.*, at p. 75.

[169] *Op. cit.*, at p. 272, Note 1; p. 280, Note 32; p. 283, Appendix.

[170] *Op. cit.* at p. 171. See, too, A Service for the Feast of the Baptism of the Lord at p. 210, Note 4.   [171] *Op. cit.* at p. 12.

[172] See the Alternative Service Book at pp. 239, 250 and 251.

[173] *In re St John the Evangelist, Chopwell* (1995) in **Appendix 6** at **pp. 286–288** *infra*. See, too, *Patterns for Worship* at p. 222.

[174] *Martin* v. *Mackonochie* (1868) LR 2 A & E 116 at p. 215, on appeal (1868) LR 2 PC 365 at p. 387; *Sumner* v. *Wix* (1870) LR 3 A & E 58 at p. 66; *Rector and Churchwardens of Capel St Mary, Suffolk* v. *Packard* [1927] P 269 at p. 305; see, too, *Gore-Booth* v. *Bishop of Manchester* [1920] 2 KB 412.

[175] *Martin* v. *Mackonochie* (1868) LR 2 A & E 116 at p. 215 *per* Sir Robert Phillimore.

[176] *The Archbishops on The Lawfulness of the Liturgical Use of Incense and the Carrying of Lights in Procession* at p. 10. See, for example, *In re St Mary, Tyne Dock* [1956] P 369 at p. 380.

[177] *Op. cit.* at pp. 12–13.

become probable when our toleration of one another had risen to a higher level, which are not probable at present.

That time fortunately seems now to have come. Moreover, in the light of the archbishops' comments it can hardly be suggested that the ceremonial use of incense is doctrinally unacceptable[178]. Just as processions and the ceremonial use of candles are permissible, the reverent and seemly use of incense is also permissible by reason of Canon B 5[179]. Such use would include the censing of the clergy and congregation.

(iv) Holy water

Although in the circumstances not found to be proved, the use of a holy water stoup seems to be assumed to be illegal in *Hebbert* v. *Purchas*[180]; moreover, in *Davey* v. *Hinde*[181] two holy water stoups were removed 'as having been introduced without a faculty, and as inappropriate ornaments for an English church'. In *Rector and Churchwardens of Capel St Mary, Suffolk* v. *Packard*[182], in reliance on these authorities, a holy water stoup was held to be an illegal ornament.

It is unclear whether a stoup[183] was regarded as illegal because it was used in illegal ceremonies or, in addition, because any use would be doctrinally unacceptable. In the latter case, for example, no explication is given, although the children were apparently being taught:

to use the 'Holy Water' from the stoup, by making the sign of the Cross with it on entering and leaving the church.

However, because in *In re St Mary, Tyne Dock*[184] the principle of *de minimis* was applied to a water stoup in a vestry, the use of such a stoup can hardly be contrary to doctrine even though it was 'very small and inconspicuously situated'. What is more, the making of the sign of the Cross, certainly outside a service, would seem only to be a matter of private devotion[185].

This is, in fact, borne out by A Service for the Feast of the Baptism of the Lord in *A Promise of His Glory*, although it also goes much further[186]:

---

[178] See Canon B 5, para. 3.
[179] *In re St John the Evangelist, Chopwell* (1995) in **Appendix 6** at **pp. 289–291** *infra*.
[180] (1871) 3 PC 605 at p. 651.   [181] [1903] P 221 at p. 237.
[182] [1927] P 289 at p. 306.
[183] The use of holy water stoups seems to be connected with the ancient religious practice of ritual bathing: see Crouch, *Water Management in Ancient Greek Cities* (Oxford University Press, 1993) at p. 290.   [184] [1954] P 369 at p. 382.
[185] See **p. 40, footnote 65** *supra*.
[186] *Op. cit.*, at p. 221, Note 30. Note 4 at p. 210 and Note 20 at p. 216 seem to suggest that the water may be poured into the font itself. However, unless *de minimis*, that would be contrary to Canon F 1, para. 3: 'The font bowl shall only be used for the water at the administration of Holy Baptism and for no other purpose whatsoever.' Rather, Note 30 at p. 221 (see text to this footnote) should be seen as clarifying the position so that the water is poured out at the font but not into the font bowl itself.

The water may be sprinkled over the people, or placed in vessels by the door for them to make the Sign of the Cross as they leave, or poured out over the threshold.

In all these circumstances, and especially in the light of the demise of the previous rigorist approach, the use of holy water is now legal, if only after reliance on Canon B 5[187]. This includes the sprinkling of the clergy and congregation from an aspergill[188].

(v)   Anointing with oil

There is no provision within the Book of Common Prayer for the use of holy oil, although that does not mean that it might not be used at a death bed. Presumably that is why in *In re St Mary, Tyne Dock*[189] Chancellor Hylton-Foster was 'not satisfied that any illegality attaches to the cruet of holy oil'. In any event such anointing is now provided for in the service of *The Laying on of Hands and Anointing* in *Ministry to the Sick*[190] and Canon B 37, para. 3, states that the oil used in the ministry to the sick is to be 'pure olive oil consecrated by the bishop of the diocese or otherwise by the priest himself'.

In the Alternative Service Book provision is not only made for a collect and readings for The Blessing of the Oils[191] but it also provides for the anointing by the bishop of candidates for confirmation who have already been baptised 'with oil which he has previously blessed for this purpose'[192]. Thus, not only must a ceremony of blessing of such oils now be legal, but its use in similar circumstances within the confirmation service according to the Book of Common Prayer must also be legal by reason of Canon B 5.

(vi)   Bells

The ringing of a bell to signify the beginning or end of a service is not illegal as it does not form part of the service itself[193]. On the other hand the ringing of

---

[187] *In re St John the Evangelist, Chopwell* (1995) in **Appendix 6** at **pp. 293–296** *infra*. Of course, Canon B 5 cannot permit anything that is contrary to, or indicative of any departure from, 'the doctrine of the Church of England in any essential matter': see Canon B 5, para. 3.

[188] *In re St John the Evangelist, Chopwell* (1995) in **Appendix 6** at **p. 298** *infra*. As to an earlier case relating to the ceremony of asperges (although the case predates the possibility of any service other than those authorised by the Book of Common Prayer), see *Matthews* v. *King* [1934] 1 KB 505.

[189] [1954] P 369 at p. 382. Of course, this was a decision within the faculty jurisdiction but it must reflect liturgical law. In *In re St John the Evangelist, Bierley* [1989] Fam. 60 the faculty granted included the use of the old aumbry for the storage of holy oil: see pp. 61G–62B and p. 76E–F.

[190] At pp. 33 and 35. Note 11 *The Anointing* states at p. 28: 'Canon B 37 provides that the anointing should be made on the forehead with the sign of the cross, but other parts of the body may be anointed in addition to the forehead.'   [191] *Op. cit.* at pp. 555–557.

[192] *Op. cit.* at p. 252.

[193] See *Sumner* v. *Wix* (1870) LR 3 A & E 58 at p. 66; see, too, Canon F 8, para. 1.

a sanctus bell or gong, or the ringing of any other bell as part of the eucharist, was an illegal ceremony[194]. However, *Lent, Holy Week, Easter* suggests that bells may be rung as part of the Easter Liturgy[195]. In the light of what is permissible under Canon B 5 in relation to other ceremonies the ringing of a bell to focus the attention of worshippers, or to draw the attention of those unable themselves to attend church, is now legal[196].

(vii)   Liturgical dance and mime

There is no doubt that the inclusion of mime[197] or liturgical dance into a service according to the Book of Common Prayer would have been illegal. However, as long as its introduction is in such circumstances as to fall within the provisions of Canon B 5[198], the introduction of mime or liturgical dance into any service would seem now to be legal as long as it is reverent, glorifies God and is edifying. This is particularly so as *A Service of the Word and Affirmations of Faith* provides for the dramatisation of readings[199].

F   Music

As has already been seen[200], even in relation to the Book of Common Prayer the singing of psalms and hymns during a service is legal, even where they may not be expressly authorised[201]. The same position is reflected in the general notes to the Authorised Service Book[202]. Equally that service book provides that, where

---

[194] *Elphinstone* v. *Purchas* (1870) LR 3 A & E 66 at pp. 98–99 (see, too, *Hebbert* v. *Purchas* (1872) LR 4 PC 301 at p. 307); *Rector and Churchwardens of Capel St Mary, Suffolk* v. *Packard* [1927] P 289 at p. 305; *In re St Mary, Tyne Dock* [1954] P 369 at p. 379; *Vicar and Churchwardens of St John the Evangelist, Clevedon* v. *All Having Interest* [1909] P 6 at p. 14 (an external bell 'rung at the like moments and for the like purpose'). Contrast, however, *Re St Mary's, West Fordington* (1956) reported briefly in *Opinions of the Legal Advisory Commission* (5th ed.) at p. 143: the installation of a church bell 'although its ringing on occasions at Holy Communion might strictly be a breach of good order'.   [195] See Note 8 at p. 227.

[196] *In re St John the Evangelist, Chopwell* (1995) in **Appendix 6** at **pp. 291–292** *infra*.

[197] As to signing for the deaf see **p. 67** *supra*.   [198] See **p. 48** *et seq. supra*.

[199] Note 5 at p. 8.   [200] See **p. 38** *supra*.

[201] *Hutchins* v. *Denziloe and Loveland* (1792) 1 Hag. Co. 170 at pp. 175–180; see, too, *Read* v. *Bishop of Lincoln* [1892] AC 644 at pp. 659–661. This includes antiphonal singing; indeed, as Pliny noted, antiphonal singing was a practice of the ancient Christians (*Epistles*, tit. 10, 97): see *Hutchins* v. *Denziloe and Loveland* (1792) 1 Hag. Co. 170 at pp. 175–180. The antiphonal signing of the *Veni, Creator Spiritus* is specifically enjoined by the rubric in the Form and Manner of Ordering of Priests and the Form of Ordaining or Consecrating of an Archbishop or Bishop annexed to the Book of Common Prayer. Although it may be argued that what is expressly permitted on one occasion is implicitly illegal elsewhere, Canon B 5, para. 1, would now certainly permit antiphonal singing on other occasions.

[202] Note 9 at p. 32. See also, for example, Note 8 at p. 242 in relation to the Baptism of Children and Notes 20 and 12 at pp. 117 and 178 respectively in relation to Holy Communion.

the rubrics indicate that a section may be said, the section may also be sung, or vice versa[203].

By Canon B 20, para. 3:

> It is the duty of the minister to ensure that only such chants[204], hymns, anthems, and other settings are chosen as are appropriate, both the words and the music, to the solemn act of worship and prayer in the House of God as well as to the congregation assembled for that purpose; and to banish all irreverence in the practice and performance of the same[205].

This Canon seems to be imposing a duty on the incumbent[206]; nonetheless, it is clearly only reflecting the general canon law[207] and the same duty falls on anyone taking a service. Similarly, the organist is under a duty to devote his best efforts towards securing a devout and appropriate rendering of the musical portions of the services so far as the means at his disposal permit[208]. If, for example, an officiating minister were to realise that bawdy words were being sung to the hymn tune he would be under a duty to ensure that it stopped; if necessary he ought to discontinue the service until all danger of such behaviour has ceased.

Where there is an organist, choirmaster or director of music, the minister[209] must:

> pay due heed to his advice and assistance in the choosing of chants, hymns, anthems, and other settings, and in the ordering of the music of the Church; but at all times the final responsibility and decision in these matters rests with the minister[210].

---

[203] Note 2 at p. 32. Note 5 of *A Service of the Word and Affirmations of Faith* at p. 8 provides that readings may be sung.

[204] The Alternative Service Book even gives guidance in relation to the chanting of the psalms and canticles; in particular it provides for the omission of Jewish doxologies where a Christian doxology is used: see Note 10 at p. 33.

[205] In *Matthews* v. *King* [1934] 1 KB 505 the organised loud singing of hymns, which lasted throughout the service so as to make the officiating minister's voice inaudible, was held to be an offence under the Ecclesiastical Courts Jurisdiction Act 1860, s. 2. See, too, **p. 248** *infra*.

[206] This is because 'the minister' in Canon B 20, paras 1 and 2, can only be referring to the incumbent; moreover, the reference to banishing all irreverence 'in the practice' of the music would not seem, for example, to refer to a visiting minister.   [207] See **p. 65** *et seq. supra*.

[208] *Legal Opinions concerning the Church of England* at p. 189. It is also his duty to recognise the authority of the incumbent in all matters relating to the conduct of the service, including what parts are to be said and sung respectively and the amount of musical elaboration suited to the needs of the congregation: *ibid*. As to the the use of the organ at weddings, funerals, etc. see *op. cit.* at pp. 190–191.

[209] The Canon speaks of 'the minister' but it is clearly referring to the incumbent: see, also, Canon B 20, para. 1.

[210] This rules out any legal appeal to the Ordinary such as was envisaged by Sir Robert Phillimore in *Wyndham* v. *Cole* (1875) 1 PD 130 at p. 134.

Indeed, an organist[211] may not play the organ immediately before, during or immediately after a service contrary to the directions of the incumbent[212]. There is a reciprocal duty in the organist to recognise the authority of the incumbent in all matters relating to the conduct of the service, including what parts are to be said and sung and the amount of musical elaboration suited to the needs of the congregation[213]; indeed, this would also be so in relation to any other minister taking the service[214]. If, as occasionally happens, the organ is used in a dispute between the organist and the incumbent so as to make the minister inaudible,[215] the organist is always in breach of the law.

In the case of a wedding it is solely the incumbent's decision what music may be played and what hymns or anthems sung[216].

G Bells

The ringing of the church bells[217] is always within the general control of the incumbent[218] and bells may never be rung contrary to his direction[219]. Nevertheless, as long as no such contrary direction has been given[220], it seems that churchwardens may in limited circumstances give such permission[221]. A charge may be levied for the ringing of the bells[222].

H Notices and Banns

Ministers having a cure of souls must give general notice of feasts and fasts. The additional duties in relation to notices in services may on occasion now be dispensed with; notices may also be given by members of the laity. However, the rules as to the calling of banns must be strictly adhered to.

---

[211] The same would apply *mutatis mutandis* to any musician.

[212] *Wyndham* v. *Cole* (1875) 1 PD 130.

[213] *Legal Opinions concerning the Church of England* at p. 189. It should always be borne in mind that silence is an important part of any service: see **p. 39, footnote 58,** and **p. 66** *supra*.

[214] Contrast, however, Canon B 35, para. 5.

[215] Cp. *Matthews* v. *King* [1934] 1 KB 505 at p. 507 (hymns).   [216] Canon B 35, para. 5.

[217] As to the ringing of a bell as a sanctus bell, see **p. 78** *et seq. supra.*

[218] *Harrison* v. *Forbes and Sissons* (1860) 6 Jur NS 1353; *Redhead* v. *Wait* (1862) 6 LT 580.

[219] Canons F 8, para. 2, and F 15, para. 1.

[220] *Harrison* v. *Forbes and Sisson* (1860) 6 Jur NS 1353 *per* Dr Lushington: 'Supposing that these gentlemen were clothed with the character and office of churchwardens, I am still inclined to agree with Dr Phillimore that they would not, generally speaking, have authority to order the bells of the parish to be rung without the consent of the minister. At the same time, I can imagine cases in which they would be justified in giving such an order without his leave.'.

[221] For example, if there is no incumbent or if he is absent. See *Opinions of the Legal Advisory Commission* (6th ed.) at 10; this opinion must be read in the light of the cases already cited.

[222] *Ibid.*

(i) Notices

(a) Generally

Canon B 7 states that:

> The minister having the cure of souls shall give adequate public notice, in any way which is locally convenient, of the feast days and fast days to be observed and of the time and place of services on those days.

This Canon is an enormous improvement upon its predecessor which contained many ambiguities; nonetheless, it is in addition to any duty imposed by a rubric upon an officiating minister[223].

Notice given during a service is not of itself sufficient notice, as people other than those in the congregation, such as vistors, are also entitled to be informed of intended services. Similarly, the same stricture would apply to notice given only in a parish magazine that was not generally available. On the other hand, in many cases a notice on a notice board, or in a newspaper that circulates in the relevant district[224], will suffice to satisfy the Canon.

However, the question still has to be asked as to which services must be notified. Is it solely notice of the feasts and fasts specified in the prayer books to be observed (whichever prayer book is used) or does it include those which will actually be observed in addition to those actually specified[225]? Although it will be seen[226] that there is a difficulty as to what notices can lawfully be given during service time, Canon B 7 is clearly dealing with publication in a wider context. In addition, the words 'and of the time and place of services on those days' make it clear that notice must be given of all celebrations being observed, whether set out in the service book being used or not.

Where the holding of a service of Holy Communion presided over by a non-Anglican minister has been authorised in a local ecumenical project[227], upon the preceding Sunday notice must so far as is practical be given of the service, together with an indication of the rite to be used and the Church to which the presiding minister belongs[228].

(b) Services

(α) Generally

Quite apart from the obligation under Canon B 7 there are the provisions in the rubrics as to the giving of notices. Notices may, however, be given out either

---

[223] See *infra*.   [224] This would include a national newspaper.

[225] There is a separate obligation in relation to Morning and Evening Prayer on days other than Sundays, principal feast days, Ash Wednesday and Good Friday. Canon B 11, para. 2, provides that 'Public notice must be given in the parish, by tolling the bell or other appropriate means, of the time and place where the prayers are to be said or sung.' The provision applies to these days only because it appears in para. 2 and not in para. 1 or separately.   [226] *Infra*.

[227] Canon B 44, para. 4(1)(f).   [228] Canon B 44, para. 4(3)(a).

before or after a service by a minister or lay person as long as good order is observed[229].

(β) Holy Communion

In *Elphinstone* v. *Purchas*[230] it was held that in the Holy Communion service according to the Book of Common Prayer notice could only lawfully[231] be given of those feasts and fasts:

> which are to be found after the preface of the prayer-book, under the head of 'A Table of all the Feasts that are to be observed in the Church of England throughout the year'.

Indeed, the rubric after the Creed specifies that ' . . . nothing shall be proclaimed or published . . . but what is prescribed by the Rules of this Book . . . '. On the other hand, the Alternative Service Book[232] not only gives a list of 'Festivals and Greater Holidays' and 'Lesser Festivals and Commemorations' but also adds that 'Diocesan, local, or other commemorations may be added to these lists.'[233]

In the result it seems that, in relation to the notices within a Holy Communion service according to the Alternative Service Book, notice may[234] be given of any celebrations that will take place. However, it cannot be said in relation to notices within a Holy Communion service according to the Book of Common Prayer that the wording of Canon B 7 by itself overruled the previous rigorist interpretation[235] so as to impose a duty[236] to announce additional celebrations, even though the purpose of the Canon is that people may know that a celebration is to take place[237]. Nonetheless, to make an announcement of celebrations other than those set out after the preface must now be permissible under Canon

---

[229] See **p. 237** *et seq. infra*. There seems no reason why the notices should not now be printed: see *Patterns of Worship* at p. 231.   [230] (1870) LR 3 A & E 66 at pp. 111–112.

[231] Sir Robert Phillimore also stated at p. 111: 'It appears to me that the epithet "high" [added to describe a eucharist] has no sanction from the rubric, and, though perhaps in itself not very material, cannot legally be used.' Such a description would surely now be regarded as *de minimis*.

[232] See *op. cit.* at pp. 17–21. Father Robert Ombres, OP, has pointed out that, in spite of *In re St. Edmund's Churchyard, Gateshead* [1995] 3 WLR 253 at p. 257B-D, Thomas More (who was executed on 6 July 1535) is described in the Alternative Service Book at p. 17 as 'Martyr'.

[233] See, too, Canon B 1, para. 3(v), Canon B 4, para. 4, and Canon B 5, para. 5.

[234] The rubrics merely state that 'Banns of marriage and other notices may be published . . . ': see Notes 19 and 11 at pp. 117 and 178 respectively.

[235] According to Stephens, *The Book of Common Prayer*, vol. II. at p. 1150, the first part of the rubric was 'first inserted to prevent the people's observing such holydays as had been introduced by popery, and were abrogated by the Reformation: and it has been wisely retained, to remind those of their duty, who are not disposed to observe holydays or fasting days.'

[236] This is particularly so as it could only impose such a duty on the minister who is also the incumbent.

[237] This is also the purpose of the rubric in the Book of Common Prayer, as the rubric after the Prayer for the Church Militant makes clear: 'When the Minister giveth warning for the celebration of the holy Communion . . . '.

B 5[238] because of the different celebrations now permitted by the Alternative
Service Book.

The rubric after the Creed in the Book of Common Prayer[239] states:

Then the Curate shall[240] declare unto the people what Holy-days, or Fasting-
days, are in the Week following to be observed. And then also (if occasion
be) shall notice be given of the Communion[241]; and Briefs, Citations, and
Excommunications read. And nothing[242] shall be proclaimed or published in
the Church, during the time of Divine Service[243], but by the Minister[244]: nor
by him at any time, but what is prescribed in the Rules of this Book, or
enjoined by the Queen, or by the Ordinary of the Place.

[238] This view is, of course, supported by the provisions of Canon B 7. The conclusion stands in
spite of the wording of the rubric: 'And nothing shall be proclaimed or published in the Church,
during the time of Divine Service, but by the Minister: nor by him any thing, *but what is prescribed
in the Rules of this Book* ...' (emphasis supplied).

[239] As to previous history see Stephens, *Book of Common Prayer*, vol. II at pp. 1150 *et seq.*.

[240] The rubric is imperative: see *Elphinstone* v. *Purchas* (1870) LR 3 A & E 66 at p. 111. Notices
may now be omitted in some circumstances in reliance upon Canon B 5.

[241] It has been suggested that this is in conflict with the rubric immediately preceding the first
Exhortation but this may be doubted: see Stephens, *op. cit*, vol. II at p. 1150; even if it is, any variation
would now be covered by Canon B 5. That rubric states: 'When the Minister giveth warning for the
celebration of the holy Communion (which he shall always do upon the Sunday, or some Holy-day,
immediately preceding,) after the Sermon or Homily ended ...'. Nevertheless, the Sacrament Act
1547, s. 8, provides: 'And also the priest which shall minister [Holy Communion] shall at least
one day before exhort all which likewise be present to resort and prepare themselves to receive
the same ...'. This latter provision cannot be varied in reliance upon Canon B 1, para. 1, as it is
a statutory obligation apart from a form of service. Impossibility of performance, for example, by
a priest visiting only for the particular celebration, would presumably be complete mitigation.

[242] 14 Halsbury's Laws of England (4th ed.) at para. 948 suggests nevertheless that notices 'which
concern the congregation and ordinary church business' might be added by analogy with *Read* v.
Bishop of Lincoln [1892] AC 644 at p. 660; even if this argument is wrong, such notices may
nonetheless now be given: see *infra*.

[243] It seems that the expression 'divine service' has in the past been used to include the choir
offices (and hence mattins and evensong) as well as the eucharist: see *The Oxford Dictionary of the
Christian Church*, 'divine service'. Nonetheless, that term was clearly used in the 1603 Canons to
embrace all services according to the Book of Common Prayer: see, for example, the heading before
Canon 13 and Canons 14, 16, 18 and 19. Moreover, in the Preface to the Book of Common Prayer,
Concerning the Church, it is made clear that in that service book 'divine service' means 'the
Common Prayers in the Church'; see, too, *Matthews* v. *King* [1934] 1 KB 505. (In Canon B 10,
however, the phrase 'the Common Prayer' is used differently in order to refer to Morning and
Evening Prayer alone.) It seems, therefore, that this rubric is intended to refer to all services in
church and not just to the Holy Communion; it is in fact a rubric dealing with a general matter of
good order. It cannot be argued that, as rubrics concerning notices are omitted from other services
and this rubric speaks of 'What is prescribed in the Rules of this Book', the rubric is confined to
the Holy Communion because the rubric also goes on to envisage directions from the Queen and
the Ordinary. Similarly, although the rubric at the commencement of the Form of Solemnization of
Marriage, as originally published, spoke of banns being published 'in the time of Divine Service,
immediately before the sentences for the Offertory', this did not mean that 'divine service' was
restricted to the Holy Communion; rather, it was unnecessary further to identify the Holy Communion as in no other service was there an offertory. The present canons clearly use the term to include
all services: see Canon B 9.   [244] See *Williams* v. *Glenister* (1824) 2 B & C 699.

However, now that the rigorist interpretation of the rubrics no longer applies[245] and bearing in mind the wider obligation under Canon B 7[246], it would seem that notices may on occasions be omitted in reliance on Canon B 1, para. 1.

Lay ministration of the Ante-Communion is permitted by a lay person in a service according to the Alternative Service Book[247] and in such circumstances he or she may also give out any notices. Indeed, if it is right that lay ministration is now permitted of Ante-Communion according to the Book of Common Prayer, it would seem that notices may also be now given by that lay person[248]. In fact, although in relation to the participation of the laity the rubric is clearly one relating to good order, in the light of the participation now generally permitted to the laity by the Alternative Service Book Canon B 5 would now permit the giving of notices by any lay person in a service according to any rite.

Some consideration has already been given to what celebrations should be notified[249]. The rubric also states that 'Briefs, Citations, and Excommunications' are to be read. However, from 1837 until the commencement of the Care of Churches and Ecclesiastical Jurisdiction Measure 1991, it was illegal[250] for such items to be 'read or published in any church or chapel during or immediately after divine service'[251]. Nonetheless, the previous law as set out in the rubric has now been reinstated[252], although it should be noted that excommunication as a legal sentence[253] has now in effect been

[245] See p. 11 et seq. supra.

[246] Although the rubrics are concerned with general Church order, they must be seen within the wider context of Canon B 7.   [247] See p. 100 infra.

[248] If this were not so, no notice during divine service might be given of forthcoming feasts and fasts if there is no member of the clergy present; such an omission would clearly be contrary to the intention of the rubric.   [249] Supra.

[250] Parish Notices Act 1837, s. 4.

[251] That is, the Common Prayers in the Church: see supra.

[252] This seems to be the effect of the most unusual provisions of the 1991 Measure. Although section 24 has a marginal note reading 'Repeal of section 4 of the Parish Notices Act 1837', the repeal is actually achieved by s. 32(2) and Sch. 8. Section 24 enacts that: 'Section 4 of the Parish Notices Act 1837 (decrees, etc. of ecclesiastical courts not to be read in churches) shall cease to have effect.' If this unwieldy mechanism had not been adopted, the provisions of the Interpretation Act 1978, s. 16(1)(a) would have applied to the repeal and the law prior to the 1837 Act would have remained abrogated.

[253] This refers to greater excommunication only. 'Excommunication ... is a Censure of the Church, pronounced, and inflicted by the Canon or some Ecclesiastical Judge lawfully Constituted, whereby the party against whom it is so pronounced, is pro tempore deprived of the lawful participation and Communion of the Sacraments. And is also sometimes (as to Offenders) a deprivation of their Communion, and sequestration of their persons from the converse and society of the Faithful. And therefore it is distinguish'd into the Greater and Lesser Excommunication; the Greater comprizing as well the latter as the former part of the abovesaid definition or description; the Lesser comprizing only the former part thereof': Godolphin, Reportorium Canonicum or An Abridgment of the Ecclesiastical Laws (London, 1680) (2nd ed.) at p. 624; see, too, p. 239, footnote 15. See, also, Briden & Hanson, Moore's Introduction to English Canon Law (3rd ed.) at p. 85, footnote 9. It is there suggested that a person excommunicated by a Church of competent jurisdiction outside England and dying in that state in England would still be caught by the rubric at the beginning of The Order for the Burial of the Dead in the Book of Common Prayer; indeed, this view receives support from the fact that the rubric is reflected in Canon B 38, para. 2, as the Canon was promulgated after the

abolished[254]. The end result is, for example, that the result of a faculty case involving the parish may now be published during the usual notices. This, of course, applies whatever service is being taken or rite used. On the other hand the prohibition relating to certain notices which prior to 1838[255] by virtue of any law or statute, or by custom or otherwise, had been made or given in churches or chapels during or after divine service technically still remains in force[256].

There is, in addition, the general restriction in the rubric against the proclamation or publication during divine service of:

> ... any thing, but what is prescribed in the Rules of this Book, or enjoined by the Queen, or by the Ordinary of the place.

The Alternative Service Book provides[257] at what places in the Holy Communion service 'Banns of marriage and other notices may be published ... ' It does not, however, state what notices may be given. It may be argued, therefore, that the rubric in the Book of Common Prayer also governs those rites, even though (and in spite of that rubric[258]) it is likely that lay persons may give notices during services according to the Alternative Service Book[259]. If that is so, these rubrics should not be interpreted in too restrictive a manner. Indeed, this view gains support from the repeal of section 1 of the Parish Notices Act 1837. That section had enacted that:

> ... No proclamation or other public notice for a vestry meeting or any other matter shall be made or given in any church or chapel during or after divine service ...

This repeal clearly envisages that public notices on 'any other matter ... during divine service' may now be given. This must also apply during a rite according to the Alternative Service Book. Similarly, such a publication is now permissible by reason of Canon B 5 in a rite according to the Book of Common Prayer.

Ecclesiastical Jurisdiction Measure 1963: see, too, **p. 199** *infra*. It also receives some support from Canon B 15A, para. 1(a) which speaks of 'members of the Church of England'. See, however, *Kemp v. Wickes* (1808) 3 Phillim. 264 at pp. 271–272 *per* Sir John Nicholl.

[254] This is because section 49 of the Ecclesiastical Jurisdiction Measure 1963 no longer permits such a sentence. This does not embrace what is sometimes called lesser excommunication: see **p. 239** *et seq. infra*. Presumably this is why the 1963 Measure does not specifically abolish excommunication but (even though it is no longer available as a censure) states at s. 82(4): 'No person shall be liable to imprisonment in consequence of being excommunicated.'

[255] See the wording of the Parish Notices Act 1837, s. 4.

[256] See Burn, *Ecclesiastical Law* (London, 1767) (2nd ed.), vol. III at pp. 257–258. 'Provided always ... that nothing in this act shall extend to or be construed to extend to the publication of banns': Parish Notices Act 1837 s. 5, as amended by the Church of England (Miscellaneous Provisions) Measure 1992, s. 17(2), Sch. 4, Pt I.

[257] Notes 19 and 11 at pp. 117 and 178 respectively.

[258] See **p. 85, footnote 246** *supra*.   [259] See *supra*.

It follows that any notice[260] may now properly be given as long as it is edifying[261], reverent and seemly[262].

In addition there remains a duty to publish that which is lawfully enjoined by the Queen or by the Ordinary[263]. This applies whichever rite is being followed.

(γ) Services other than Holy Communion

It should be noted that consideration has so far only been given to notices during the Holy Communion service. This is because the rubrics do not specify the occasions upon which notices should be given other than in those services[264]. Nonetheless, if it be right that the rubric after the Creed in Holy Communion according to the Book of Common Prayer is concerned with notices during any service[265], other occasions must have been envisaged. Indeed, that would seem to be the common sense of the situation in relation to both service books. Moreover, even if it were not so envisaged, it would now be permissible pursuant to Canon B 5, as long as care is taken as to the time when the notices are given within the service. This view would also accord with Canon B 7 in so far as it may be locally convenient to give out notices during a service other than Holy Communion[266].

(ii) Banns of marriage[267]

Banns of marriage are matters of particular importance as the marriage itself alters the legal status of those involved[268]. Indeed, this importance is recognized by the fact that the Church of England (Worship and Doctrine) Measure 1974, section 1(1)(b), excludes 'the publication of banns of marriage' from the General Synod's general powers to make provision in relation to any matter to which the rubrics in the Book of Common Prayer relate.

Canon B 35, para. 2[269], also states:

---

[260] Notice of a forthcoming church fete would, therefore, not be illegal: cp. Briden & Hanson, *op. cit.* at p. 97.   [261] Canon B 1, para. 2.

[262] Canon B 5, para. 3.

[263] See **p. 85, footnote 253** *supra* and see Phillimore, *Ecclesiastical Law* vol. I at p. 1420.

[264] Although Canon 22 of the 1603 Canons spoke of notice being given 'publicly in the Church at Morning Prayer', no provision is made in the Book of Common Prayer for notices to be given during that service.

[265] See **p. 84, footnote 243** *supra* concerning the meaning of 'during the time of Divine Service'.

[266] Although Canon B 7 is concerned with 'the minister having the cure of souls', in relation to some at least of the notices what is convenient for him must be equally convenient for the minister actually taking the service.

[267] For the general law as to banns see **p. 164** *et seq. infra*; 14 Halsbury's Laws of England (4th ed.) at para. 1015 *et seq.*; *Anglican Marriage in England and Wales A Guide to the Law for Clergy* (The Faculty Office of the Archbishop of Canterbury, 1992) at para. 7.

[268] That is, the fact of the marriage means that the parties and their children are treated differently both under English law and by that of other countries if they change their domicile. For example, it may affect inheritance.

[269] The Canon reflects the Marriage Act 1949, s. 7(2). See also Canon B 35, para. 1: 'In all matters pertaining to the granting of licences of marriage every ecclesiastical authority shall observe the law relating thereto.'

In all matters pertaining to the publication of banns of marriage ... every minister shall observe the law relating thereto, including, so far as they may be applicable, the rules prescribed by the rubric[270] prefixed to the office of Solemnisation of Matrimony in the Book of Common Prayer.

Indeed, the words 'so far as they may be applicable' do not seem merely to refer to such occasions as those when the service is conducted according to the Book of Common Prayer; if that were so, they would be otiose. Rather, they seem to impose a duty to incorporate those provisions into any service[271].

Banns of marriage must be published 'in an audible manner', even if the service is only for those who are deaf[272]. The form of words to be used[273] is:

I publish the banns of marriage between N. of—[274] and N. of—. If any of you know cause, or just impediment[275], why these persons should not be joined together in holy Matrimony, ye are to declare it. This is for the first [*second, or third*] time of asking.

It is sufficient if the substance of this form is followed, rather than its use word for word[276]. It is unnecessary to give the marital status of the parties[277]; the requirement to state the parish from which each party comes reflects the requirements[278] concerning residence[279] and the need for the parties to be properly

---

[270] This seems to refer to the first such rubric, although the second is also concerned with the publication of banns. Nevertheless, the Marriage Act 1949, s. 7(2), suggests that all those rubrics are included.   [271] See **p. 165** *et seq. supra*.

[272] Marriage Act 1949, s. 7(2). This cannot be varied by Canon B 5 as a canon cannot abrogate a statute. Signing may be utilised in addition: see **p. 67**, *supra*.

[273] Whatever service is used: see the rubric at the commencement of the Form of Solemnization of Matrimony in the Book of Common Prayer; Marriage Act 1949, s. 7(2); Canon B 35, para. 2. Note 1 at p. 285 of the Alternative Service Book suggests an alternative form, namely: 'I publish the banns of marriage between *N* of ... and *N* of ... This is the first (second)(third) time of asking. If any of you know any reason in law why these persons may not marry each other you are to declare it now.' *Anglican Marriage in England and Wales A Guide to the Law for Clergy* at para. 7.6 casts doubt upon the legality of this alternative because of section 1(1)(b) of the Church of England (Worship and Doctrine) Measure 1974, and recommends that it should not be used. However, although the subsection does indeed cast doubt upon the legality of Note 1, the use of the suggested form of words may nevertheless be permissible as it follows the statutory requirements in their substance: see *infra*.

[274] Where the person does not reside in the parish but is on the electoral roll of the area in which the parish church or chapel is situated the words 'on the electoral roll of this parish' may be used rather than 'of this parish' or 'of the parish of —': *Legal Opinions concerning the Church of England* at p. 162.   [275] As to what is a 'cause or just impediment' see **p. 168** *infra*.

[276] *Standen* v. *Standen* (1791) Peake 45.   [277] Contrast the Marriage Act 1949, s. 27(3).

[278] For these requirements, see 14 Halsbury's Laws of England (4th ed.) at para. 1007; *Anglican Marriage in England and Wales A Guide to the Law for Clergy* at para. 5.

[279] The term has its ordinary and natural meaning and is normally a matter of fact and degree. It usually embraces something more than a casual visit but the existence of a home is a highly significant factor, even though it may not have been visited for some time: see *Rayden and Jackson on Divorce and Family Matters* (16th ed.) at para. 5.2; *Legal Opinions concerning the Church of England* at pp. 166–169. See, too, *Cripps on Church and Clergy* (8th ed.) at pp. 544–545.

identifiable[280]. Indeed, the whole purpose of the banns is so that those hearing the banns may know whether to object[281]. Therefore to use a name which has been used for a considerable time is entirely proper, as there is no deception as to identity[282].

All banns must be published from the actual register book of banns[283] and after each publication the entry in the book must be signed by the person publishing the banns or by some person under his direction[284].

There is a duty upon a clerk in Holy Orders to publish banns[285] but only if, at least seven days days before the date on which they wish the banns to be published for the first time, the persons to be married deliver or cause to be delivered to him a notice in writing, dated on the day on which it is delivered, stating the Christian name[286] and surname and the place of residence of each of them, and the period during which each of them has resided at his or her address[287]. The clergyman may, however, waive such notice. However, if (as a result of not using due diligence to ascertain the accuracy of the banns that he calls) he marries persons who do not reside within the parish, he commits an ecclesiastical offence[288]. A lay person is under no obligation to publish banns but may do so in the circumstances set out below.

The banns must be published on three Sundays preceding the solemnisation of the marriage[289] but these need not be consecutive[290]. Where the marriage is

[280] See, generally, 14 Halsbury's Laws of England (4th ed.) at para. 1017.

[281] See, generally, 14 Halsbury's Laws of England (4th ed.) at para. 1017. 'The intention of the publication of banns is to make known that a marriage is about to take place between the individual parties – if, therefore, the publication is such as not to designate, but to conceal the parties – it is no publication': per Sir John Nicholl in *Fellowes* v. *Stewart* (1815) 2 Phillim. 238 at p. 240. For this reason, if one or both of the parties is a foreigner, the banns should be called in both English and the relevant foreign language: *Legal Opinions concerning the Church of England* at p. 171.

[282] *Cope* v. *Burt, falsely calling herself Cope* (1809) 1 Hag. Con. 434, affd (1811) 1 Phillim. 224.

[283] The register book must be provided in every parish church and chapel: Marriage Act s. 7(3), (4); Canon F 11. Register books must be provided, maintained and kept in accordance with Statutes and Measures relating thereto, and the rules and regulations made thereunder and from time to time in force: Canon F 11, para. 2.   [284] Marriage Act 1949, s. 7(3).

[285] Whether or not the person whose banns are to be called is divorced (see *Anglican Marriage in England and Wales A Guide to the Law for Clergy* at para. 7.12) or, indeed, is not Christian. As to the place where they must be published see **p. 165 et seq. infra.**

[286] A non-Christian resident is also entitled to have banns called and in such circumstances the notice requires such person's first name.   [287] Marriage Act 1949, ss. 8, 78(1).

[288] '. . . if a Clergyman, not using due diligence marries people, neither of whom are resident in the parish, he is liable at least to ecclesiastical censure; perhaps to other consequences' – per Lord Eldon in *Nicholson* v. *Squire* (1809) 16 Ves. 259 at p. 261; see, also, *Priestley* v. *Lamb* (1801) 6 Ves. 421; *Wynn* v. *Davies and Weever* (1835) 1 Curt. 69 at pp. 83–84 per Sir Herbert Jenner. See, too, 14 Halsbury's Laws of England (4th ed.) at para. 1015, note 2.

[289] Marriage Act 1949, s. 7(1).

[290] They must be consecutive if published on one of Her Majesty's ships at sea: s. 14(1); for further details concerning banns published at sea see **p. 167 infra.** A similar view of the law is stated in *Legal Opinions concerning the Church of England* at p. 162 and in *Anglican Marriage in England and Wales A Guide to the Law for Clergy* at para. 7.4; contrast, however, *Anglican Marriage in England and Wales A Guide to the Law for Clergy* at para. 7.12. In fact there is a duty upon a clergyman to publish banns and, therefore, it would seem sensible to publish them as soon as

not solemnised within three calendar months of their completion, that publication is void and no clergyman may solemnise the marriage on the authority of those banns[291].

Publication must[292] be during 'morning service' or, if there is no morning service on a Sunday on which the banns are to be published, during 'evening service'[293]. At one time, the banns had to be published during the Holy Communion service[294] and the Alternative Service Book also makes provision[295] for their publication during the eucharist[296]. No definition is given of 'morning' or 'evening' service but, nevertheless, the legislation clearly means such service as is celebrated at that particular time of day[297]. Moreover, because the intention is clearly to provide the greatest opportunity for the banns to be heard, this should include the Sunday service at which it is usual in that parish to publish banns[298]; there is, however, no reason why the banns should not be published at more than one service. Publication must be during a service performed according to the rites of the Church of England or duly authorised by canon[299].

Usually only a clerk in Holy Orders may publish banns[300]. However, when on any Sunday in any church or other building in which banns may be published[301] a clerk in Holy Orders does not officiate at the service at which it is usual to publish banns, other considerations may apply. In those circumstances the

possible unless requested for some good reason (for example, the absence of a relative who wishes to hear them) not so to do. *Pace Anglican Marriage in England and Wales A Guide to the Law for Clergy* at para. 7.12, however, it may be doubted whether there is a breach of duty unless the clergyman fails to use due diligence; the choice of dates seems to be that of the clergyman rather than that of the parties.

[291] Marriage Act 1949, s. 12(2); Interpretation Act 1978, s. 5, Sch. 1. The marriage is void if the parties thereto knowingly and wilfully intermarry on the authority of those banns: Marriage Act 1949, s. 25(c); *Rayden and Jackson on Divorce and Family Matters* (Butterworths, 1992) (16th ed.) at 9.15.   [292] See, however, the provisions where a clergyman is not available: *infra*.
[293] Marriage Act 1949, s. 7(1).
[294] See the rubric at the commencement of the Form of Solemnization of Matrimony in the Book of Common Prayer. It would seem that this statutory provision overrides the necessity otherwise to publish the banns in the Holy Communion service according to the Book of Common Prayer if, for example, such a celebration occurs in addition to that at which the banns must be published by reason of the Marriage Act 1949, s. 7(1). Even if this is not so, their omission would certainly be justified under Canon B 5.   [295] This is permissive rather than directory.
[296] See Notes 19 and 11 at pp. 117 and 178 respectively.
[297] Contrast the specific wording of the Marriage Act 1949, s. 9(2)(b) as to 'morning or evening prayer'; see, too, *ibid*, s. 6(3).   [298] Cp. Marriage Act 1949, s. 9(2)(b).
[299] *Legal Opinions concerning the Church of England* at p. 163.
[300] Marriage Act 1949, ss. 9, 78(1). This does not apply to banns published on one of Her Majesty's ships: Marriage Act 1949, s. 14.
[301] As to which these places are, see **p. 165 *et seq. infra***; 14 Halsbury's Laws of England (4th ed.) at para. 1007 *et seq.*; *Anglican Marriage in England and Wales A Guide to the Law for Clergy* at para. 7. Where by virtue of a designation made by a pastoral scheme or otherwise a parish has more than one parish church, the bishop may give directions with respect to the publication of banns in the parish churches: Pastoral Measure 1983, s. 27(5)(b). The marriage is void if the parties thereto knowingly and wilfully intermarry in any place other than a church or other building in which banns may be published: Marriage Act 1949, s. 25(a); *Rayden and Jackson on Divorce and Family Matters* (16th ed.) at 9.15.

banns may be published either by a clergyman at some other service at which banns may be published or by a lay person during the course of a public reading authorised by the diocesan bishop[302] of a portion or portions of morning or evening prayer; in this latter case the public reading of the service must be at the same time of day as the service at which banns are usually published is commonly held or at such other time as the bishop may authorise[303]. Even so, banns may not be published[304] by a lay person unless the incumbent or minister in charge of the church or building, or some other clergyman nominated in that behalf by the bishop, has made or authorised to be made the requisite entry in the register book of banns in relation to that church or building[305].

I Collections

Both in the Book of Common Prayer and the Alternative Service Book the only provision made for a collection[306] is at the Offertory during Holy Communion[307]. However, in *Marson* v. *Unmack*[308] the Dean of the Arches said:

> A collection during Mattins or Evensong – I exclude an offertory during the Communion service because that is expressly provided for by rubric, and may therefore perhaps be regarded as part of the service – is not provided for in the Prayer Book. It is an incident occuring during a service or interposed between different portions of it, but it is no more part of the service than a voluntary played on the organ or the action of a verger closing windows or lighting the gas while the service is in progress. Though varying greatly in degree of importance, they are all alike in being matters, not in themselves

---

[302] Because authorisation must be given, it is illegal for the banns to be published by a lay person without that authorisation, even if that lay person is otherwise legally taking the service. According to Canons D 1, para. 4(d), E 4, para. 2(b), and Canon E 7, para. 5(d), the bishop may so authorise a deaconess, reader or lay worker. However, this does not flow merely from their being a deaconess, reader or lay worker; they must be specifically authorised. By reason of the Marriage Act 1949, s. 9(2), it would seem that the bishop may similarly authorise other members of the laity.

[303] Marriage Act 1949, ss. 9(2), 78(1).

[304] If a lay person purports to publish banns in circumstances outside these provisions, the marriage is void if the parties thereto knowingly and wilfully intermarry without banns having been duly published: Marriage Act 1949, s. 25(b); *Rayden and Jackson on Divorce and Family Matters* (16th ed.) at 9.15.

[305] Marriage Act 1949, s. 9(2) proviso. Where a lay person publishes banns he must sign the register book and for that purpose is deemed to be the officiating clergyman: Marriages Act s. 9(3).

[306] Money given at services of Holy Communion form part of the general funds of the parochial church council: Church of England (Legal Aid and Miscellaneous Provisions) Measure 1988, s. 13; Canon B 17A. The allocation of all other collections is a matter for that council and the incumbent jointly; in the case of any disagreement the bishop may give directions: Parochial Church Councils (Powers) Measure 1956, s. 7(iv); *Legal Opinions concerning the Church of England* at p. 69; *Howell* v. *Holdroyd* [1897] P 198 at p. 207. [307] See **p. 119** *infra*.

[308] [1923] P 163 at pp. 167–168. This overlaps with both *de minimis* and long practice: see **p. 4, footnote 28**, and **p. 35** *supra*.

irreverent or unseemly, but outside the rites and ceremonies of public worship. Such a collection is an interlude entirely at the option of the minister, and has its sole justification in the sanction of long custom.

At institutions, inductions and confirmations it is for the bishop to decide whether there is to be a collection[309]. If Holy Communion is coupled with another service, a collection may be made at that other service as well as at the Offertory[310].

The rubric in the Book of Common Prayer after the Offertory Sentences states:

While these Sentences are in reading, the Deacons, Churchwardens, or other fit person appointed for that purpose[311], shall receive the Alms for the Poor, and other devotions of the people, in a decent bason to be provided by the Parish for that purpose; and reverently bring it to the Priest, who shall humbly present and place it upon the holy Table.

In *Cope* v. *Barber*[312] it was decided that, although the collection might be made by the priest, he is not ministering the divine office at that time; however, the whole rubric must now be read in the light of Canon B 5, para. 1. The Alternative Service Book merely states that 'the offerings of the people may be collected and presented'[313]. Nevertheless long standing practice ought to be followed[314].

The Legal Advisory Commission of the General Synod states that the churchwardens are the proper officers to make the collection, either alone or with the aid of the sidesmen or other persons selected by them[315]. However, this opinion cannot override the position as to the Offertory during a Holy Communion service according to the Book of Common Prayer.

These provisions only apply to money given or collected in church[316].

Alms collected in the course of, or in connection with, the performance of offices and services pursuant to the provisions of the Extra-Parochial Ministry

[309] *Legal Opinions concerning the Church of England* at p. 69.
[310] *Marson* v. *Unmack* [1923] P 163 at p. 168. Indeed, two collections may now be justified within the same service by reason of Canon B 5, para. 1.
[311] In *Cope* v. *Barber* (1872) LR 7 CP 393 at p. 403 it is suggested that the appointment should be by the priest.   [312] (1872) LR 7 CP 393 at p. 403.
[313] Notes 34, 15 and 27 at pp. 129, 182 and 189 respectively.
[314] *Howell* v. *Holdroyd* [1897] P 198.
[315] *Legal Opinions concerning the Church of England* at p. 69. After the service the moneys should be handed to the treasurer of the parochial church council, who must keep accounts of such money so collected: *ibid.*
[316] See the Parochial Church Councils (Powers) Measure 1956, s. 7(iv), as amended by the Church of England (Legal Aid and Miscellaneous Provisions) Measure 1988, s. 13. 'Churchwardens had, and Parochial Church Councils have, no more control or authority over religious gatherings in a school room or mission hall, than over a drawing-room meeting for a religious purpose in a private house': *Marson* v. *Unmack* [1923] P 162 at p. 170 *per* the Dean of the Arches.

Measure 1967[317], in a university, college, school, hospital or public or charitable institution must be disposed of in such manner as the minister performing the office or service may determine, subject to the direction of the diocesan bishop[318].

J Vesture

(i) Generally

The question of vesture has in the past caused much legal controversy[319]. Fortunately, however, most of the legal dispute has now been resolved and Canon B 8, para. 1, now declares that:

The Church of England does not attach any particular doctrinal significance to the diversities of vesture permitted by this Canon, and the vesture worn by the minister in accordance with the provisions of this Canon is not to be understood as implying any doctrines other than those now contained in the formularies of the Church of England.

Nevertheless, no minister[320] may change the form of vesture used in the church or chapel in which he officiates[321] unless he has ascertained by consultation[322] with the parochial church council that such changes will be acceptable[323]. If there is a disagreement, the minister must refer the matter to the diocesan bishop and his direction must be obeyed[324].

According to Canon B 8, para. 3:

At Holy Communion the presiding minister must wear either a surplice[325] or alb with scarf or stole. When a stole is worn other customary vestments[326]

---

[317] See **p. 220** *et seq. supra.*   [318] Extra-Parochial Ministry Measure 1967, s. 2(3).

[319] See Phillimore, *Ecclesiastical Law*, vol I at pp. 711 *et seq*; 14 Halsbury's Laws of England (4th ed.) at paras 960, note 3, and 970.

[320] It might be argued that these words refer to the minister having the cure of souls as a visiting minister would not normally have access to the parochial church council and that the words 'in which he officiates' import some regularity. However, the provisions are most likely to apply to any minister as Canon B 8, para. 2, is designed to protect the sensibilities of the congregation; moreover, the subsequent references to 'the presiding minister' (para. 3) and 'the minister' (paras 4 and 5) certainly refer to any minister. Thus the words 'in which he officiates' are probably to be read as meaning 'in which he officiates at any time'.   [321] See **the previous footnote**.

[322] Although a vote may not be necessary, a full and sufficient opportunity must be given to the council or its nominees to ask questions and submit their opinions: see *Re Union of Benefices of Whippingham and East Cowes, St James, Derham v. Church Commissioners for England* [1954] AC 245.   [323] Canon B 8, para. 2.

[324] Canon B 8, para. 2 proviso.

[325] It is the duty of the parochial church council to provide surplices and to maintain them 'in a clean condition for the use of the minister': Canons F 6 and 14.

[326] It is the duty of the sexton, if any, to care for the vestments (see 14 Halsbury's Laws of England (4th ed.) at para. 559) but it also falls on the parochial church council: Canon F 14.

may be added. The epistoler and gospeller (if any) may wear surplice or alb to which other customary vestments may be added.

The previous Canon B 8 mentioned a cassock as vesture that should be worn both at Morning and Evening Prayer and at Holy Communion[327]; however, the omission of any mention of a cassock from the present Canon should not be seen as making them illegal[328]. Rather, the wearing of a cassock seems to be assumed[329]. Moreover, although 'the presiding minister' is mentioned, the Canon is again silent in relation to any other minister who may be participating, save as an epistoler or gospeller. Once again, however, the intention must be that such a minister should wear vesture similar to that worn by the presiding minister, as long as that minister is ordained[330]. Finally, although the Canon speaks of 'other customary vestments', it is not referring to any legal custom[331] but, rather, to those vestments that have traditionally been so worn[332]. This would certainly include a cope as the previous Canon[333] specifically referred to its use.

In relation to other services Canon B 8 states:

4. At Morning Prayer and Evening Prayer on Sundays the minister shall normally wear a surplice or alb with scarf or stole.
5. At the Occasional Offices[334] the minister shall wear a surplice or alb with scarf or stole.

No provision is made as to occasions other than normal Sundays[335] but in any event Canon C 27 would still apply:

[327] *Ibid*, paras 1 and 2.   [328] 14 Halsbury's Laws of England (4th ed.) at para. 970.

[329] Canon C 27 (see *infra*) may be seen as permitting the wearing of a cassock in any event; see, too, **p. 97** *infra*. Moreover, as was quoted with approval in *Ridsdale* v. *Clifton* (1877) 2 PD 276 at p. 331: 'Usage, for a long series of years, in ecclesiastical customs especially, is entitled to the greatest respect; it has every presumption in its favour; but it cannot contravene or prevail over positive law, though, where doubt exists, it might turn the balance': see, too, **p. 4, footnote 28** *supra*. Even if this were to be an incorrect understanding of the law, as cassocks have been worn for so many years to continue so to wear them would certainly be regarded as *de minimis*.

[330] As to the vesture of readers, see **p. 96** *infra*.

[331] See **p. 4, footnote 28,** *supra*. Note 7 at p. 338 of the Alternative Service Book states that: 'Where it is agreed that those to be ordained are to be clothed in their customary vesture, it is appropriate that this should take place at any time after the Declaration.' This in practice means the vesture usually worn according to the tradition of churchmanship that each candidate represents. See, too, **p. 234** *infra*.

[332] Thus, it seems that at least the wearing of a chasuble is envisaged: see 14 Halsbury's Laws of England (4th ed.) at para. 970, note 10. A humeral veil was regarded as outside the faculty jurisdiction (and, therefore, presumably as *de minimis*) in *St Mary, Tyne Dock* [1954] P 369. In any event such a veil would presumably fall within the description of 'customary vestments', as would a maniple, even though they are now less commonly worn. It does not refer to those vestments customarily worn in that particular church or chapel, as those must be worn unless a change is agreed with the parochial church council: see Canon B 8, para. 2.   [333] Canon B 8, para. 3.

[334] For the meaning of this term see **p. 61** *supra*.

[335] However, Canon B 10 states: 'In every cathedral church the Common Prayer shall be said or sung ... the officiating ministers and others of the clergy present in choir being duly habited.'

The apparel of a bishop, priest or deacon shall be suitable to his office; and, save for purposes of recreation and other justifiable reasons, shall be such as to be a sign and mark of his holy calling and ministry as well to others as to those committed to his spiritual charge.

In the normal course of events such apparel would include a clerical collar and, optionally, a cassock.

As has been seen, the mere fact that a form of apparel is not mentioned by the Canon does not mean that its wearing is therefore illegal[336]. Indeed, the wearing of a black robe when preaching has been held not to be illegal[337]. Similarly, although the wearing of an academic hood is no longer provided by Canon on occasions when a scarf is worn[338], its continued use would still be legal[339]. The carrying of a biretta[340] in the hand of a minister during a service is not illegal[341]; on the other hand, to wear one has been held to be illegal[342], although possibly not if the minister were to wear the biretta due to some infirmity[343]. In fact, Sir Robert Phillimore seems to have considered a biretta to be no different from any other head covering[344] and, although he was at that time overruled, his view may well now prevail since a different approach to vestments has also prevailed. Any apparel must, of course, be seemly[345] and all behaviour reverent[346] but the wearing of head gear is not itself unseemly or irreverent; for example, bishops wear

[336] This is in spite of the fact that the decisions about to be cited predated Canon B 8. The previous law was particularly rigorist but other practices were nevertheless permitted in very limited circumstances: see, for example, 14 Halsbury's Laws of England (4th ed.) at para. 970. This being so, Canon B 8 should not be given an even more rigorist interpretation today.

[337] 'The "warrant of law" for the black gown is constant user for centuries. Inasmuch as no positive law exists, and no objection against the legality of the use of the black gown in the pulpit, which has ranged over 300 years, can be found, and there is no decision that its use is illegal, I agree . . . that its use is not illegal . . .' per A.L.Smith LJ in *In re Robinson. Wright* v. *Tugwell* [1897] 1 Ch 85 at p. 98. See, too, **p. 4, footnote 28**, and **p. 93** *infra*.

[338] Contrast the previous Canon B 8, para. 4; see, too, **p. 96** *infra*.

[339] The same may be said as to the wearing of a black (non-silk) tippet, if the minister is not a graduate (see Canon 58 of the 1603 Canons), or preaching bands.

[340] Or, presumably, an academic hat or mortar board.

[341] *Hebbert* v. *Purchas* (1871) LR 3 PC 605 at p. 651.

[342] See the monition by Lord Penzance that led to *Enraght's Case* (1881) 6 QBD 376, affd *Sub. nom. Enraght* v. *Lord Penzance* (1882) 7 App. Cas. 240.

[343] *Elphinstone* v. *Purchas* (1870) LR 3 A & E 66 at pp. 94–95 *per* Sir Robert Phillimore (*obiter*). This view depended, however, upon the wording of Canon 18 of the 1603 Canons (now repealed).

[344] ' . . . it appears to me as innocent as a hat or wig, or as a velvet cap, which latter is not uncommonly worn by bishops, clergy, and laity as a protection to the head when needed': *Elphinstone* v. *Purchas* (1870) LR 3 A & E 66 at p. 94 *per* Sir Robert Phillimore (*obiter*).

[345] This flows from the general canon law (see **p. 65** *supra*) and from the words 'suitable to his office' in Canon C 27. See, also, the rubric at the commencement of the Churching of Women in the Book of Common Prayer as to the the woman being 'decently apparelled': see **p. 223** *infra*.

[346] See **the previous footnote**. In relation to Canon 18 of the 1603 Canons headed 'A Reverence and Attention to be used within the Church in the time of Divine Service' (now repealed), Bullard, *Constitutions and Canons Ecclesiastical 1604* (Faith Press, 1934) comments at p. 169 that it is 'an essay in good manners'.

mitres[347] during a service, other than when their public prayers are addressed directly to God.

(ii)   Bishops

The provisions in relation to vesture in general apply to archbishops and bishops but those provisions are not exhaustive and he may therefore wear episcopal robes[348], namely, a rochet, chimere and mitre[349]. In addition, he may carry a pastoral staff. Indeed, as the Alternative Service Book provides for the presentation of such a staff at his consecration[350], this would now be legal even if the ordinal annexed to[351] the Book of Common Prayer is being used[352].

(iii)   Priests and deacons

The Alternative Service Book speaks of those to be ordained being clothed 'in their customary vesture'[353] but this adds nothing to what has already been set out. As has been seen, in practice this means the vesture usually worn according to the tradition of churchmanship that each candidate represents.

(iv)   Readers

The normal dress for readers is cassock, surplice, degree hood (where appropriate) and blue scarf[354].

(v)   Official robes

Until 1978 statutory provision was made whereby any person holding any judicial, civil or corporate office might attend divine service in the robe, gown or other habit peculiar to his office, together with the appropriate ensign or insignia[355]. However, the necessity for that provision was historical[356] and it did not in any

---

[347] The wearing of a mitre was legal (see Phillimore, *Ecclesiastical Law*, vol. I, at p. 49) in spite of Canon 18 of the 1603 Canons (now repealed).

[348] A bishop usually nowadays wears an episcopal ring and pectoral cross (see 14 Halsbury's Laws of England (4th ed.) at para. 477). These are part of 'the apparel ... suitable to his office' (Canon C 27) and, therefore, may also be worn during the time of divine service.

[349] See, further, 14 Halsbury's Laws of England (4th ed.) at para. 477. See, also, Note 7 at p. 338 of the Alternative Service Book and *infra*.   [350] Note 8 at p. 338.

[351] See Canon A 4. The Clergy (Ordination and Miscellaneous Provisions) Measure 1964, s. 3 (now repealed) described it as being 'Contained in' the Book of Common Prayer.

[352] By reason of Canon B 5.   [353] Note 7 at p. 338.

[354] Regulations respecting Readers accepted by the House of Bishops on 15 January 1991, at p. 14. The previous regulations included the wearing of 'the badge of his office' but excluded the blue scarf: see 14 Halsbury's Laws of England (4th ed.) at para. 971. The wearing of such a badge would still be legal.

[355] Office and Oath Act 1867, s. 4 (repealed by the Statute Law (Repeals) Act 1978).

[356] It was necessary to ensure that anyone so attending did not forfeit his office or incur some other penalty: see *ibid*.

event prevent the wearing of other uniforms, such as military uniforms and medals. The wearing of such official robes is, therefore, still permissible.

Nonetheless, the duty imposed by the canons cannot be ignored and, if a minister is also the holder of such an office[357], he is still under a duty to wear his ecclesiastical robes when taking a service. Similarly, a minister who is also a diocesan chancellor may wear a chancellor's robes when preaching or reading a lesson; if he were, for example, a non-ecclesiastical judge, he might wear his judicial robes when preaching or reading a lesson in the latter capacity.

K Offences

The canons bind the clergy and their breach is an ecclesiastical offence[358]. The canons do not of their own force bind the laity[359] but they may form the basis of a legal obligation on those who celebrate, or take part in, any service[360].

This general duty is also made specific in relation to particular canons. Canon B 1, para. 2, for example, states:

Every minister[361] shall use only the forms of service authorised by this Canon, except so far as he may exercise the discretion permitted by Canon B 5.

In addition, other canons make it an ecclesiastical offence not to comply with the civil law[362]. Moreover, the civil law itself impinges on a number of matters concerning liturgy[363].

---

[357] For example, if he is a mayor or alderman.
[358] *Matthew* v. *Burdett* (1703) 2 Salk. 412.   [359] *Middleton* v. *Crofts* (1736) 2 Atk 650.
[360] See 14 Halsbury's Laws of England (4th ed.) at para. 308. See, too, **p. 65, footnote 59** *supra*.
[361] This includes lay ministers.
[362] See Canon B 35, para. 2 (marriage), Canon B 38, para. 1 (burial) and Canon B 39, para. 1 (registrations of baptisms, marriages and burials).
[363] See **pp. 196** *et seq.* and **237** *et seq. infra*.

4

HOLY COMMUNION

A   General

Many of the ritual and doctrine cases in the nineteenth century and the beginning of the present century were concerned in whole or in part with the Holy
Communion[1]. Nonetheless, as a number of the questions that were raised also
affected other services, they have already been considered[2]. For example, the
general matter of ceremonies has already been dealt with as it may impinge
upon any service; similarly, notices may have to be given[3], and sermons preached[4],
other than in the Communion service. This chapter will therefore generally be
confined to matters concerning the Holy Communion service itself.

B   Ministers

Holy Communion can only be celebrated and administered[5] by an episcopally
ordained priest[6]; it cannot be celebrated by a layman, even in an emergency[7]. If
present[8] at a celebration of Holy Communion according to a rite contained in the

---

[1] For a historical discussion of these cases see Rodes, *Modernization in the Church of England
Charles II to the Welfare State* (University of Notre Dame Press, 1991) at pp. 243–316.
[2] See **p. 71** *et seq. supra.*   [3] See **p. 81** *et seq. supra.*
[4] See **p. 24** *et seq.* and **p. 69** *et seq. supra.*
[5] It is unclear what the word 'administer' means in this context, especially as it is omitted in
Canon B 40. It may merely be tautologous, as the Book of Common Prayer speaks of 'The Order
of the Administration of the Lord's Supper' rather than 'The Order of the Celebration of the Lord's
Supper'. The word cannot refer to the distribution of the sacrament within the actual service: see
Canon B 12, para. 3. Nor can the mere *distribution* of the reserved sacrament to the sick be such
an administration: see *Ministry of the Sick* at p. 3, note 6(a). That being so, it is inconceivable that
it refers to such a distribution other than to the sick: see, for example, *Re Lapford (Devon) Parish
Church* [1954] P 416 at p. 419. It is, however, possible that it refers to a form of service to accompany such distribution but resembling an actual celebration. Certainly Ante-Communion may only
be used where there is no Communion (see **p. 118** *infra*) but it might be argued that such a service
resembling Holy Communion at which the reserved sacrament is distributed may be authorised
under Canon B 4 or Canon B 5, para. 2: see **p. 217** *et seq. infra.* Canon B 12, para. 1, may therefore
prevent the authorisation of such a service, unless it is 'administered' by an episcopally ordained
priest – although in that case the word would seem to be unnecessary. Clearly the latter question
is a matter of doubt and, at the least, should be referred to the diocesan bishop: see **p. 31** *et seq.
supra.* See, too **p. 110, footnote 115**.
[6] Canon B 12, para. 1. The ordination must be in accordance with the provisions of Canon C 1.
[7] *Escott* v. *Mastin* (1842) 4 Moo. PCC 104 at p. 128; see, too, **p. 43, footnote 96** *supra.*
[8] It is most likely that the words are intended to mean 'present and taking part': contrast Canon
C 26, para. 1; if this were not so, a suffragan bishop attending a cathedral as a canon would always

Alternative Service Book 1980, a bishop should act as president[9]. The question of concelebration is nowhere addressed[10] and must therefore be resolved by the diocesan bishop[11].

In the rite according to the Alternative Service Book the president, who must be an episcopally ordained priest[12], presides over the whole service. He says the opening Greeting, the Collect, the Absolution, the Peace and the Blessing; he must himself take the bread and cup before placing them upon the holy table, say the Eucharistic Prayer and break the consecrated bread[13]. In the Book of Common Prayer the reading of different parts of the service by different ministers is justified by Canon B 5, para. 1[14].

A deacon or lay person may also preside[15] over the Ministry of the Word 'when necessity dictates'[16]. However, no guidance is given as to what such a 'necessity[17]' may be. It would probably encompass pastoral considerations as well, for example, as a situation where the priest is struggling with loss of voice. Nevertheless, it is unclear whether this is a matter of Church order and therefore also applicable to the rite according to the Book of Common Prayer. Presumably it is, if a layman may take Ante-Communion in the same rite[18]. Nonetheless, as there is doubt, it is a matter to be resolved by the diocesan bishop[19].

Subject to the general directions of the bishop, the Epistle, Gospel[20] and the

have to preside at the eucharist unless the diocesan bishop were there. In The Ordering of Priests in the Book of Prayer the rubric before the laying on of hands speaks of 'the priests present'. Presumably this has the same meaning (namely, taking an active part and not merely being in the congregation), in spite of the rubric before the Veni Creator which speaks of 'the Priests, and others that are present'; fortunately a strict statutory interpretation is no longer necessary and the latter rubric only emphasises the participation of the whole congregation. This is confirmed by the rubrics in The Ordination of Priests in the Alternative Service Book at pp. 378–379 which make it clear that the reference to those laying on hands is, in fact, to the priests who are assisting the bishop: see, too, Canon C 3, para. 4. Contrast the clearer wording of Canon C 2, para. 1: 'present together and joining in the act of consecration'. See, also, **p. 18, footnote 120** *infra*.

[9] Although he would no doubt ordinarily do so at a service celebrated according to the rite in the Book of Common Prayer, this rubric cannot be seen as laying down a rule of Church order as the rubrics in the Book of Common Prayer specify the necessary role of a bishop who is present: see **p. 18** *supra*.

[10] It would certainly have been illegal under the rigorist interpretation of the Book of Common Prayer. [11] See **p. 21** *supra*.

[12] See *supra* and Canon B 12, para. 1.

[13] Note 1 at p. 115 of the Alternative Service Book. The president may delegate the remaining parts of the service: *ibid*. In spite of the wording of this Note, Canon B 5, para. 1, would seem to permit delegation of other parts of the service as well. Such delegation may be withdrawn as long as no disorder is caused thereby: see **p. 237** *et seq. infra*.

[14] Similarly, as is implicit in Canon B 12, para. 3, the distribution of the sacrament may be made by more than one minister. As to consecration see **p. 21** *supra*.

[15] It is unclear precisely what this means but it would not permit a lay person to preach without the licence or specific permission of the diocesan bishop: see Canon B 18, para. 2, and **p. 24** *et seq. infra*. [16] See Note 2 at p. 115 of the Alternative Service Book. See, too, **the next footnote**.

[17] This cannot amount to legal necessity as the Note would then be otiose: see **p. 42** *et seq. supra*. Presumably it would embrace the necessity to train the deacon in the best way to take the service.

[18] See *infra*. [19] See **p. 31** *et seq. supra*.

[20] See, too, Canon E 7, para. 4(b) (lay workers).

Prayer of Intercession may at the invitation of the minister be read by a lay person at the celebration of Holy Communion[21].

No provision has been made by canon in relation to lay persons ministering at Ante-Communion[22], although the notes to both Rites A and B in the Alternative Service Book state[23]:

> When there is no communion, the minister reads the service as far as the Absolution . . . , and then adds the Lord's Prayer, the General Thanksgiving, and/or other prayers . . . at his discretion, ending with the Grace. When such service is led by a deacon or lay person, 'us' is said instead of 'you' in the Absolution.

Clearly such lay ministration is permitted in relation to those two rites but it is far from clear whether, in the absence of specific regulation by canon, it is permissible in relation to the rite in the Book of Common Prayer. In spite of the Ante-Communion in the Book of Common Prayer including the Absolution and ending with a Blessing, it is nonetheless likely that the notes in the Alternative Service Book should now be regarded as indicative of proper Church order[24] and that someone other than a priest may therefore now minister at the service[25]. When this is so the Absolution ought to be varied as in the Alternative Service Book and the Blessing altered to a similar inclusive form[26].

The distribution of the holy sacrament is dealt with separately[27].

C Location

Other than the celebration of Holy Communion as provided for by Canon B 37[28] in a private house where there is someone sick, dying or so impotent that he cannot go to church, no minister may celebrate Holy Communion elsewhere than in a consecrated building within his cure[29] or other building licensed for the purpose, except with the permission of the diocesan bishop[30].

---

[21] Canon B 12, para. 4; see, further, Canon E 7, para. 4(b) (lay workers). There is, of course, no specific 'Prayer of Intercession' in the Holy Communion according to the rite contained in the Book of Common Prayer, although Canon B 12 may well embrace the Prayer for the Church Militant; on the other hand, the reading of the latter prayer by a lay person would seem now to fall within the ambit of Canon B 5, para. 1, in any event: see **p. 48** *et seq. supra.*   [22] See **p. 118** *infra.*

[23] See Notes 24 and 14 at pp. 118 and 178 respectively.

[24] See p. 26 *et seq.* Being in doubt this is a matter for the diocesan bishop to decide: see **p. 31** *et seq. supra.*

[25] Being a matter of doubt it is for the diocesan bishop to resolve: see **p. 31** *et seq. supra.*

[26] See, too, **p. 124** *et seq. infra*; Canon B 5, para. 1.   [27] See **p. 110** *et seq. infra.*

[28] See **p. 117** *et seq. infra.*

[29] This Canon is badly drafted. In spite of the words 'within his cure' apparently only qualifying the words 'a consecrated building' and not 'other building licensed for the purpose', the Canon does not mean that the minister is entitled to celebrate in a consecrated building within another cure without the bishop's permission as that would defeat the whole purpose of the Canon.

[30] Canon B 40.

No chaplain, ministering in any house where there is a chapel dedicated and allowed by the ecclesiastical law, may celebrate Holy Communion in any part of the house other than the chapel[31]; moreover, so that the residents in the house may resort to their parish church and there attend divine service, he should seldom celebrate Holy Communion on Sundays or other greater[32] Feast Days[33].

In any college, school, hospital, or public or charitable institution the diocesan bishop may license a minister to celebrate Holy Communion[34]; such a celebration does not require the consent, nor is it subject to the control, of the minister of the parish in which it is performed[35].

D   Occasions

(i)   Generally

Holy Communion must be celebrated in every parish church at least on Sundays and principal Feast Days[36] as well as on Ash Wednesday and Maundy Thursday[37]; such a celebration may only be dispensed with in particular circumstances[38]. In churches and chapels dependent on a parish church Holy Communion must be celebrated as regularly and frequently as may be convenient; however, this is subject to the direction of the Ordinary[39].

Holy Communion must be celebrated in every cathedral church at least on all Sundays and other Feast Days[40], on Ash Wednesday and on all other days as often as may be convenient, according to the statutes and customs of each church[41].

(ii)   Attendance

Every member of the clergy must celebrate, or be present at[42], Holy Communion on all Sundays and other principal Feast Days[43]; in addition, unless they have a

[31] Canon B 41, para. 1.
[32] Presumably this refers to the principal Feasts set out in Canon B 6, para. 2; cp. Canon B 13, para. 1.   [33] *Ibid.*
[34] Canon B 41, para. 2. The licence may also relate to other offices and services: *ibid.*
[35] Canon B 41, para. 3.
[36] That is, on Christmas Day, Epiphany, the Annunciation of the Blessed Virgin Mary, Easter Day, Ascension Day, Whitsunday or Pentecost, Trinity Sunday and All Saints' Day: see Canon B 6, para. 2.
[37] Canon B 14, para. 1. It must be celebrated distinctly, reverently and in an audible voice: *ibid*; see, too, **p. 65** *et seq. supra.*
[38] See Canon B 14, para. 2, and Canon B 14A, para. 1. See, too, **p. 64** *supra.*
[39] Canon B 14, para. 3, and Canon B 14A, para. 2.
[40] This provision is wider than the 'principal Feast Days' referred to in Canon B 14, para. 1. See *supra* and cp. Canon B 6, para. 2.
[41] Canon B 13, para. 1. The reference to 'customs' may in the context be to pre-Reformation custom rather than to local practice: see, further, **p. 4, footnote 28 supra**. The service must be celebrated distinctly, reverently and in an audible voice: *ibid*; see, too, **p. 65** *et seq. supra.*
[42] See, too, **p. 18, footnote 120**, and **p. 98, footnote 8,** *supra.*
[43] Canon C 26, para. 1. The obligation is subject to the proviso: ' . . . not being let by sickness or some other urgent cause . . . ': *ibid.*

reasonable cause to the contrary, in every cathedral church the dean or provost, the canons residentiary, and the other ministers of the church being in Holy Orders, must all receive the Holy Communion at least every Sunday[44].

Every minister must receive the sacrament himself as often as he celebrates Holy Communion[45]. However, the minister who distributes communion to those who are absent from a celebration may receive communion at the same time but does not have to do so[46].

Similarly, it is the duty of all those who have been confirmed to receive Holy Communion regularly and especially at the festivals of Christmas, Easter and Whitsunday or Pentecost[47].

E Admission to Holy Communion

By reason of Canon B 15A, para. 1, those entitled to be admitted to Holy Communion are[48]:

(a) members of the Church of England who have been confirmed in accordance with the rites of that Church, or are ready and desirous to be so confirmed[49], or who have been otherwise episcopally confirmed with unction or with the laying on of hands . . [50];

(b) baptised persons who are communicant members of other Churches which subscribe to the doctrine of the Holy Trinity and who are in good standing in their own Church[51];

[44] Canon B 13, para. 2. As this provision is in addition to the obligation under Canon C 26, para. 1 (see *supra*), Canon B 13, para. 2, must refer to receiving Holy Communion in the cathedral itself. Clearly, however, to attend elsewhere to preach at, or to participate in, the celebration of the eucharist would normally be 'a reasonable cause to the contrary'.

[45] Canon B 12, para. 2; see, too, the rubrics after the Gospel in The Communion of the Sick in the Book of Common Prayer and Note 1 at p. 115 of the Alternative Service Book. Such a celebration would not seem to include the distribution of the reserved sacrament.

[46] *Ministry to the Sick* at p. 4, Note 6(c). The same would seem to apply even outside a sick communion.

[47] Canon B 15, para. 1; this now supersedes the rubrics at the end of Holy Communion in the Book of Common Prayer. The minister must teach the people from time to time (and especially before those festivals) that they must come to the sacrament with such preparation as is required by the Book of Common Prayer: Canon B 15, para. 2; see, further, the Exhortation after the Prayer for the Church Militant.

[48] Where any minister is in doubt as to the application of Canon B 15A, he must refer the matter to the bishop of the diocese or other Ordinary and follow his guidance: Canon 15A, para. 3.

[49] See, too, the rubric at the end of The Order of Confirmation in the Book of Common Prayer; and **p. 16** *supra*.

[50] Canon B 15A, para. 1(a). This is specifically subject to the provisions of Canon B 16: see **p. 240** *et seq. infra*.

[51] Canon B 15A, para. 1(b). If such person regularly receives the Holy Communion over a long period of time which appears to continue indefinitely, the minister must set before him the normal requirements of the Church of England for communicant status in that Church: Canon B 15A, para. 2. See, too, Canon B 28 and **p. 153** *et seq. infra*.

(c) any other baptised persons authorised to be admitted under regulations of the General Synod[52];

(d) any baptised person in immediate danger of death[53].

Indeed, because of the Sacrament Act 1547, section 8[54], such persons must be admitted to Holy Communion, save in relation to any mentioned in paragraph (a) who are subject to lesser excommunication[55].

The rubric at the beginning of Holy Communion in the Book of Common Prayer states:

So many as intend to be partakers of the holy Communion shall signify their names to the Curate[56], at least some time the day before.

This practice has fallen into abeyance and, indeed, seems to have been no more than a courtesy or convenience[57]. Especially as there is no equivalent in the Alternative Service Book, it would therefore not be lawful for a minister to refuse the sacrament on the grounds that such notice had not been given[58].

F Numbers

The rubrics at the end of Holy Communion in the Book of Common Prayer state:

And there shall be no celebration of the Lord's Supper, except there be a convenient number to communicate with the Priest, according to his discretion.

And if there be not above twenty persons in the Parish of discretion to receive the Communion; yet there shall be no Communion, except four (or three at least) communicate with the Priest.

As Stephens' *The Book of Common Prayer* points out[59], these rubrics[60] were directed against solitary masses at which only the priest received the sacrament; indeed, although there are no similar rubrics in the other eucharistic rites, such solitary masses are still illegal. This is made plain in the Alternative Service Book when it states[61]: 'The president and people receive the communion.' The

---

[52] Canon B 15a, para. 1(c).   [53] Canon B 15A, para. 1(d).

[54] For the exceptions to this section see **p. 240** *et seq. infra*.

[55] Canon B 15A, para. 1(a) proviso and Canon B 16. See **p. 240** *et seq. infra*.

[56] That is, the minister of the parish: Stephens, *The Book of Common Prayer*, vol. II, at p. 1056.

[57] 'Those, therefore, who intend to receive the Holy Sacrament are *invited* to give notice of their intention . . .': *Clifton* v. *Ridsdale* (1876) 1 PD 316 at p. 345 *per* Lord Penzance (emphasis supplied).

[58] *Stewart* v. *Crommelin* (1852), cited in *Clifton* v. *Ridsdale* (1876) 1 PD 316 at pp. 331 and 346–347; see, too, **p. 239** *et seq. infra*.   [59] *Op. cit.*, vol. II, at p. 1231.

[60] In *Clifton* v. *Ridsdale* (1876) 1 PD 316 at p. 344 Lord Penzance treats them as one rubric.

[61] See Notes 46 and 37 at pp. 143 and 196 respectively. It is particularly clear in Rite B.

reception of the sacrament by the people and the priest is therefore a matter of Church order[62]. It would not be an ecclesiastical offence, however, to complete a service if those who the priest believed would communicate all thereafter failed to do so[63]; nevertheless, he ought first to request members of the congregation to receive the sacrament, as such an interpolation would now be legal[64].

Is it necessary, however, that there should still be at least three persons other than the priest to communicate? In fact, the minimum of three was not invariable. The first rubric to the Communion of the Sick in the Book of Common Prayer provides that there should be three communicants in addition to the priest 'or two at the least'. However the final rubric states:

> In the time of the Plague, Sweat, or such other like contagious times of sickness or diseases, when none of the Parish or neighbours can be gotten to communicate with the sick of their houses, for fear of the infection, upon special request of the diseased, the Minister may only communicate with him.

Although the latter rubric is clearly dealing with a time of danger, it is not necessarily concerned with a matter of necessity, for example, when the sick person is in immediate danger of death[65]. In any event the precise number in addition to the priest does not seem to be of primary importance: it was the fact that there should be other communicants that was paramount.

It has been suggested[66] that the second of the two rubrics at the end of Holy Communion in the Book of Common Prayer quoted above constitutes the minister as 'a judge as to the maximum of persons who may be considered as forming a convenient or proper number ... ' However, this seems to be a misreading of the rubrics[67] both of which seem, in fact, to deal with the minimum required. Although the rubrics give the minister a discretion as to the minimum number, that minimum[68] may not number less than three even when there are only

---

[62] Sacrament Act 1547, s. 8: ' ... and also it is more agreeable to the first institution of Christ and to the usage of the apostles and the primitive Church that the people being present should receive the same with the priest than that the priest should receive it alone ... '. Although Canon B 12, para. 2, does not read 'shall *first* receive [the] sacrament' as Canon 21 of the 1603 Canons did, such an omission cannot override the clear intention of the rites themselves. Canon B 12, para. 2, stresses that the priest must always receive the sacrament whenever he celebrates. As the question of solitary masses is also one of doctrine, neither Canon B 5, para. 1, nor the duties under Canons B 13 and 14 (see **p. 101 *supra***) can be relied upon to excuse such a celebration.

[63] *Parnell* v. *Roughton* (1874) LR 6 PC 46 at p. 54; *Clifton* v. *Ridsdale* (1876) 1 PD 316 at pp. 343–349. As the elements would by then be consecrated, to do so would seem to be a matter of necessity.   [64] Compare *Clifton* v. *Ridsdale* (1876) 1 PD 316 at p. 348.

[65] Nevertheless, it is possible that such an immediate danger should be inferred from the opening words. See, further, **p. 42, footnote 82 *supra***. At times of death special rules, of course, apply: see Canon B 15A, para. 1(d), and **p. 103 *supra***.

[66] Jebb, *Choral Service* at p. 516, quoted in Stephens, *The Book of Common Prayer*, vol. II, at p. 1231.

[67] It is not considered by other text book writers nor adverted to in *Parnell* v. *Roughton* (1874) LR 6 PC 46 at p. 54 or *Clifton* v. *Ridsdale* (1876) 1 PD 316 at pp. 343–349.

[68] Canon B 5, para. 1, apart.

twenty who may be admitted to the sacrament in the parish[69]. That this is so is emphasised by the fact that the most number of communicants is likely to occur at the principal festivals when communicants are under a duty to receive the sacrament[70].

Bearing in mind both the primary purpose of the rubrics and the omission of any similar rubrics from the other rites, it therefore seems that the precise number of other communicants is no longer a matter of Church order. Therefore, to celebrate with a congregation of only one or two communicants would seem now to fall within the ambit of Canon B 5, para. 1, even in so far as a celebration according to the rite in the Book of Common Prayer is concerned[71].

There is no similar discretion as to a minimum number greater than three in the other rites. However, it seems strange if there were to be such a discretion in relation to one rite but not in relation to any other. For this reason the discretion would seem to be a matter of Church order and apply to all rites[72]. Nevertheless, now that the rubric no longer has statutory force, it cannot be used to circumvent the provisions as to when Holy Communion must be celebrated[73].

G The Holy Table and Communion Plate

In every church and chapel a Holy Table, or altar, must be provided for the celebration of Holy Communion[74]. It must be kept in a sufficient and seemly manner and must be covered in the time of divine service with a covering of silk or other decent stuff; at the time of the celebration of Holy Communion it must be covered with a fair linen cloth[75]. Altar frontals may be used[76].

In every church and chapel there must be provided[77] for the celebration of Holy Communion a chalice for the wine and a paten, or other suitable vessel, for the bread; these must be made of gold, silver or other suitable material[78]. There

---

[69] This is the reason for the words '*yet* shall there be' (emphasis supplied). That this is the correct interpretation is emphasised by the fact that Lord Penzance read the two rubrics as one: *Clifton* v. *Ridsdale* (1876) 1 PD 316 at p. 344.

[70] See **p. 102** *supra*. The priest's discretion could not be used to circumvent this duty, imposed also in a subsequent rubric at the end of Holy Communion in the Book of Common Prayer.

[71] The precise number of communicants in addition to the priest cannot be a matter of doctrine, as the rubrics in the Book of Common Prayer demonstrate.

[72] As there is doubt it is a matter to be resolved by the diocesan bishop: see **p. 31** *et seq. supra*.

[73] See Canons B 13 and 14; see, too, **p. 101** *supra*.

[74] It must be convenient and decent and must be of wood, stone, or other suitable material. In addition, it must stand in the main body of the church or in the chancel where Morning and Evening Prayer are appointed to be said. Any dispute as to the position where the table shall stand is to be decided by the Ordinary: Canon F 2, para. 1. See, too, the rubrics before Holy Communion in the Book of Common Prayer.   [75] Canon F 2, para. 2. It must also be kept in repair: *ibid*.

[76] *Westerton* v. *Liddell* (1857) Moore's Special Report 1 at p. 188. These now fall within the faculty jurisdiction: see Newsom & Newsom, *Faculty Jurisdiction of the Church of England* (2nd ed.) at p. 127.   [77] At the expense of the parochial church council: Canon F 14.

[78] Canon F 3, para. 1.

must also be provided[79] a bason for the reception of alms and other devotions[80] of the people, as well as a convenient cruet or flagon for bringing the wine to the communion table[81]. It is the duty of the minister of every church or chapel to see that the communion plate is kept washed, clean and ready for the celebration of the Holy Communion[82].

H   Position of Celebrant

(i)   Position

The rubrics before the Holy Communion in the Book of Common Prayer state:

... the Priest standing at the north side of the Table shall say the Lord's Prayer, with the Collect following, the people kneeling[83].

In addition, the rubric immediately before the Prayer of Consecration in the Book of Common Prayer states:

When the Priest, standing before the Table, hath so ordered the Bread and Wine, that he may with the more readiness and decency break the Bread before the people, and take the Cup into his hands, he shall say the Prayer of Consecration ...

In the past the first of these rubrics caused much controversy[84], especially as in 1662 the altar was not orientated in the same way in every church[85]. However, in *Read* v. *Bishop of Lincoln*[86] the Privy Council decided that the rubric did not:

... render it obligatory on a clergyman who thinks it desirable during the Prayer of Consecration to stand at the side of the table which now ordinarily faces westward to stand during the earlier part of the service at a different part of the table. Their Lordships are not to be understood as indicating an opinion that it would be contrary to the law to occupy a position at the north end of the table when saying the opening prayers. All that they determine is that it

---

[79] At the expense of the parochial church council: Canon F 14.

[80] See, too, the rubric before the Prayer for the Church Militant in the Book of Common Prayer. These 'devotions' are the same as the 'oblations' referred to in that prayer and include 'all contributions for the support of the clergy, or for the maintenance of the fabric of the church, or for the supply of the sacramental elements, or for the general purposes of religion and charity': see Stephens, *The Book of Common Prayer*, vol. II, at pp. 1169 and 1175.   [81] Canon F 3, para. 1.

[82] Canon F 3, para. 2.   [83] As to the posture of the congregation see **p. 51 *et seq. supra*.**

[84] See *Hebbert* v. *Purchas* (1871) LR 3 PC 605; *Ridsdale* v. *Clifton* (1877) 2 PD 276.

[85] Yates, *Buildings, Faith and Worship* at p. 32; 14 Halsbury's Laws of England (4th ed.) at para. 983, note 2.   [86] [1892] AC 644 at p. 665.

is not an ecclesiastical offence to stand at the northern part of the side which faces westwards.

Moreover, in *Ridsdale* v. *Clifton*[87] the Privy Council decided in relation to the second rubric:

There is, in the opinion of their Lordships, a rule sufficiently intelligible to be derived from the directions which are contained in the rubric as to the acts which are to be performed. The minister is to order the elements 'standing before the table': words which, whether the table stands 'altarwise' along the east wall, or in the body of the church or chancel, would be fully satisfied by his standing on the north side and looking towards the south; but which also, in the opinion of their Lordships, as the tables are now usually, and in their opinion lawfully, placed, authorize him to do those acts standing on the west side and looking towards the east. Beyond this and after this there is no specific direction that, during this prayer, he is to stand on the west side, or that he is to stand on the north side. He must, in the opinion of their Lordships, stand so that he may, in good faith, enable the communicants present, or the bulk of them, being properly placed, to see, if they wish it, the breaking of the bread and the performance of the other manual acts mentioned. He must not interpose his body so as intentionally to defeat the object of the rubric and to prevent this result. It may be difficult in particular cases, to say exactly whether this rule has been complied with; but where there is good faith the difficulty ought not to be a serious one; and it is, in the opinion of their Lordships, clear that a protection was in this respect intended to be thrown around the body of the communicants, which ought to be secured to them by an observance of the plain intent of the rubric.

Thus, even during the time of the rigorist interpretation of the Book of Common Prayer, a certain latitude was allowed, as long as at the Consecration the congregation were able to see the Fraction[88] and everything was done reverently.

The Alternative Service Book says nothing about the position of the celebrant[89] but, in the light of the fact that even cylindrical altars are now legal[90], it cannot be that the rubrics in the Book of Common Prayer are indicative of Church order, save possibly in relation to the Fraction[91]. Thus, any reverent and convenient position for the celebrant at any stage of the service is now lawful.

By reason of Canon B 5, para. 1, it would be lawful to adopt an eastward

---

[87] (1877) 2 PD 276 at pp. 343–344.
[88] The rubric states specifically that the bread should be broken 'before the people'.
[89] 'Posture' alone is mentioned: see Note 3 at p. 115. See, further, *infra*.
[90] *Re St Stephen's, Walbrook* [1987] Fam. 146.
[91] This is particularly so as the Fraction has a more significant place in Rites A and B: see Notes 43 and 34 at pp. 142 and 195 respectively of the Alternative Service Book.

facing position if that has been the practice in the particular parish, at least as long as it is not done intentionally so as to prevent the bulk of the congregation from seeing the Fraction[92]. On the other hand, where such a practice has not been prevalent, the minister ought not to introduce it unilaterally[93].

(ii) Posture

In *Martin* v. *Mackonochie*[94] the Privy Council applied a rigorist interpretation to the question of posture of the celebrant during the Prayer of Consecration. However, for the reasons already given[95], posture is no longer a matter of substantial importance[96].

I   The Elements

(i) Provision

The churchwardens must, with the advice and direction of the minister, provide a sufficient quantity of bread and wine for the number of communicants who shall from time to time receive the same[97].

The bread must be brought to the communion table in a paten or convenient box; the wine must be brought in a convenient cruet or flagon[98].

(ii) Bread

Whether leavened or unleavened, the bread must be of the best and purest wheat flour that may conveniently be gotten[99]. No uniformity of size is required and,

---

[92] Such a practice would indicate that being able to see the Fraction was not of substantial importance to that particular congregation.

[93] See *Howell* v. *Holdroyd* [1987] P 198. Cp. Canon B 3; see, too, **p. 60** *et seq. supra.*

[94] (1868) LR 2 PC 365 at p. 382.   [95] See **p. 51** *et seq. supra.*

[96] As long as it does not indicate a departure from the doctrines of the Church of England: see Canon B 5, para. 3; see, too, *In re St John the Evangelist, Bierley* [1989] Fam. 60 at pp. 70H–71B (reverencing the sacrament); *Martin* v. *Mackonochie* (1870) LR 3 PC 409 at p. 418 (adoration of the sacrament); Article XXVIII of the Articles of Religion. Fortunately, it is therefore unnecessary to consider the differences between bowing, kneeling, bowing the knee, genuflecting and prostration: see *Martin* v. *Mackonochie* (1868) LR 3 PC 52 at p. 66; *Martin* v. *Mackonochie* (1869) LR 3 PC 409 at p. 418.

[97] Canon B 17, para. 1. The rubrics at the end of Holy Communion in the Book of Common Prayer require the bread and wine to be provided by the curate and churchwardens at the charge of the parish. Canon B 17, para. 1, may be seen as more specifically setting out their various functions; if this is incorrect, now that the rubrics no longer have statutory force the Canon must prevail.

[98] Canon B 17, para. 3. Canon B 5, para. 1, cannot be appealed to in order to justify a procession in which, for example, a loaf is carried on a tray and not in a paten or box. It may be, however, that such a practice would be regarded as *de minimis* as long as reverently done.

[99] Canon B 17, para. 2.

therefore, the use of wafers is legal[100]; as no uniformity of shape is required either, the use of wafers carrying the shape of the crucifix must be similarly legal. Clearly, a broken or cut loaf may similarly be used. Those unfortunate enough to suffer from coeliac disease of necessity can only eat gluten[101] free bread and, therefore, the use of a separate gluten free wafer for such communicants would be legal[102].

(iii) Wine

The wine, being the fermented juice of the grape, must be good and wholesome[103]. This renders illegal, for example, the use of unfermented grape juice[104] or similar beverages[105]. If the merest drop of alcohol such as would be taken by intincture would be medically harmful[106], it would be legal to administer non-alcoholic wine as a matter of necessity to that particular communicant[107]. In no circumstances may water be used instead of wine[108].

(iv) Mixing water with the wine

In *Martin* v. *Mackonochie*[109] Sir Robert Phillimore said:

> ... the mingling a little pure water with the wine is an innocent and primitive custom, and one which has been sanctioned by eminent authorities in our church, and I do not say that it is illegal to administer to the communicants wine in which a little water has been previously mixed; my decision upon this point is, that the mixing may not take place during the service, because such mixing would be a ceremony designedly omitted in and therefore prohibited by the rubrics of the present prayer-book.

Moreover, this view of the law was finally confirmed[110] by the Privy Council in *Read* v. *Bishop of Lincoln*[111]:

---

[100] *Ridsdale* v. *Clifton* (1877) 2 PD 276 at pp. 345–346, approving in this regard *Hebbert* v. *Purchas* (1870) LR 3 A & E 66 (at pp. 102–105) and, on appeal, disapproving of *Hebbert* v. *Purchas* (1870) LR 3 PC 605 (at pp. 653–656); cp., too, *Clifton* v. *Ridsdale* (1876) 1 PD 316.

[101] That is, the nitrogenous part of the flour.

[102] Care must, however, be taken that nothing is done which may be seen as divisive of unity: see, further, **p. 116** *infra*. See, too, **p. 42** *et seq. supra*. If no such wafer is provided, the communicant may legally receive the wine only: see **p. 117** *infra* and *Ministry to the Sick* at p. 4, Note 7.

[103] Canon B 17, para. 2. It may be either red or white wine, fortified or unfortified.

[104] Briden & Hanson, *Moore's Introduction to English Canon Law* (3rd ed.) at p. 68.

[105] Moreover, each rite speaks specifically of 'wine'. See, however, **p. 43** *et seq. supra*.

[106] For example, to an alcoholic.

[107] See **p. 43** *et seq. supra*. Any case of doubt must be resolved by the diocesan bishop: see **p. 31** *et seq. supra*. If the use of a separate chalice is seen as too divisive, the alcoholic may of necessity receive the bread only: see **p. 117** *infra* and *Ministry to the Sick* at p. 4, Note 7.

[108] Canon B 17, para. 2; *Beddoe* v. *Hawkes* (1888) 4 TLR 315. Each rite, of course, speaks specifically of 'wine'.   [109] (1868) LR 2 A & E 116 at p. 218.

[110] See *Elphinstone* v. *Purchas* (1870) LR 3 A & E 66 at p. 102 and, on appeal, *Hebbert* v. *Purchas* (1871) LR 3 PC 605 at pp. 652–653.   [111] [1892] AC 644 at p. 658.

... the archbishop[112] accurately states the law when he says that the mixing of the wine in, and as part of the service, is against the law of the Church, but that the use of a cup mixed beforehand does not constitute an ecclesiastical offence.

The rigorist interpretation of the rubrics has now disappeared and, in these circumstances, whichever rite is used the mixing of a little water with the wine during the service prior to consecration is now permitted by Canon B 5, para. 1.

(v) Distribution

No person may distribute the holy sacrament[113] of the Lord's Supper to the people unless he has been ordained in accordance with Canon C 1, or is otherwise authorised by Canon[114], or unless he has been specifically authorised to do so by the bishop[115] acting under such regulations[116] as the General Synod may make from time to time[117]. A person appointed under the present regulations may only distribute the sacrament in his own parish[118].

When the consecrated bread and wine are to be conveyed directly from a

---

[112] *Read* v. *Bishop of Lincoln* [1891] P 9 at p. 30. See, too, *The Archbishops on the Lawfulness of the Liturgical Use of Incense and the Carrying of Lights in Procession* (MacMillan and Co., 1899) at p. 12.

[113] This must include the reserved sacrament. See, too, *Ministry to the Sick* at p. 3, note 6(a), and **p. 20** *supra*.

[114] See Canon D 1, para. 3(b) (deaconesses); Canon E 4, para. 2(c) (readers); and Canon E 7, para. 4(b) (lay workers).

[115] *Legal Opinions concerning the Church of England* at p. 4 states: 'With regard to the ancient tradition of penitence followed by absolution before receiving communion, it is suggested that the bishop's authorisation should provide that when the Sacrament is distributed by someone other than a priest and a BCP form of words is used, the communicant should make an act of penitence and the person administering the Sacrament should say some such prayer as the collect for Trinity XXI or XXIV in the BCP. Where the form of words used is taken from an ASB form of service (as when the service cards for 'Holy Communion at Home or in Hospital', Rite A or Rite B, are used) the word 'you' in the absolution should be replaced by 'us'. See, too, *Ministry to the Sick* and **p. 117** *et seq.* and **p. 225** *infra*.

[116] The present regulations are the Regulations on the Administration of Holy Communion made by the Church Assembly in November 1969; these remain in operation: see *The Canons of the Church of England* at pp. 26 and 181. An application to the bishop to authorise a baptised and confirmed person to distribute the holy sacrament in any parish must be made in writing by the incumbent or priest-in-charge of the parish, supported by the churchwardens; it must specify the name and give relevant particulars of the person to whom the application relates: reg. 1(1). Where the cure is vacant and no priest-in-charge is appointed, an application may be made by the rural dean and supported by the churchwardens: reg. 1(2). It is in the discretion of the bishop to grant or refuse the application and to specify the circumstances or conditions in or on which the authority is to be available: reg. 2. In the regulations 'the bishop' means the diocesan bishop or a person appointed by him for the purpose, being a suffragan or assistant bishop or archdeacon of the diocese: reg. 3.   [117] Canon B 12, para. 3.

[118] See the wording of reg. 1(1) in **footnote 116** *supra*.

celebration to those not present, they are given to the ministers after the breaking of the bread, or after the distribution, or after the end of the service[119].

(vi) Consumption

The rubrics at the end of Holy Communion in the Book of Common Prayer state:

And if any of the Bread and Wine remain unconsecrated, the Curate shall have it to his own use[120]; but if any remain of that which was consecrated, it shall not be carried out of the Church, but the Priest and such other of the Communicants as he shall then call unto him, shall, immediately after the Blessing, reverently eat and drink the same.

The second part of this rubric was one of the main arguments against the legality of reservation of the sacrament[121]. However, the original purpose of the rubric was described in *Bishop of Oxford* v. *Henly*[122] as '[t]he danger of irreverence rather than of superstition'; moreover, Chancellor Garth Moore stated in *In re St Michael and All Angels, Bishopwearmouth*[123] that the rubric did 'no more than forbid the profanation of the sacrament'.

The various cases concerning reservation show that there is nothing doctrinally wrong with reservation of the sacrament[124]. Moreover, there is no precisely

---

[119] *Ministry to the Sick* at p. 4, note 6(b). If the service is presided over by a non-Anglican, the elements may only be conveyed to the sick person at his express wish: Canon B 44, para. 4(3)(c). It must be conveyed during or immediately after the service or as soon as practicable on the same day: *ibid.*

[120] Although the rubric speaks of such bread and wine as 'remain unconsecrated' at the end of each eucharist, it is unlikely to apply to wafers and wine provided for future celebrations, especially as parish finances are involved. It therefore seems best to interpret the rubric as referring to such bread and wine as may spoil before the next service, for example, if loaves of bread (rather than wafers) are used. It is in any event unclear whether it applies to all rites, although it appears to be a matter of Church order.

[121] As to reservation see *Sheppard* v. *Bennett* (1870) LR 4 PC 350 at p. 414; *Davey* v. *Hinde* [1901] P 95, [1903] P 221; *Bishop of Oxford* v. *Henly* [1907] P 88; *Gore-Booth* v. *Bishop of Manchester* [1920] 2 KB 412; *Rector and Churchwardens of Capel St Mary, Suffolk* v. *Packard* [1927] P 289; *Roffe-Sylvester* v. *King* [1939] P 64; *In re St Mary Magdalene, Altofts* [1958] P 172n; *Re Lapford (Devon) Parish Church* [1954] P 416, on appeal at [1955] P 205; *Bishopwearmouth, Rector and Churchwardens* v. *Adey* [1958] 3 All ER 441; *In re St Nicholas, Plumstead* [1961] 1 WLR 916; *Re St Peter and St Paul, Leckhampton* [1968] P 495; *Re St Matthew's, Wimbledon* [1985] 3 All ER 670; *In re St John the Evangelist, Bierley* [1989] Fam. 60; *In re St Thomas, Pennywell* [1995] 2 WLR 154; *Re St Mary the Virgin, Lewisham* (1995) unreported. See too, Canon B 44, para. 4(3)(c). See, generally, 14 Halsbury's Laws of England (4th ed.) at para. 986.

[122] [1907] P 88 at p. 97 *per* the Dean of the Arches. See, too, *Re Lapford (Devon) Parish Church* [1954] P 416 at p. 424 *per* Chancellor Wigglesworth.   [123] [1958] 1 WLR 1183 at p. 1187.

[124] Moreover, the ornaments rubric at the commencement of Morning and Evening Prayer in the Book of Common Prayer no longer has statutory force and is not a matter of Church order. Articles may now be allowed the use of which is required in the services and ministrations of the Church: *In re St Thomas, Pennywell* [1995] 2 WLR 154 at p. 171F–G.

similar rubric concerning consumption in the other eucharistic rites. The Alternative Service Book merely states[125]:

> Any consecrated bread and wine which is not required *for the purposes of*
> *communion* is consumed at the end of the distribution, or after the service
> (emphasis supplied).

Thus, as long as the the reserved sacrament is for the purposes of communion[126],
the consecrated elements that remain unused need not be consumed if one of the
rites according to the Alternative Service Book is being used. It also follows that
their consumption cannot be of 'substantial importance' in any other rite, as long
as they are required for the same purpose. Canon B 5, para. 1, therefore, permits
the minister not to consume them even when using the rite according to the
Book of Common Prayer[127], as long as the sacrament is required for the purposes
of communion.

J   Eucharistic Rites

(i)   Generally

The Book of Common Prayer provides an Order of the Administration of the
Lord's Supper, or Holy Communion[128], as well as a service for the Communion
of the Sick. The Alternative Service Book provides two Orders of Holy Communion[129], Rites A[130] and B[131]; it also makes provision for the ministration of
Holy Communion to the sick[132], as well as an Order following the pattern of the

---

[125] Notes 49 and 42 at pp. 144 and 198 respectively. These words were, of course, chosen against
the background of the widespread practice of reservation, a practice based in part on a similarly
worded rubric in the Alternative Services (series two): see *In re St Thomas, Pennywell* [1995] 2
WLR 154 at p. 166A–C.

[126] '[T]he incumbent's and the congregation's attitude towards the sacrament once reserved [must]
be theologically acceptable according to the tenets of the Church of England': *In re St Thomas,
Pennywell* [1995] 2 WLR 154 at p. 165D–E. See, too, *In re St John the Evangelist, Bierley* [1989]
Fam. 60 at pp. 70H–71B (reverencing the sacrament); *Martin* v. *Mackonochie* (1870) LR 3 PC 409
at p. 418 (adoration of the sacrament); Article XXVIII of the Articles of Religion.

[127] *In re St Thomas, Pennywell* [1995] 2 WLR 154 at p. 170C–F. See, too, *Ministry to the Sick*
at p. 4, Note 6(b).

[128] In the Latin version of Article XXVIII of the Articles of Religion the word 'eucharistia' (*lit.*,
thanksgiving) is twice used as the equivalent of 'the Lord's Supper', words which it otherwise
translates as 'Cena Domini': see *Liber Precum Communium et Administrationis Sacramentorum*. In
Rite A in the Alternative Service Book the description 'Eucharistic Prayer' is used for what is
otherwise called 'The Thanksgiving' in Rite B: cp., for example, *op. cit.*, at pp. 130 and 190.

[129] *Op. cit.*, at p. 115 *et seq.*   [130] *Op. cit.*, at p. 119 *et seq.*

[131] *Op. cit.*, at p. 179 *et seq.*

[132] See Note 23 at p. 118. See, too, **pp. 117 *et seq.*** and **225 *et seq. infra*.**

Book of Common Prayer[133] for use with Rite A. In addition, the General Synod has authorised the use of the *Ministry to the Sick*[134].

Furtheremore, the House of Bishops has commended the use[135] of both *Lent, Holy Week, Easter: Services and Prayers* and *The Promise of His Glory*[136].

(ii) Variations[137]

As has been seen the Legal Advisory Commission of the General Synod has given some guidance in relation to the Book of Common Prayer. It suggests that such well known variations as the substitution of the Summary of the Law for the Ten Commandments, the omission of the Exhortation and, perhaps, the addition of certain psalms and Old Testament readings as well as the use of a revised Prayer for the Church may fall within the ambit of Canon B 5, para. 1[138].

An alternative collect for Christmas Eve and an additional Alternative Lectionary are already authorised[139].

(iii) Communion vessels

Canon F 3, para. 1, only makes provision for one chalice but the rubrics concerning the manual acts during the Prayer of Consecration in the Book of Common Prayer make it clear that more than one communion vessel may be used:

And here to lay his hand upon every vessel (be it Chalice or Flagon) in which there is any Wine to be consecrated.

Indeed, the use of more than one chalice, or paten, is conducive of reverence and good order when there are a large number of communicants. However, that is not to say that each different communicant may have a separate vessel. Not only is it implied in the Book of Common Prayer that communicants will receive the wine from a common vessel, or vessels, but to depart from such a long standing practice[140] would be divisive of the unity of the holy sacrament itself[141].

---

[133] Alternative Service Book p. 146 *et seq.*

[134] *Public Worship in the Church of England* at p. 12. Only rites authorised in accordance with Canon B 1 may lawfully be celebrated: *In re St John the Evangelist, Chopwell* (1995) in **Appendix 6** at **p. 297** *infra*. The use of the Roman Catholic missal has never been lawful: see Vaisey, *'Lawful Authority', A Memorandum* in *The Canon Law of the Church of England* (S.P.C.K., 1947) at p. 218.

[135] For the effect of such a commendation see **pp. 58** *et seq. supra* and **221** *et seq. infra*.

[136] *Public Worship in the Church of England* at p. 13. This is out of date and, therefore, does not refer to *The Promise of His Glory*. See, too, *Patterns for Worship*.

[137] See, generally, **p. 47** *et seq. supra*.

[138] *Legal Opinions concerning the Church of England* at p. 235. As to the use of other collects or passages of Scripture, as well as other variations, see *ibid* and **p. 52** *supra*.

[139] *Further Alternative Rules to Order the Service together with an Additional Alternative Lectionary* (CIO Publishing, 1981).

[140] See *Howell* v. *Holdroyd* [1897] P 198; *Legal Opinions concerning the Church of England* at p. 140.   [141] *Legal Opinions concerning the Church of England* at p. 140.

The communion vessel may, of course, be replenished from a flagon containing consecrated wine[142] and, when necessary, administration may be from more than one chalice at a time[143].

(iv) Manual acts

The Book of Common Prayer provides specific manual acts in relation to the elements in the Prayer of Consecration; indeed, in reliance upon these acts it was held in *Martin* v. *Mackonochie*[144] that to elevate the chalice was illegal. The reasons for this were twofold: first, that the elevation of the sacrament so that it might be adored is contrary to the tenets of the Church of England[145] and, second, that the physical act went further than the rubric required. As the Privy Council stated in relation to the original charge[146]:

> That would have been ... a charge which would have raised a distinct and definite issue, whether the elevation of the Paten or the elevation of the Cup were or were not a bona fide raising it so far only as is necessary for anything to be raised, that is, to be taken from the table, or whether or not there was some ulterior purpose, that is to say, an act of elevation wholly distinct from, and going beyond what is necessary, for the mere purpose of taking the Paten and Cup into the hands of the officiating Minister.

Although the 'traditional manual acts' may be still be used[147], save for the minister's taking the bread and cup into his hands before the Prayer of Thanksgiving and replacing them on the holy table, Rite A in the Alternative Service Book does not provide for the use of manual acts, except in relation to the Fraction[148]. Rite B follows the rubrics in the Book of Common Prayer in the First Thanksgiving[149], except that the Fraction may be postponed until later in the service[150]; the Second Thanksgiving has more limited manual acts[151], followed by a separate Fraction.

In so far as the Alternative Service Book is concerned it seems that the manual acts may not be of substantial importance and that by reason of Canon B 5, para. 1, they may therefore be omitted, or varied within the ambit of the rubrics, in either Rite. In so far as the Book of Common Prayer is concerned their omission or variation may be far more difficult to justify[152]. However, now that the

---

[142] *Legal Opinions concerning the Church of England* at p. 140.

[143] *Legal Opinions concerning the Church of England* at p. 141. The same, of course, applies to the use of more than one paten.

[144] (1868) LR 2 A & E 116 at pp. 202–210; (1869) LR 3 PC 52 at pp. 62–64; (1870) LR 3 PC 409 at pp. 413–419; see, too, *Matthews* v. *King* [1934] 1 KB 505.

[145] See the cases referred to at **p. 111** *et seq. supra*.   [146] (1869) LR 3 PC 52 at p. 62.

[147] Note 16 at p. 117 of the Alternative Service Book.   [148] Note 43 at p. 142.

[149] *Op. cit.*, at p. 191.   [150] Note 34 at p. 195.   [151] *Op. cit.*, at p. 194.

[152] See **p. 52** *supra*.

rigorist interpretation of the Book of Common Prayer is past, the lifting of the sacrament higher than strictly necessary in order to raise them from the table, for example, in a dramatic gesture would seem now to be legal in any Rite unless by so doing the minister were intending to convey, or promote, a doctrine contrary to the tenets of the Church of England[153].

In the Book of Common Prayer the Fraction was always intended to be 'before the people' and, therefore, should be carried out visibly[154]. Particularly as the Fraction is an act separate from the other eucharistic prayers in Rites A and B save where the traditional acts are being used[155], this must be regarded as a matter of Church order and therefore applicable to all rites.

(v) Reception

(a) Generally

Every minister must receive the sacrament himself as often as he celebrates Holy Communion[156].

The rubric after the Prayer of Consecration in the Book of Common Prayer states:

> Then shall the Minister first receive the Communion in two kinds, and then proceed to deliver the same to the Bishops, Priests, and Deacons[157], in like manner, (if any be present,) and after that to the people also in order, into their hands ...

There are no similar provisions in the other Rites[158].

In so far as precedence is concerned the rubric in the Book of Common Prayer is unlikely to be a matter of Church order such as to apply to all Rites; indeed, in this day and age it is likely not to be a matter of substantial importance even in a service according to the Book of Common Prayer and Canon B 5, para. 1, therefore applies. What matters is good order, reverence and seemliness. On the other hand, the practice of some priests to reserve the priest's wafer for the sole consumption of those who are ordained seems to give a special significance to

---

[153] See *In re St John the Evangelist, Chopwell* (1995) in **Appendix 6** at **pp. 292–293** *infra*; see, too, Canon B 5, para. 3.

[154] See the rubric before the Prayer of Consecration; see, too, **p. 106** *et seq. supra.*

[155] Notes 43 and 34 at pp. 142 and 195 respectively.

[156] Canon B 12, para. 2; see, too, the rubrics after the Gospel in The Communion of the Sick in the Book of Common Prayer and Note 1 at p. 115 of the Alternative Service Book. Such a celebration would not seem to include the distribution of the reserved sacrament.

[157] It is unclear whether this rubric is concerned with precedence within the clergy themselves. However, in this day and age hopefully precedence is not a matter of substantial importance and therefore falls within the ambit of Canon B 5, para. 1; nevertheless, the primacy of the bishop may particularly be argued to be a matter of doctrine.

[158] Rite B says that 'One of the ministers then delivers' the bread and cup to the communicant but this does not necessarily imply that they must be placed into the communicants' hands.

that particular wafer; whether or not this is on doctrinal grounds, it is illegal as it is divisive of the unity of the holy sacrament itself[159].

The delivery of the bread or cup without its touching the hands of the communicant would seem equally not to be a matter of Church order[160]; it may therefore also be excused in a service according to the Book of Common Prayer by reason of Canon B 5, para. 1[161].

Intinction is lawful as long as it is not indicative of division[162].

(b)   Reception in two kinds

The Sacrament Act 1547, section 8, requires that the sacrament is distributed:

> under both the kinds, that is to say of bread and wine, except necessity otherwise require ...

Indeed, each Rite clearly envisages reception in two kinds[163]. Although it is feasible that such a necessity may arise by reason of some pressing danger, the Act nonetheless has in mind that some celebration is possible. Therefore, especially bearing in mind the duty upon communicants to receive Communion[164], the words 'except necessity otherwise requires' should be seen as embracing physical and medical necessities as well. Indeed, *Ministry to the Sick* states[165]:

> **Reception of Consecrated Bread and Wine** Communion should normally be received in both kinds separately, but where necessary may be received in either of the following ways:
>
> (a)   by intinction[166], in which case the minister says 'The body and blood ...';
>
> (b)   in one kind, whether of bread or, where the communicant cannot receive solid food, wine.

[159] See, too, *Legal Opinions concerning the Church of England* at p. 141.

[160] See, further, Stephens, *The Book of Common Prayer*, vol. II, at pp. 1209–1210.

[161] For a different view in relation to all Rites see *Legal Opinion concerning the Church of England* at pp. 138–140.

[162] See *Ministry to the Sick* at p. 4, Note 7. See, further, *Legal Opinions concerning the Church of England* at p. 141; in spite of what is there said, the practice of intinction is now so widespread that it seems doubtful whether the doctrine of necessity need be relied upon. It seems now to follow long standing practice: see *Howell v. Holdroyd* [1897] P 198. See, too, *Ministry to the Sick*, Note 7 at p. 4 and *Patterns for Worship* at p. 227.

[163] The rubric after the Prayer of Consecration in the Book of Common Prayer specifically states: 'Then shall the Minister first receive the Communion in two kinds, and then proceed to deliver the same to ...' the other communicants.   [164] See **p. 101** *supra*.

[165] Note 7 at p. 4.

[166] Rather than intinct some alcoholics touch the bread or wafer against the chalice. However, this procedure seems to be doctrinally inappropriate.

This being so, a similar procedure is legal whatever Rite is used[167]. It also applies in relation to coeliacs, alcoholics and such people as suffer from a mental handicap[168].

(vi) Ablutions

The rubric after the Distribution in Holy Communion in the Book of Common Prayer provides that the priest must:

> ... reverently place upon [the Lord's Table] what remaineth of the consecrated Elements, covering the same with a fair linen cloth.

The rubrics at the end of that service then provide for their reverent consumption[169] immediately after the Blessing[170]; there is no express mention of any ablutions. However, as the Alternative Service Book provides that the ablutions may be done 'at the end of the distribution or after the service'[171], a similar latitude would be permissible by reason of Canon B 5, para. 1, in a service according to the Book of Common Prayer.

K Ministry to the Sick

When any person sick or in danger of death or so impotent that he cannot go to church desires to receive the holy sacrament, the priest[172], having knowledge thereof, must as soon as may be visit him and, unless there is any grave reason to the contrary, reverently minister the same to him at such place and time as may be convenient[173].

---

[167] The alteration of the words would then fall within Canon B 5, para. 1.

[168] See **p. 109** *et seq. supra.*

[169] In *Read* v. *Bishop of Lincoln* [1891] P 9 at p. 32 it is suggested that this should be done at the credence table or 'the place where [the elements] were prepared. Nevertheless the Court cannot hold that the minister, who, after the service was ended and the benediction given, in order that no part of the consecrated elements should be carried out of church, cleansed the vessels of all remnants in a reverent way without ceremony or prayers before finally leaving the holy table, would have subjected himself to penal consequences by doing so.' In the light of the alternative time for the ablutions in the Alternative Service Book, carrying out the ablutions at the altar must be as acceptable as anywhere else. Any accompanying 'ceremonies or prayers' would now be subject to Canon B 5, para. 1.

[170] See *Read* v. *Bishop of Lincoln* [1891] P 9 at pp. 30–32; [1892] AC 644 at p. 659. See, too, **p. 111** *supra.*   [171] Notes 68 and 42 at pp. 150 and 198 respectively.

[172] This must refer to a minister licensed to the parish: see Canon B 37, para. 1; see, too, the rubric before The Communion of the Sick in the Book of Common Prayer.

[173] Canon B 37, para. 2; see, too, Canon B 40 and **p. 100** *supra.* Where the service of Holy Communion is presided over by a non-Anglican minister, the consecrated elements may only be conveyed to the sick person at his express wish: Canon B 44, para. 4(3)(c). This must be done either during or immediately after or as soon as practicable on the same day: *ibid.* See, too, **pp. 110–111** *supra.*

The Alternative Service Book particularly provides for Holy Communion to be ministered to the sick[174]; the service may be shortened if the needs of the patient require it[175]. The Book of Common Prayer also provides a shortened form of Holy Communion entitled 'The Communion of the Sick', which may be coupled with the Visitation of the Sick; however, Canon B 5, para. 1, would also allow further shortening.

In addition *Ministry to the Sick*[176] provides particular forms of service for the sick in accordance with Rites A and B in the Alternative Service Book[177]; it also provides forms of distribution to those not present at such celebrations[178], together with a service of Laying on of Hands with Prayer, and Anointing, at the Holy Communion[179]. The forms provided may be modified or shortened in the light of pastoral need[180]. In addition it deals with the mode of distribution of the sacrament[181], as well as its reception[182].

Lent, Holy Week, Easter provides for services of the Imposition of Ashes, the Procession of Palms and a Service of Light, together with the Renewal of Baptismal Vows, normally to be combined with Holy Communion[183]. When a priest is not available, they should be combined with the Ministry of the Word in the Alternative Service Book and a deacon or lay person may preside. It also states[184] 'Similarly a deacon or lay person may preside on Good Friday.' This latter provision, however, must be a reference to Ante-Communion[185] or to a combination of the relevant service with the Ministry of the Word.

L Ante-Communion

The Book of Common Prayer makes provision for occasions when the service of Holy Communion is read without there being any actual Communion[186]. In this case the service proceeds until the Prayer for the Church Militant, which is

---

[174] Note 23 at p. 118. There is a special Eucharistic Prayer for use with the Sick as an alternative for use in Rite A: *op. cit.,* at p. 171 *et seq.*   [175] Note 23 at p. 118.

[176] At p. 4, Note 8, it draws attention to the fact that 'Believers who cannot physically receive the sacraments are . . . assured that they are partakers by faith of the body and blood of Christ and of the benefits he conveys to us by them'. See, similarly, the rubrics at the end of The Communion of the Sick in the Book of Common Prayer.

[177] *Ministry to the Sick,* at pp. 7 and 13 respectively

[178] *Op. cit.,* at pp. 19 and 23 respectively.   [179] *Op. cit.,* at p. 29.

[180] *Op. cit.,* at p. 3, Note 3. Whichever order is followed, the Greeting, Confession, Absolution and Lord's Prayer must always be used. When there is a celebration in the presence of the sick, sections 11–14 must always be included: *ibid.*

[181] *Op. cit.,* at pp. 3–4, Note 6. See, too, **p. 110** *supra.*

[182] *Op. cit.,* at p. 4, Note 7. See **p. 115** *et seq. supra.*

[183] *Lent, Holy Week, Easter,* at p. 6, Note 9.   [184] *Ibid.*

[185] See Canon B 12, para. 1. As to who may preside in Rites A and B see **p. 98** *et seq. supra.*

[186] 'Upon the Sundays and other Holy-days (if there be no Communion) . . . ': see the rubrics at the end of Holy Communion in the Book of Common Prayer. Other than on Good Friday this should rarely occur in a parish except when the benefice is vacant: see Canon B 14, para. 1.

then followed by one or more of the Collects[187] and the Blessing[188]. The Alternative Service Book makes a similar provision although neither a deacon nor a lay person should give the Blessing[189].

M   Collections

Not withstanding any rubric in the Book of Common Prayer moneys given or collected in church at Holy Communion form part of the general funds of the parochial church council and must be disposed of by the council in accordance with the provisions of the Parochial Church Councils (Powers) Measure 1956, section 7(iv)[190]. This applies in relation to all eucharistic rites[191].

The rubric in the Book of Common Prayer after the Offertory Sentences states:

> While these Sentences are in reading, the Deacons, Churchwardens, or other fit person appointed for that purpose[192], shall receive the Alms for the Poor, and other devotions of the people, in a decent bason to be provided by the Parish for that purpose; and reverently bring it to the Priest, who shall humbly present and place it upon the holy Table.

In *Cope* v. *Barber*[193] it was decided that, although the collection might be made by the priest, he is not ministering the divine office at that time; however, the whole rubric must now be read in the light of Canon B 5, para. 1. The Alternative Service Book merely states that 'the offerings of the people may be collected and presented'[194]. Nevertheless long standing practice ought to be followed[195].

The Legal Advisory Commission of the General Synod states that the churchwardens are the proper officers to make the collection, either alone or with the

---

[187] See the rubrics after the Blessing and immediately before the Prayer for the Church Militant. The same collects may be used after the collects either of Morning or Evening Prayer, Communion or the Litany at the discretion of the minister: *ibid*. As to the Absolution see **p. 100** *supra*.

[188] See the rubrics at the end of Holy Communion in the Book of Common Prayer.

[189] 'When there is no communion . . . ': Notes 24 and 14 at pp. 118 and 178 respectively. See, too, **pp. 20** and **100** *supra*.

[190] Church of England (Legal Aid and Miscellaneous Provisions) Measure 1988, s. 13; Canon B 17A. See, further, **p. 91** *et seq. supra*.

[191] See *Legal Opinions concerning the Church of England* at p. 69.

[192] In *Cope* v. *Barber* (1872) LR 7 CP 393 at p. 403 it is suggested that the appointment should be by the priest.   [193] (1872) LR 7 CP 393 at p. 403.

[194] Notes 34, 15 and 27 at pp. 129, 182 and 189 respectively. The presentation does not necessarily include the placing of the collection on the altar and therefore, as it does not seem to be a matter of Church order, failure so to do may be excused in a Holy Communion service according to the Book of Common Prayer by reason of Canon B 5, para. 1.

[195] *Howell* v. *Holdroyd* [1897] P 198.

aid of the sidesmen or other persons selected by them[196]. This opinion cannot override the position as to the Offertory during a Holy Communion service according to the Book of Common Prayer, if the rubric after the Offertory Sentences is a matter of church order; however, it seems best now to regard the rubric as a general directive[197].

An announcement may be made as to the objects to which the alms will be applied[198].

[196] *Legal Opinions concerning the Church of England* at p. 69; cp. **footnote 192** *supra*. After the service the monies should be handed to the treasurer of the parochial church council: *Legal Opinions concerning the Church of England* at p. 69.   [197] See **p. 16** *et seq. supra*.

[198] *Marson* v. *Unmack* [1923] P 163 at pp. 168–169 *per* the Dean of Arches; see, too, **p. 35** *et seq. infra*.

5

MORNING AND EVENING PRAYER AND A SERVICE OF THE WORD

A   Generally

By the end of the last century doubts had arisen as to whether the services of Morning Prayer, the Litany and Holy Communion according to the Book of Common Prayer might be used separately. These doubts were resolved by the Act of Uniformity Amendment Act 1872[1], and, in spite of its repeal[2], it is clear that they may still be used separately[3]. Indeed, this is indirectly confirmed by rule 2 of the Rules to Order the Service in the Alternative Service Book[4].

The shortened forms of Morning and Evening Prayer set out in the Schedule to the Act of Uniformity Amendment Act 1872[5], may still be used; in addition, the Alternative Service Book provides shorter forms of these service[6].

Since 1993 A Service of the Word has been authorised 'as an alternative[7] to Morning and Evening Prayer', although it is not intended for daily use but, rather, 'to provide a structure for Sunday services and weekday services of an occasional nature'[8]. The service is very flexible in its structure[9] and may also be used with Holy Communion according to the rite in the Alternative Service Book[10].

---

[1] 'Whereas doubts have arisen as to whether the following services, that is to say, the order for morning service, the litany, and the order for the administration of the Lord's Supper or holy communion, may be used as separate services, and it is expedient to remove such doubts: be it therefore enacted and declared that any form of such services may be used together or in varying order as separate services, or that the litany may be said after the third collect in the order for evening prayer, either in lieu of or in addition to the use of the litany in the order of morning prayer, without prejudice nevertheless to any legal powers vested in the ordinary; and any of the said forms of service may be used with or without the preaching of a sermon or lecture, or the reading of a homily': s. 5.

[2] Church of England (Worship and Doctrine) Measure 1974, s. 6(3), Sch. 2.

[3] See **p. 34 et seq. supra**.

[4] See p. 26 of the Alternative Service Book: 'Principal Holy Days, Festivals, and greater Holy Days are observed with their own proper service of Morning and Evening Prayer, and *may also* be observed with a celebration of Holy Communion . . . ' (emphasis supplied).

[5] Church of England (Worship and Doctrine) Measure 1974, s. 6(4), Sch. 3, para. 3; Canon B 1, para. 1(b). As the Act of Uniformity Amendment Act 1872, s. 2, has been repealed, they may now be used at any time.   [6] See *op. cit.*, pp. 73 and 82.

[7] See *infra*.   [8] *A Service of the Word and Affirmations of Faith* at p. 7.

[9] See, especially, *op. cit.* at pp. 8–9.

[10] Page 71 of the Alternative Service Book has been amended by *A Service of the Word and Affirmations of Faith* at p. 10; see, too, *Patterns for Worship passim*. Only A Service of the Word may now be used with services of Baptism and Confirmation: *ibid*, last rubric.

B Occasions

In addition to the obligation[11] on every member of the clergy to say Morning and Evening Prayer daily, either privately or openly, every priest having a cure of souls must, in the absence of reasonable hindrance, provide those services daily in the church[12] of which he is the minister[13].

At least on every Sunday and principal feast days, together with Ash Wednesday and Good Friday, Morning and Evening Prayer must in addition be said or sung in every parish church[14]. Where the cure is vacant or the minister incapacitated the churchwardens may invite a reader, a lay person authorised by the diocesan bishop or some other suitable lay person to take these services, although the Absolution must be omitted[15]. On all other days the minister of the parish[16], together with all other ministers licensed to serve in the parish, must make provision for Morning and Evening Prayer to be said or sung either in the parish church or, after consultation[17] with the parochial church council, elsewhere as may best sustain the corporate spiritual life of the parish and the pattern of life enjoined upon ministers by Canon C 26[18]. Public notice must be given in the parish of the time and place where the prayers are to be said or sung by tolling the bell or other appropriate means[19].

The Rules to Order the Service in the Alternative Service Book also lay down[20] that the principal Holy Days, Festivals and Greater Holy Days are to be observed with their own proper service of Morning and Evening Prayer. However, this has now been affected[21] by *A Service of the Word and Affirmations of Faith*[22] which states that:

---

[11] Canon C 26, para. 1, and the Preface to the Book of Common Prayer, *Concerning the Service of the Church*. The obligation is subject to the proviso: '. . . not being let by sickness or some other urgent cause . . .': *ibid*. Amongst other things the clergy must also be diligent in daily prayer and intercession: *ibid*.   [12] Or one of the churches.

[13] Canon C 24, para. 1. The litany must also be said on appointed days: *ibid* and see **p. 126 *et seq. infra*.   [14] Canon B 11, para. 1.

[15] Canon B 11, para. 1; see, too, the third rubric before the Order of Morning and Evening Prayer in the Book of Common Prayer.

[16] This expression is not defined but is wide enough to embrace the minister in charge of a suspended benefice.

[17] Although a vote may not be necessary, a full and sufficient opportunity must be given to the council or its nominees to ask questions and give opinions: see *Re Union of Benefices of Whippingham and East Cowes, St James, Derham* v. *Church Commissioners for England* [1954] AC 245.   [18] Canon B 11, para. 2.

[19] *Ibid*.   [20] At p. 26, rule 2.

[21] The Rules have not, however, been amended: contrast the wording at *op. cit.* pp. 7 and 10. The latter specifically amends the Alternative Service Book and the former does so by implication, although only to a limited extent.

[22] For difficulties that arise in relation to the provisions of this rite in relation to 'historic creeds and other Affirmations of Faith' (*op. cit.* at p. 23) see *In re St John the Evangelist, Chopwell* (1995) in **Appendix 6** at **pp. 297 *infra*; see, too, **p. 57 *supra*.

This service is authorised as an alternative to Morning Prayer and Evening Prayer. It is not intended for daily prayer, but to provide a structure for Sunday services and weekday services of an occasional nature.

Nevertheless, although an authorised service cannot amend the canons, it is probable that Canons B 11 and C 26 will be interpreted so as to embrace the new service within their provisions[23]; however, this can only be to the limited extent envisaged by the rubric to the service itself, namely, occasionally on weekdays.

The reading of Morning and Evening Prayer[24] in any parish church as set out in the last but one paragraph[25] may, however, be dispensed with in certain circumstances[26].

Morning and Evening Prayer must also be said or sung daily in every cathedral church[27].

In the chapels of the colleges subsisting in the universities of Oxford, Cambridge and Durham on 16 June 1871, Morning and Evening Prayer according to the Book of Common Prayer must be used daily, although the college visitor may[28] from time to time instead authorise[29] the use of any abridgement or adaption of those services[30].

C Minister

Readers[31], lay persons authorised by the bishop[32] and other suitable lay persons may at the invitation of the minister of the parish[33] or, where the cure is vacant or the minister is incapacitated, at the invitation of the churchwardens say or

---

[23] This is on the analogy that the Canons already embrace the shortened forms of those services.

[24] Although expressed conjunctively, it is likely that either one or both of the services may be dispensed with.

[25] Canon B 14A does not apply to Canon C 24. Canon B 11, para. 3, states that 'The reading of Morning and Evening Prayer in any parish church as required by this Canon may only be dispensed with in accordance with the provisions of Canon B 14A.' 'Reading' embraces both saying and singing the services.   [26] Canon B 14A, para. 1 and **p. 64** *et seq. supra.*

[27] Canon B 10. The Canon is headed 'Of Morning and Evening Prayer in Cathedral Churches' whereas the body of the Canon speaks of 'the Common Prayer ... every morning and evening'.

[28] At the request of the governing body.   [29] The authorisation must be in writing.

[30] Universities Tests Act 1871, as amended by the Church of England (Worship and Doctrine) Measure 1974, s. 6(3), Sch. 2. The use of such services is legal in spite of the word 'only' in Canon B 1, para. 2; the statute overrides the Canon: see **p. 3, footnote 14** *supra.*

[31] They may only do so if licensed or with written temporary permission: Canon E 6, para. 1; Canon E 4, para. 2(b).

[32] This includes deaconesses and lay workers: Canon D 1, para. 3(a), and Canon E 7, para. 4(a).

[33] At the least this certainly includes the incumbent. On balance it is thought that it does not embrace a minister licensed to a suspended benefice. If it were to do so, as the cure would be vacant, it would mean that the invitation might be by either the minister or the churchwarden.

sing Morning and Evening Prayer, save for the Absolution[34]. When they do so they are as much bound by the ecclesiastical law as any ordained person[35].

D   Presentation

As has been seen[36], the provision[37] that Morning and Evening Prayer are to be taken 'distinctly, reverently and in an audible[38] voice' is a reflection of the general canon law. In addition, the services may be either 'said or sung', whether in a cathedral[39], parish church[40] or any other church or chapel[41]. Hymns, of course, may be sung where appropriate, even when not expressly authorised[42].

E   Absolution and Blessing

If there is a bishop present[43], it would seem that he should give the absolution and blessing. Provision is specifically made in this regard in the Holy Communion service according to the Book of Common Prayer[44], although no similar provision is made in the services of Morning and Evening Prayer[45]; nevertheless, the rubric in the Holy Communion service is a rubric dealing with Church order, if not with dogma[46].

A lay person may not give the Absolution[47]. Instead, when using the Book of Common Prayer, he must use the collect for the twenty-first Sunday after Trinity[48]. There was originally no such provision in relation to the Alternative Service

---

[34] Canon B 11, para. 1; see, too, the third collect before the Order of Morning and Evening Prayer in the Book of Common Prayer and *infra*.

[35] See **p. 65, footnote 59,** *supra* and 14 Halsbury's Laws of England (4th ed.) at para. 308.

[36] See **p. 65** *et seq. supra.*   [37] Canon B 10 and Canon B 11, para. 1.

[38] The rubrics in the Book of Common Prayer before both Morning and Evening Prayer set down that one or more of the Sentences should be read 'with a loud voice'.   [39] Canon B 10.

[40] Canon B 11, para. 1.

[41] *Hutchins* v. *Denziloe and Loveland* (1792) 1 Hag. Con. 170. This is why it is also called evensong: *ibid* at p. 177 *per* Sir William Scott.   [42] See **p. 79** *supra.*

[43] See Note 3 of *A Service of the Word and Affirmation of Faith* at p. 8 and **p. 18, footnote 120** *supra.*   [44] See the rubrics immediately before the Absolution and the Blessing.

[45] The rubrics before the Absolution in both services refer to 'the Priest alone'.

[46] See **p. 16** *et seq. supra.*

[47] Canon B 11, para. 1; see, too, the third rubric before the Order of Morning and Evening Prayer in the Book of Common Prayer; and see *Ministry at the Time of Death,* note 2(a) at p. 3; *Services of Prayer and Dedication after Civil Marriage,* Section 7 at p. 8 (see **p. 226** *infra*); *Lent, Holy Week, Easter,* Note 2 at p. 38. Indeed, in the Book of Common Prayer the rubric before the Absolution in the Forms of Prayer to be used at Sea states: 'Then shall the Priest, if there be any in the Ship, pronounce this Absolution.'

[48] See the rubric inserted after the Absolution in Morning and Evening Prayer according to the Book of Common Prayer by the Prayer Book (Further Provisions) Measure 1968, s. 1(2). Although this Measure has been repealed, the provision remains in force: Church of England (Worship and Doctrine) Measure 1974, s. 6(4), Sch. 3, para. 4.

Book[49]. Although the use of the same collect would be justifiable under Canon B 5, para. 1, the matter is now regulated by the Appendix to *A Service of the Word and Affirmation of Faith*[50].

There is no specific suggestion in the canons that a deacon ought not to give the Absolution. However, prior to 1968 when the rubric was inserted into the Book of Common Prayer in relation to the use of the collect for the twenty-first Sunday after Trinity, a deacon would not have been justified in omitting it. The new rubric commences with the words 'when no priest is present . . . ' Although the word 'priest' is used interchangeably with the word 'minister' elsewhere within the same services, on this occasion it is likely to be used intentionally so as to exclude a deacon[51]. Although originally the Alternative Service Book did not provide alternative forms of Absolution[52], this is now done by the Appendix to *A Service of the Word and Affirmations of Faith*. The Appendix makes it clear that alterations are to be made when there is no ordained priest; these alterations in effect alter the Absolution into a joint petition for absolution[53].

In the Book of Common Prayer the services of Morning and Evening Prayer end with the Grace[54]. However, the Alternative Service Book specifically provides that those services may end with a Blessing[55]. By reason of Canon B 5, para. 1, therefore, to give a final Blessing is also legal when using the Book of Common Prayer. Such a Blessing may not, however, be given by a layman[56] and, if used at all, 'the customary alterations should be made'[57].

---

[49] Although provision was made for alternative Confessions: see Notes 7 and 30 at pp. 49 and 62. See now *A Service of the Word and Affirmations of Faith* at pp. 12–20 and *Patterns for Worship* at pp. 37–52 and 240.

[50] 'One of the forms in the ASB should normally be used. It may sometimes be helpful to vary the form on particular occasions, in which case a Confession and an Absolution from this authorized list should be used. If possible, an Absolution should be chosen which reflects the style, in language and length, of the Confession. "Us" and "our" are said by those who are not ordained priest: words in italics indicate the points where changes are necessary': *op. cit.* at p. 11.

[51] Note 2(a) in *Ministry at the Time of Death* at p. 3 specifically applies to deacons; compare, however, *Services of Prayer and Dedication after Civil Marriage*, para. [7] at p. 8 where 'Minister' clearly includes a deacon by reason of Note 7 at p. 4. See, too, the rubric before the Absolution in the Order for the Visitation of the Sick in the Book of Common Prayer: 'After which Confession, the Priest shall absolve him (if he humbly and heartily desires it) after this sort . . . ', and the Absolution itself, namely, 'And by [Our Lord Jesus Christ's] authority committed to me, I absolve thee from thy sins . . . '

[52] Although provision was made for alternative Confessions: see Notes 7 and 30 at pp. 49 and 62.　　　　　　　　　　　　　　　　　　　　　　　　　　　　　　[53] See **footnote 50** *supra*.

[54] See the two final rubrics.　　　　[55] Notes 23, 46, 61 and 75 at pp. 60, 70, 81 and 87.

[56] This is in spite of Note 15 at pp. 22 and 26 and Note 14 at p. 42 of *Ministry to the Sick*; as alternatives are given, the rubrics cannot abrogate the usual rule. This is underlined by the Note at p. 37 which applies to the use of *A Commendation at Time of Death* by any Christian person: 'The commendation may be accompanied by the sign of the cross by those present on the forehead of the dying person, recalling his baptism into Christ.' See, too, Canon B 25.

[57] See *Ministry at the Time of Death*, note 3 at p. 3; the reference to 'section 12' is clearly a misprint. The 'customary alterations' are to make the wording inclusive: for example, 'May God grant us . . . '. See, too, the prayer for a blessing at the end of Night Prayer in *Lent, Holy Week, Easter* at p. 69 (and *Night Prayer A Service for Late Evening* (Church House Publishing, 1986) at p. 17): see **p. 224** *et seq. infra*.

Although it may be argued that theologically a deacon may not give a blessing, a deacon used to be under an obligation to do so when celebrating a wedding according to the rite in the Book of Common Prayer[58]; moreover, the archbishops have stated that, where a priest is present, the blessing of the couple and any ring may be delegated to a deacon[59]. Indeed, as they also state that no variations ought to be made in the service, this seems to bear out that any such variation would be contrary to Canon B 5, para. 3[60], whichever rite is used.

However, especially as provision is now made in *Services of Prayer and Dedication after Civil Marriage*[61] and *Ministry at the Time of Death*[62] for a deacon to use the Grace instead of the Blessing, if no priest is present at Morning or Evening Prayer according to the Alternative Service Book[63] a deacon may[64] now alter the final Blessing to a similar inclusive form by reason of Canon B 5, para. 1. Nevertheless, as he is not obliged to do so, he may legally pronounce a Blessing.

F   Litany

Canon C 24, para. 1, states that every priest having a cure of souls must provide[65] that in the absence of reasonable hindrance:

Morning and Evening Prayer daily and on appointed days the Litany shall be said in the church, or one of the churches, of which he is the minister.

This applies whichever rite is being used, although the Alternative Service Book does not specify when the Litany is actually to be used. It follows that the rubric in the Book of Common Prayer before the Litany must be a rubric concerned

---

[58] See **p. 189** *infra*.

[59] The blessing of the congregation, however, should be by the priest: *Guidelines issued jointly by the Archbishops of Canterbury and York*, paragraph 4, printed in *The Canons of the Church of England* at p. 187.

[60] *Guidelines issued jointly by the Archbishops of Canterbury and York*, paragraph 3, printed in *The Canons of the Church of England* at p. 187; see, too, **p. 177** *et seq. infra*.

[61] See Note 7 at p. 4; paragraphs 13 and 18 are, therefore, best seen as prayers for a blessing. See, too, *Lent, Holy Week, Easter*, Note 2 at p. 38. See, too, Notes 24 and 14 at pp. 118 and 178 respectively of the Alternative Service Book in relation to Ante-Communion: see **p. 119** *supra*.

[62] Note 2(c) at p. 3 which provides that 'the customary alterations are to be made': see the text *supra*.

[63] Contrast the position in Morning and Evening Prayer according to the Book of Common Prayer where a Blessing is not included: see **p. 124** *supra*.

[64] This is not obligatory as *Services of Prayer and Dedication after Civil Marriage* and *Ministry at the Time of Death* are not authorised under Canon B 1 and therefore the notes do not have general force as rubrics concerned with Church order: see **p. 16** *supra*.

[65] This is in spite of the rewording of Canon B 11, para. 3, which used to read: 'On all other days the minister of the parish, together with all other ministers licensed to serve in the said parish, being at home and not otherwise reasonably hindered, shall resort to the church morning and evening, and, warning being given by the tolling of the bell, say or sing the Common Prayers and on the appointed days the Litany.'

with Church order[66] and thus applicable to both rites[67]. This provides that the Litany[68] is to be said or sung after Morning Prayer on Sundays, Wednesdays and Fridays and at other times when the Ordinary commands. The rubric after the third collect in Morning Prayer provided for its incorporation into that service.

The Alternative Service Book provides for the incorporation of the Litany[69] into either Morning or Evening Prayer in their longer forms[70]. For the avoidance of doubt the Act of Uniformity Amendment Act 1872 provided that the litany might also be incorporated into Evening Prayer[71] and, in spite of its repeal[72], any renewed doubt is answered by reference to the Alternative Service Book and Canon B 5, para. 1.

The 1872 Act also resolved a doubt as to whether the Litany might be used separately, with or without a sermon, lecture or the reading of a homily[73]. The Alternative Service Book is unclear in this regard[74] but the Litany is probably best seen as a separate service[75], as was specifically recognised by section 5 of the 1872 Act[76]. In any event such a use would be *de minimis* after such a long period of use and might in addition be permitted by the minister having the cure of souls under Canon B 5, para. 2[77].

G Lectionary and Psalms

In 1871 a different Table of Lessons[78] was substituted for that originally contained in the Book of Common Prayer[79] and in 1922 an alternative Table of Lessons was authorised[80] to be followed at the discretion of the minister[81]. In

---

[66] See **p. 16** *et seq. infra.*

[67] *In re St Thomas, Pennywell* [1995] 2 WLR 154 at p. 169B-D. It may, therefore, be embraced within the words 'all else proper to the service' in the Rules to Order the Service, r. 1(a), at p. 26 of the Alternative Service Book.

[68] Certain prayers and thanksgivings may be used before the two final prayers: see the rubric at the beginning of the Prayers and Thanksgivings upon Several Occasions.

[69] Certain additions may be made: see the Note at p. 102.   [70] See Note 10 at p. 46.

[71] Section 5 (now repealed): see **p. 121, footnote 1** *infra.*

[72] See **p. 121, footnote 2** *supra.*

[73] Section 5 (now repealed): see **p. 121, footnote 1** *supra.*   [74] See the Note at p. 102.

[75] This would accord with the definition of 'form of service' in the Church of England (Worship and Doctrine) Measure 1974, s. 5(2).   [76] See **p. 121** *supra.*

[77] See **p. 200** *et seq. infra.*

[78] As to the use of different versions of the Bible, see **p. 63** *et seq. supra.*

[79] The Prayer Book (Tables of Lessons) Act 1871, s. 2, Schedule, Second Part. Substituted a new 'Order How the Rest of Holy Scripture is Appointed to be Read'. If Evening Prayer is said at two different times in the same place of worship on any Sunday (except a Sunday for which alternative Second Lessons are specially appointed in the new table), the Second Lesson at the second time may, at the discretion of the minister, be any chapter from the four Gospels, or any Lesson appointed in the Table of Lessons from the four Gospels; on occasions approved by the Ordinary other Lessons may with his consent be substituted for those which are appointed in the Calendar: *ibid.*

[80] Revised Tables of Lessons Measure 1922, s. 1, Schedule. Once adopted it must be continued at least until the end of the ecclesiastical year: s. 1.

[81] The expression 'minister' is defined as 'the rector vicar or perpetual curate of a parish or the curate in charge of a parish': s. 2.

addition Canon B 1 includes 'the lessons designated in any Table of Lessons' within the definition of a 'form of service'; thus new tables may now be authorised by canon for use with the Alternative Service Book, and probably also with the Book of Common Prayer[82]. Indeed, the use of such lessons in Morning or Evening Prayer according to the Book of Common Prayer might in any event be justified under Canon B 5, para. 1[83], by comparison with the lectionary in the Alternative Service Book, especially for a particular occasion[84].

In 1973 the General Synod purported to authorise a lectionary but it is without legal authority[85]. Nevertheless, it may be argued that its use is permitted in Morning and Evening Prayer according to the Book of Common Prayer by the consent of the Ordinary, implied[86] until withdrawn, pursuant to 'The Order How the Rest of Holy Scripture is Appointed to be Read'[87]; if this is so, it may similarly be used with the Alternative Service Book by reason of Canon B 5, para. 1. In any event, since the amendment of the canons to include a definition of 'form of service'[88], its use may in future be authorised pursuant to Canons B 4 and 5[89].

On occasions to be approved by the Ordinary psalms other than those appointed in the Psalter may be used with his consent[90].

H   Miscellaneous

Various prayers are provided for inclusion within Morning and Evening Prayer both in relation to the Book of Common Prayer[91] and the Alternative Service Book[92]; whether those from one rite may equally be used in another depends

---

[82] See **p. 8** *supra*.

[83] '[T]he lessons designated in any Table of Lessons' are in themselves a 'form of service' by reason of Canon B 1, para. 3(ii) and this would seem also to include individual lessons, especially as Canon B 1, para. 3(iii), embraces 'any other matter to be used as part of a service'. Nevertheless, an individual lesson must remain part of the whole rite and therefore also part of the 'form of service' as a whole. This being so Canon B 5, para. 1, permits variation in the choice of a lesson in spite of Canon B 5, para. 5. This is unaffected by the fact that Note 6 to the Ordinal in the Alternative Service Book at p. 338 specifically permits the presiding bishop to choose alternative Old and New Testament readings 'suitable to the occasion', although that Note makes a choice of a different Gospel more difficult to justify as 'not [being] of substantial importance' under Canon B 5, para. 1.   [84] See the Alternative Service Book at p. 980 *et seq.*.

[85] See the *Further Alternative Rules to Order the Service together with an Additional Alternative Lectionary*; see, too, **p. 6** *et seq. supra*. The Suggested Calendar and Lectionaries in *The Promise of His Glory* at p. 369 *et seq.* had no authorisation for liturgical use (*ibid*, note) but now may be authorised under Canons B 4 or 5.

[86] By reason of the authorisation of the General Synod. See, however, **p. 5** *infra*.

[87] See **p. 127, footnote 79** *supra*.   [88] See **p. 3, footnote 19** *supra*.

[89] See *Patterns for Worship* at pp. 53–56. See **p. 6** *et seq. supra* and **p. 220** *et seq. infra*.

[90] See the new 'Order How the Rest of Holy Scripture is Appointed to be Read' substituted by the Prayer Book (Tables of Lessons) Act 1871, s. 2, Schedule, Second Part.

[91] See the rubric at the commencement of the Prayers and Thanksgivings upon Several Occasions.

[92] See Notes 23 and 46 at pp. 60 and p. 70; Prayers for Various Occasions at pp. 97 *et seq.*

upon the factors already considered concerning Canon B 5, para. 1[93]. In addition, the Book of Common Prayer provides that the Athanasian Creed is to be used instead of the Apostles' Creed on particular feast days and on Trinity Sunday[94]; in the past this provision has been honoured more in the breach[95] than in the observance but the failure may now be justified by a comparison with the Alternative Service Book and reliance upon Canon B 5, para. 1.

The position concerning who may read the lessons has already been considered[96].

---

[93] See **p. 48** *et seq. supra.*

[94] See the rubrics before the Creed and prior to the Quicunque Vult.

[95] Unless the rubrics in the Book of Common Prayer are ones pertaining to church order and are therefore to be embraced already within the words 'all else proper to the service' in the Rules to Order the Service, r.1(a), at p. 26. [96] See **p. 21** *supra.*

6

BAPTISM AND CONFIRMATION

A Baptism[1]

(i) Generally

Baptism provides a 'legal and valid initiation into the Christian Church'[2] from which a number of consequences flow[3]. In particular, the rubric before the Order for the Burial of the Dead in the Book of Common Prayer[4] states:

> Here it is to be noted, that the Office ensuing is not to be used for any that die unbaptized, or excommunicate, or have laid violent hands upon themselves.

It is for this reason that the law relating to baptism has mostly been considered in cases concerning refusals to bury.

In *Kemp* v. *Wickes*[5], for example, the Dean of the Arches decided that baptism

---

[1] See, too, p. 349 *et seq. infra.*

[2] *Kemp* v. *Wickes* (1809) 3 Phillim. 264 at p. 275 *per* Sir John Nicholl.

[3] For example, only a baptised person may be confirmed or ordained: Canons B 27, para. 4, and C 4, para. 1. It has even been suggested that baptism is a prerequisite to marriage in an Anglican church. However, that has in fact never been the law: see **p. 183** *infra* and letters to the Church Times on 26 August and 9 September 1994.

[4] The rubric was only drawn up in 1661. Until then none of its regulations were specified in any ecclesiastical canon or constitution, save that relating to persons dying excommunicate which appears in Canon 68 of the 1603 Canons. Nonetheless, according to Stephens, *The Book of Common Prayer*, vol. III at p. 1708, the regulations are merely 'explanatory of the ancient canon law and of the previous usage in England'; see, too, *Bland* v. *Archdeacon of Cheltenham* [1972] Fam. 157 at p. 165E–F. If this view is correct, in so far as previous usage is concerned the regulations would have become part of the canon law by reason of the force of custom: see **p. 4, footnote 28,** *supra.* On the other hand the Privy Council expressed a somewhat different view as an *obiter dictum* in *Escott* v. *Mastin* (1842) 4 Moo. PCC 104 at pp. 124–125: 'In the first place, no prohibition of the Burial Service for unbaptised persons, or indeed for any class of persons, is to be found in the Liturgies of Edward and Elizabeth. The exception of unbaptised persons and suicides first occurs in the rubric of 1661, and consequently first received the force of law from the Uniformity Act of 1662, after the Restoration ... The Statutes of Edward VI and Elizabeth recognised the right of every person to burial with the Church Service; and the 68th Canon, enforcing the civil statutory right, only excepting persons excommunicate and impenitent. Unbaptised persons, – persons baptised in no way whatever, – would have had the right of burial according to the service of the Church, if they were not excluded by those portions of the service which appear to regard Christians alone. Those portions would probably exclude persons not Christians; but if an unbaptised person could be regarded as a Christian, then would he not be excluded prior to the Rubric and Statute of 1661 and 1662'; so, too, *ibid* at p. 129: 'A right formerly existing was thus taken away, at least in some cases.'. See, too, Daniel, *The Prayer Book Its History, Language and Contents* at p. 507 and **p. 199** *et seq. infra.*   [5] (1809) 3 Phillim. 264.

with water in the name of the Trinity by a dissenting minister is a valid baptism and that, therefore, a minister of the Church of England was under a legal duty to bury a child so baptised. Similarly, in *Escott* v. *Mastin*[6] a Church of England clergyman was suspended for refusing to bury a parishioner baptised by a lay person.

The reasoning behind the rubric in the Book of Common Prayer was explained in *Kemp* v. *Wickes*[7]:

> ... [T]aking the context of the law, putting unbaptized persons in association with excommunicated persons and with suicides, both of whom are considered as no longer Christians, it leads to the same construction as the general import of the words; namely, that burial is refused to those who are not Christians at all, and not to those who are baptized according to the forms of any particular Church.

The importance of this was in part doctrinal, as baptism may well have been regarded by some as a prerequisite of salvation[8].

Of course, in *Sheppard* v. *Bennett*[9] Lord Hatherley LC said:

> [T]he Church of England has wisely left a certain latitude of opinion in matters of belief, and has not insisted on a rigorous uniformity of thought which might reduce her communion to a narrow compass.

Moreover, the doctrines of the Church of England may be altered[10] and section 13 of the Burial Laws Amendment Act 1880, permitted the use of a service approved by the Ordinary[11] in such cases as are covered by the rubric. Indeed,

---

[6] (1842) 4 Moo. PCC 104. See, too, *Nurse* v. *Henslowe* (1844) 3 Notes of Cases 272; *Titchmarsh* v. *Chapman* (1844) 3 Notes of Cases 370; and *R* v. *Vicar of Bassingbourne* (1845) 9 JP Jo. 83.

[7] (1809) 3 Phillim. 264 at p. 273.

[8] 'Ingredientibus hoc mare magnum, mundum videlicet naufragiis plenum, prima tabula nos ad portum salutis adducens, Baptismus esse dignoscitur ... ': *Constitutiones Legatinae ... D. Othonis et D. Othobonis* (Oxford, 1779) at p. 80; 'As to the Effects of Baptism, the Person is, *First*, deliver'd from the Power and Tyranny of the Devil, according to the *Canon* Law': Ayliffe, *Parergon Juris Canonici Anglicani* (London, 1726) at p. 104. Moreover, the rubric immediately after The Ministration of Public Baptism in the Book of Common Prayer states: 'It is certain by God's Word, that Children *which are baptized*, dying before they commit actual sin, are undoubtedly saved' (emphasis supplied). Nonetheless, 'Over the centuries there has been considerable speculation and controversy about [baptism's] precise theological significance, to all of which the Church of England sits somewhat lightly and is not swift to condemn any view provided it is not inconsistent with the little that is stated in the Book of Common Prayer and the Thirty-nine Articles': Briden and Hanson, *Moore's Introduction to English Canon Law* at p. 62. See Articles IX, XVI, XXII, XXVII and XXXIII of the Articles of Religion. See also *Gorham* v. *Bishop of Exeter* (1849) 2 Rob. Eccl. 1.

[9] (1871) LR 4 PC 371 at p. 404.

[10] *Ex parte Williamson*, *The Times*, 9 March 1994 (for a full transcript see Hill, *Ecclesiastical Law* at p. 77).

[11] See, also, the Prayer Book (Further Provisions) Measure 1968, s. 5 (as amended) and Canon B 37, para. 2, and **p. 219** *et seq. infra.*

even if such a draconian doctrinal view as to the effects of baptism was ever in fact consistent with the tenets of the Church of England, it is clearly no longer so as the Alternative Service Book requires that parents:

> ... should be assured that questions of ultimate salvation or of the provision of a Christian funeral for an infant who dies do not depend upon whether or not *he* had been baptised.

This in its turn is important in construing the present law.

Canon 68 of the 1603 Canons had provided[12]:

> No Minister shall refuse or delay to christen any child, according to the form of the Book of Common Prayer, that is brought to the Church to him upon Sunday or Holy-days[13] to be christened ... And if he shall refuse to christen ... he shall be suspended by the Bishop of the diocese from his ministry for a space of three months.

This, of course, left open the position of sickly children although this in turn was covered by Canon 69 which stated:

> If any Minister, being duly, without any manner of collusion, informed of the weakness and danger of death of any infant unbaptized in his parish, and thereupon desired to go or come to the place where the said infant remaineth, to baptize the same, shall either wilfully refuse so to do, or of purpose, or of gross negligence, shall defer the time, as when he might conveniently have resorted to the place, and have baptized the said infant, it dieth, through such his default, unbaptized; the said Minister shall be suspended for three months; and before his restitution shall acknowledge his fault, and promise before his Ordinary, that he will not wittingly incur the like again. Provided, that where there is a Curate, or a Substitute, this Constitution shall not extend to the Parson or Vicar himself, but to the Curate or Substitute present.

What is more, the pre-Reformation canon law provides[14] that women at the time of their confinement should have water ready for baptising the child in case of

---

[12] For a case brought under this Canon see *Bland* v. *Archdeacon of Cheltenham* [1972] Fam. 157.

[13] The rubric at the commencement of The Ministration of Public Baptism of Infants originally stated: 'The people are to be admonished, that it is most convenient that Baptism should not be administered but upon Sundays and other holy-days ... Nevertheless (if necessity so requires) children may be baptized on any other day.' This followed the rubric in the 1548 Prayer Book. The present rubric was inserted by section 3(1) of the Prayer Book (Further Provisions) Measure 1968 (now repealed, but with savings, by the Church of England (Worship and Doctrine) Measure 1974, s. 6(3), (4), Schs 2, 3).

[14] This remains the law even though there is no provision for its enforcement against the laity: see 14 Halsbury's Laws of England (4th ed.) at para. 308, notes 10 and 11. No doubt it is of less importance today in the light of the ready availability of water and better national education.

necessity[15] and that the clergy should instruct the laity in the proper form[16] of baptism[17].

The new rubric[18] at the commencement of the Ministration of Public Baptism of Infants in the Book of Common Prayer provides:

No Minister shall refuse or, save for the purpose of preparing or instructing the parents or guardians or godparents, delay to baptize any infant within his cure that is brought to church to be baptized, provided that due notice has been given[19] and the provisions relating to godparents are observed. If the Minister shall refuse or unduly delay to baptize any such Infant, the parents or guardians may apply to the Bishop of the diocese who shall, after consultation with the Minister, give such directions as he thinks fit.

There is no similar provision in the Alternative Service Book but the rubric in the Book of Common Prayer is clearly one dealing with Church order. In the light of Canons B 22 and 24 this in fact makes little difference, save that the rubric demonstrates that Canon B 22, para. 2, should be read after paragraph 4.

(ii) Notice

Canon B 22, para. 1, requires that 'due notice, normally of at least a week' be given before a child is brought to the church to be baptised[20]. The precise length

[15] Lyndwood, *Provinciale Angliae* at p. 63; Phillimore, *Ecclesiastical Law* (2nd. ed.), vol. I, at p. 491.

[16] Namely, 'I christen thee in the name of the Father, and of the Son, and of the Holy Ghost': Lyndwood, *Provinciale Angliae* at p. 245; Phillimore, *Ecclesiastical Law* (2nd ed.), vol. I, at p. 491. The proper form is now set out in The Ministration of Private Baptism of Children in Houses: 'N. I baptize thee In the Name of the Father, and of the Son, and of the Holy Ghost. Amen.' See, too, Emergency Baptism in the Alternative Service Book at p. 280, Note 108.

[17] *Constitutiones Legatinae . . . D. Othonis et D. Othobonis* at pp. 11 and 80; Phillimore, *Ecclesiastical Law* (2nd ed.), vol. I, at p. 491.

[18] The present rubric was inserted by section 3(1) of the Prayer Book (Further Provisions) Measure 1968 (now repealed, but with savings, by the Church of England (Worship and Doctrine) Measure 1974, s. 6(3), (4), Schs 2, 3).

[19] By reason of the new rubrics this is 'normally [notice] of at least one week': see, too, Canon B 22, para. 1, and *infra*.

[20] See *Titchmarsh* v. *Chapman* (1844) 3 Notes of Cases 370; *Nurse* v. *Henslowe* (1844) 3 Notes of Cases 272; *R* v. *Vicar of Bassingbourne* (1845) 9 JP Jo. 83. An offence is committed, even if the child is not brought to church, as long as the minister has 'evinced a clear and final intention not to baptise the child if and when brought to the church for baptism': *Bland* v. *Archdeacon of Cheltenham* [1972] Fam. 157 at p. 166A–C. The rubrics before The Ministration of Publick Baptism of Infants in the Book of Common Prayer also state that: 'At the time appointed, the godfathers and the godmothers and the parents or guardians with the child must be ready at the Font . . . '; there is a similar provision in the rubrics before The Ministration of Publick Baptism to such as are of Riper Years. There is no equivalent to this requirement in the Alternative Service Book but presumably the rubric is stressing that there is no obligation on the minister to baptise unless the participants are ready for the service to proceed and in a location which demonstrates that this is so. Merely to congregate outside the church may be insufficient: see, too, **p. 143, footnote 110**, and **p. 145** *et seq.* *infra*. Nevertheless, the rubrics in the Book of Common Prayer (inserted as they were by s. 3 of the Prayer Book (Further Provisions) Measure 1968) deal with a matter of Church order and, as such, should be followed in relation to the Alternative Service Book: see, too, **p. 146** *infra*.

of notice must depend upon the particular circumstances. For example, in relation to a child whose parents reside outside the parish contact may have to be made with the minister of the other parish[21]. The notice must therefore be reasonable; it cannot be 'due' notice if it is contrary to a court order issued by the civil courts[22].

Although the Canon is silent as to whom this notice should be given, Canon B 22, para. 5, leads to the inference that it is to any minister having a cure of souls in the parish. Paragraph 5 states that:

A Minister who intends to baptise any infant whose parents are residing outside the boundaries of his cure, unless the names of such persons[23] or one of them be on the electoral role of the same, shall not proceed to the baptism without having sought the good will of the minister of the parish in which such parents reside.

Baptism need not be administered by the incumbent[24] and Canon B 22, para. 5, draws a distinction between 'the parish' of the minister where the parents reside and 'the cure' of the baptising minister[25]. Nevertheless, subject to the general cure of the bishop[26], it is usually only the incumbent who has an exclusive cure of souls within a parish[27]; it follows that an assistant curate has no cure of souls except when, for example, by reason of a vacancy he is the minister in charge of the parish[28]. Equally, any other minister in charge of the parish during a vacancy has the cure of that parish[29]. However, notice to an assistant curate or licensed deaconess would seem to be sufficient as he, or she, would receive it on behalf of the incumbent[30].

In relation to those who are of riper years[31] the minister must give notice of

---

[21] See **p. 135** *et seq. infra*.

[22] Moreover, a minister who is told that such an order is to be applied for should await the civil court's decision.

[23] Unfortunately, this paragraph speaks only of 'parents' whereas Canon B 22, paras 2, 3 and 4, make it plain that children may also be brought by their guardians. Although the Latin maxim *expressio unius, exclusio alterius* would usually apply, there seems no doubt that paragraph 5 should be read so as to include guardians.   [24] See **p. 144** *et seq. infra*.

[25] The distinction is the greater as Canon B 22, para. 9, also speaks of 'the minister of every parish'. As to Canon B 22, para. 7, see **p. 222** *infra*.

[26] See, too, Diocesan Stipends Funds Measure 1953, s. 5.

[27] 14 Halsbury's Laws of England (4th ed.) at. para. 690; see, too, the recent opinion of the Legal Advisory Commission of the General Synod. The minister of a conventional district has a cure of souls (see *Legal Opinions concerning the Church of England* at p. 70) as does a vicar in a team ministry where a special cure of souls in respect of the parish has been assigned to him by a scheme under the Pastoral Measure 1983 or by his licence from the bishop: Church of England (Miscellaneous Provisions) Measure 1992, s. 2(6); see, too, the Pastoral Measure 1983, ss. 20(7), (8), 21(1), 23(5). As to hospital chaplains see **p. 140, footnote 84** *infra*.

[28] *Pinder* v. *Barr* (1854) 4 E & B 105 at pp. 115–116. In relation to joint worship, however, **see p. 228** *infra*. See, too, **p. 199, footnote 3** *infra*.   [29] *Ibid*.

[30] See *Pinder* v. *Barr* (1854) 4 El. & Bl.105 at p. 116 *per* Coleridge J, where he speaks of an assistant curate 'representing' the incumbent.   [31] See **p. 137** *et seq. infra*.

the baptism to the diocesan bishop, or to the person appointed by the bishop in his place, at least a week before[32].

(iii)   Non-parishioners[33]

By reason of Canon B 22, para. 5, a minister intending to baptise any infant whose parents[34] reside outside the boundaries of his cure[35] must seek the good will[36] of the actual incumbent or other minister in charge (rather than of any representative such as a curate), unless the names of those parents or of one of them are on the electoral roll of the parish[37].

Similarly a minister, who in an emergency[38] baptises a child in a hospital or nursing home when the parents do not live within his cure and their names are not on its electoral roll[39], must send their names and addresses to the minister of the parish in which they reside[40].

It will be noted that there is no express provision for the situation where the infant has guardians rather than parents. However, it is most probable that each of these paragraphs in the Canon will be interpreted on the basis that it should be implied. Canon B 22, para. 1, certainly does not limit baptism to those whose parents or guardians reside within the parish and Canon B 22, para. 4, should not be interpreted as an extension of an otherwise limited duty to baptise.

A further problem may arise when, for whatever reason, only one parent resides within the cure or parish. Nonetheless, it is inconceivable that these provisions are not intended to apply when, for example, one parent has died. The Canon should therefore be interpreted so as to include the singular within the plural, save where it is expressly excluded[41].

[32] See Canon B 24, para. 2, and the rubrics preceding The Ministration of Baptism to such as are of Riper Years in the Book of Common Prayer. No doubt this is because of the provision relating to confirmation: see Canon B 24, para. 3, and **p. 138** *infra*.   [33] See, too, **p. 152** *infra*.
[34] As to where only one parent lives within the cure see *infra*.
[35] Although special considerations thereafter apply in relation to the registration of baptisms performed within a conventional district (see **p. 151, footnote 188** *infra*), the minister of a conventional district has a cure of souls and therefore does not need first to seek the goodwill of the minister of the parish: see *Legal Opinions concerning the Church of England* at p. 70.
[36] These words are not defined further but seem reasonably clear. What is unclear, however, is how the baptising minister should proceed in the absence of such good will. Presumably he still has the right to proceed, although he would be well advised to seek his diocesan bishop's guidance if it is withheld on reasonable grounds. The diocesan bishop can then contact the other minister or, if he is from another diocese, that minister's own bishop.
[37] See **p. 134** *supra* concerning the meaning of this paragraph of the Canon.
[38] See **p. 140** *et seq. infra*.
[39] Canon B 22, para. 7, uses the words 'on the electoral role of the same' referring back to the words 'in his cure'. Although this might suggest that 'in his cure' means 'in his parish', this cannot be so by reason of the distinction drawn in Canon B 22, para. 5: see *supra*.
[40] Canon B 22, para. 7. Unlike Canon B 22, para. 5, this Canon requires that the names of both parents should be on the electoral roll. It might be argued that this is to rule out the danger of rebaptism but, if this were so, it might also be expected that Canon B 22, para. 5, would expressly apply where only one parent resides outside the cure. The difference may be due to the fact that the dangers of rebaptism are greater after an emergency baptism.
[41] See, for example, Canon B 22, para. 5, in which the situation is expressly addressed where the name of only one of the parents is on the electoral role.

(iv) Parents and guardians

The ecclesiastical law does not itself define who are parents and guardians and therefore follows the general law in relation to parental responsibility[42]. The Children Act 1989 provides that where a child's father and mother are married to each other at the time of the birth each has parental responsibility[43]; if they are not married at that time the father can only gain such a parental responsibility under the provisions of the Act[44]. An adoption order gives parental responsibility to the adopters[45]. A guardian can be appointed by the civil courts, by a person having parental responsibility or by a guardian[46].

This necessarily causes difficulties for a minister but it is probable that there is no duty to enquire into the bona fides of those holding themselves out as parents or guardians unless, and until, something arises to throw doubt upon the matter[47]; once it does, the minister should be careful not to proceed until the parental responsibility has been clarified. Nevertheless, if the minister is approached by one parent or guardian alone[48], enquiry should then be made concerning the existence, and attitude towards the proposed baptism, of the other so that at the least the other parent or guardian may be instructed in his or her responsibilities.

The minister must instruct the parents or guardians of an infant to be admitted to Holy Baptism that the same responsibilities rest on them as are in the service of Holy Baptism required of the godparents[49].

(v) Godparents and sponsors

Every child to be baptised must have at least three godparents[50], of whom at least two must be of the same sex as the child and of whom at least one must be of the opposite sex; nonetheless, when three cannot conveniently be had, one

---

[42] See the recent opinion of the Legal Advisory Commission of the General Synod.

[43] Section 2(1).

[44] See sections 4 and 12. This must be by order of the court or by a parental responsibility agreement with the mother made and recorded in the prescribed manner.

[45] Adoption Act 1976, s. 12(1) (as amended). The rights, powers and obligations of the natural parents or any other guardian are extinguished by such an order: *ibid*, ss. 39 and 41.

[46] Children Act 1989, s. 5.

[47] This is in accordance with the legal maxim *omnia praesumuntur rite esse acta*.

[48] Section 2(7) of the Children Act 1989 states: 'Where more than one person has parental authority for a child, each of them may act alone and without the authority of the other (or others) in meeting that responsibility; but nothing in this Part shall be taken to affect the operation of any enactment which requires the consent of more than one person in a matter affecting the child.' The consent of a parent, although no doubt usual, does not seem to be a necessary prerequisite to baptism; indeed, in the case of an emergency baptism the consent of both parents, or indeed one of them, must have often been impossible to obtain.

[49] Canon B 22, para. 3; see, too, **p. 138** *et seq. infra*.

[50] A godparent cannot be removed or substituted: *Legal Opinions concerning the Church of England* at p. 137.

godfather and one godmother is sufficient[51]. The godparents must be persons who will faithfully fulfil their responsibilities both by their care for the children committed to their charge and by the example of their own godly living[52].

In relation to a person who is of riper years he must choose two or three[53] sponsors who must be ready to present him at the font and afterwards put him in mind of his Christian profession and duties.

No person may be admitted to be a sponsor or godparent who has not been baptised and confirmed[54]. Nevertheless the minister has power to dispense with the requirement of confirmation in any case in which in his judgment need so requires[55].

(vi) Age

The Book of Common Prayer draws a distinction between those who are 'infants'[56] or ,'children'[57] on the one hand and 'such who are of riper years'[58] on the other, whereas the Alternative Service Book distinguishes between 'children who are not old enough to answer for themselves'[59] and 'adults'[60]; Canon B 22 seems to use the words 'child' and 'infant' indiscriminantly, whereas Canon B 24, para. 1, speaks of a person who is 'of riper years and able to answer for himself'.

Usually this is unlikely to cause difficulty but problems may arise, for example, in relation to the mentally disabled. Each case must be considered on its own particular merits but there is no reason why baptism should be refused to those who are mentally disabled but no longer children in age. Rather than mere age the test is one relating to both age and understanding[61]. Indeed, this is borne out, not only by the description in the Alternative Service Book of 'children who

[51] Canon B 23, para. 1. Parents may be godparents for their own children provided that each child has at least one other godparent: *ibid.* See, too, the rubrics before The Ministration of Publick Baptism of Infants in the Book of Common Prayer.

[52] Canon B 23, para. 2. See, too, the rubrics before The Ministration of Publick Baptism of Infants in the Book of Common Prayer.

[53] It seems that there may not be more than three: see Canon B 23, para. 3. It seems also that parents may not be sponsors as there is no similar provision to that in relation to parents being godparents; cp. Canon B 23, para. 1.

[54] As any baptism with water in the name of the Trinity is a valid baptism, whether or not administered by an Anglican (see *Kemp* v. *Wickes* (1809) 3 Phillim. 264 *per* Sir John Nicholl) confirmation by a bishop of any Christian Church would seem to be sufficient.

[55] Canon B 23, para. 4; see, too, the rubrics before The Ministration of Publick Baptism of Infants in the Book of Common Prayer. As long as a child is baptised after its parent, as 'is fitting', it follows that a parent may still be the child's godparent even when the two are being baptised at the same time: see Note 2 at p. 225 of the Alternative Service Book.

[56] See The Ministration of Publick Baptism of Infants.

[57] See The Ministration of Private Baptism of Children in Houses.

[58] See The Ministration of Baptism to such as are of Riper Years.

[59] See Note 2 at p. 225.   [60] See Note 1 at p. 225.

[61] See Stephens, *The Book of Common Prayer*, vol. II, at p. 1422.

are not old enough to answer for themselves'[62], but also by the rubric at the end
of the Ministration of Baptism of such as are of Riper Years in the Book of
Common Prayer. This directs that one of the forms of infant baptism[63] is to be
used for those not baptised in their infancy but who have not 'come to years of
discretion to answer for themselves'[64]. In addition, Canon B 24, para. 1, states[65]:

> When any such person as is of riper years and able to answer for himself[66]
> is to be baptized, the Minister shall instruct such person, or cause him to be
> instructed, in the principles of the Christian religion, and exhort him so to
> prepare himself with prayers and fasting that he may receive this holy sacra-
> ment with repentance and faith.

This is also underlined by the requirement in Canon B 24, para. 3, that any such
baptised person as is of riper years must be confirmed 'so soon after his baptism
as conveniently may be'[67]. Any doubt is be resolved by the diocesan bishop to
whom notice must be given[68].

(vii)   Refusal and delay

Because of the order of the wording in the rubric before the Ministration of
Public Baptism of Infants in the Book of Common Prayer it is clear that Canon
B 22, para. 2, should be read after Canon B 22, para. 4. These, therefore read
as follows:

> 4. No minister shall refuse[69] or, save for the purposes of preparing or in-
> structing the parents or guardians or godparents, delay to baptise any infant
> within his cure[70] that is brought to the church to be baptised, provided due

---

[62] The Alternative Service Book envisages some 'children who are not old enough to answer for
themselves' as nevertheless being 'old enough to respond', presumably either from memory or by
their being able to read: see Note 2 at pp. 225 and 241. This underlines that an understanding of
the actual Christian profession is necessary before a person is to be treated as an adult for the
purposes of baptism.

[63] The Office for Private Baptism is only to be used 'in case of extreme danger'.

[64] In this case the word 'infant' is to be changed to 'child' or 'person' as is required: *ibid.*

[65] See, too, the rubric in the Book of Common Prayer before the Ministration of Baptism to such
as are of Riper Years.

[66] He must also be able to choose his sponsors: Canon B 23, para. 3.

[67] This is so that 'he may be admitted to the Holy Communion': *ibid.* See, too, **p. 145** *infra.*

[68] See Canon B 24, para. 2, and the rubrics preceding The Ministration of Baptism to such as are
of Riper Years; see, too, **p. 135** *supra.*

[69] Even if the child is not brought to church, as long as the minister has 'evinced a clear and final
intention not to baptise the child if and when brought to the church for baptism, it would constitute
a refusal': *Bland* v. *Archdeacon of Cheltenham* [1972] Fam. 157 at p. 166A–C. (Although concerned with the old Canon, this case is still very relevant to the present law, especially as there were
Acts of Convocation to an effect similar to the present Canons.) It is unclear whether a refusal is
a continuing offence or whether 'a refusal a second time is a fresh offence': see *Titchmarsh* v.
Chapman (1844) 3 Notes of Cases 370 at p. 376 *per* Sir H. Jenner Fust.

[70] See **p. 134** *et seq. supra.*

notice[71] is given and the provisions relating to godparents in these Canons[72] are observed.

2. If the minister shall refuse or unduly delay to baptise any such infant, the parents or guardians may apply to the bishop of the diocese, who shall, after consultation with the minister, give such directions as he thinks fit[73].

The order of these paragraphs may be important as otherwise it might be suggested[74] that the minister is under a duty, other than in an emergency, to baptise a child brought with due notice by someone other than a parent or guardian[75].

It is clear that the only valid reason for refusal or delay is that relating to preparation and instruction[76]. What this encompasses is set out in Canon B 22[77]. Paragraph 2 provides:

The minister shall instruct the parents or guardians of an infant to be admitted to Holy Baptism that the same responsibilities rest on them as are in the service of Holy Baptism required of the godparents[78].

[71] See Canon B 22, para. 1, and **p. 133** *et seq. supra*.

[72] Canon B 23 and see, too, **p. 136** *et seq. supra*.

[73] A problem may arise if one parent requires baptism but the other either cannot be found, does not so require it or refuses to be prepared or instructed. The fact that Canon B 22, paras 2 and 4, cater for a refusal as well as for delay seems to underline at the least that, if one parent will not co-operate, it may be ground for a denial of baptism; it is, after all, unlikely that, having brought the child to baptism, both parents will thereafter be unreasonably unco-operative. In cases of doubt the minister may always seek the advice of his bishop, just as the parents or guardians may apply to him under Canon B 22, para. 2. No doubt the bishop's final decision will depend upon how and by whom the child is to be brought up, although in the final analysis the bishop and minister must accept any ruling made by the civil courts.

Canon 68 of the 1603 Canons, unlike Canon B 22, paras 2 and 4, provided no ground at all for refusal or delay. Indeed, especially as a child might be brought for baptism by anyone, this raised the question whether a minister might ever refuse baptism. In 1806 an eminent canonist was consulted as to whether a minister was bound to baptise the child of a dissenter, knowing that the child was to be brought up in dissent from the doctrines of the Church of England. Dr Lawrence gave as his opinion: 'By the 68th Canon, any minister who shall refuse or delay to christen any child brought to him on Sundays or holydays, after due notice, is liable to be suspended from his ministry for three months. The phrase "any child" is general. There is no distinction of parishioners who frequent the church or any other place of divine worship. The reasons given by the clergyman himself in this case might be easily shown to be weak and fallacious. But the authority of the law is clear and express on this point. The objection would of course be much stronger against the children of papist recusants (that is, of persons convicted by law of being Papists), than of those parents supposed to be Protestant Dissenters. Yet by the 3 Jac.1, c.5, s. 14, all popish recusants are compelled to bring their children to be baptised by a lawful minister in the parish church': quoted in Phillimore, *Ecclesiastical Law*, at pp. 494–495. See, further, **p. 142** *et seq. infra*.

[74] Because of the words 'any such infant' in Canon B 22, para. 2.

[75] As to emergencies see **p. 140** *et seq. infra*.

[76] See *Cripps on Church and Clergy* (Sweet & Maxwell, 1937, 8th ed.) at pp. 521–522.

[77] See, too, the rubrics before the Ministration of Publick Baptism of Infants in the Book of Common Prayer.

[78] It is in this context that the attitude of someone without parental responsibility, but for example with whom the parent is living, becomes of relevance. Parents and guardians are also under a duty to take care that their children receive instruction in the doctrine, sacraments and discipline of Christ, as the Lord has commanded and as they are set forth in the holy Scriptures, in the Book of Common Prayer, and especially in the Church Catechism: Canon B 26, paras 1 and 2.

In addition, Canon B 23, para. 2, provides:

The godparents shall be persons who will faithfully fulfil their responsibilities[79] both by their care for the child committed to their charge and by the example of their own godly living.

Precisely what preparation is envisaged, other than instruction, is unclear especially as Canon B 22, para. 3, merely speaks of instruction[80]. Moreover, Canon B 24, para. 1, particularly states in relation to the baptism of a person of riper years that he should be exhorted 'to prepare himself with prayers and fasting' so that he may receive the sacrament 'with repentance and faith'. Presumably what Canon B 22, para. 4, has in mind is that the parents and godparents should also be prepared in relation to a reverent approach to the sacrament[81].

(viii)   Emergency[82]

Canon B 22, para. 6, states[83]:

No minister being informed of the weakness or danger of death of any infant within his cure[84] and therefore desired to go to baptise the same shall either refuse or delay to do so.

Moreover, as has been seen, the pre-Reformation canon law provides[85] that women at the time of their confinement should have water ready for baptising the child

---

[79] This includes a duty to bring the child to the bishop to be confirmed: see **p. 153** *infra*.

[80] It is therefore possible that the wording in Canon B 22, para. 4, is tautologous.

[81] In *Bland* v. *Archdeacon of Cheltenham* [1972] Fam 157 at p. 166F–G it was said: 'In this particular case, therefore, [the minister] would have been quite justified, not in a blunt refusal to baptise the child but in asking for some delay so that he could instruct the parents further and consider with them all that is involved in the solemn rite of baptism, for the child, for the parents and godparents, and for the Church community.'

[82] See the recent opinion of the Legal Advisory Commission of the General Synod. See, too, **p. 151** *infra*.   [83] See **p. 46** *supra*.

[84] The paragraph therefore only applies to ministers with actual cures: see **p. 134** *et seq. supra*. As there is a distinction drawn between a minister's 'parish' and 'cure', hospital chaplains who are licensed under the Extra-Parochial Ministry Measure 1967, are to be regarded as having a cure for these purposes. Contrast Canon 69 of the 1603 Canons which specifically applied to other ministers: see **p. 132** *supra*. In modern day practice, however, there is unlikely to be any difference in the actual effect of the old and new Canons. Canon 69 of the 1603 Canons (now repealed) specifically applied to curates: 'Provided, that where there is a Curate, or a Substitute, this Constitution shall not extend to the Parson or Vicar himself, but to the Curate or Substitute present.'

[85] This remains the law even though there is no provision for its enforcement against the laity: see Halsbury's Law of England (4th ed.) at para. 308, notes 10 and 11. No doubt it is of less importance today in the light of the ready availability of water and better national education.

in case of necessity[86] and that the clergy should instruct the laity in the proper form[87] of baptism[88]. Nonetheless, Canon B 22, para. 9, also states[89]:

> The minister of every parish shall warn the people that without grave cause and necessity they should not have their children baptised privately in their houses.

Thus it is clear that private baptism should only occur 'in case of great danger'[90] or 'emergency'[91].

However, the general canon law, and the Alternative Service Book[92] in particular, lays down the requirements for such an emergency baptism[93]. An emergency baptism should, if possible, be performed by a duly authorised minister[94] but it may lawfully be performed by a lay person[95]. Strictly the only other requirements are the use of water and the invocation of the Trinity[96]. The rubric in the

---

[86] Lyndwood, *Provinciale Angliae* at p. 63; Phillimore, *Ecclesiastical Law* (2nd ed.), vol. I, at p. 491.

[87] Namely, 'I christen thee in the name of the Father, and of the Son, and of the Holy Ghost': Lyndwood, *Provinciale Angliae* at p. 245; Phillimore, *Ecclesiastical Law* (2nd ed), vol. I, at p. 491. The proper form is now set out in The Ministration of Private Baptism of Children in Houses: 'N. I baptize thee In the Name of the Father, and of the Son, and of the Holy Ghost. Amen.'. See, too, Emergency Baptism in the Alternative Service Book at p. 280, note 108.

[88] *Constitutiones Legatinae ... D. Othonis et D. Othobonis* at pp. 11 and 80; Phillimore, *Ecclesiastical Law* (2nd ed.), vol. I, at p. 491.

[89] See, too, the rubrics before The Ministration of Private Baptism of Children in Houses in the Book of Common Prayer.

[90] See the rubric at the end of The Ministration of Publick Baptism to such as are of Riper Years in the Book of Common Prayer. The rubrics at the commencement of The Ministration of Private Baptism of Children in Houses also direct that 'The Lord's Prayer, and as many of the Collects appointed to be said before in the Form of Publick Baptism, *as the time and present exigence will suffice* should be said' (emphasis supplied): see, too, *Escott* v. *Mastin* (1842) 4 Moo. PCC 104 at p. 126.   [91] Notes 106 and 107 at p. 280 in the Alternative Service Book.

[92] See Notes 106–111 at pp. 280–281.

[93] Although the Book of Common Prayer deals specifically with emergency baptism 'in houses', the general canon law required a similar form whenever it took place, namely, 'I christen thee in the name of the Father, and of the Son, and of the Holy Ghost': Lyndwood, *Provinciale Angliae* at p. 245; Phillimore, *Ecclesiastical Law* (2nd ed.), vol. I, at p. 491. The general canon law restricts such emergency baptism to children; indeed, this is also reflected in the Alternative Service Book by its change from the use of the word 'infant' to 'person' in Notes 106 and 108 at p. 280.

[94] This seems to be implied by Note 106 at p. 280 of the Alternative Service Book: 'The parents are responsible for *requesting* emergency baptism for an infant' (emphasis supplied). The rubric before The Ministration of Private Baptism of Children in Houses in the Book of Common Prayer speaks of 'the Minister of the Parish (or, in his absence, any other lawful Minister that can be procured)': see, too, *Escott* v. *Mastin* (1842) 4 Moo. PC 104 at p. 125, Gibson, *Codex Iuris Ecclesiastici Anglicani* (2nd ed., Oxford, 1761), vol. I, at p. 369, note.

[95] *Escott* v. *Mastin* (1842) 4 Moo. PCC 104. See, too, *Nurse* v. *Henslowe* (1844) 3 Notes of Cases 272; *Titchmarsh* v. *Chapman* (1844) 3 Notes of Cases 370; and *Cope* v. *Barber* (1872) LR 7 CP 393 at p. 402 (which unnecessarily stresses that it may be 'performed by a layman or woman'). See, further, Note 107 at p. 280 of the Alternative Service Book: 'In an emergency a lay person may be the minister of baptism ...'

[96] Indeed, the final rubric in The Ministration of Private Baptism of Children in Houses in the Book of Common Prayer describes baptism with 'Water, In the Name of the Father, and of the Son and of the Holy Ghost' as the 'essential parts of baptism'; see, too, Note 105 at p. 279 in the Alternative Service Book.

Book of Common Prayer at the commencement of the Ministration of Private Baptism in Houses states:

> And then, the Child being named by some one that is present, the Minister shall pour Water upon it, saying these words;
> N. I baptize thee In the Name of the Father, and of the Son, and of the Holy Ghost. Amen.

Nevertheless, the giving of a name is not essential[97]. As the Alternative Service Book says[98]:

> When, through the absence of parents, or for some other reason, there is uncertainty as to the name of the person, the baptism can properly be administered without the use of the name (so long as the identity of the person baptized can be duly recorded).

This also makes it clear that the presence of the parents is not required[99]. Nor is there a requirement for any godparents at the moment of baptism as these are supplied later[100].

It must be borne in mind that there is no exception to the duty upon a minister to attend upon an emergency under Canon B 22, para. 6, for example, to await the presence of parents, guardians or godparents; indeed, the summons may come from someone entirely unconnected with the family[101]. However, if upon attendance the minister were to find that the child was perfectly healthy, he would not be under an obligation to administer baptism then and there. Canon B 22, para. 6, obliges the minister to attend without refusal or delay rather than expressly to administer the sacrament. Nevertheless, if the child is indeed in danger of death, or will remain at risk[102], there is a clearly implied duty[103] to administer the sacrament[104]. If there is any doubt as to the emergency, the child should still be baptised[105].

Does this duty exist in relation to every child? There have always been a

---

[97] The wording of the rubric in The Ministration of Private Baptism of Children in Houses in the Book of Common Prayer before the questions of the godparents may be read as a request for such name as may have been given.   [98] Note 109 at p. 280.

[99] This is unaffected by Canon B 22, para. 9.

[100] See The Ministration of Private Baptism of Children in Houses in the Book of Common Prayer: *passim*, but especially before the Renouncement of the devil and all his works. See, also, Notes 110 and 111 at pp. 280–281 of the Alternative Service Book.

[101] Although Note 106 at p. 280 of the Alternative Service Book states that 'The parents are responsible for requesting emergency baptism', this cannot impose a duty upon the laity; moreover, Note 109 at p. 280 makes it clear that the parents may be absent.

[102] This would seem to be the purport of the word 'weakness' in Canon B 22, para. 6.

[103] See Canon B 22, para. 7.

[104] Unless there is an order in existence from the civil courts forbidding such a baptism. If told of the existence of such an order, a minister who nevertheless administered baptism would be in danger of having to answer to the civil court for a breach. The decision as to whether the child should be baptised, however, is in no way dependent upon whether it is 'within his cure'; these words only delimitate upon whom the duty of attendance falls.

[105] Clearly the minister should not set himself up with a medical expertise that he does not possess.

number of people in England who are not Christians[106], for example, the Jewish community. No doubt in the ordinary course of events a Jewish or Muslim child would rarely, if ever, be brought for baptism by its parents but what if someone other than the parents summons a minister in an emergency? In fact, by very reason of the emergency it is unlikely that it will be apparent that the parents are not themselves Christian, although it may be more readily apparent if the summons is to a hospital as admission documents may reveal the situation. Nevertheless, in an emergency the duty imposed by Canon B 22, para. 6, on the minister is paramount: in the case of an emergency he may not refuse or delay baptism in order to ascertain whether the parents wish a baptism to take place. The one possible exception to this duty is when it is likely that the parents will not bring the child up as a Christian[107].

When the parents of the child are not resident in his cure and their names are not on the electoral roll, a minister so baptising a child in a hospital or nursing home must send their names and address to the minister of the parish in which they reside[108]. In practice most emergencies are likely to arise in hopitals and nursing homes but they may arise anywhere and emergency baptism may also be administered by those not having cures[109]. However, there is an obligation, presumably resting primarily[110] upon the parents or guardians[111], subsequently to

[106] It is thought that, if the parents are Christian but non-Anglican, there is no real problem as baptism gives membership within the universal Church: see, also, the opinion of Dr Lawrence quoted at **p. 139, footnote 73** *supra*.

[107] On balance it is thought there is no duty to baptise in these circumstances. Dr Lawrence's opinion quoted at **p. 139, footnote 73,** *supra* was specifically concerned with a child of Christian parents but it may be noted that he did not base his opinion on a universal approach. Furthermore, it is now clear that Anglican doctrine does not embrace the view that an unbaptised child is without ultimate salvation: see Note 107 at p. 280 of the Alternative Service Book. Baptism is 'the sacrament instituted by Christ *for those who wish to become* members of his Church': see Note 1 at p. 212 *op. cit.* (emphasis supplied) and the rubric after the questions to those who bring a child to church after emergency baptism in The Ministration of Private Baptism of Children in Houses in the Book of Common Prayer ('. . . shall receive him as one of the flock of true Christian people'). This being so, it can no longer be argued that baptism ought to be administered against the wishes or beliefs of the child's parents on the ground that the salvation of the child must be of paramount concern. Rather, the minister should be concerned with the feelings of his non-Christian neighbours who will in any event be distraught at the sickness or death of their child. It should be noted that the obligation to attend is absolute, even if it is suspected that the child's parents may not be Christian. Only when present will the minister be in a position fully to appraise the situation.

[108] Canon B 22, para. 7. For the problems of interpretation in relation to this paragraph see **p. 135, footnote 40** *supra*.   [109] See *infra*.

[110] The rubric in the Ministration of Private Baptism in Houses in the Book of Common Prayer after the questions relating to the baptism speaks of 'the answers of such as bring the Child'. An earlier rubric says 'it is expedient that [the child] be brought into the Church'. This might also suggest that the child should be brought to the parish church; indeed, Canon B 22, para. 8, states: 'If any infant which is privately baptised do afterwards live, it shall be brought to the church and there, by the minister, received into the congregation of Christ's flock according to the form and manner prescribed in and by the office for Private Baptism authorised by Canon B 1.' However, Note 110 at p. 280 of the Alternative Service Book merely states that 'If *he* lives, a person so baptised shall afterwards come to church, or be brought to church . . . ' Thus any church seems to be sufficient. This would certainly accord with the modern practice by which persons frequently worship other than in their own parishes. See, too, **footnote 113** *infra*.

[111] This may be inferred from Note 111 at p. 281 of the Alternative Service Book; it cannot rest on the godparents as they only gain responsibilities thereafter.

bring the child to church. As the subsequent service is described in the Alternative Service Book as 'the baptism service', although with certain omissions and additions[112], Canon B 22, para. 5, then comes into play[113].

(ix)   Lawful minister

The Book of Common Prayer is silent as to who should administer Holy Baptism and its rubrics speak both of 'the minister' and 'the priest'. The Alternative Service Book, however, states[114] that:

> Holy Baptism is normally administered by the parish priest in the course of public worship on Sunday; but it may be administered at other times, and he may delegate its administration to other lawful ministers. Where rubrics indicate that a passage is to be said by 'the priest', this must be understood to include any other minister authorized to administer Holy Baptism.

Being a matter of Church order this provision also governs the proper practice when the rite according to the Book of Common Prayer is used[115]. In addition to those who are ordained[116], a deaconess may be authorised to perform baptisms[117]. As has been seen, an emergency baptism should, if possible, be performed by a duly authorised minister[118] but it may lawfully be performed by a

---

[112] See Note 110 at p. 280 of the Alternative Service Book.

[113] See **p. 134** *supra*. In addition, Note 107 at p. 280 of the Alternative Service Book provides that 'In an emergency a lay person may be the minister of baptism, and should subsequently inform those who have the pastoral responsibility for the person so baptized.'

[114] Note 1 at p. 241.

[115] This is also implied by Canon B 21: 'It is desirable that every minister having a cure of souls shall normally administer the sacrament of Holy Baptism on Sundays at public worship when the most number of people come together, that the congregation there present may witness the receiving of them that be newly baptised into Christ's Church, and be put into remembrance of their own profession made in God in their own baptism.' In the Ordering of Deacons annexed to the Book of Common Prayer the bishop after the examination of the ordinands describes their duties as including 'in the absence of the Priest to baptize infants . . . ' However, this seems to be superseded by the general wording of Canon B 21 and the bishop's description of the duties of deacons in the Alternative Service Book, namely: 'He may baptize when required to do so' (see pp. 344 and 370). Ayliffe, *Parergon Juris Canonici Anglicani* (London, 1726) at 104 states: ' . . . for by the *Canon Law*, Deacons ought not to baptize without the command of the Bishop or Priest, unless a Bishop or Priest should happen to be at a great Distance, or extreme Necessity should require it . . . '

[116] For the ecumenical position see **p. 26** *et seq. supra*. Until a special joint service of baptism is authorised an ecumenical service must be one of the rites in the Book of Common Prayer or the Alternative Service Book: see **p. 228** *et seq. infra*.

[117] See Canon D 1, para. 4(b). She may only do so at the invitation of the minister of the parish or of the relevant extra-parochial place and in his absence: *ibid.* When the cure is vacant the reference to 'the minister of the parish' is to be construed as a reference to the rural dean.

[118] This seems to be implied by Note 106 at p. 280 of the Alternative Service Book: 'The parents are responsible for *requesting* emergency baptism for an infant' (emphasis supplied). The rubric before The Ministration of Private Baptism of Children in Houses in the Book of Common Prayer speaks of 'the Minister of the Parish (or, in his absence, any other lawful Minister that can be procured)'. In relation to this rubric *Escott* v. *Mastin* (1842) 4 Moo. PCC 104 at p. 131 states: 'Doubtless it is required that a Minister shall perform the ceremony if he can be procured . . . ' See, too, Gibson, *Codex Iuris Ecclesiastici Anglicani* (2nd ed., Oxford, 1761), vol. I, at p. 369, note.

lay person[119]; however, a lay person is not an authorised minister when there is no emergency.

In the rite of Baptism, Confirmation, and Holy Communion in the Alternative Service Book, where it is prescribed that anything other than the actual confirmation is to be said or done by the bishop, the bishop may delegate the baptism to other ministers[120].

(x) Time and location

Canon B 21 states[121]:

> It is desirable that every minister having a cure of souls shall normally administer the sacrament of Holy Baptism on Sundays at public worship when the most number of people come together, that the congregation there present may witness the receiving of them that be newly baptised into Christ's Church, and be put into remembrance of their own profession made in God in their own baptism.

The Alternative Service Book provides that, when baptism is not to be administered on its own[122] or with the rite of confirmation[123], the Baptism of Children should be administered during Holy Communion[124] or Morning or Evening Prayer[125]. There is no similar provision in relation to the baptism of adults, no doubt because it should normally occur at the same time as confirmation[126]. However, this is not invariably so[127] and Canon B 5, para. 1, would permit the baptism of an adult in similar parts of the same services. The Book of Common Prayer used to provide for the administration of public baptism within Morning

---

[119] *Escott* v. *Mastin* (1842) 4 Moo. PCC 104. See, too, *Nurse* v. *Henslowe* (1844) 3 Notes of Cases 272 and *Titchmarsh* v. *Chapman* (1844) 3 Notes of Cases 370; see, further, Note 107 at p. 280 of the Alternative Service Book: 'In an emergency a lay person may be the minister of baptism . . . ' Note 108 then describes whoever administers the sacrament as '[t]he minister'; similarly, the rubric after the form of certification by the minister of the parish in the Ministration of Private Baptism of Children on Houses according to the Book of Common Prayer proceeds to address the situation where the child has been baptised by 'any other lawful minister'.   [120] Note 8 at p. 226.

[121] See, too, Note 1 at p. 241 of the Alternative Service Book: 'Holy Baptism is normally administered by the parish priest in the course of public worship on Sunday; but it may be administered at other times, and he may delegate its administration to other lawful ministers. Where rubrics indicate that a passage is to be said by "the priest", this must be understood to include any other minister authorized to administer Holy Baptism.'

[122] The Baptism of Children in the Alternative Service Book should normally be used at Holy Communion or Morning or Evening Prayer; at other times representatives of the regular congregation should attend the service so that they may welcome the newly baptised infant and be put in mind of their own baptism: Note 7 at pp. 242–242. In spite of the concluding words of this Note it is probably not indicative of Church order as The Welcome is a specific part of the service: see Note 58 at p. 248.   [123] See the Note at p. 223.

[124] See *op. cit.* at p. 250.   [125] See *op. cit.* at p. 251.   [126] See Note 1 at p. 225.

[127] See Note 1 at p. 225 and Canon B 24, para. 3.

or Evening Prayer[128]. As the sacrament should be administered 'on Sundays at public worship when the most number of people come together'[129], not only may the same continue to occur but public baptism according to the Book of Common Prayer may now be administered with the Holy Communion service also.

The Book of Common Prayer provides[130] that:

At the time appointed[131], the godfathers and godmothers and the parents or guardians with the child must be ready at the Font, and the Priest coming to the Font (which is then to be filled with pure Water[132]), and standing there, shall proceed . . .

The Alternative Service Book is silent on the precise location where the baptismal party should be but the rubrics in the Book of Common Prayer are probably ones dealing with Church order and therefore govern the position in both rites[133]. Nonetheless, the rubric must refer to whatever font is used in the particular church; if a moveable font[134] is commonly used, presentation should be at that font rather than any other[135].

There is no doubt that the Book of Common Prayer requires a baptism, other than an emergency baptism, to take place in the church itself; indeed, the rite for the public baptism of infants is entitled 'The Ministration of Publick Baptism of Infants to be used in the Church'[136]. Moreover, not only must the candidate be brought to the font but the service commences with the minister 'standing there'[137]. This is also reflected in the rubric requiring due notice 'before a child is brought to the church to be baptised'[138]. As has been seen, the Alternative Service Book is silent as to the precise location but Canon B 22, para. 1[139], applies to rites in that service book as well. What is more, baptism in the church itself

---

[128] See the old rubrics before the Ministration of Publick Baptism of Infants and The Ministration of Baptism to such as are of Riper Years. The service was held immediately after the second lesson: *ibid.*   [129] See Canon B 21 and **p. 145** *infra.*

[130] Rubrics before The Ministration of Publick Baptism of Infants. There is a similar provision before the Ministration of Publick Baptism to such as are of Riper Years.

[131] That is, appointed by the minister after due notice given.

[132] This is to underline that the font should be filled afresh. This would seem to be a matter of Church order but it is nonetheless probable that, if the font were to be filled immediately before the service (for example, so that hot water might have time to cool), it would be regarded as *de minimis.* See, too, **p. 77, footnote 186** *infra.*   [133] See **p. 133 footnote 20** *supra.*

[134] See *In re St Andrew's Church, Cheadle Hulme*, [1994] 1 WLR 880.

[135] Notes 17 and 52 at pp. 231 and 246 respectively merely speak of the minister standing 'before the water of baptism'.

[136] This is not referring to the Church universal but to the location, as the title to 'The Ministration of Private Baptism in Houses' makes clear.

[137] See the rubrics before The Ministration of Publick Baptism of Infants and The Ministration of Publick Baptism to such as are of Riper Years.

[138] See the rubrics before The Ministration of Publick Baptism of Infants and Canon B 22, para. 1.

[139] Canon B 22, para. 1, states: 'Due notice . . . shall be given before a child is brought to the church to be baptised'.

is implied in the Note on the Administration of Baptism[140] in the Alternative Service Book:

> Holy Baptism is normally administered by the parish priest in the course of public worship on Sundays . . .

It cannot be argued that baptism elsewhere, for example, at a swimming pool is a necessity in order to provide for total immersion[141], as both rites provide for either 'dipping or pouring'[142] and 'dipping' is clearly envisaged within the context of a font[143].

(xi) Re-baptism

As the rubric in the Ministration of Private Baptism of Children in Houses makes clear, a child once baptised ought not to be baptised again[144]. This reads:

> And let them not doubt, but that the Child so baptised is lawfully and sufficiently baptized, and ought not to be baptised again. Yet nevertheless, if the Child, which is after this sort baptised, do afterwards live, it is expedient that it be brought into the Church, to the intent that, if the Minister of the same Parish did himself baptise that Child, the congregation may be certified of the true Form of Baptism, by him privately before used . . .

If the baptism has been performed by the minister of the parish[145] he must certify that the baptism was performed according to law:

[140] Note 1 at p. 241. It may be noted that it states that baptism 'may be administered at other times' but does not speak of its administration elsewhere.

[141] Such a baptism would nonetheless be valid. Total immersion is of itself legal, if that is physically possible in the church itself: see, too, **pp. 148–149** *infra*.

[142] Note 11 and 9 at pp. 226 and 242 in the Alternative Service Book; see, too, the rubrics immediately before the actual baptism in both rites of public baptism in the Book of Common Prayer.

[143] It might be argued that the rubrics are now primarily directives and, therefore, are not the final arbiters of the matter. However, when the present rubrics at the commencement of The Ministration of Publick Baptism of Infants were inserted into the Book of Common Prayer in 1968, the rubrics were not so to be interpreted: see **pp. 11** *et seq.* and **130** *et seq. supra*. Moreover, Canon B 22, para. 1, reflects the first of those rubrics and requires the child to be brought to the church. Not only does this apply to all rites but it clearly implies that the church is the location for the subsequent ceremony. Although Canon B 24 is silent as to location, at the time of its promulgation in 1969 the Book of Common Prayer was still to be interpreted rigorously and required the service for those of riper years to be in church. There is nothing in the Alternative Service Book to suggest that the previous law as to location was being altered and, indeed, Note 1 at p. 241 militates against such a suggestion. It cannot be argued with much force that its silence is in marked contrast to Series 2 Baptism and Confirmation as these are still authorised: *Public Worship in the Church of England* at p. 13. Series 2 makes it clear that the baptism is to be at the font. See, too, Canon F 1, para. 2.

[144] See the rubric after the form of emergency baptism. In *In re St Barnabas, Kensington* [1991] Fam.1 at p. 4A Chancellor Newsom QC stated: 'Baptism can be received only once.' See, too, *In re St Nicholas' Church, Gosforth* (1989) 1 Ecc. LJ (5) 4 (cited in *In re St George's, Deal* [1991] Fam.6 at pp. 11H–12A); *Re St Michael and All Angels, Tettenhall Regis* [1995] Fam. 179.

[145] This may well include any minister licensed to the parish as the concern is with a knowledge of the correct form rather than with the actual cure of souls.

I certify you, that according to the due and prescribed Order of the Church[146], *at such a time*, and *at such a place*, before divers witnesses I baptised this Child.

Similarly, the first question to be asked by the minister in the Ministration of Public Baptism according to the Book of Common Prayer relates to whether the child has already been baptised; only if it has not is the minister to proceed with the baptism[147]. If there is doubt as to whether the proper form were used, the minister must use a form of conditional baptism[148].

(xii)   The rites of baptism

The Book of Common Prayer provides[149] that the godparents should certify whether the child is able 'well [to] endure' being dipped in water or whether it is 'weak'. In the former case the minister is to dip the child in the water 'discreetly and warily' and in the latter it is sufficient for him to 'pour' water upon it. In practice such a certification is rarely given; indeed, not only do godparents often come from far afield, but it is usually recognised that very young children are liable to catch a chill and, therefore, at least in one sense 'weak'[150]. However, as the Alternative Service Book makes clear[151], there is nowadays no preference for either form of administration when a young child is to be baptised[152]:

The Administration of Baptism A threefold administration of water (whether by dipping or pouring[153]) is a very ancient practice of the Church and is commended as testifying to the faith of the Trinity in which candidates are baptized. Nevertheless, a single administration is also valid and lawful.

---

[146] As is made clear in the questions asked of lay persons who bring the child to church after an emergency baptism, the concern is with the use of water and the invocation of the Holy Trinity rather than the other prayers provided for in The Ministration of Private Baptism of Children in Houses. It follows that the same procedures are to be followed wherever the emergency arose and the child was baptised.

[147] So, too, the rubric after the questions to be asked of those other than the minister of the parish in The Ministration of Private Baptism of Children in Houses in the Book of Common Prayer states that: 'And if the Minister shall find by the answers of such as bring the child, that all things were done as they ought to be; then shall not he christen the Child again, but shall receive him as one of the flock of true Christian people . . .'

[148] See the final rubric in The Ministration of Private Baptism of Children in Houses in the Book of Common Prayer and Conditional Baptism in the Alternative Service Book at p. 279. See, too, Canon B 27, para. 5. Canon B 28, para. 1, states: 'Any person desiring to be received into the Church of England, who has not been baptised or the validity of whose baptism can be held in question, shall be instructed and baptised or conditionally baptised, and such baptism, or conditional baptism, shall constitute the said person's reception into the Church of England.'

[149] See the rubric after the Naming in The Ministration of Publick Baptism of Infants.

[150] This seems, however, to be recognised by the rubric immediately before the administration by dipping in The Ministration of Publick Baptism of Infants in the Book of Common Prayer: ' . . . (if they shall certify him that the child may well endure it) he shall dip it in the water *discreetly and warily* . . . ' (emphasis supplied).

[151] See Notes 11 and 9 at pp. 226 and 242 respectively. This rubric is one dealing with Church order.

[152] The Ministration of Baptism to such as are of Riper Years in any event states that the minister 'shall dip him in the water, or pour water upon him': see the rubric immediately before the actual baptism.   [153] Notes 20 and 55 at pp. 232 and 247 respectively treat the two as alternatives.

This now applies whichever rite is used as the Alternative Service Book is indicative of Church order.

All the rites for public baptism provide for the candidate to be dipped into the water or for the water to be poured over him[154]; that is not to say that baptism may not be administered by total immersion[155], if that is physically possible in the church[156].

Each rite[157] provides for the minister's signing of the child's forehead with the sign of the cross after the actual baptism; this is 'for the remembrance of the Cross'[158]. The Alternative Service Book states that the signing may be made in oil blessed for the purpose[159]. The Alternative Service Book also provides for the giving of a lighted candle[160], which may be the Paschal candle[161]; a similar presentation would now be legal within the rite according to the Book of Common Prayer by reason of Canon B 5, para. 1.

In a baptism of children according to the rite in the Alternative Service Book the parents and godparents answer for the children and, when they are old enough themselves to respond, the children may answer at the discretion of the minister[162]. In a baptism of a family according to the rite in the Alternative Service Book the parents should answer both for themselves and the children when the children are not old enough to answer for themselves; when the children are old enough to respond, the children may at the discretion of the minister answer in addition to their parents and godparents[163]. In these circumstances the children ought to be baptised after their parents[164]. Being a matter of Church order it would seem that similar procedures should be adopted when the rite according to the Book of Common Prayer is being used[165].

Each of the rites for public baptism in the Alternative Service Book may be used at Morning or Evening Prayer[166] as well as with A Service of the Word[167].

---

[154] See Notes 11 and 9 at pp. 226 and 242 respectively in the Alternative Service Book and the rubrics immediately before the actual baptism in the rites of public baptism in the Book of Common Prayer.

[155] '... baptism may be by affusion, immersion or submersion ...': *In re St George's, Deal* [1991] Fam. 6 at p. 12H *per* Chancellor Newey QC. It must, of course, be done with due decorum: the rubric before the administration by dipping in The Ministration of Publick Baptism of Infants reflects general Church order: '... he shall dip it in the water *discreetly and warily* ...' (emphasis supplied).

[156] See *In re St George's, Deal* [1991] Fam.6 and *In re St Barnabas, Kensington* [1991] Fam.1; *In re St James, Shirley* [1994] Fam.134; *Re Emmanuel, Loughborough* (1995) 3 Ecc.LJ 430; see, too, **p. 147** *et seq. supra* and 'Response by the House of Bishops to Questions raised by Diocesan Chancellors' (June 1992).

[157] Including the reception of a child baptised in an emergency: see the Ministration of Private Baptism of Infants in Houses in the Book of Common Prayer and Note 110 at p. 280 in the Alternative Service Book.

[158] See Canon B 25 and the rubric at the end of the Ministration of Publick Baptism of Infants in the Book of Common Prayer.

[159] Note 3 at pp. 225 and 241. This would also be legal in the rite according to the Book of Common Prayer either as *de minimis* or by reason of Canon B 5, para. 1. See, also, Canon B 37, para. 3.

[160] See Notes 22 and 57 at pp. 233 and 248 respectively.

[161] See Note 4 at pp. 225 and 241.   [162] Note 2 at p. 241.   [163] See Note 2 at p. 225.

[164] *Ibid.*   [165] It would in any event be lawful by reason of Canon B 5, para. 1.

[166] See *op. cit.* at pp. 239 and 251.

[167] *A Service of the Word and Affirmations of Faith* at p. 10.

Specific provision is made for Baptism and Confirmation[168], either with[169] or without[170] the Holy Communion, and for the Baptism of Children at Holy Communion[171]. The Book of Common Prayer used to provide for the administration of public baptism within Morning or Evening Prayer[172] but it may now also be administered with the Holy Communion service[173].

The Alternative Service Book not only provides a service of Renewal of Baptismal Vows on Various Occasions[174] but parts of the service may also be used in conjunction with the rites of Baptism, Confirmation, and Holy Communion and the rite of Confirmation and Holy Communion[175].

(xiii) Names

The giving of a name is not essential[176] to the validity of baptism; a name must, of course, be given in a public baptism[177] and should, if possible, be given in an emergency baptism[178]. The name should not be wanton[179]. There may be more than one part to the Christan name[180].

(xiv) Fees

It is unlawful[181] for the minister, clerk in orders, parish clerk, vestry clerk, warden or any other person to demand any fee or reward for the celebration of the sacrament of a baptism or for its registration[182]. A fee may, however, be

---

[168] Series 2 Baptism and Confirmation may still be used: *Public Worship in the Church of England* at p. 13. These services are in traditional language.
[169] See the Alternative Service Book at p. 227 *et seq.*   [170] See *op. cit.* at p. 236 *et seq.*
[171] See *op. cit.* at p. 250.
[172] See the old rubrics before the Ministration of Publick Baptism of Infants and The Ministration of Baptism to such as are of Riper Years. The service was held immediately after the second lesson: *ibid.* It may still take place at that time: see, too, **footnote 174 *infra*.**
[173] See **p. 145 *supra*.**
[174] It may be used 'at Easter, at New Year, and on other suitable occasions': Note 1 at p. 275. When it is used at Holy Communion, it may be used after the sermon; the Creed may be omitted, as may the Prayers of Intercession and of Penitence: Note 2 at p. 275. When it is used at Morning or Evening Prayer, it may be used 'after a Sermon, either after the Second reading or at the end of the service': Note 3 at p. 275 and **p. 69 *et seq. supra*.**   [175] Note 1 at p. 275.
[176] The wording of the rubric in The Ministration of Private Baptism of Children in Houses in the Book of Common Prayer before the questions to the godparents may be read as a request for such name as may have been given.   [177] See the baptismal words in each rite.
[178] See the opening words in The Ministration of Private Baptism of Children in Houses in the Book of Common Prayer and Note 108 at p. 280 in the Alternative Service Book.
[179] The pre-Reformation canon law forbids the giving of such names, 'lasciva nomina'; if given they may be changed at confirmation: see Gibson, *Codex Juris Ecclesiatici Anglicani* (Oxford, 1761) (2nd ed.) at p. 363. See **p. 156 *infra*.**
[180] See *Legal Opinions concerning the Church of England* at p. 182; this resolves the difficulty alluded to by Vaisey J, in *In re Parrott. Cox* v. *Parrott* [1946] Ch 183 at p. 187.
[181] It is an ecclesiastical offence to demand or accept such a fee: *Burgoyne* v. *Free* (1829) 2 Hag. Ecc. 456 at pp. 464–467.   [182] Baptismal Fees Abolition Act 1872, s. 1.

charged by the incumbent for a certificate of baptism[183] and searches of the baptismal register[184].

(xv) Registers

(a) Generally

Every minister must observe the law from time to time in force in all matters pertaining to the registration of baptisms[185].

Where a ceremony of baptism according to the rites of the Church of England is performed in the parish church[186] or in any other place in a parish by a minister[187] of the parish[188], the person by whom the ceremony was performed shall as soon as possible thereafter enter in the appropriate register book[189] of baptisms the particulars required[190]; he must also sign the register[191].

Where the ceremony is performed in any place in a parish other than a parish church by a person who is not the minister of the parish, the person by whom the

---

[183] The Baptismal Registers Measure 1961, s. 2(1), Sch., Pt 2, provides for the issue of a shortened form of certificate.

[184] See the Ecclesiastical Fees Measure 1986 and the current Parochial Fees Order made thereunder. Any such fee is recoverable as a debt: *ibid*, s. 7. During a vacancy in a benefice the fees which, but for the vacancy, would be paid to the incumbent must be paid to the diocesan board of finance or to such other person as the board, after consultation with the bishop, may direct: *ibid*, s. 3(1). See, too, *Legal Opinions concerning the Church of England* at p. 15; Baptismal Registers Measure 1961, s. 2(1).   [185] Canon B 39, para. 1.

[186] Or, in the case of a parish having more than one such church, any parish church: Parochial Registers and Records Measure, 1978, s. 2(1)(a).

[187] For the purposes of these provisions 'minister', in relation to a parish, means the incumbent of the benefice to which the parish belongs, a vicar in a team ministry in the area of that benefice, the priest in charge of the parish and any curate licensed to officiate in the parish: Parochial Registers and Records Measure 1978, s. 2(5).

[188] There is no statutory provision removing a conventional district from the scope of the 1978 Measure. Therefore, where a baptism is performed in the place of worship of a conventional district by the minister of that district, the minister who perfoms the ceremony must as soon as possible thereafter send to the incumbent or priest-in-charge of the parish a certificate signed by him certifying when and where the ceremony was performed: see *Legal Opinions concerning the Church of England* at p. 16. If the minister of the conventional district keeps a form of record of baptisms performed within the district, it should be clearly marked as a copy of the entries in the actual parish register: *ibid*.

[189] A register book must be provided in every parish church and chapel: Canon F 11, para. 1; Canon F 14; Parochial Registers and Records Measure 1978, s. 1. Register books must be provided, maintained and kept in accordance with Statutes and Measures relating thereto, and the rules and regulations made thereunder and from time to time in force: Canon F 11, para. 2.

[190] Where a person's name appears on a birth certificate as the child's father, the baptismal register should follow the birth certificate. If no birth certificate is produced, or if the birth certificate does not show who the father is, no person's name can be entered as father of an illegitimate child on the baptismal register without his consent. The same principle should be followed where a married woman has a child by a man other than her husband. The register cannot be altered in a case where a man accepts the child of a previous relationship and desires the entry in the baptismal register to be altered, for example, to save the child from later knowledge that he is not in fact the father: see *Legal Opinions concerning the Church of England* at p. 15. There is no power to enter the name of a child born abroad to parents in the foreign service or in the armed services in the register of a parish in England in which they normally reside: *ibid*.

[191] Parochial Registers and Records Measure 1978, s. 2(1). Canon B 39, para. 1, states: 'In all matters pertaining to the registration of baptisms, marriages, and burials every minister shall observe the law from time to time in force relating thereto.'

ceremony was performed must as soon as possible thereafter send to the incumbent or priest in charge of the parish a certificate signed by him certifying when and where the ceremony was performed and containing the required particulars[192].

Where the ceremony is performed in an extra-parochial place, unless it is performed in a church or chapel for which a register book has been provided[193], the person by whom the ceremony was performed must, as soon as possible thereafter, send to the incumbent or priest in charge of such of the adjoining parishes as the bishop in whose diocese that place is may direct, a certificate signed by him certifying when and where the ceremony was performed and containing the required particulars[194].

On receiving such a certificate the incumbent or priest in charge must enter particulars of the baptism to which the certificate relates in the appropriate register book of baptisms[195].

As long as certain conditions are fulfilled[196], a person having custody of the register of baptisms[197] must without fee make a statutory annotation[198] to the relevant baptismal register showing that a person has been legitimated since baptism[199]. Otherwise, a person required to register a baptism who discovers an error in the form of substance of an entry is not liable to any penalty under the Forgery Act 1913[200], by reason only that within one month after the discovery of the error he corrects the erroneous entry[201] by an entry in the margin of the register book[202] but without altering the original entry[203].

[192] Parochial Registers and Records Measure 1978, s. 2(2): see, too, **p. 144, footnote 113 *supra***. As to conventional districts see **p. 151, footnote 188 *supra***.

[193] By virtue of the 1978 Measure or any enactment repealed by it: Parochial Registers and Records Measure 1978, s. 2(3).   [194] *Ibid.*

[195] Parochial Registers and Records Measure 1978, s. 2(4). He must add the following words: 'According to the certificate of
received by me on the   day of   '.

[196] The legitimated person, either of his parents or anyone having a reasonable interest must: (a) produce a certified copy of an entry in a register maintained under the Births and Deaths Registration Act 1953, or which is in the custody of the Registrar General, being an entry in which the birth of the baptised person is re-registered as that of a legitimated person; and (b) identify to the custodian in the registers in his custody the entry showing the baptism requiring annotation. The custodian must be satisfied that the certified copy relates to the birth of the person whose baptism is recorded in the entry so identified to him: Baptismal Registers Measure 1961, ss. 1(1), 3.

[197] By virtue of the Parochial Registers and Records Measure 1978, ss. 6 or 14: Baptismal Registers Measure 1961, s. 3.

[198] 'Certificate showing re-registration of birth, produced to me this   day of   19 , showing father's name as A.   B.
(signed)
Officiating minister': Baptismal Registers Measure 1961, s. 1(2), Schedule, Pt I.

[199] Baptismal Registers Measure 1961, s. 1. Thereafter any certificate of the baptism, other than a short certificate, must set out the annotation in full: *ibid*, s. 1(3).

[200] Now repealed but see the Forgery and Counterfeiting Act 1981, s. 30, Schedule, Pt I.

[201] In the presence of the parents of the child to whom the entry relates or, in the case of the death or absence of both of them, the churchwardens of the parish to which the register book belongs: Parochial Registers and Records Measure 1978, s. 4(1), (2).

[202] The marginal entry must be signed by whoever the entry is made and must be attested by the persons in whose presence the entry is required to be made; the date of the entry must be added by the person by whom it is made: Parochial Registers and Records Measure 1978, s. 4(3).

[203] Parochial Registers and Records Measure 1978, s. 4.

(b)   Cathedrals, etc.

So far as is applicable and with necessary modifications the provisions concerning registers apply for any cathedral or collegiate church or any other church or chapel which does not belong to a parish[204].

B   Confirmation

(i)   Generally

It is the duty of every minister having a cure of souls[205] diligently to seek out children and other persons whom he thinks meet to be confirmed and to use his best endeavours to instruct them in the Christian faith and life as set forth in the holy Scriptures, the Book of Common Prayer and the Church Catechism[206]. Once a child is able to say the Creed, the Lord's Prayer and the Ten Commandments and to be further instructed in the Catechism it is the duty of the parents and guardians[207], as well as the godparents, to bring it to the bishop for confirmation[208].

When any person as is of riper years and able to answer for himself[209] is baptised, he should be confirmed 'so soon after his baptism as conveniently may be' so that he may be admitted to Holy Communion[210].

If any person who desires formally to be admitted into the Church of England has been baptised but not episcopally confirmed[211], he must after appropriate instruction be received by the rite of confirmation[212].

---

[204] Parochial Registers and Records Measure 1978, s. 5.   [205] See **p. 134** *et seq. supra.*

[206] Canon B 27, para. 2. Every minister must take care that the children and young people within his cure are instructed in the doctrine, sacraments, and discipline of Christ, as the Lord has commanded and as they are set forth in the holy Scriptures, in the Book of Common Prayer, and especially in the Church Catechism; to this end he, or some godly and competent persons appointed by him, must on Sundays (or, if need be, at other convenient times) diligently instruct and teach them in the same: Canon B 26, para. 1. A priest having a cure of souls must 'instruct the children, or cause them to be instructed, in the Christian faith; and shall use such opportunities of teaching and visiting in schools within his cure as are open to him': Canon C 24, para 4. See, also, the rubrics at the end of the Catechism in the Book of Commmon Prayer and *Sanders* v. *Head* (1843) 3 Curt. 565. All parents and guardians must take care that their children receive such instruction: Canon B 26, para. 2.   [207] Canon B 22, para. 3.

[208] See the final exhortation in The Ministration of Publick Baptism of Infants in the Book of Common Prayer. The rubrics before Series 2 Infant Baptism (a service which is still authorised: see *Public Worship in the Church of England* at p. 13) provide that the minister must ask the parents and godparents ('sponsors') 'whether they will encourage [the child] in due time to come to Confirmation and Communion'. See, too, paragraphs 53 and 59 at pp. 246–247 and 248 respectively in the Alternative Service Book. It is also implicit in Canons B 26, para. 2, and Canon B 27, para. 3.

[209] See **p. 137** *et seq. supra.*

[210] Canon B 24, para. 3, and the final rubrics to The Ministration of Publick Baptism to such as are of Riper Years in the Book of Common Prayer and Note 1 at p. 225 of the Alternative Service Book.

[211] If he has been episcopally confirmed with unction or with the laying on of hands, he must be instructed and, with the permission of the bishop, received into the Church of England according to the Form of Reception approved by the General Synod, or with other appropriate prayers; if the person is a priest, he must be received only by the bishop of the diocese or by his commissary: Canon B 28, para. 3. There is no such approved Form of Reception at present.

[212] Canon B 28, para. 2. If he is not ready to be presented for confirmation, he must be received by the parish priest with appropriate prayers: *ibid.*

(ii)   Pre-requisites

A minister may only present a candidate for confirmation who has come to years of discretion[213], who can say[214] the Creed, the Lord's Prayer and the Ten Commandments and who can also render an account of his faith according to the Catechism[215]. He must satisfy himself that those whom he is to present to the bishop have been validly baptised[216], ascertaining the date and place of such baptism. Before or at the time assigned for the confirmation he must give to the bishop their names, together with their age and the date of their baptism[217].

The Book of Common Prayer states[218] that: ' . . . every one shall have a God-father, or a Godmother, as a Witness of their Confirmation.'. However, particularly as this requirement does not appear in the canons or in the Alternative Service Book, the presence of a godparent is not a *sine qua non* to a valid confirmation[219].

(iii)   Confirmation

Only a bishop can administer the rite of confirmation[220]. A diocesan bishop must be faithful in celebrating the rite of confirmation as often and in as many places

---

[213] Cp. also the rubrics at the end of the Holy Communion in the Book of Common Prayer: 'And if there be not above twenty persons in the Parish of discretion to receive the Communion . . . ' This implies a measure of understanding, as the necessity for the candidate to be able to 'render an account of [his] faith' makes clear. Any doubts are to be resolved by the bishop: see the last rubric at the end of the Catechism in the Book of Common Prayer – 'And, if the Bishop approve of them, he shall confirm them in manner following.'

[214] It is unnecessary that the candidate has committed them to memory.

[215] Canon B 27, para. 3. It is unclear whether Canon C 24, para. 5, adds to these requirements. It states that every priest having a cure of souls 'shall carefully prepare, or cause to be prepared, all such as desire to be confirmed and, if satisfied of their fitness, shall present them to the bishop for confirmation.' See, too, Canon B 27, para. 1, by which the bishop is to lay his hand on those 'who have been baptised and instructed in the Christian faith.' *Cripps on Church and Clergy* (8th ed.) at p. 83 states: ' . . . it seems that if the minister should refuse or neglect to comply with the bishop's directions as to preparing and sending his parishoners for confirmation, this might be good cause for the non-approval of such persons by the bishop. Consequently, in different ways, the bishop has the entire power of directing the preparation of candidates for confirmation in any manner he may think fit; and all the various circumstances connected with it; and the mode of bringing them to be confirmed: and this independently of the minister, if any difficulty should arise respecting his co-operation and concurrence.'

[216] If the minister is doubtful about the baptism of a candidate for confirmation, he must conditionally baptise him in accordance with the form of service authorised by Canon B 1 before presenting him to the bishop: Canon B 27, para. 5. See, too, Canon B 28, para. 1, and **p. 153** *supra*.

[217] Canon B 27, para. 4. The rubrics at the end of the Catechism in the Book of Common Prayer also state: ' . . . whensoever the Bishop shall give knowledge for Children to be brought unto him for their Confirmation, the Curate of every Parish shall either bring, or send in writing, with his hand subscribed thereunto, the names of all such persons within his Parish, as he shall think fit to be presented to the Bishop to be confirmed. And, if the Bishop approve of them, he shall confirm them in manner following.' 'Curate' here means the minister having the cure of souls.

[218] See the rubrics at the end of the Catechism in the Book of Common Prayer.

[219] Indeed, this must be so as all the godparents may be dead.

[220] See Note 8 at p. 226 of the Alternative Service Book: ' . . . only the Bishop is to confirm'. This makes explicit that which is in any event clear from the use of the word 'bishop' in all the rites of confirmation. See, too, Canon C 18, para. 6.

as is convenient[221], laying his hands upon children and other persons who have been baptised and instructed in the faith[222]; however, he may also cause it to be ministered by some other bishop lawfully deputised in his stead[223]. The bishop must give due notice of the confirmation[224].

The choice of which rite of confirmation[225] to use is to be made by the officiating bishop after consultation with the minister of the church where the service is to be held[226].

The Book of Common Prayer only provides for the delegation of the reading of the Preface to another minister[227] but the Alternative Service Book permits the delegation of any part of the bishop's duties to other ministers[228], other than the actual confirmation[229]. Indeed, such further delegation would now be lawful in any rite by reason of Canon B 5, para. 1.

The rite of confirmation may be used as a separate service[230]. The Alternative Service Book makes provision for confirmation alone with or without Holy Communion[231] or during Morning or Evening Prayer[232]; it also makes provision for confirmation with or without Baptism together with Holy Communion[233] or during Morning or Evening Prayer[234]. When it is used at the same time as the rite of baptism the Alternative Service Book provides that the precise ordering of the service and the place of baptism[235] is to be determined by consultation between the bishop and the parish priest[236]. The bishop may direct the use of other readings[237]. At his discretion the Renewal of Baptismal Vows may be used[238].

In the rite according to the Alternative Service Book the bishop may anoint the candidates with oil which he has previously blessed for that purpose[239]; a similar anointing may now be adopted when using the rite according to the Book of Common Prayer by reason of Canon B 5, para. 1.

[221] Canon C 18, para. 6.   [222] Canon B 27, para. 1.   [223] *Ibid.*
[224] See the last rubric at the end of the Catechism in the Book of Common Prayer which states: '... whensoever the Bishop shall give knowledge for Children to be brought unto him for their Confirmation ...' In addition, the rubric at the commencement of The Order for Confirmation begins: 'On the day appointed ...'
[225] Series 2 Baptism and Confirmation may still be used: *Public Worship in the Church of England* at p. 13. These services are in traditional language.
[226] See Canons B 3, paras 4 and 5, and p. 97 *supra*.   [227] See the introductory rubric.
[228] Notes 8 and 3 at pp. 226 and 252 of the Alternative Service Book respectively.
[229] That is, sections 23–25 and 78–80 at pp. 233–234 and 256 respectively.
[230] See the Note at p. 223 of the Alternative Service Book. Indeed, The Order of Confirmation in the Book of Common Prayer makes no mention of any immediately subsequent eucharist.
[231] See *op. cit.* at pp. 253 and 258 respectively.   [232] See *op. cit.* at p. 260.
[233] See *op. cit.* at pp. 227 and 236 respectively.   [234] See *op. cit.* at p. 239.
[235] This must mean the location for the baptism. Paragraph 17 at p. 231 merely states: 'The Bishop stands before the water of baptism ...'   [236] Note 10 at p. 226.
[237] See Notes 9 and 4 at pp. 226 and 252 respectively. For the set readings see *op. cit.* at p. 261 *et seq.*
[238] See Notes 9 and 5 at pp. 226 and 252 respectively. See also the Notes at p. 275.
[239] See Notes 7 and 2 at pp. 226 and 252 respectively: see **p. 78** *supra*. Being part of the actual confirmation this cannot be delegated by the bishop: see *supra*.

(iv)   Re-confirmation

Once confirmed a person may not be re-confirmed[240].

(v)   Change of name

Other than by Act of Parliament a person's Christian name may only be altered at confirmation[241]. Canon B 27, para. 6, states:

> If it is desired for sufficient reason[242] that a Christian name be changed, the bishop may, under the laws of this realm, confirm a person by a new Christian name[243], which shall be thereafter deemed the lawful Christan name of such person.

This may be done even though, unlike the Alternative Service Book[244], the rite according to the Book of Common Prayer makes no provision for the use of the candidate's name[245]. The change may be by the addition or substitution of the whole or part of the baptismal name[246].

(vi)   Registers

When any person is presented for confirmation, the minister presenting the candidate must record and enter the confirmation in his register book of confirmations[247].

A record of any change of name must be made in the register book of confirmations[248]. It is also advisable that a note of the change of name is made in the margin of the relevant baptismal register, although the register itself must not be altered[249].

---

[240] Lyndwood, *Provinciale Angliae* at pp. 40–41; see, too, Canon B 28, para. 3.

[241] See 14 Halsbury's Laws of England (4th ed.) at para. 1000 and *In re Parrott. Cox* v. *Parrott* [1946] Ch 183 at pp. 186–187 *per* Vaisey J.

[242] This seems to reflect the content of the pre-Reformation canon law to the effect that wanton names, 'lasciva nomina', might be changed at confirmation: see Gibson, *Codex Juris Ecclesiatici Anglicani* (Oxford, 1761) (2nd ed.) at p. 363. Clearly it should not be done merely on a whim.

[243] He should confirm using the whole of the new name: see *Legal Opinions concerning the Church of England* at p. 182.   [244] See Notes 25 and 80 at pp. 234 and 256 respectively.

[245] *In re Parrott. Cox* v. *Parrott* [1946] Ch 183 at p. 186 *per* Vaisey J. See, too, **p. 39** *supra*.

[246] See *Legal Opinions concerning the Church of England* at p. 182. An accidental change of name is not possible as the change must be intentional: *ibid*. See, too, **p. 150** *supra*.

[247] Canon B 39, para. 2. A register book is to be provided for every parish church and chapel: Canon F 11, para. 3.   [248] Canon B 39, para. 2.

[249] See *Legal Opinions concerning the Church of England* at p. 182. Although not strictly necessary, it is advisable that a statutory declaration is also made in order further to evidence the change of name: *ibid*.

7

MARRIAGE

A Generally

(i) Duties

In all matters pertaining to the publication of banns of marriage[1] and to the solemnisation of matrimony every minister must observe the law relating thereto, including in so far as is applicable the rules prescribed by the rubric prefixed to the Office of Solemnisation of Matrimony in the Book of Common Prayer[2]. Indeed, the law relating to matrimony is particularly important as a marriage alters the legal status of those involved[3]; it is for this reason that the only matter to which any of the rubrics in the Book of Common Prayer relate and in respect of which the General Synod cannot make provision by Canon or regulation is the publication of banns of matrimony[4].

It is the duty of the minister, when application is made to him for matrimony to be solemnised in the church of which he is the minister[5], to explain to the two persons who desire to be married the Church's doctrine of marriage and the need

---

[1] As to the publication of banns see **p. 87 et seq. supra**.

[2] Canon B 35, para. 2. The Canon reflects the Marriage Act 1949, s. 7(2). Canon B 5, para. 1, cannot be relied upon to excuse a failure in compliance as a canon cannot abrogate a statute. See, too, Canon B 35, para. 1: 'In all matters pertaining to the granting of licences of marriage every ecclesiastical authority shall observe the law relating thereto.'

[3] See **p. 87 et seq. supra**. 'Failure to comply with [the] legal requirements can easily invalidate an apparent marriage in the eyes of the temporal law; and since the Church requires compliance with the temporal law before she will recognise a marriage as canonically valid, the consequences of laxity in the observance of these requirements, if sufficient to invalidate the ceremony, can be very serious both spiritually and temporally': Briden & Hanson, *Moore's Introduction to English Canon Law* (3rd ed.) at p. 77.

[4] Church of England (Worship and Doctrine) Measure 1974, s. 1(1)(b).

[5] It is unclear to whom this relates; 14 Halsbury's Laws of England (4th ed.) at para. 1002, note 4, merely speaks of an application 'to a minister for marriage in his church'. The words certainly embrace a minister having a cure of souls and a minister under whose authority the church falls: cp. the Marriage Act 1949, s. 17 proviso; see, too, Canon B 33; Marriage Act 1949, s. 5A; Matrimonial Causes Act 1965, s. 8(2). The Canon speaks of 'the church of which he is *the* minister' (emphasis supplied), rather than 'the church of which he is *a* minister'. However, as other Canons specifically refer to ministers having a cure of souls and, as the intention must be that all those intending to be married are given the explanation, it is possible to argue that the duty is upon the person to whom the application is actually made as long as he is licensed to minister at that church, such as an assistant curate. However, Canon B 36, para. 1, speaks of 'the church or chapel in which he is authorised to exercise his ministry' and such wording would seem to be necessary in order to embrace an assistant curate. Nonetheless, there is clearly a difference between an actual application and an enquiry; moreover, there is no reason why the explanation should not be given by someone else, although the duty itself would remain upon the minister of the relevant church. Cp., too, the Extra-Parochial Ministry Measure 1967, s. 3 ('minister of a parish') and **p. 23, footnote 162 supra**.

of God's grace in order that they may discharge aright their obligations as married persons[6]. In this regard, the teaching of our Lord affirmed by the Church of England is expressed and maintained in the Form of Solemnisation of Matrimony contained in the Book of Common Prayer[7]. The Church of England affirms, according to our Lord's teaching, that marriage is in its nature a union permanent and life-long, for better for worse, till death them do part[8], of one man with one woman, to the exclusion of all others on either side, for the procreation and nurture of children, for the hallowing and right direction of the natural instincts and affections, and for the mutual society, help and comfort which the one ought to have of the other, both in prosperity and adversity[9].

It is also the duty of the minister, when application is made to him for matrimony to be solemnised in the church or chapel of which he is the minister, to inquire whether there is any impediment either to the marriage or to its solemnisation[10].

If the rite according to the Alternative Service Book is to be used, the minister must enquire before the day of the marriage which form of vows the couple have agreed to use[11].

(ii)   Foreigners

Where one of the parties to the intended wedding is a foreigner[12], or has his permanent home outside the United Kingdom, it is advisable that the marriage should be by licence rather than by banns[13]. This is to ensure that the legal requirements of the foreigner's country are observed[14].

---

[6] Canon B 30, para. 3. Regulation 2(C) concerning Marriage and Divorce passed by the Convocation of Canterbury on 1 October 1957, states: 'Recognizing that pastoral care may well avert the danger of divorce if it comes into play before legal proceedings have been started, this House urges all clergy in their preparation of couples for marriage to tell them, both for their own sakes and for that of their friends, that the good offices of the clergy are always available.' See *The Canons of the Church of England* at p. 183.   [7] Canon B 30, para. 2.

[8] The Convocation of Canterbury has in consequence declared an Act of Convocation stating, *inter alia*, that re-marriage after divorce during the lifetime of a former partner always involves a departure from the true principle of marriage as declared by our Lord: Regulations concerning Marriage and Divorce, reg. 1(3). See *The Canons of the Church of England* at p. 182. An Act of Convocation has moral force only: *Bland* v. *Archdeacon of Cheltenham* [1972] Fam. 157 at p. 166D.

[9] Canon B 30, para. 1.

[10] Canon B 33. For the special rules applying to marriages of the Royal Family see Phillimore, *Ecclesiastical Law*, (2nd ed.) vol. I, at pp. 578–580; 8 Halsbury's Laws of England (4th ed.) at para. 868.   [11] Note 6 at p. 285.

[12] As to banns see **p. 87 *et seq. supra.*** As to interpreters see **p. 191 *infra.***

[13] *Anglican Marriage in England and Wales: A Guide to the Law for the Clergy* (Faculty Office of the Archbishop of Canterbury, 1992) at paras 1.5 and 9.3. Before granting such a licence a surrogate should consult with the diocesan registrar: *Legal Opinions concerning the Church of England* at p. 165. The Marriage with Foreigners Act 1906, s. 2, is so far of no effect as no regulations have as yet been made thereunder. Where one of the parties to the intended marriage is a British subject resident in certain of Her Majesty's dominions a certificate of publication of banns, or of notice of marriage, has the same effect as a certificate of marriage issued by a Superintendent Registrar: Marriage of British Subjects (Facilities) Act 1915, s. 1; 22 Halsbury's Laws of England (4th ed.) at para. 950.

[14] *Anglican Marriage in England and Wales: A Guide to the Law for the Clergy* at para. 9. 3; *Legal Opinions concerning the Church of England* at p. 165.

B Pre-Condition to Marriage

(i) Generally

In order to be married the parties.

(a)   must be respectively male and female[15];
(b)   must not be within the prohibited degrees of relationship[16];
(c)   must both be over sixteen[17];
(d)   must not at the time of the marriage be lawfully married[18];
(e)   must have fulfilled certain formalities[19].

Since 31 July 1971, any marriage in England in contravention of these pre-conditions is void without a decree of nullity from an English court[20] but before any party to such a relationship goes through a further ceremony of marriage in an Anglican church the minister should require to see such a decree or seek legal advice. Marriages may also be voidable for such reasons as non-consummation or duress but they remain valid until a decree of nullity is pronounced[21].

Because matrimonial questions depend in law upon a person's domicile[22] it is advisable when one party to an intended marriage is a foreigner that the marriage is by licence rather than by banns. This is to ensure that all the legal requirements of that person's country are observed[23].

(ii) Sex

English law does not recognize a marriage between two men or two women, whatever their sexual proclivities. The test is a biological one and, at least for the purposes of marriage, a person cannot change his or her sex by a medical operation[24]. Whether any service of blessing may be used in relation to such

---

[15] Matrimonial Causes Act 1973, s. 11(c); Canon B 30, para. 1.
[16] Marriage Act 1949, s. 1; Matrimonial Causes Act 1973, s. 11(a)(i); Canon B 31, para. 2.
[17] Marriage Act 1949, s. 2; Matrimonial Causes Act 1973, s. 11(a)(ii); Canon B 31, para. 1.
[18] Matrimonial Causes Act 1973, s. 11(b); Canon B 30, para. 1. As to conditional marriages see
p. 194 *et seq. infra.*   [19] Matrimonial Causes Act 1973, s. 11(a)(iii); Canon B 34.
[20] Matrimonial Causes Act 1973, s. 11; *Rayden and Jackson on Divorce and Family Matters* (16th ed.) at p. 94. Also void is any marriage celebrated after 31 July 1971, which is a polygamous marriage entered into outside England and Wales when either party was domiciled at the time in England or Wales: Matrimonial Causes Act 1973, s. 11(d).
[21] For a discussion as to the difference between void and voidable marriages, see Briden & Hanson, *Moore's Introduction to English Canon Law* (3rd ed.) at pp. 74–76. In practice a minister should always require to see the relevant decree.
[22] 'Domicile is the legal and normally also the factual relationship between a person and a territorial area subject to one system of law ...': *Rayden and Jackson on Divorce and Family Matters* (16th ed.) at p. 59.
[23] *Legal Opinions concerning the Church of England* at p. 165.
[24] *Corbett* v. *Corbett (Otherwise Ashley)* [1971] P 83; see, further, *Rayden and Jackson on Divorce and Family Matters* (16th ed.) at pp. 91–92.

people by reason of Canon B 5, para. 2, will depend, in part at least, upon the extent to which the service resembles one of marriage[25].

(iii) Prohibited degrees

Marriages between persons within the prohibited degrees are void[26]. Canon B 31, para. 2, is specifically subject to the provisions of the Marriage (Prohibited Degrees of Relationship) Act 1986, but the Table of Kindred and Affinity[27] set out in the Canon does not completely reflect the provisions of that Act; moreover, it ignores further changes made by the Children Act 1975[28]. Nevertheless, by reason of Canon B 35, para. 2, both those Acts take precedence over the Table in Canon B 31[29].

What is more, the matter is further complicated by provisions relating to those who have attained the age of twenty-one. Firstly, the marriage of any person to another within certain degrees of affinity[30] is void for that reason, except if both have reached the age of twenty-one and the younger of the two has at no time before reaching the age of eighteen been a child of the family[31] in relation to the other[32]. Secondly, the marriage of certain persons to others within particular degrees of affinity[33] are void, except if both parties to the marriage are over twenty-one and the marriage is solemnised:

(a)   in the case of a marriage between a man and the mother of a former wife of his, after the death of both the former wife and the father of the former wife;
(b)   in the case of a marriage between a man and the former wife of his son, after the death of both his son and the mother of his son;
(c)   in the case of a marriage between a woman and the father of a former husband of hers, after the death of both the former husband and the mother of the former husband;
(d)   in the case of a marriage between a woman and a former husband of her daughter, after the death of both her daughter and the father of her daughter[34].

As has been seen, it is the duty of the minister, when application is made to him for matrimony to be solemnised in the church or chapel of which he is the minister, to inquire whether there is any impediment either to the marriage or to its solemnisation[35].

---

[25] See Canon B 5, para. 3, and **p. 220** *infra*.   [26] See **p. 159** *supra*.
[27] This Table must be set up and fixed in every parish church at the expense of the parish: Canon B 31, para. 2.   [28] Section 108(1), Sch. 3, para. 8.
[29] The Table in **Appendix 5, Part I**, at **p. 283** *infra* reflects the provisions of both these Acts.
[30] See **Appendix 5, Part II**, at **p. 283** *infra*.
[31] A 'child of the family' in relation to a marriage means a child of both parties to the marriage (including an illegitimate or adopted child) or any other child, not being a child who has been placed with those parties as foster parents by a local authority or voluntary organisation, who has been treated by them as a child of their family: see the Matrimonial Causes Act 1973, s. 52(1).
[32] Marriage Act 1949, s. 1(2), (3).   [33] See **Appendix 5, Part III, at p. 284** *infra*.
[34] Marriage Act 1949, s. 1(4), (5).   [35] Canon B 33.

Nevertheless, no minister is obliged to solemnise a marriage which, apart from the 1986 Act, would have been void by reason of the relationship of the persons to be married, nor to permit such a marriage to be solemnised in the church or chapel of which he is the minister[36]. If, in spite of this provision, a minister decides that he will solemnise such a marriage, he should be very careful either to solemnise the marriage on the authority of a special or common licence, a Superintendent Registrar's certificate or himself to obtain evidence similar to that which is required in relation to a common licence[37].

(iv) Nonage

No person under the age of sixteen shall marry and all such purported marriages are void[38].

Furthermore, no minister shall solemnise matrimony between two persons either of whom (not being a widow or widower) is under eighteen years of age otherwise than in accordance with the requirements of the law relating to the consent of parents or guardians in the case of the marriage of a person under eighteen years of age[39]. Unfortunately, this provision is out of touch with the modern law in relation to infants and persons having parental responsibility[40] but, in the light of Canon B 35, paras 1 and 2, it must nevertheless be read in accordance with it[41]. That being so, only specified persons may now legally forbid the publication of banns[42].

---

[36] Marriage Act 1949, s. 5A. This includes all those marriages referred to in **Appendix 5, Parts II and III**.

[37] See the Marriage Act 1949, s. 16 (1A), (1B) and **p. 174, footnote 186** *infra*; see, too, Marriage Act 1949, s. 27B and s. 27C.   [38] Canon B 31, para. 1; see, too, **p. 159** *supra*.

[39] Canon B 32. A marriage celebrated without the requisite consents is nevertheless valid: *R* v. *Birmingham Inhabitants* (1828) 8 B. & C. 29: see, too, *Rayden and Jackson on Divorce and Family Matters* at paras 9.10 and 41.55.   [40] See **p. 136** *supra*.

[41] See the Marriage Act 1949, s. 3(3), (4). See, too, *Anglican Marriage in England and Wales* at para. 7.8.

[42] See the Marriage Act 1949, s. 3(1A), (3), (4). Generally these persons are:

(a)   subject to paragraphs (b) and (d):
    (i)   each parent (if any) of the child who has parental responsibility for him; and
    (ii)   each guardian (if any) of the child;
(b)   where a residence order is in force with respect to the child, the person or persons with whom he lives, or is to live, as a result of that order (in substitution for the persons mentioned in (a) above);
(c)   where a care order is in force with respect to the child, the consent of the local authority designated in the order;
(d)   where neither (b) nor (c) above applies but a residence order was in force with respect to the child immediately before he reached the age of sixteen, the person or persons with whom he lived, or was to live, as a result of that order (in substitution for the persons mentioned in (a) above).

Those who must consent to the marriage are, of course, the same, save that the consent of the local authority in (c) is in addition to those of parents and guardians in (a).

Different considerations may apply if there is an order in force predating 14 October 1991.

If one of the parties to the intended marriage is a ward of court, the consent of the High Court is always required: Marriage Act 1949, s. 3(6).

Nonetheless, a clergyman is not liable to ecclesiastical censure for solemnising the marriage of a child after the publication of banns without the consent of the parents or guardians of the child unless he has notice of the dissent of any person who is entitled to give notice of dissent[43].

Consent may be implied[44] although it lapses on death[45]. Consent may also be retracted[46] but rarely at the actual ceremony[47]. If consent is refused, a court can give its consent instead of the person having the right to give consent but in these circumstances the marriage must be solemnised on the authority of a Superintendent Registrar's certificate[48]. The consent of the court has the same effect as if it had been given by the person whose consent is refused[49].

If the person whose consent is required is absent or inaccessible or under a disability, the Superintendent Registrar[50] may dispense with consent in which case the marriage must be solemnised on the authority of a Superintendent Registrar's Certificate[51]. However, in this latter instance if the marriage is to be solemnised on the authority of a common licence, the dispensing power lies with the ecclesiastical authority[52] by whom the licence was granted[53].

---

[43] Marriage Act 1949, s. 3(4).

[44] *Smith* v. *Huson* (1811) 1 Phillim. 287 at pp. 299–300 *per* Sir John Nicholl.

[45] *Ex parte Reibey* (1843) 12 LJ Ch 436.

[46] 'It is undoubtedly true that consent may be retracted; since the parental authority continues up to the time of marriage. This principle, however, must be taken with reasonable limitations; for it cannot be maintained that this power can be arbitrarily resumed at any moment: that if a parent gives consent on Monday for a marriage the next day, and it is deferred, it would be necessary to renew that consent, or that it would be considered as wearing out or expiring by mere lapse of a short time. When consent has actually been given, it will be necessary that dissent afterwards should be distinctly expressed, and that it should be proved so to have been in the clearest manner . . . ': *Hodgkinson* v. *Wilkie* (1795) 1 Hag. Con. 262 at p. 265 *per* Sir William Scott; see, too, *Smith* v. *Huson* (1811) 1 Phillim. 287 at p. 300 *per* Sir John Nicholl.

[47] ' . . . it must be justifiable for persons in loco parentis to change their minds if circumstances come to their knowledge in respect of the proposed [spouse] which, if they had been within their knowledge at the time the consent was given, would have fairly and properly operated to induce them not to give their consent . . . On the other hand . . . a retraction of consent must not be, as was expressed in one case, ad libitum, or, as it was, I think, expressed in another case, a mere caprice . . . ': *In re Brown. Ingall* v. *Brown* [1904] 1 Ch 120 at 129 *per* Byrne J. See, too, the **previous footnote**, Marriage Act 1949, s. 7(2) and **p. 187** *infra*. Some of the relevant criteria seem to be: has the parent had a previous chance to express dissent and, if so, to what extent has he availed himself of it, for example, by forbidding the banns?

[48] Marriage Act 1949, s. 3(1) proviso (b).

[49] Marriage Act 1949, s. 3(1) proviso (b). See, too, *Rayden and Jackson on Divorce and Family Matters* at pp. 1098–1099.

[50] This is only if other consents are also required; if not, the Registrar General has the dispensing power: Marriage Act 1949, s. 3(1) proviso (a).

[51] Marriage Act 1949, s. 3(1) proviso (a); *Rayden and Jackson on Divorce and Family Matters* at p. 1098.

[52] See, further, **p. 172** *et seq. infra*. A surrogate may not dispense with consent because, as a deputy, he is not the actual 'ecclesiastical authority'.

[53] Marriage Act 1949, s. 3(2). If there are no other consents required the dispensing authority is the Master of the Faculties, i.e., the Dean of the Arches: *ibid*, Ecclesiastical Jurisdiction Measure 1963, s. 13(1).

(v) Lawfully married

It is the fact that a marriage is monogamous[54] that matters, not that it is a Christian one[55]. Such a marriage can only be brought to an end by a decree of a competent court; in England this is by a decree of nullity or by a decree absolute of divorce[56]. More particularly, a decree of nullity made by a Roman Catholic tribunal is not a decree by such a competent court and does not affect the marital status of the parties[57].

Nevertheless, a religious ceremony between the same parties may be performed after a civil ceremony[58].

What is more, no clergyman of the Church of England or the Church of Wales is compelled to solemnise a marriage of any person whose former marriage has been dissolved and whose former spouse is still living nor to permit the marriage of such a person to be solemnised in the church or chapel of which he is the minister[59]. However, he is obliged to marry a person whose marriage has been annulled[60].

(vi) Relevant formalities

Unless certain formalitites as to the formation of marriage are complied with the marriage is void[61]. Oddly, these formalities are not specified but, in so far as the Anglican church is concerned, a marriage is void[62]:

(a) if any persons knowingly and wilfully consent or acquiesce in the solemnisation of the marriage by any person who is not in Holy Orders[63]; or

(b) if any persons knowingly and willingly intermarry according to the rites of the Church of England (otherwise than by special licence):

(α) in any place other than a church or other building in which banns may be published[64];

[54] See, also, R v. Bham [1966] 1 QB 159 at p. 163C.
[55] Rayden and Jackson on Divorce and Family Matters at p. 96. A decree nisi is insufficient.
[56] Anglican Marriage in England and Wales at paras 11.1–11.5. A minister should always insist upon seeing the original decree. [57] Anglican Marriage in England and Wales at paras 11.4.
[58] Marriage Act 1949, s. 46(1), (2); Canon B 36; Piers v. Piers (1849) 2 HL Cas. 331 at pp. 354, 384–385 per Lord Campbell, at p. 363 per Lord Cottingham LC and at pp. 371–373 per Lord Brougham; Hewett v. Hewett (1929) 73 Sol. Jo. 402 per Hill J: 'If people went through a second ceremony it was their own look-out. It could not be a marriage, because they had already been married.' See, too, p. 192 et seq. infra. As to conditional marriages see p. 194 et seq. infra.
[59] Matrimonial Causes Act 1965, s. 8(2).
[60] Anglican Marriage in England and Wales at para. 11.2.
[61] Matrimonial Causes Act 1973, s. 11(a)(iii).
[62] A marriage is valid unless'there is a specific provision declaring it to be void: R v. Birmingham Inhabitants (1828) 8 B. & C. 29. As to marriages declared to be void see the Marriage Act 1949, s. 25. [63] Marriage Act 1949, s. 25. See, too, p. 194 et seq. infra.
[64] Marriage Act 1949, s. 25(a). This is subject to the exception of a marriage solemnised on the authority of a Superintendent Registrar's certificate at the place where a person who is house-bound or is detained usually resides: Marriage Act 1949, ss. 25(a), 26(1)(dd).

(β)   without banns having been duly published[65], a common licence having been obtained, or a Superintendent Registrar's certificate having been duly issued[66];

(γ)   on the authority of a publication of banns which are void[67], on the authority of a common licence that is void[68], or on the authority of a Superintendent Registrar's certificate that is void[69];

(δ)   in the case of a marriage on the authority of a Superintendent Registrar's certificate, in any place other than the church building or other place specified in the notice of marriage and certificate as the place where the marriage is to be solemnised[70].

C   Preliminary Requirements Prior to a Ceremony

(i)   Generally

A marriage according to the rites of the Church of England may only be solemnised[71]:

(a)   after the publication of banns[72];
(b)   on the authority of a special licence[73];
(c)   on the authority of a common licence[74]; or
(d)   on the authority of a certificate issued by a Superintendent Registrar[75].

In all matters pertaining to the granting of licences of marriage every ecclesiastical authority must observe the law relating thereto[76].

(ii)   Banns

(a)   Generally

Where banns have been published, the marriage must normally be solemnised in the church or chapel or, as the case may be, one of the churches or chapels

---

[65] The notice of banns must state the Christian name and surname of both persons to be married, their places of residence and their periods of residence there: Marriage Act 1949, s. 8. The marriage is void if to the knowledge of both parties a false name is used in order to conceal: *Chipchase* v. *Chipchase* [1942] P 37. As to the publication of banns see **p. 87** *et seq. supra*.

[66] Marriage Act 1949, s. 25(b).

[67] Through lack of consent (including the fact that they have been forbidden: see **p. 168** *et seq. infra*) or the lapse of three calendar months after publication: Marriage Act 1949, ss. 3(3), 12(2); Interpretation Act 1978, s. 5, Sch. 1.

[68] Through the lapse of three calendar months after its issue: Marriage Act 1949, s. 16(3); Interpretation Act 1978, s. 5, Sch. 1.

[69] Through the lapse of three calendar months since the entry of the notice of marriage: Marriage Act 1949, s. 33(2); Interpretation Act 1978, s. 5, Sch. 1. See the Marriage Act 1949, s. 25(c).

[70] Marriage Act 1949, s. 25(d).   [71] Marriage Act 1949, s. 5.

[72] Canon B 34, para. 1(a).

[73] Granted by the Archbishop of Canterbury or any person by virtue of the Ecclesiastical Licences Act 1533: Canon B 34, para. 1(b). See, too, the Marriage Act 1949, ss. 5(b), 25, 79(6).

[74] Canon B 34, para. 1(c).   [75] Canon B 34, para. 1(d).   [76] Canon B 35, para. 1.

in which the banns have been published[77]. However, where a marriage is not solemnised within three calendar months after their publication, that publication is void and no clergyman may solemnise the marriage on the authority thereof[78].

(b) Publication[79]

(α) Generally

In all matters pertaining to the publication of banns every minister must observe the law in relation thereto, including, in so far as they are applicable, the rules prescribed by the rubric prefixed to the Office of Solemnisation of Matrimony in the Book of Common Prayer[80].

A clergyman may still refuse to publish banns in relation to a proposed marriage between a man and his deceased wife's sister, his deceased wife's widow or between persons and their nephews and nieces by marriage[81].

(β) Residence

If the persons to be married reside[82] in the same parish, the banns must be published in the parish church[83] of that parish[84]; otherwise they must be published in the parish church[85] of each parish in which they reside[86]. However, if either of them reside in a chapelry or in a district licensed by the bishop for the publication of banns[87], the banns may be published in an authorised chapel in

---

[77] Marriage Act 1949, s. 12(1).

[78] Marriage Act 1949, s. 12(2); Interpretation Act 1978, s. 5, Sch. 1. That is not to say that banns may not be republished, however.

[79] Matters relating to the content and mode of publication of banns have already been considered: see **p. 87** *et seq. supra.*

[80] Canon B 35, para. 2. This must mean whichever rite is being used. The rubric referred to seems to be the first rubric, although the second is also concerned with the publication of banns. However, the Marriage Act 1949, s. 7(2), suggests that each of those rubrics is in fact included: see, too, **p. 87** *et seq. supra.*   [81] 14 Halsbury's Laws of England (4th ed.) at para. 1005.

[82] See **pp. 87** *et seq.* and **134** *et seq. supra*; *Legal Opinions concerning the Church of England* at pp. 166–169; *Anglican Marriage in England and Wales* at para. 5. A minimum of fifteen continuous days is likely to be required: cp. the Marriage Act 1949, ss. 15(1), 16(1)(b). Merely to deposit a suitcase is insufficient.

[83] Where by virtue of a designation made by a pastoral scheme or otherwise a parish has more than one parish church, the bishop may give directions with respect to the publication of banns in the parish churches: Pastoral Measure 1983, s. 27(5)(b). The sharing of a church under the Sharing of Church Buildings Act 1969 merely has the effect that the building may in addition be registered for non-conformist marriages; in so far as marriages according to the rites of the Church of England are concerned the law remains the same: *op. cit.*, s. 6; *Anglican Marriage in England and Wales* at para. 3.5.   [84] Marriage Act 1949, s. 6(1)(a).

[85] Where a parish has no parish church the bishop may designate a parish centre of worship which thereupon is deemed to be a parish church for the purposes of the Marriage Act 1949. If persons to be married so elect, they may proceed under ss. 6 and 15 of the Marriage Act 1949, as if it has not been so designated and as if there is no church licensed for marriage or in which divine service is usually solemnised every Sunday: Pastoral Measure 1983, s. 29(2), (3). See, too, *Legal Opinions concerning the Church of England* at p. 166.   [86] Marriage Act 1949, s. 6(1)(b).

[87] Under the Marriage Act 1949, s. 20. Such a licence is deemed to have been revoked by a declaration of redundancy: Pastoral Measure 1983, Sch. 3, para. 14(3). A guild church in the City of London may similarly be licensed: City of London (Guild Churches) Act 1952, s. 22(1). A chapel belonging to the armed forces may be licensed, if it has first been certified as a military chapel by the Ministry of Defence: Marriage Act 1949, s. 69; *Anglican Marriage in England and Wales* at para. 3.2.

that chapelry or district instead of in the relevant parish church[88]. Where a person resides in an extra-parochial place, publication must be in an authorised[89] chapel of that place[90]. If any parish does not have a parish church or chapel, or no church or chapel in which divine service is usually solemnised every Sunday, it is deemed to belong to any adjoining parish or chapelry[91]; the position is the same if any extra-parochial place has no authorised chapel[92].

Where two or more benefices are held in plurality[93], or where there are two parishes or parish churches in the area of a single benefice[94], the diocesan bishop[95] may direct in writing where banns of persons entitled to be married in any of those churches may be published[96].

(γ) Usual place of worship

Banns of marriage may be published in any parish church or authorised chapel which is the usual place of worship[97] of the persons to be married, or of one of them, although neither of those persons resides in the parish or chapelry to which it belongs but any such publication must be in addition to the publication of their banns in their parish churches[98].

(δ) Repair and rebuilding[99]

Where any church or chapel in which banns may be published and marriages solemnised is being rebuilt or repaired and for that reason not being used for divine service, banns which could otherwise have been published there may be published:

(a)   in any building licensed[100] by the bishop for the performance of divine service during the disuse of the church or chapel, being a building within the

---

[88] Marriage Act 1949, s. 6(1) proviso.   [89] That is, under the Marriage Act 1949, s. 21.
[90] Marriage Act 1949, s. 6(2).   [91] Marriage Act 1949, s. 6(3).   [92] Ibid.
[93] Under the Pastoral Reorganisation Measure 1949 (now repealed).
[94] By reason of the Pastoral Measure 1983: ibid, s. 27(5)(b), Sch. 3, para. 14(4). The provisions of the 1949 Act then apply subject to the necessary modifications: ibid.
[95] Or, during a vacancy in see, the guardian of the spiritualities.
[96] Marriage Act 1949, s. 23. However, nothing in the section may deprive a person of the right to be married in any church in which he would have been entitled to be married if no directions had been given, even if the banns were published only in some other church: ibid, proviso. In the absence of any such election the incumbent may decide: Legal Opinions concerning the Church of England at p. 161.
[97] This can only be a parish church or chapel in an area where the person is on the electoral roll; if a person is on the electoral roll, that is sufficent evidence that his or her usual place of worship is a parish church or chapel in that area: Marriage Act 1949, s. 72. Where a bishop has licensed a guild church in the City of London for the publication of banns and the solemnisation of marriages and a person is on the electoral roll it is deemed to be that person's usual place of worship: City of London (Guild Churches) Act 1952, s. 22(2). A clerk in Holy Orders cannot have his name on an electoral roll: Church Representation Rules, r. 1(1); see, further, r. 44(3). See, too, Legal Opinions concerning the Church of England at p. 169. A list of habitual worshippers at a cathedral under the Church Representation Rules, r. 22, is probably not an electoral roll: Legal Opinions concerning the Church of England at p. 170; Anglican Marriage in England and Wales at para. 4.3.
[98] Marriage Act 1949, s. 6(4).
[99] As to churches injured by war damage see the Marriage Act 1949, s. 19. This provision does not apply to damage caused by terrorists.
[100] There is a rebuttable presumption that the building is licensed if divine service has been performed there on several occasions: R. v. Cresswell (1876) 1 QBD 446. A minister should always endeavour to ascertain the correct position.

parish or other ecclesiastical district in which the disused church or chapel is situated[101];

(b) if no building has been so licensed, in any consecrated chapel as the diocesan bishop may in writing direct, being a chapel within that parish or district[102];

(c) if no building has been so licensed and no such direction given, in a church or chapel of any adjoining parish or other ecclesiastical district, being a church or chapel in which banns may be published and marriages solemnised[103].

(ε) Completion

Where publication has begun in any church, the publication may in some circumstances be completed in the same church or in any church which has at the time of completion taken the place of the first mentioned church[104] for the purposes of banns either generally or in relation to the parties to the intended marriage[105]. Where publication has been duly commenced in any building which ceases to be a parish church[106] or, as the case may be, ceases to be licensed for marriages, the publication may be completed in such other building, being either a parish church or a building licensed for marriages, as may be directed by the diocesan bishop to take the place of the first mentioned building for the purposes of the publication of banns[107].

. *(ζ) Military chapels*

Banns may be published and marriages solemnised in military chapels[108] between parties at least one of whom is military personnel[109], or the daughter[110] of such a person[111], at the time of the notice of publication of banns[112] or, if it is without such notice, at the date of the first publication of banns[113].

(η) At sea

Where a marriage is intended to be solemnised in England after the publication of banns between parties of whom one is residing in England and the other is an officer, seaman or marine borne on the books of one of Her Majesty's ships

---

[101] Marriage Act 1949, s. 18(1)(a).   [102] Marriage Act 1949, s. 18(1)(b).
[103] Marriage Act 1949, s. 18(1)(c).
[104] By virtue of the Union of Benefices Measure 1923, or the New Parishes Measure 1943: Marriage Act 1949, s. 10(1). These Measures are now all repealed but section 10(1) has effect as if the Pastoral Measure 1983 were included amongst the Measures there mentioned: Pastoral Measure 1983, Sch. 3, para. 14(1).   [105] Marriage Act 1949, s. 10(1).
[106] By virtue of a reorganisation scheme under the Reorganisation Areas Measure 1944: Marriage Act 1949, s. 10(2).   [107] Marriage Act 1949, s. 10(2).
[108] The chapel must be licensed in accordance with the Marriage Act 1949, ss. 68, 69.
[109] The person must be (a) serving in any of the regular armed forces of the Crown; or (b) have served in any such force, other than with a commission granted or under an engagement entered into only for the purpose of war or other national emergency; or (c) is called out on actual or permanent service or embodied as a member of a reserve of officers, a reserve force, the Territiorial Army or the Auxiliary Air Force: Marriage Act 1949, s. 68(2)(a)–(c).
[110] As no contrary intention appears, the feminine includes the masculine: Interpretation Act 1978, s. 6(b). The provision does not apply to a step daughter (or step son): Marriage Act 1949, s. 68(3).
[111] Marriage Act 1949, s. 68(2)(e).
[112] See Marriage Act 1949, s. 8; see **p. 87** *et seq. supra.*
[113] Marriage Act 1949, s. 68(3), (a), (b).

at sea, the banns may be published on three successive[114] Sundays during morning service on board that ship by the chaplain or, if there is no chaplain, by the
captain or other officer commanding the ship[115].

(c) Forbidding banns

Section 3 of the Marriage Act 1949 declares that, where the marriage of a child,
not being a widower or widow, is intended to be solemnised after the publication
of banns, then, if any person whose consent is required[116], openly and publicly
declares or causes to be declared in the church or chapel in which the banns are
published, at the time of publication, his dissent from the intended marriage the
publication of banns is void[117].

However, the actual calling of the banns requires any person knowing
any 'cause' or 'just impediment'[118], not merely a lack of consent, to the marriage
to declare it. Such an objection therefore seems to be any cause or impediment which would make the marriage void if the ceremony were to proceed[119].
The necessity for the statutory provision concerning consent is that those
banns would not otherwise be void[120]. It, therefore, seems that if any other
cause or just impediment is raised the banns are equally of no effect[121]; if this
were not so, the minister might proceed in the face of the objection[122]. Of

---

[114] In this regard the rules are different from the publication of ordinary banns: see **p. 89** *supra*.
[115] Marriage Act 1949, s. 14(1). This is subject to any adaptation made by Order in Council: *ibid*,
s. 14(2).
[116] It must be noted that this may be wider than merely a parent or guardian: see **p. 161, footnote
42** *supra*. The minister ought always to ascertain all the facts and then consult the diocesan registrar.
[117] Marriage Act 1949, s. 3(3).
[118] In this context the words seem to be used as loosely interchangeable: see the rubric before the
Vows in The Form of Solemnisation of Matrimony in the Book of Common Prayer and **p. 186** *et
seq. infra*.
[119] *Cripps on Church and Clergy* (8th ed.) at p. 546; this is borne out by the wording of the rubric
before the Vows in the Form of Solemnisation of Matrimony in the Book of Common Prayer: see
p. 186 *et seq. infra*. They would include the matters (ignoring for present purposes the mental ele-
ment of the actual couple) that are found in **paragraph B(vi)(c)***supra*: see, too, the Marriage Act
1949, s. 25(c).   [120] It is thus an additional 'cause'.
[121] This is borne out by comparison with section 14(1) of the Marriage Act 1949: ' . . . where
banns have been published, the person who published them shall, unless the banns have been
forbidden on any of the grounds on which banns may be forbidden, give a certificate of publication.'
For a different view see *Anglican Marriage in England and Wales* at para. 7.8: 'The dissent of a
qualified parent or guardian is the only ground which can render the publication of banns void.
However, other allegations of legal impediments . . . should be investigated before the marriage is
due to take place if they are prima facie supported by evidence'; *Legal Opinions concerning the
Church of England* at p. 164; see, too, the Marriage Act 1949, s. 25(c). The end result is, of course,
likely to be the same but, if the view in the text is incorrect, the publication of the banns would be
valid although there is no duty on a minister to inform another minister of the impediment, etc. The
result might be that the ceremony might nevertheless then go ahead. In *Legal Opinions concerning
the Church of England* at p. 163 it is suggested that the certificate of banns must be issued 'subject
to indorsement or amendment clearly stating that an objection has been made, and the circumstances
alleged must be fully investigated before a marriage ceremony takes place'.
[122] The objection should be noted in the banns' register: *Anglican Marriage in England and
Wales* at para 7.8.

course, if upon investigation there is no valid or sufficient cause, the publication stands[123].

The cause or impediment may be put forward by anyone[124] and, by analogy with the statutory provision as to consent, on behalf of someone else[125]. It should be declared during the service at the time of publication, although its amplification ought to be left until the end of the service[126]. If an objection (other than on the statutory ground) is made otherwise than during the service, the objection is not therefore to be ignored but, on balance, the publication of the banns may very well still stand[127].

(d) Certificates of publication

Where a marriage is intended to be solemnised after publication of banns and the persons to be married do not reside in the same parish or other ecclesiastical district, a clergyman must not solemnise the marriage in the parish or district in which one of them resides unless there is produced to him a certificate that the banns have been properly[128] published in the parish or other ecclesiastical district in which the other person resides[129].

Where a marriage is intended to be solemnised in a church or chapel of a parish or other ecclesiastical district in which neither of the persons to be married resides, after the publication of banns[130] a clergyman must not solemnise the marriage unless there is produced to him:

(i) if the persons to be married reside in the same parish or other ecclesiastical district, a certificate that the banns have been properly[131] published in that parish or district[132]; or

(ii) if the persons to be married do not reside in the same parish or other ecclesiastical district, certificates that the banns have been properly[133] published in each parish and district in which one of them resides[134].

---

[123] *Cripps on Church and Clergy* (8th ed.) at p. 546. If the ceremony is to take place in another parish, the minister of that parish ought to be informed if only so that he is properly prepared in case the objection is proceeded with at the ceremony: see **p. 186** *et seq. infra*.

[124] *Ibid.* See, too, *Cole* v. *Police Constabe 443A* [1937] 1 KB 316 at p. 335 *per* Goddard J.

[125] The fact that the objection is delegated to somebody else may very well be explicable, for example, by ill health or infirmity. Nevertheless, it may be a factor to be considered when deciding whether the objection is genuine.

[126] See, generally, **p. 237** *et seq. infra*; *Anglican Marriage in England and Wales* at para. 7.8.

[127] Unlike section 3(4) of the Marriage Act 1949, the words of publication (see **p. 87** *et seq. supra*) do not specify when the objection is to be made; nevertheless, the statute is likely to reflect the general position.

[128] That is, in accordance with Part II of the Marriage Act 1949: Marriage Act 1949, s. 11(1).

[129] Marriage Act 1949, s. 11(1). See, too, **p. 156** *et seq. infra*.

[130] By virtue of the Marriage Act 1949, s. 6(4): see **p. 166** *supra*.

[131] See **p. 87** *et seq.* and **p. 164** *et seq. supra*.   [132] Marriage Act 1949, s. 11(2)(a).

[133] See **p. 87** *et seq.* and **p. 164** *et seq. supra*.   [134] Marriage Act 1949, s. 11(2)(b).

Where banns are published in a parish or chapelry adjoining the parish or extra-parochial place in which the banns would otherwise have been published[135], a certificate that the banns have been published in that parish or chapelry is the same as a certificate that banns have been published in a parish in which one of the persons to be married resides[136].

Any such certificate must be signed by the incumbent or minister in charge of the building in which the banns were published or by a clergyman nominated in that behalf by the diocesan bishop[137]. It should, therefore, be noted that a certificate by the person who actually published the banns is not necessarily sufficient.

Where a marriage is intended to be solemnised in England after the publication of banns between parties of whom one is residing in Scotland, Northern Ireland or the Republic of Ireland, then, if the banns have been published or proclaimed in any church of the parish or place in which that other person is residing according to the law or custom there prevailing, a certificate given in accordance with that law or custom that the banns have been so published or proclaimed shall as respects that party be a sufficient certificate[138].

Where the banns of one of the parties to an intended marriage have been published at sea[139], the person who published them must give a certificate unless they were forbidden[140]; in so far as the officer, seaman or marine whose banns were called is concerned the certificate is the equivalent of banns published in England[141].

(iii)　Special licence

(a)　Generally

Special licences are rarely[142] mentioned by the Marriage Act 1949, save that[143]:

Nothing in this Act shall affect the right of the Archbishop of Canterbury or any other person by virtue of the Ecclesiastical Licences Act 1533 to grant special licences to marry at any convenient time or place or to affect the validity of any marriage solemnised on the authority of such licence.

---

[135] By reason of section 6(3) of the Marriage Act 1949: see **p. 166** *supra*. This also includes the situation where the parties have made their election under the Pastoral Measure 1983, s. 29(3): see **p. 165, footnote 85** *supra*.　　　　　　　　[136] Marriage Act 1949, s. 11(3).
[137] Marriage Act 1949, s. 11(4).
[138] Marriage Act 1949, s. 13. Unless the minister to solemnise the marriage is put on notice to the contrary he is entitled to assume that everything has been correctly done pursuant to the legal maxim *omnia praesumuntur rite esse acta*. The marriage is not void by reason only that the banns have been published in the manner required for the publication of banns in England: *ibid.*
[139] See **p. 167** *supra*.　　　　[140] Marriage Act 1949, s. 14(1).
[141] Marriage Act 1949, s. 14(2)　　　[142] See the Marriage Act 1949, ss. 5(b), 25, 79(6).
[143] Marriage Act 1949, s. 79(6).

The grant of such a licence is the particular[144] privilege of the Archbishop of Canterbury[145] and his successors 'by theym selff or by theire sufficient and sub-stanciall comissarye or deputye by theire discreacions'[146]. Nevertheless, if the licence is unreasonably refused, an appeal lies to the Lord Chancellor[147].

The archbishop may grant special licences for the solemnisation of matrimony without the publication of banns at any convenient time or place not only within the province of Canterbury but throughout all England[148].

As a matter of discretion a special licence is not granted where both parties to the intended marriage are unbaptised or where either party is divorced and the former spouse is still living[149].

In all matters pertaining to the granting of licences of marriage every ecclesiastical authority must observe the law relating thereto[150].

(b)   Effect

A special licence may permit the solemnisation of a marriage without the publication of banns wherever and whenever it is convenient[151]; in spite of Canon B 35, para. 3[152], the licence is not necessarily restricted to the the hours of 8.0a.m. to 6.0p.m.[153] and a special licence may therefore give particular authorisation to solemnise the marriage outside those hours.

In practice authority is very rarely given for a solemnisation outside the statutory hours[154] or for a marriage other than in a building customarily used for Anglican worship[155]. A real connection is usually required with the parish, church or chapel before a licence is granted[156].

It is also the practice that the special licence is made conditional upon the marriage being solemnised within three months of the grant of the licence[157].

---

[144] See *Anglican Marriage in England and Wales* at para. 10.1. As to the Bishop of Sodor and Man's powers within the Isle of Man see *Piers* v. *Piers* (1849) 2 HL Cas. 331 at pp. 362 and 364 *per* the Lord Chancellor.

[145] During a vacancy in see the licence is granted by the guardian of the spiritualities: Ecclesiastical Licences Act 1533, s. 10.

[146] Ecclesiastical Licences Act 1533, s. 3; Canon C 17, para. 7; Canon B 34, para. 1(b).

[147] Ecclesiastical Licences Act 1533, ss. 11 and 12.   [148] Canon B 34, para. 2.

[149] *Anglican Marriage in England and Wales* at paras 10.3 and 9.4.

[150] Canon B 35, para. 1.

[151] Marriage Act 1949, s. 79(6); 14 Halsbury's Laws of England (4th ed.) at para. 1023; *Anglican Marriages in England and Wales* at paras 3.3 and 10.1 *et seq.*

[152] This is both because the Ecclesiastical Licences Act 1533 Act has precedence over a Canon (see, further, Canon C 17, para. 7) and because such a licence is also a form of dispensation: see the Ecclesiastical Licences Act 1533, s. 3; 14 Halsbury's Laws of England (4th ed.) at para. 433; *Legal Opinions concerning the Church of England* at p. 165. The provisions of section 4 of the Marriage Act 1949 do not preclude it because of the saving in *ibid*, s. 79(6).

[153] See **p. 184** *et seq. infra.*

[154] *Anglican Marriage in England and Wales* at para. 10.1. It is usually only permitted in the case of serious illness: *ibid.*   [155] *Op. cit.* at para. 3.3.

[156] *Op. cit.* at para. 10.1.   [157] *Op. cit.* at para. 10.5.

(c)   Application

Application is made to the Faculty Office of the Archbishop of Canterbury[158] but before an application form is requested the parties to the intended marriage ought to obtain the views of the clergy where they reside or worship[159]. The form must be completed by the parties and the officiating clergyman[160]; an affidavit is required verifying the details and the absence of any impediment[161]. Prescribed fees are also payable[162].

(d)   Minister

The officiating minister ought always to insist upon seeing the original licence[163]. Although he has no right to question the authority or propriety of the licence[164], if there is a variation in the licence he may properly hesitate to act upon it[165]; if he suspects fraud, it is justifiable for him to delay in order to make enquiry into it[166].

(iv)   Common licences

(a)   Generally

A common licence for the solemnisation of matrimony without the publication of banns at a lawful time and at a lawful place may be granted by the archbishop of each province and by each diocesan bishop[167] within the area of their own jurisdictions; the Archbishop of Canterbury may grant common licences throughout all England[168]. This is a dispensing power[169] and may, therefore, be exercised by the Vicar-General who normally in turn delegates the hearing to a surrogate[170].

---

[158] 1, The Sanctuary, Westminster, London SW1P 3JT.

[159] *Anglican Marriage in England and Wales* at para. 10.2.

[160] This may, of course, be other than the minister actually having the cure of souls.

[161] *Ibid.* The affidavit may be sworn locally before a specially appointed commissary or by appointment at The Faculty Office: *ibid.*   [162] *Op. cit.* at para. 10.6.

[163] Cp. the provisions relating to a Superintendent Registrar's certificate: **p. 176, footnote 206** *infra*.

[164] See *Tuckniss* v. *Alexander* (1863) 32 LJ Ch 794 at p. 806 *per* Kindersley VC (common licence).

[165] *Ewing* v. *Wheatley* (1814) 2 Hag. Con. 175 at p. 185 *per* Sir William Scott (common licence).

[166] *Argar* v. *Holdsworth* (1758) 2 Lee 515 at p. 517 *per* Sir George Lee (common licence).

[167] During a vacancy licences may be granted by the guardian of the spiritualities: 14 Halsbury's Laws of England (4th ed.) at para. 1023, note 5.

[168] Ecclesiastical Licences Act 1533, s. 9; Ecclesiastical Jurisdiction Act 1847, s. 5; Canon B 34, paras 1(c) and 3.   [169] See the Ecclesiastical Licences Act 1533, s. 9.

[170] Marriage Act 1949, s. 16(4); 14 Halsbury's Laws of England (4th ed.) at para. 1023; *Anglican Marriage in England and Wales* at para. 9.6. The Vicar-General is the ecclesiastical authority 'having power to grant such a licence' within the meaning of the Marriage Act 1949, s. 5(c); Vicars-General are therefore also the 'others who of ancient right have been accustomed to issue a common licence' within the meaning of Canon B 34, para. 3.

The issue of common licences is a matter of favour, not of right[171], and therefore no appeal lies from its refusal[172]. However, in all matters pertaining to the granting of licences of marriage every ecclesiastical authority must observe the law relating thereto[173].

Unlike a special licence a common licence only dispenses from the need for banns; it cannot authorise a marriage to be solemnised outside the normal hours or in a special place[174]. Where a marriage is not solemnised within three calendar months after the grant of a common licence the licence is void and no minister should solemnise the marriage on its authority[175].

As a matter of discretion a common licence is usually not granted where both parties to the intended marriage are unbaptised or where either party is divorced and the former spouse is still living[176].

(b) Surrogates

A surrogate is a deputy of the Vicar-General[177] and his appointment lapses with that of the Vicar-General. He is appointed under the seal of the Vicar-General[178] but before the surrogate may grant any licence he must take an oath before the Vicar-General, or a commissioner appointed under the seal of that judge, faithfully to execute his office according to law to the best of his knowledge[179].

(c) Pre-requisites

A common licence must not be granted unless one of the persons to be married has sworn before a person having authority to grant such a licence:

(i) that he or she believes that there is no impediment of kindred or alliance or any other lawful cause, nor any suit commenced in any court, to bar or hinder the solemnisation of the marriage in accordance with the licence[180];
(ii) that one of the persons to be married has had his or her usual place of residence[181] in the parish or other ecclesiastical district in which the

---

[171] In cases of difficulty, such as the marriage of a foreigner (if such cases are delegated to him), a surrogate is well advised to seek advice from the diocesan registrar: see *Legal Opinions concerning the Church of England* at p. 165.
[172] 14 Halsbury's Laws of England (4th ed.) at para. 1023, note 7.
[173] Canon B 35, para. 1.
[174] Canon B 34, para. 3; 14 Halsbury's Laws of England (4th ed.) at para. 1023.
[175] Marriage Act 1949, s. 16(3); Interpretation Act 1978, s. 5, Sch. 1.
[176] *Anglican Marriage in England and Wales* at para. 9.4. In such cases the application should always be referred to the Vicar-General.
[177] 14 Halsbury's Laws of England (4th ed.) at para. 1275, note 1. *Anglican Marriage in England and Wales* at para. 9.6.   [178] Nowadays this is usually the seal of the consistory court.
[179] Marriage Act 1949, s. 16(4).   [180] Marriage Act 1949, s. 16(1)(a).
[181] This is a different criterion from that of 'residence': cp. Marriage Act 1949, ss. 6 and 34; see, too, **p. 165 *et seq. supra*.** Although actual residence is required, the party need not be actually resident at the relevant time; particular care is therefore required in relation to members of the armed forces, students and the like: see *Anglican Marriage in England and Wales* at para. 5.3.

marriage is to be solemnised for fifteen days immediately before the grant of the licence or that the parish or authorised chapel in which the marriage is to be solemnised is the usual place of worship of those persons or one of them[182];

(iii) where one of the persons to be married is a child and is not a widower or widow, that the consent of the person or persons whose consent to the marriage is required has been obtained, that the necessity of obtaining any such consent has been dispensed with, that the court has consented to the marriage[183], or that there is no person whose consent to the marriage is required[184].

In relation to those whose marriage would otherwise be void by reason of affinity but who fall within the exceptions for those over twenty-one years of age[185], no common licence may be granted unless evidence is produced to satisfy the issuing authority that the relevant preconditions are fulfilled[186].

(d) Foreigners

It is most advisable that surrogates should in the first instance refer applications in relation to foreigners to the diocesan registrar[187].

(e) Consent

If consents cannot be obtained by reason of absence or inaccessibility of the person whose consent is required, or by reason of his being under a disability, the ecclesiastical authority[188] by whom the licence is to be granted may dispense with its necessity if the marriage is to be under the authority of a common licence[189].

---

[182] Marriage Act 1949, s. 16(1)(b).   [183] See, too, **p. 162** *supra.*

[184] Marriage Act 1949, s. 16(1)(c). The consents, etc. referred to are those under *op. cit.*, s. 3. Those whose consents are necessary are the same as those who may forbid the banns (see **p. 161, footnote 42** *supra*), save that the consent of the local authority is in addition to that of any parent having parental authority or of any guardian.   [185] See **p. 160** *supra.*

[186] Marriage Act 1949, s. 16(1A), (1B). As to the preconditions see **p. 160** *supra.* In relation to section 1(2) there must be a written declaration by both persons specifying their affinial relationship and declaring that the younger of those persons has not at any time before attaining the age of eighteen been a child of the family in relation to the other: Marriage Act 1949, s. 16(1A)(b). No such written declaration is necessary where, after application by one of the parties, the ecclesiastical judge out of whose office the licence is to issue has himself issued a declaration that there is no impediment of affinity to the solemnisation of the marriage: Marriage Act 1949, s. 16(2B). See, too, p. 270 *et seq. infra.*   [187] *Anglican Marriage in England and Wales* at para. 9.3.

[188] See, too, **p. 172, footnote 170** *supra.* A surrogate cannot dispense with consent: see **p. 162, footnote 52** *supra.*

[189] Marriage Act 1949, s. 3(1), (2). If there is no other person whose consent is required, the dispensing authority is the Dean of the Arches: *ibid.* See, too, **p. 162** *et seq. supra.*

(f) Caveats

A caveat may be entered against the grant of a common licence[190]; it must be signed by, or on behalf of, the person by whom it is entered[191] and must state his place of residence and the ground of the objection on which the caveat is founded[192]. Once this has been done no licence may be granted until the caveat, or a copy, is transmitted to the ecclesiastical judge out of whose office the licence is to issue and the judge has certified to the registrar of the diocese[193] that he has examined into the matter and is satisfied that it ought not to obstruct the grant of the licence[194].

A caveat may also be withdrawn[195]. However, even if a caveat that the marriage would be void on the grounds of affinity as either the parties were not over twenty-one or that one of them at any time before attaining the age of eighteen has been a child of the family in relation to the other[196] is withdrawn, no licence may be granted until the judge has certifed that he has examined into that ground of objection and is satisfied that that ground ought not to obstruct the grant of the licence[197].

(g) Minister

The officiating minister ought always to insist upon seeing the original licence[198]. Although he has no right to question the authority or propriety of the licence[199], if there is a variation in the licence he may properly hesitate to act upon it[200]; if he suspects fraud, it is justifiable for him to delay in order to make enquiry into it[201].

---

[190] Marriage Act 1949, s. 16(2). Presumably the caveat should be lodged both with the appropriate surrogate and, out of an abundance of caution, at the provincial and diocesan registries. In *Anglican Marriage in England and Wales* at para. 9.8 it is stated that the caveat must be lodged in the registry. To be fully effective the caveat should be entered in the provincial registry and the Faculty Office of the Archbishop of Canterbury as well: *ibid*. It is an offence for a person to forbid the issue of a licence falsely representing, knowing it to be false, that he is a person whose consent is required: Perjury Act 1911, s. 3(1)(c). Similarly, it is an offence to enter a caveat against a declaration under the Marriage Act 1949, s. 16(1A) knowing it to be false in a material particular: Perjury Act 1911, s. 3(1)(d).

[191] It therefore must be in writing although no particular form is required: see *Anglican Marriage in England and Wales* at para. 9.8.   [192] Marriage Act 1949, s. 16(2).

[193] Presumably in appropriate cases this embraces the provincial registrar.

[194] Marriage Act 1949, s. 16(2).   [195] *Ibid*.   [196] See **p. 160** *supra*.

[197] Marriage Act 1949, s. 16(2A).

[198] Cp. the provisions relating to a Superintendent Registrar's certificate: **p. 176, footnote 206** *infra*.

[199] See *Tuckniss* v. *Alexander* (1863) 32 LJ Ch 794 at p. 806 *per* Kindersley VC. What matters is that the parties are sufficiently identified, not that all the particulars are accurate: *Bevan* v. *M'Mahon* (1861) 2 Sw. & Tr. 230 at pp. 239–340 *per* the Judge Ordinary.

[200] *Ewing* v. *Wheatley* (1814) 2 Hag. Con. 175 at p. 185 *per* Sir William Scott.

[201] *Argar* v. *Holdsworth* (1758) 2 Lee 515 at p. 517 *per* Sir George Lee.

(v)   Superintendent Registrar's certificate

A marriage according to the rites of the Church of England may be solemnised on the authority of a Superintendent Registrar's certificate[202] in any church or chapel[203] in which banns of marriage may be published[204]. However, a marriage may not be solemnised on the authority of a Superintendent Registrar's certificate within twenty-one days of the notice being entered in the marriage notice book[205] nor once three calendar months thereafter has expired[206].

A marriage must not be solemnised on the authority of such a certificate in any church or chapel without the consent of the minister thereof; moreover, it can only be solemnised by a clergyman[207].

D   Minister

(i)   Generally

A marriage must be solemnised by a person in Holy Orders[208]. Deacons as well as priests may validly solemnise marriage[209], although neither may solemnise their own wedding[210].

[202] A Superintendent Registrar may not issue a licence dispensing with the requirement of the twenty-one days waiting period in relation to marriages according to the rites of the Church of England: Marriage Act 1949, s. 26(2) proviso.

[203] A Superintendent Registrar's licence cannot authorise a marriage elsewhere (Marriage (Registrar General's Licence) Act 1970, s. 1(1) proviso) except that in relation to a person who is housebound or who is a detained person the certificate may also permit it to be be solemnised in the place where he usually resides: Marriage Act 1949, ss. 17 and 26(1)(dd).

[204] Marriage Act 1949, s. 17; Canon B 34, para. 1(d). The Superintendent Registrar may issue a certificate notwithstanding that the church or chapel is not within a registration district in which either of the persons to be married resides: *op. cit.*, s. 35(3).

[205] Marriage Act 1949, s. 31(4). See, too, **p. 196 *et seq. infra.***

[206] Marriage Act 1949, s. 33; Interpretation Act 1978, s. 5, Sch. 1. The notice and certificate are then both void: Marriage Act 1949, s. 33(2). The certificate or certificates must be delivered to the officiating clergyman (s.50(1)(f)) unless the service is in a chapel of the armed forces in which case it must be delivered to the appointed clergyman in whose presence the marriage is to be solemnised: *op. cit.*, s. 69(1), Sch. 4, Pt II. See, too, **p. 196 *et seq. infra.***

[207] Marriage Act 1949, s. 17 proviso.

[208] Marriage Act 1949, s. 75(1)(d). See, too, the different rites *passim*; Marriage Act 1949, s. 17 proviso. The clergyman must be 'in orders recognised by the Church of England': *R* v. *Millis* (1844) 10 Cl. & Fin. 534 at p. 906 *per* Lord Cottenham. See, also, **p. 193 *infra*.**

[209] *R* v. *Millis* (1844) 10 Cl. & Fin. 534 at pp. 656 *per* Lord Tindal CJ, 746 *per* Lord Abinger and 859–860 *per* Lord Lyndhurst LC; *Cope* v. *Barber* (1872) LR 7 CP 393 at p. 403 *per* Willes J; 14 Halsbury's Laws of England (4th ed.) at para. 664. The position remains the same in spite of the repeal of the Act of Uniformity 1662. For reservations see Briden & Hanson, *Moore's Introduction to English Canon Law* (3rd ed.) at p. 76, especially footnote 12, although the authors conclude that ' . . . if a clear case were to arise, it seems almost certain that a marriage at which a deacon officiated would be held to be valid.'

[210] *Beamish* v. *Beamish* (1861) 9 HL Cas. 274.

The Archbishops have issued guidelines in relation to the solemnisation of marriage by deacons[211]. These state:

1. The minister officiating at a marriage service in the Church of England should normally be a bishop or priest[212];
2. A deacon may officiate at a marriage only if the consent of the incumbent and/or minister is first given[213];
3. The authorised services should be used without variation[214] whether the officiating minister is bishop, priest or deacon;
4. When a priest is present he may delegate to a deacon parts of the service including:

> (i)   the blessing of the ring(s);
> (ii) the pronouncement of the blessing(s) on the couple.

The priest should pronounce the blessing of the congregation at the end of the service.

These, of course, are no more than guidelines but they incorporate matters of law and doctrine and should therefore only be departed from with great hesitation. For example, the pronoucement of an inclusive blessing of the congregation might now be justified under Canon B 5, para. 1; nevertheless, by reason of Canon B 5, para. 3, the same would not be the case in relation to the blessing of the couple whichever rite is used[215].

Unless he is a clerk in Holy Orders of the Church of England[216] no person can

---

[211] *Guidelines issued jointly by the Archbishops of Canterbury and York* in July 1992, printed in *The Canons of the Church of England* at pp. 187–188; *Anglican Marriage in England and Wales* at para. 14.3.

[212] 'Where the incumbent or minister has colleagues who are in holy orders (priests as well as deacons) the decision as to who should solemnise the marriage of a particular couple belongs to the incumbent or minister. Consideration should be given to the wishes of the couple and there should be discussion at the parish staff meeting or other consultation between colleagues. In considering who should be officiating minister, pastoral considerations are important. A significant factor may be that the person who is to solemnise the marriage should also have prepared the couple for the wedding; in the case of a newly ordained deacon (man or woman) it needs to be noted that training to undertake marriage preparation is at present primarily a post-ordination task and colleges and courses do not require students to develop skills in this area before ordination. In the first year following ordination as deacon therefore, a deacon should rarely, if ever, solemnise a marriage and should only do so for exceptional reasons': *op. cit.* at p. 187, note 1.

[213] 'Reference to the incumbent and minister mean the incumbent of the parish to which the deacon is licensed and minister means minister or priest-in-charge of the church in which the service is to take place': *op. cit.* at p. 188, note 2.

[214] See, too, *Beamish* v. *Beamish* (1861) 9 HL Cas. 274 at 330: ' . . . we must protest against its being supposed to be . . . either wise or right to leave out any part of the service.' However, this cannot affect the minister's limited powers under Canon B 5, para. 1.

[215] See, too, **p. 126** *et seq. supra.*

[216] This includes a clergyman given written permission to officiate by the Archbishop of Canterbury under the Overseas and Other Clergy (Ministry and Ordination) Measure 1967: see Halsbury's Laws of England (4th ed.) at para. 667. The Anglican minister would be well advised to require sight

solemnise a marriage according to the rites of the Church of England[217]. Canon B 43, para. 1(1)(e), therefore, states:

> A minister or lay person who is a member in good standing of a Church to which this Canon applies and is a baptised person may, subject to the provisions of this Canon[218], be invited ...
>
> (e)   to assist at ... the solemnisation of Matrimony ...

In the result the Anglican minister must as a bare minimum take paragraphs 6–19 in the Alternative Service Book, or their equivalent in the Book of Common Prayer, together perhaps[219] with the final blessing[220].

Other than under the Sharing of Church Buildings Act 1969[221], a ceremony of marriage according to a rite other than that of the Church of England or by a person who is not a clerk in Holy Orders in the Church of England is illegal[222].

(ii)   Military chapel

In a military chapel the ceremony must take place in the presence of a clergyman specially appointed for the purpose of registering such marriages[223].

E   Location

(i)   Generally

Save when the marriage is solemnised under the authority of a special licence[224], a marriage must be solemnised in a church or other building[225] in which banns may

---

of that permission. A clergyman in the Episcopal Church of Scotland may solemnise the marriage if invited to do so by the minister having the cure of souls: Episcopal Church (Scotland) Act 1964, s. 1(1). The position of clergymen in the Church of Ireland who do not have written permission under the 1967 Act is unclear: *Legal Opinions of the Church of England* at p. 174; *Anglican Marriage in England and Wales* at para. 14.1. See, too, **p. 17, footnote 115** *supra*.

[217]   Church of England (Ecumenical Relations) Measure 1988, s. 3(b). The Anglican minister must therefore sign the register book as the officiating minister although the other minister may, of course, sign as a witness: *Legal Opinions concerning the Church of England* at p. 173.

[218]   See **p. 26** *supra*.

[219]   *Anglican Marriage in England and Wales* at para. 14.5 states: ' ... as a minimum, the charge to the couple should be read and the vows tendered by the Anglican minister, who should also pronounce (or invoke) the blessing of the couple'.

[220]   *Legal Opinions concerning the Church of England* at pp. 172–173.

[221]   See 14 Halsbury's Laws of England (4th ed.) at para. 1190.

[222]   *Legal Opinions concerning the Church of England* at pp. 172–174.

[223]   Marriage Act 1949, s. 69(4).   [224]   Marriage Act 1949, ss. 5(b), 25, 79(6).

[225]   Where a parish has no parish church the bishop may designate a parish centre of worship which thereupon is deemed to be a parish church for the purposes of the Marriage Act 1949. If persons to be married so elect, they may proceed under ss. 6 and 15 of the Marriage Act 1949, as if it has not been so designated and as if there is no church licensed for marriage or in which divine service is usually solemnised every Sunday: Pastoral Measure 1983, s. 29(2), (3). See, too, *Legal Opinions concerning the Church of England* at p. 166.

be called[226]. The only other exception is in relation to a person who is housebound or who is a detained person; in these cases the ceremony may take place where the person usually resides but only on the authority of a Superintendent Registrar's certificate[227].

A cathedral which is also a parish church is in the same position as any other parish church; any other cathedral, however, must be licensed by the diocesan bishop[228].

If a parish has more than one parish church marriages may be solemnised in any of them[229].

(ii) After publication of banns

Where banns have been published the marriage must normally be solemnised in the church or chapel or, as the case may be, in one of the churches or chapels in which the banns have been published[230]. However, where after completion of publication another church has become a church in which they could have been published[231] in relation to those parties, the marriage may be solemnised in that other church[232].

Moreover, where two or more benefices are held in plurality[233], or where there are two parishes or parish churches in the area of a single benefice[234], the diocesan bishop[235] may direct in writing where marriages of persons entitled to be married in any of those churches may be solemnised[236].

Where any church or chapel in which banns may be published and marriages solemnised is being rebuilt or repaired[237] and for that reason not being used for

---

[226] See the Marriage Act 1949, ss. 25(a), 75(2), (a). As to where banns may be called see **p. 164** *et seq. supra*. A minister who solemnises a marriage elsewhere commits both a civil and an ecclesiastical offence: Marriage Act 1949, s. 75(1)(c), (4); *Middleton* v. *Crofts* (1736) 2 Atk. 650; see, too, **p. 196** *et seq. infra*. The diocesan bishop may license a public chapel for the publication of banns and the solemnisation of marriages under section 20 of the Marriage Act 1949. As to authorisation in extra-parochial places see *op. cit.*, s. 21.

[227] Marriage Act 1949, ss. 25(a), 26(1)(dd). See, too, **p. 196** *et seq. infra*.

[228] Marriage Act 1949, s. 21; *Legal Opinions concerning the Church of England* at p. 170. A resident in a diocese possibly has the right to be married in the cathedral: see *Re the Pews of the Cathedral of St Columb, Londonderry* (1863) LT 861 *per* Dr Todd at p. 864.

[229] Pastoral Measure 1983, s. 27(5).

[230] Marriage Act 1949, s. 12(1). A guild church in the City of London may be licensed for the publication of banns: City of London (Guild Churches) Act 1952, s. 22(1).

[231] By reason of the Pastoral Measure 1983.

[232] Pastoral Measure 1983, Sch. 3, para. 14(2).

[233] Under the Pastoral Reorganisation Measure 1949 (now repealed).

[234] By reason of the Pastoral Measure 1983: *ibid*, s. 27(5)(b), Sch. 3, para. 14(4). The provisions of the Marriage Act 1949 then apply subject to the necessary modifications: *ibid*.

[235] Or, during a vacancy in see, the guardian of the spiritualities.

[236] Marriage Act 1949, s. 23. However, nothing in the section may deprive a person of the right to be married in any church in which he would have been entitled to be married if no directions had been given, even if the banns were published only in some other church: *ibid*, s. 23 proviso.

[237] As to churches injured by war damage see the Marriage Act 1949, s. 20. This provision does not apply to damage caused by terrorists.

divine service, marriages which could otherwise have been solemnised there may be solemnised[238]:

(a) in any building licensed[239] by the bishop for the performance of divine service during the disuse of the church or chapel, being a building within the parish or other ecclesiastical district in which the disused church or chapel is situated[240];

(b) if no building has been so licensed, in any consecrated chapel as the diocesan bishop may in writing direct, being a chapel within that parish or district[241];

(c) if no building has been so licensed and no such direction given, in a church or chapel of any adjoining parish or other ecclesiastical district, being a church or chapel in which banns may be published and marriages solemnised[242].

(iii) Special licence

A special licence may permit the solemnisation wherever it is convenient[243]. However, only rarely is permission given for solemnisation other than in a building used for Anglican worship[244].

(iv) Common licence

Except when churches are disused[245], a common licence must not be granted for the solemnisation of a marriage in any church or chapel other than:

(i) the parish church of the parish, or an authorised chapel of the ecclesiastical district, in which one of the persons to be married has had his or her usual place of residence[246] for fifteen days immediately before the grant of the licence; or

(ii) a parish church or authorised chapel which is the usual place of worship of the persons to be married or of one of them[247].

For these purposes any parish in which there is no parish church or chapel belonging to it or no church or chapel in which divine service is usually solemnised

---

[238] Any such marriage must be registered in the marriage register book kept by the incumbent of the disused church or chapel: Marriage Act 1949, s. 18(3).

[239] As to licensing see **p. 166** *supra*.   [240] Marriage Act 1949, s. 18(1)(a).

[241] Marriage Act 1949, s. 18(1)(b). Any fees payable for the solemnisation must be applied as the bishop, with the consent of the incumbent of the disused church or chapel, may in writing direct: Marriage Act 1949, s. 18(2).   [242] Marriage Act 1949, s. 18(1)(c).

[243] Marriage Act 1949, s. 79(6).   [244] See **p. 171** *supra*.

[245] See the Marriage Act 1949, ss. 19 and 20, and **p. 166** *et seq. supra*.

[246] See **p. 165** *supra*.

[247] Marriage Act 1949, s. 15(1). A guild church in the City of London may be licensed for the solemnisation of matrimony and a person on the electoral roll of that church is deemed to have that church as his or her usual place of worship: City of London (Guild Churches) Act 1952, s. 22(2).

every Sunday, and any extra-parochial place which has no authorised chapel, is deemed to belong to any adjoining parish or chapelry[248].

Where, after the issue of a common licence for the solemnisation of a marriage in a church, another church has taken the place of that church as a church in which the marriage of those parties ought to be solemnised, the marriage may be solemnised in that other church[249].

(v) Military chapels

When the marriage is in a military chapel the relevant party[250] must qualify at the relevant date[251].

(vi) During the ceremony

The rubric at the commencement of the Form of Solemnization of Matrimony in the Book of Common Prayer states that the service should begin in 'the body of the Church', whereas later rubrics indicate that the minister and the married couple should proceed to the Lord's Table after the psalm[252]. The Alternative Service Book merely indicates that after the psalm 'the husband and wife kneel before the holy table'[253]. Because such emphasis is placed throughout the law relating to matrimony on the openness of the ceremony, the commencement of the service in the body of the church seems to be a matter of Church order and therefore to apply to both rites[254]. Indeed, for the same reason it would not seem to be a matter capable of falling within the ambit of Canon B 5, para. 1[255]; the same may be said in relation to the procession to the altar, as the Alternative Service Book seems to go out of its way to stress it.

F Duty to Marry

Subject to the exceptions set out below, a minister is under a duty to solemnise a marriage in accordance with a special or common licence[256]. Similarly, after

---

[248] Marriage Act 1949, s. 15(2).   [249] Pastoral Measure 1983, Sch. 3, para. 14(5).

[250] This does not include a step son or step daughter of the military person: see Marriage Act 1949, s. 68(2); **p. 167 *supra*.**

[251] See *ibid*. Where the marriage is by common licence the relevant date is the date of taking the oath under section 16: Marriage Act 1949, s. 68(3)(c).

[252] See the rubrics before and after the Psalm.

[253] Note 24 at p. 296. Series 1 Solemnisation of Matrimony (Cambridge University Press; Oxford University Press; SPCK) follows the rubric in the Book of Common Prayer: *op. cit.* at pp. 3 and 8.

[254] See *R* v. *James* (1850) 3 Car. & Kir. 167 at p. 177 *per* Alderson B. Indeed, the reference to kneeling before the holy table may be seen as implying that the couple are to be elsewhere until that time.

[255] Nevertheless, a marriage that takes place in the vestry is valid: *Wing* v. *Taylor* (1861) 2 Sw. & Tr. 278 at p. 286.

[256] *Argar* v. *Holdsworth* (1758) 2 Lee 515 at p. 517 *per* Sir George Lee: ' ... I was of opinion a licence was a legal authority for marriage, and that a minister was guilty of a breach of duty who should refuse to marry pursuant to a proper licence from his ordinary', namely, the diocesan chancellor. *Tuckniss* v. *Alexander* (1863) 32 LJ Ch 794 at p. 806 *per* Kindersley VC: 'Therefore it

the publication of banns there is a duty to solemnise a marriage in the church or chapel, or in one of them[257], in which the banns have been published[258]. There is no duty to solemnise a marriage on the grounds of a Superintendent Registrar's certificate[259].

A minister who is in breach of this duty is guilty of an ecclesiastical offence[260]. It is unclear whether such a breach is also an indictable offence[261] or whether it gives rise to an action in damages[262].

Nevertheless, no minister is obliged to solemnise a marriage which, apart from the Marriage (Prohibited Degrees of Relationship) Act 1986, would have been void by reason of the relationship of the persons to be married[263]. What is more, no clergyman of the Church of England or the Church of Wales is compelled to solemnise a marriage of any person whose former marriage has been dissolved and whose former spouse is still living[264].

---

appears to me that . . . if the licence is duly framed and presented to him, [the minister] has no right to question the authority or propriety of that licence; he is bound to marry the parties according to it; and . . . the minister has no option but to perform the marriage according to the bishop's licence.' On the other hand, if there is a variation in the licence, the minister may properly hesitate to act upon it: *Ewing* v. *Wheatley* (1814) 2 Hag. Con. 175 at p. 1185 *per* Sir William Scott. He may also delay the ceremony if he has reason to suspect fraud (*Argar* v. *Holdsworth* (1758) 2 Lee 515 at p. 517 *per* Sir George Lee) or if a party is clearly under age: *Millet* v. *Rowse* (1802) 7 Ves. 419.

[257] The choice must be that of the parties to the intended marriage: cp. Pastoral Measure 1983, s. 29(3).

[258] Marriage Act 1949, s. 12(1); *R* v. *James* (1850) 3 Car. & Kir. 167 at p. 175 *per* Alderson B; *R* v. *Ellis* (1888) 16 Cox CC 469; 14 Halsbury's Laws of England (4th ed.) at para. 1003. The latter at note 2 is perhaps infelicitously worded; it does not mean that unbaptised persons may be refused marriage if they have actually obtained a licence. The question of the propriety of issuing a licence, however, is one solely for the issuing authority: see the quotations from *Argar* v. *Holdsworth* (1758) 2 Lee 515 and *Tuckniss* v. *Alexander* (1863) 32 LJ Ch 794 (cited in **footnote 256 supra**) and **p. 171 et seq. supra**.

[259] See the Marriage Act 1949, ss. 17, 26(2) proviso. Cp. *R* v. *James* (1850) 3 Car. & Kir. 167.

[260] *Argar* v. *Holdsworth* (1758) 2 Lee 515; *Tuckniss* v. *Alexander* (1863) 32 LJ Ch 794; *R* v. *James* (1850) 3 Car. & Kir. 167. There is probably no offence unless a definite request has been made and the parties have presented themselves at the church or chapel when the minister is not engaged in another duty: *Davis* v. *Black* (1841) 1 QB 900 at p. 906 *per* Kindersley VC: ' . . . if a licence is produced to a clergyman from his ordinary, from his diocese, directing him, or in terms authorizing him, to marry two persons in his church or chapel, his canonical obedience requires him, as well as the rights of the parties require him, to perform the marriage according to that licence'. Similarly, the other canonical requirements must first have been fulfilled: Canon B 35, para. 4: *R* v. *James* (1850) 3 Car. & Kir. 167. It would seem to be the obligation of the parties to provide witnesses: see Canon B 35, para. 5. The rubrics at the commencement of The Form of Solemnization of Matrimony in the Book of Common Prayer state that 'At the day and time appointed for the solemnization of Matrimony, the persons to be married shall come into the body of the Church with their friends and neighbours . . . ' The minister cannot escape his duty by failing to agree a day or time: see **supra**.   [261] *R* v. *James* (1850) 3 Car. & Kir. 167.

[262] *Argar* v. *Holdsworth* (1758) 2 Lee 515 at p. 516 *per* Sir George Lee; *Davis* v. *Black* (1841) 1 QB 900. However, in *R*. v. *Ellis* (1888) 16 Cox CC 469 at p. 471 Pollock B, described it as 'a duty which . . . they cannot decline to perform without being made liable to civil consequences.' Different considerations may arise if the minister has agreed to take the service and then fails to do so. If an action for damages can be brought, it would be irrelevant that the wedding has been insured.

[263] Marriage Act 1949, s. 5A. This includes all those marriages referred to in **Appendix 5, Parts II and III**.   [264] Matrimonial Causes Act 1965, s. 8(2).

The fact that one of the parties[265] intending to be married is not baptised[266], confirmed[267] or a member of the Church of England[268] is irrelevant[269]. However, these matters may be taken into consideration by the minister of the church or chapel where the marriage is intended to be solemnised when considering whether to give his consent[270].

Where one of the parties to the intended wedding is a foreigner[271], or has his permanent home outside the United Kingdom, it is advisable that the marriage should be by licence rather than by banns[272]. This is to ensure that the legal requirements of the foreigner's country are observed[273]. Moreover, if the officiating minister has good reason to doubt whether the congregation or parties understand the essential parts of the service, it would seem that he should delay the ceremony until an interpreter is to hand[274].

G   Time

(i)   Generally

Where a marriage is not solemnised within three calendar months after the completion of the publication of banns that publication is void and no clergyman may solemnise marriage on its authority[275]. Similarly, a common licence is only valid for three calendar months and no marriage may be solemnised thereafter on its authority[276]. A marriage may not be solemnised on the authority of a Superintendent Registrar's certificate within twenty-one days of the notice being entered in the marriage notice book[277] nor once three calendar months thereafter has expired[278]. A special licence expires after the time therein specified[279].

---

[265] Or both of them.

[266] See *Jenkins* v. *Barrett* (1827) 1 Hag. Ecc. 12 at p. 21. See, too, **p. 130, footnote 3**, and **p. 181, footnote 256** *supra*.   [267] See *R* v. *James* (1850) 3 Car. & Kir. 167.

[268] See *Jones* v. *Robinson* (1815) 2 Phillim. 285.

[269] As the Marriage Act ss. 8, 12(1), are imperative; see, too, the cases cited in **p. 181, footnote 256** *supra* concerning licences; Briden & Hanson, *Moore's Introduction to English Canon Law* (3rd ed.) at p. 76. The authority issuing a licence may, however, take such matters into consideration: see **p. 173** *supra*; *Anglican Marriage in England and Wales* at paras 9.4 and 10.3.

[270] See the Marriage Act 1949, s. 17.

[271] As to banns see **p. 87** *et seq. supra*. As to interpreters see **p. 191** *infra*.

[272] Before granting such a licence a surrogate should consult with the diocesan registrar: *Legal Opinions concerning the Church of England* at p. 165.   [273] *Ibid.*

[274] See **p. 191** *infra*.

[275] Marriage Act 1949, s. 12(2); Interpretation Act 1978, s. 5, Sch. 1. See, too, **p. 196** *et seq. infra*.

[276] Marriage Act 1949, s. 16(1); Interpretation Act 1978, s. 5, Sch. 1.

[277] Marriage Act 1949, s. 31(4). This requirement cannot be dispensed with if the marriage is to be according to the rites of the Church of England: Marriage Act 1949, s. 26(2) proviso.

[278] Marriage Act 1949, s. 33(2); Interpretation Act 1978, s. 5, Sch. 1. The notice and certificate are then both void. See, too, **p. 196** *et seq. infra*.

[279] In practice a special licence is only granted for three months: *Anglican Marriage in England and Wales* at para. 10.5.

(ii) Hours

The Marriage Act 1949, section 4, provides that:

A marriage may be solemnised at any time between the hours of eight in the forenoon and six in the afternoon[280].

Canon B 35, para. 3, however states:

A marriage may not be solemnised at any unseasonable hours but only between the hours of eight in the forenoon and six in the afternoon.

The provision of the Canon as to 'unseasonable', or untimely, hours only seems to mean that the the minister cannot have a ceremony foisted upon him that is difficult for him to attend because of his other engagements[281]; nevertheless, the ceremony must take a high precedence particularly if he is under a duty to solemnise the marriage[282]. In this regard both the Act and the Canon are subject to the provisions of a special licence[283].

The Legal Advisory Commission has given its opinion that the minister 'must say the whole rite and perform the whole ceremony . . . by 6.00pm.' However, the registration may take place after that hour as long as it immediately follows the ceremony[284].

It is unnecessary that the marriage should take place at the time of divine service[285], although:

It is convenient that the newly-married persons should receive the holy Communion at the time of their Marriage, or at the first opportunity after their Marriage[286].

H Witnesses

The marriage must be solemnised in the presence of two or more witnesses in addition to the clergyman by whom it is solemnised[287]. It would seem to be the obligation of the parties to provide the witnesses[288].

---

[280] See, too, **p. 196 *et seq. infra*.**
[281] See, too, *Anglican Marriage in England and Wales* at para. 6.3.
[282] See **p. 181 *et seq. supra*.**   [283] See **p. 171 *supra*.**
[284] Marriage Act 1949, s. 55(1); *Legal Opinions concerning the Church of England* at p. 175.
[285] In spite of the repeal of the Canon amending Canon 62 of 1887. The Alternative Service Book is silent upon the matter whereas the Book of Common Prayer merely says 'At the day and time appointed . . . ': see the rubrics at the beginning of The Form of Solemnisation of Matrimony.
[286] See the rubrics at end of The Form of Solemnisation of Matrimony in the Book of Common Prayer; Stephens, *The Book of Common Prayer*, vol. III, at pp. 623–1625.
[287] Marriage Act 1949, s. 22; Canon B 35, para. 4.
[288] See Canon B 35, para. 5. The rubrics at the commencement of The Form of Solemnisation of Matrimony in the Book of Common Prayer state that 'At the day and time appointed for the solemnization of Matrimony, the persons to be married shall come into the body of the Church with their friends and neighbours . . . '

If an interpreter is used, it is advisable that he should be one of the witnesses to sign the register book[289].

I Rites of Matrimony

(i) Generally

The only essentials to a valid marriage are the reciprocal agreement of the parties to a marriage for life[290], the joining together of their hands[291] and the pronouncement by the minister that they are man and wife[292]. It follows that the omission of these matters, at the least, cannot be justified by Canon B 5, para. 1.

(ii) Choice

(a) Rite

There are three rites of matrimony authorised for use under Canon B 1, para. 1: the Form of Solemnisation of Matrimony in the Book of Common Prayer, the Marriage Service in the Alternative Service Book[293] and Series 1 Solemnisation of Marriage[294].

As has been seen[295], Canon B 3, para. 4, in the first instance gives the choice as to which marriage service is to be used to the minister who is to conduct the service[296] but:

> ... if any of the persons concerned objects beforehand to the use of the service selected by the minister and he[297] and the minister cannot agree as to which form is to be used, the matter shall be referred to the bishop of the diocese for his decision.

---

[289] *Legal Opinions concerning the Church of England* at p. 171.

[290] Indeed, it is arguable that this plighting of troth is all that is required: *Beamish* v. *Beamish* (1861) 9 HL Cas. 274 at pp. 329–330; *R* v. *Millis* (1844) 10 Cl. & Fin. 534 at p. 748 *per* Lord Campbell.

[291] Presumably even this would not be so in the case of a disabled person: see, further, *Beamish* v. *Beamish* (1861) 9 HL Cas.274 at pp. 329–330.

[292] *Harrod* v. *Harrod* (1854) 1 K. & J. 4 at pp. 15–16; *Beamish* v. *Beamish* (1861) 9 HL Cas. 274 at p. 339 *per* Lord Campbell. See, further, *Weld* v. *Chamberlaine* (1683) 2 Show. 300; *More* v. *More* (1741) 2 Atk. 157. In the *Legal Opinions concerning the Church of England* at p. 171 it is suggested within the context of the translation of the service for foreigners that the essentials 'include the charge, promises and vows'; it is, of course, essential to translate the charge so that the duty to disclose impediments is clearly understood.

[293] *Op. cit.* at p. 283 *et seq.*   [294] *Public Worship in the Church of England* at pp. 12–13.

[295] See **p. 62** *supra*.

[296] There may be more than one minister conducting the service but, if part of the service is to be delegated to him (for example, by the incumbent), the delegation may always be withdrawn. The final arbiter between ministers is the bishop: see **p. 31** *et seq. supra.*

[297] This expression must be taken to include the feminine.

Although no guidance is actually given on who 'the persons concerned' may be, the words must at least[298] refer to the parties to the intended marriage; they would not, for example, include the parties' parents, even if one of them were giving away the bride or acting as best man.

Clearly, the earlier such objection is communicated the better. Presumably, for example, if one of those to be married objected to the form of service selected by the minister[299] so late that a decision could not be obtained from the bishop, the minister would then have a just cause to refuse to conduct the service until such decision had been obtained[300]; that is not to say, however, that the minister might not be open to ecclesiastical discipline, if he were responsible for the parties not having an earlier opportunity to object[301].

(b)　Vows

If the rite according to the Alternative Service Book is to be used, the minister must enquire before the day of the marriage which form of vows the couple have agreed to use[302].

(iii)　Objections to the marriage

In both the rites according to the Book of Common Prayer[303] and the Alternative Service Book[304] the minister is required to ask the congregation to declare any reason why the parties may not lawfully marry. The Alternative Service Book, however, gives no guidance as to how the minister should proceed if any such reason is declared, whereas the Book of Common Prayer states[305]:

> ... if any man do alledge and declare any impediment, why they may not be coupled together in Matrimony, by God's Law, or the Laws of this Realm; and will be bound and sufficient sureties with him, to the parties; or else put in a Caution (to the full value of such charges as the persons to be married do thereby sustain) to prove his allegation: then the solemnization must be

---

[298] It may be argued that they include the minister in whose church the ceremony is to be performed. However, if he objects to the choice of service, it would seem that his proper recourse is for him to withdraw his consent to the other minister's officiating. He could not, however, do so at such a late stage that the ceremony would be disrupted.

[299] Once the rite according to the Alternative Service Book has been chosen, the choice of vows is up to the couple: *op. cit.* at p. 285, Note 6.

[300] See 14 Halsbury's Laws of England (4th ed.) at para. 1005.

[301] See 14 Halsbury's Laws of England (4th ed.) at para. 1357. On the other hand, as ignorance of the law is no excuse, it is doubtful whether the minister is under any duty to tell the parties of their right to object. Cp. the position as to choice of vows: *infra.*　　　[302] Note 6 at p. 285.

[303] At the end of the Opening Address to the Congregation: 'Therefore if any man can shew just cause, why they may not lawfully be joined together, let him now speak, or else hereafter for ever hold his peace.'

[304] Note 7 at p. 289: 'But first I am required to ask anyone present who knows a reason why these persons may not lawfully marry, to declare it now.'　　　[305] The rubric before the Vows.

deferred, until such time as the truth be tried. If no impediment be alledged, then shall the Curate say . . .

Nonetheless, a minister is under a duty to prevent an improper marriage[306] and, even when using the Alternative Service Book, he cannot ignore an objection[307].

As when banns are forbidden[308], the cause or impediment may be put forward by anyone[309]. It should be declared during the service but it would seem best then to adjourn to the vestry before any amplification is made so as to preserve good order[310].

The cause or impediment must be such as to prevent the parties being 'coupled together in Matrimony, by God's Law, or the Laws of this Realm . . . ' This clearly includes any matter that would make the marriage void if the ceremony were to proceed[311].

Nevertheless, it is not so clear whether the words embrace a lack of consent. Merely because a declaration of dissent at the time of publication of the banns would have made the publication void[312] does not change the fact that consent may be retracted, although rarely at the actual service[313]. Certainly, a clergyman is not liable to ecclesiastical censure for solemnising a marriage after the publication of banns without the consent of the parents or guardians of a child unless he has notice of the dissent of any person who is entitled to give consent[314]. This statutory provision, however, is not restricted to notice at the time of the publication of banns[315]. On balance, therefore, it seems that a lack of consent may also be raised at the time of the ceremony[316], although in practice it will usually be too late[317].

Moreover, as no minister is obliged to solemnise a marriage which, apart from the Marriage (Prohibited Degrees of Relationship) Act 1986, would have been

---

[306] See *Beamish* v. *Beamish* (1861) 9 HL Cas. 274 at pp. 333 and 347.

[307] The Book of Common Prayer in any event must reflect Church order, if not general civil order.

[308] See **p. 168** *et seq. supra*.

[309] See *Cole* v. *Police Constable 443A* [1937] 1 KB 316 at p. 335 *per* Goddard J. However, the rubric seems to suggest that it cannot be done through an agent.

[310] See **p. 237** *et seq. infra*; cp. *Anglican Marriage in England and Wales* at paras 7.8 and 15.

[311] See **p. 159** *supra*.   [312] Marriage Act 1949, s. 3(3).

[313] See **p. 162** *supra*.

[314] Marriage Act 1949, s. 3(4): 'A clergyman shall not be liable to ecclesiastical censure for solemnising the marriage of a child after the publication of banns without the consent of the parents or guardians of the child unless he had notice of the dissent of any person who is entitled to give notice of dissent under the last foregoing subsection.' This includes any notice however given.

[315] If that were so, the words 'under the last foregoing subsection' would immediately succeed the words 'until he had notice'.

[316] For a different view see *Anglican Marriage in England and Wales* at para. 15.1.

[317] See Stephens, *The Book of Common Prayer*, vol. III, at p. 1561–1562. A clergyman is not entitled to go behind a licence duly granted by authority (see **p. 181, footnote 256** *supra*). However, he may delay the ceremony if he has reason to suspect fraud: *Argar* v. *Holdsworth* (1758) 2 Lee 515 at p. 517 *per* Sir George Lee. Otherwise, he may properly hesitate to act upon the licence if there is a variation in it: *Ewing* v. *Wheatley* (1814) 2 Hag. Con. 175 at p. 1185 *per* Sir William Scott. See, too, **p. 181** *et seq. supra*.

void by reason of the relationship of the persons to be married[318] or the marriage of any person whose former marriage has been dissolved and whose former spouse is still living[319], such a revelation coming for the first time in the ceremony would also entitle the minister to stop the ceremony[320].

Of course, if no proper cause or impediment is alleged[321] the ceremony must go forward. Once a proper cause or impediment is in fact alleged, according to the rubric in the Book of Common Prayer the ceremony must be deferred if the person making the objection is prepared to back his allegation financially. The backing must be to full value of such 'charges', or costs, as the persons to be married thereby sustain[322], in other words to the full cost of any such adjournment[323].

The rubric provides for this to be done either by the objector being bound with sufficient[324] sureties, or else by his putting in a 'caution'. It is unclear upon whom the choice of backing falls but it would seem to be the choice of the objector[325]. A 'caution' is the putting forward of money then and there as a security or guarantee[326]; presumably, the minister would then act as the equivalent of the stakeholder. On the other hand, it is unclear how the objector may now be bound over, particularly as there is a necessity for sureties[327]. While the Book of Common Prayer had statutory force it might have been argued that the minister had the power to take a binding promise both from the objector and the sureties. However, this no longer would seem to be the case[328]. Therefore, in order for the objector and the sureties actually to be bound, it will be necessary for them to enter into a deed[329].

As has been noted, the ceremony must be deferred if the objector can fulfil

---

[318] Marriage Act 1949, s. 5A. This includes all those marriages referred to in **Appendix 5, Parts II and III**, see **p. 283** *infra*.   [319] Matrimonial Causes Act 1965, s. 8(2).

[320] These are the only circumstances which seem now to fall within the distinction expressed in the words 'coupled together in Matrimony, by God's Law, or the Laws of this Realm . . .'.

[321] At least a *prima facie* case should be made out: see *Anglican Marriage in England and Wales* at para. 15.2.

[322] It is likely that this includes costs incurred on their behalfs by their parents.

[323] It is likely that this includes the costs not only of hire cars and photographers but also of a postponed honeymoon and any fresh reception. However, it would seem undesirable for a lengthy, or too detailed, financial discussion to take place: see *Anglican Marriage in England and Wales* at para. 15.2.

[324] Presumably, subject to the court's supervisory jurisdiction, the decision concerning sufficiency must be that of the minister as the only uninterested party.

[325] Otherwise it might be possible, if no-one else supports the allegation, for the objection to be circumvented by an insistence upon sureties.

[326] It should, of course, be borne in mind that cheques can be stopped.

[327] The wording of the rubric suggests that the requirement for sureties cannot be dispensed with.

[328] This is especially so in relation to the Alternative Service Book.

[329] That is, a document signed, sealed and delivered. A contract would seem to be insufficient as it is unclear with whom such a contract should be if the legal requirement for consideration to move from the promisee is to be fulfilled. It may be argued that there could be a contract with the minister on his promising to postpone the ceremony if the objector and sureties make the requisite promise to pay the persons to be married; however, the minister is already under a duty to postpone the ceremony if the 'promise' is forthcoming.

the above requirements. On the other hand, if he cannot, or will not, do so it does not follow that the ceremony must therefore go ahead[330]. Such an inability or refusal may well indicate that there is no force in the allegations but, if the minister on due consideration believes that there is a danger of fraud, he would be entitled to delay the ceremony until the matter can be verified. Nonetheless, the minister should be very sure of his ground as he would do so at his peril.

These provisions in the Book of Common Prayer must be concerned with Church, as well as civil, order and therefore might be thought to apply to both rites, as the Alternative Service Book is silent on the matter[331]. However, Series 1 Solemnisation of Matrimony states:

At which day of Marriage, if any man do allege and declare any impediment, why they may not be coupled together in Matrimony, by God's law, of the laws of this realm; then the solemnization must be deferred, until such time as the truth be tried.

It therefore seems to follow that in the rites other than that according to the Book of Common Prayer, once there is an objection that is on the face of it valid, the minister must thereupon adjourn the ceremony without more[332]. It cannot be argued that the provisions in the Book of Common Prayer should not be followed on the basis of a comparison with the provisions of Series 1 Solemnisation of Matrimony, as to do so would not be a variation 'in the form of service' within the meaning of Canon B 5, para. 1.

(iv) Blessing

Although it may be argued that theologically a deacon may not give a blessing[333], a deacon used to be under an obligation to bless the couple when celebrating a wedding according to the rite in the Book of Common Prayer. This is because no variation was then permitted from the authorised service[334]. Moreover, the archbishops have stated that, where a priest is present, the blessing of the couple and any ring may be delegated to a deacon[335]. Indeed, as they also state that no variations ought to be made in the authorised service[336], this

---

[330] For what may be a different view see *Anglican Marriage in England and Wales* at para. 15.2.
[331] Note 7 at p. 289 does not even require that the ceremony be deferred.
[332] See, too, *Anglican Marriage in England and Wales* at para. 15.2.
[333] See Briden & Hanson, *Moore's Introduction to English Canon Law* (3rd ed.) at p. 76; *Anglican Marriage in England and Wales* at para. 14.3.   [334] See **p. 11 *et seq. supra***.
[335] The blessing of the congregation, however, should be by the priest: *Guidelines issued jointly by the Archbishops of Canterbury and York*, paragraph 4, printed in *The Canons of the Church of England* at p. 187.
[336] However, this cannot overrule Canon B 5, para. 1, although it underlines that caution must be used before making any such variation.

might suggest that any such variation would be contrary to Canon B 5, para. 3[337], whichever rite is used. An additional blessing of the couple by another minister would seem to fall within the variations permitted by Canon B 5, para. 1[338].

The rite according to the Alternative Service Book ends with a blessing of the couple and the congregation[339], whereas no final blessing is provided for in the rite according to the Book of Common Prayer. By reason of Canon B 5, para. 1, it would seem that a final blessing may now be included in the latter rite although it is unlikely that the same provision could justify its omission from the former rite[340].

(v)   Variations

Variations may in any event be more difficult to justify in relation to the Book of Common Prayer[341] but it must not be thought in either rite that, because a part of the ceremony is not essential to the creation of a marriage between the parties[342], it is therefore a matter which is not of substantial importance within the meaning of Canon B 5, para. 1: one is a question of civil requirements[343] and the other of theological and religious essentials[344].

The rite according to the Book of Common Prayer envisages a sermon 'declaring the duties of Man and Wife'[345] whereas the rite according to the Alternative Service Book specifies no particular topic[346]; however, as the preaching of a sermon is in any event discretionary in both rites, it is unlikely that the subject of such a sermon is obligatory[347]. Series 1 Solemnisation of Matrimony, on the other hand, provides that a sermon is to be preached if there is to be no Holy Communion[348]; nevertheless, it seems that this may be omitted by reason of Canon B 5, para. 1, and a comparison with the other rites.

Moreover, a comparison of the three rites shows that the specific vows are not by themselves an essential and, therefore, the use of the alternative vows from the rite according to the Alternative Service Book[349] in a ceremony according to

---

[337] *Guidelines issued jointly by the Archbishops of Canterbury and York*, paragraph 3, printed in *The Canons of the Church of England* at p. 187; see, too, **p. 176 *et seq. supra.***
[338] See *Anglican Marriage in England and Wales* at para. 14.5.
[339] Note 30 at p. 297. As does Series 1 Solemnisation of Matrimony: *op. cit.*, at p. 12.
[340] See *Solemnisation of Marriage by Deacons: Guidelines issued jointly by the Archbishops of Canterbury and York*, paragraph 4, printed in the *Canons of the Church of England* at p. 187.
[341] See **p. 53 *et seq. supra.***   [342] See **p. 185 *supra.***   [343] See **p. 159 *supra.***
[344] See, for example, **p. 189 *supra.***   [345] See the rubric before the final Declaration.
[346] See Notes 5 and 22 at pp. 287 and 294 respectively.
[347] Canon B 5, para. 1, would seem to excuse the choice of a different topic, if the sermon is an actual part of the service: see **p. 69, footnote 105 *supra.***   [348] *Op. cit.* at p. 12.
[349] Within themselves, however, the two sets of vows in the Alternative Service Book are not interchangeable: see Note 6 at p. 285.

the Book of Common Prayer would seem equally to be justifiable[350] by reason of Canon B 5, para. 1[351].

(vi) Double marriages

The marriages of more than one couple may take place at the same time as long as the necessary formalities[352] are separately complied with in relation to each couple[353]. The requisite variations may be made to either rite by reason of Canon B 5, para. 1, as long as the service is reverent[354] and the worship offered glorifies God and edifies the people[355].

(vii) Holy Communion

The Book of Common Prayer points out that it is convenient that the newly-married persons should receive Holy Communion at the time of their marriage or at the first opportunity after their marriage[356]. The Alternative Service Book[357] and Series 1 Solemnisation of Matrimony[358] both make particular provision for the occasion when the marriage service is combined with Holy Communion.

(viii) Foreigners

A service must be solemnised in English[359] but where one or both parties to the intended marriage, or the congregation, do not understand English[360] the officiating minister must ensure[361] that the essential parts[362] are translated by an interpreter into a language that is understood[363]. Although the obligation to provide

---

[350] The same may be argued in relation to the addition, for example, of a Blessing of the Ring in the rite according to the Book of Common Prayer.

[351] This is the more so as Series 1 Solemnisation of Matrimony provides such alternatives for the wife: *op. cit.* at p. 6. If so, it would also seem that the couple may read the vows in the rite according to the Book of Common Prayer, just as they may in the rite according to the Alternative Service Book: see Note 6 at p. 285.

[352] That is, in relation to the publication of banns or the obtaining of a licence or Superintendent Registrar's certificate.

[353] See *Suggestions for the Guidance of the Clergy with reference to the Marriage and Registration Acts, &c.* (Registrar General, 1982 ed.) at p. 3.   [354] See **p. 237** *et seq. infra.*

[355] Canon B 1, para. 2.   [356] Final rubric.

[357] Note 39 at pp. 301–304; note 4 at p. 285.   [358] *Op. cit.* at p. 12.

[359] See **p. 66** *et seq. supra.* Where Welsh is commonly spoken in England the vows may be taken in Welsh; in Wales the marriage service may be taken in either language: see *Anglican Marriage in England and Wales* at para. 13.

[360] The minister ought to err on the side of caution.

[361] If he has good reason to doubt that the congregation or parties understand the essential parts of the service, it would seem that he should delay the ceremony until an interpreter is to hand.

[362] See **p. 185** *supra*. In these circumstances it is essential that the Charge is also translated so that the duty of the congregation and parties to declare any impediment is clearly understood.

[363] *Legal Opinions concerning the Church of England* at p. 171.

an interpreter does not lie upon the minister, he should endeavour to ensure that the interpreter is independent and not a relative or friend of the couple[364].

J   Service after Civil Marriage

(i)   Generally

Canon B 36, para. 1, states:

> If any persons have contracted marriage before the civil registrar under the provisions of the statute law, and shall afterwards desire to add thereto a service of Solemnisation of Marriage, a minister may, if he see fit[365], use such form of service, as may be approved by the General Synod under Canon B 2, in the church or chapel in which he is authorised to exercise his ministry: Provided first, that the minister be duly satisfied that the civil marriage has been contracted[366], and secondly that in regard to this use of the said service the minister do observe the Canons[367] and regulations[368] of the General Synod for the time being in force.

There may be no publication of banns, licence or certificate authorising the marriage and no record of any such service may be entered in the register book of marriages provided by the Registrar General[369]. This is because the civil marriage cannot be superseded or invalidated[370]. An entry should, however, be made in the general register of services.

The provisions of Canon B 36, para. 1, are in their terms restricted to the situation where there has been a civil marriage in England[371]. However, presumably the provisions as to no banns, licence, certificate or entry in the register book of marriage should also apply to the situation where there has been any other prior legally valid marriage, for example, in a Roman Catholic church or abroad[372].

---

[364] *Ibid*. It is advisable that the interpeter should sign the register book of marriages as a witness: *ibid*.

[365] These words show that the minister has a discretion whether to take such a service; they do not give him the discretion to use another rite.

[366] Notice must be given and the parties must produce a certificate of their marriage in the registry office, together with any customary fees: Marriage Act 1949, s. 46(1).

[367] In the light of Canon B 1, para. 2, this provision is unnecessary but it at least forestalls the argument (if the words had been omitted) that only Regulations have to be complied with.

[368] There are no such applicable Regulations.

[369] Canon B 36, para. 2; Marriage Act 1949, s. 46(2); *Anglican Marriage in England and Wales* at para. 1.3.

[370] Marriage Act 1949, s. 46(2). See, too, *Hewett* v. *Hewett* (1929) 73 Sol. Jo. 402.

[371] This is the result of the words 'before the civil registrar under the provisions of the statute law'.   [372] See **p. 193** *et seq. infra*.

(ii)   Rite

The wording of Canon B 36, para. 1, suggests that only a form of service approved by the General Synod under Canon B 2 may be used, whereas in fact no such service has been so approved. In these circumstances, a form of service approved by the diocesan bishop under Canon B 4, para. 3, may be used instead[373]. This is because Canon B 4, para. 3, specifically applies:

> on occasions for which no provision is made . . . by the General Synod under Canon B 2 . . .

Alternatively, the minister having the cure of souls may use a form of service which he considers suitable and may permit other ministers similarly to use it[374]. Indeed, the House of Bishops has commended the use of *Services of Prayer and Dedication after Civil Marriage*[375] in these circumstances[376].

If the latter rite is led by a deacon, the Grace is used in place of the final Blessing[377].

(iii)   Minister

The service may only be taken by an Anglican clergman[378]. Canon B 36, para. 1, only permits a service after a civil marriage to be performed by a minister who is 'authorised to exercise his ministry' in the relevant church or chapel. At first sight this might seem to suggest that only those actually licensed to that church or chapel may take the service[379]. However, the Canon does not use the word 'licensed' and, for example, authority may equally be derived from Canon C 8, para. 2(a), or from the diocesan bishop[380]. Rather, the Canon reflects the provisions of section 46(3) of the Marriage Act, 1949, to the effect that no person who is not entitled to solemnise Church of England marriages may read or celebrate such a service.

---

[373] Of course, in so far as is possible the Canons must be interpreted in line one with each other but neither Canon B 4 nor Canon B 5 expressly includes an exception in relation to a dedication after civil marriage. Thus, although a little strained, the interpretation adopted in the text is to be preferred; otherwise the clergy would not be in the position legally to cater for the particular pastoral need.   [374] Canon B 5, para. 2.

[375] Church House Publishing, 1985; see, too, *Public Worship in the Church of England* at p. 13. See also **p. 221**, especially **footnote 56** *infra*.   [376] See, too, **p. 226** *infra*.

[377] *Op. cit.*, Note 7 at p. 4. In these circumstances the prayers at paragraphs 13 and 18 are best seen as prayers for a blessing.   [378] Marriage Act 1949, s. 46(3).

[379] Note the use of the definite, rather than the indefinite, article: 'in the church or chapel'.

[380] In any event, if the service is taking place under the provisions of Canon B 5, para. 2, the minister having the cure of souls may permit another minister the use of a form of service he considers suitable: see **p. 220** *infra*.

K Conditional Marriages

If there has been a possible breach as to the proper formalities[381] in an earlier ceremony great care must be taken before another ceremony is performed[382], especially as any subsequent ceremony will inevitably cast doubt, for example, on the legitimacy of any children born since the first ceremony[383]. No rite is provided for such an eventuality and neither that in the Book of Common Prayer nor that in the Alternative Service Book is really appropriate[384]; however, in such circumstances Canon B 5, para. 1, would seem to permit appropriate variations similar to those for conditional baptism[385].

L Fees

Fees may be charged in accordance with the current Parochial Fees Order[386]. Unless the marriage is in an extra-parochial place the incumbent[387], rather than

[381] The most likely reason why such a second ceremony may be required is the fortunately rare occasion when the person who officiated at the first ceremony is later found not to have been in Holy Orders. Section 25 of the Marriage Act 1949 states: '... if [any persons] knowingly and wilfully consent to or acquiesce in the solemnisation of the marriage by any person who is not in Holy Orders, the marriage is void'. The better view, therefore, is that in all other cases the marriage is valid: *Rayden and Jackson on Divorce and Family Matters* (16th ed.) at para. 9.20; 14 Halsbury's Laws of England (4th ed.) at para. 1030, note 1. Nevertheless the matter is not completely free from doubt, if only one of the parties is aware of the fact: *Hawke* v. *Corri* (1820) 2 Hag. Con. 280 at p. 288 *per* Sir William Scott; *Cripps on Church and Clergy* (8th ed.) at p. 558; but cp. *Tongue* v. *Allen* (1835) 1 Curt. 38; *Dormer* v. *Williams* (1838) 1 Curt. 870. See, too, *Costard* v. *Winder* (1660) Cro. Eliz. 775; *R* v. *Millis* (1844) 10 Cl. & Fin. 534 at pp. 784–785 *per* Lord Campbell, pp. 860–861 *per* Lord Lyndhurst LC, and p. 906 *per* Lord Cottenham; *R* v. *Ellis* (1888) 16 Cox CC 469.

[382] Immediately a second religious ceremony is proposed the minister should consult the diocesan registrar. It would seem preferable that the marriage should be after licence although presumably banns may be called. Of course this does not apply if the parties have been legally divorced and now wish to remarry. In these circumstances one of the authorised rites musť be used without variation: see Canon B 35, para. 2.

[383] *Suggestions for the Guidance of the Clergy with reference to the Marriage and Registration Act, &c* at p. 3.

[384] Nevertheless, it seems that an unaltered rite may be used: see *Piers* v. *Piers* (1849) 2 HL Cas. 331 at pp. 354 and 384–385 *per* Lord Campbell.

[385] See **p. 147** *et seq. supra*. The second ceremony must be recorded in the marriage register books but the marital condition should be recorded as 'Previously went through a form of marriage at:_____ on the:_____': *Suggestions for the Guidance of the Clergy with reference to the Marriage and Registration Act, &c* at p. 3.

[386] Ecclesiastical Fees Measure 1986. Any such fee is recoverable as a debt: *ibid*, s. 7. During a vacancy in a benefice the fees which, but for the vacancy, would be paid to the incumbent must be paid to the diocesan board of finance or to such other person as the board, after consultation with the bishop, may direct: *ibid*, s. 3(1). As to special licences see **p. 172** *supra*. As to services after a civil marriage see **p. 192, footnote 366** *supra*.

[387] However, as to fees when a church or chapel cannot be used because of repair or rebuilding see **p. 180, footnote 241** *supra*.

the officiating minister, is entitled to the relevant fee[388]. If the marriage is by special licence, other than in a parish church, parish centre of worship or licensed building, fees are only payable by custom[389].

According to the rite according to the Book of Common Prayer[390] the man should place the ring upon the minister's book 'with the accustomed duty[391] to the Priest and Clerk'; however, as such accustomed duties are now superseded by fees, this is in effect abrogated[392].

M   Registers

Every minister must observe the law from time to time in force in relation to the registration of marriages[393]. Register books must be provided, maintained and kept in accordance with the Statutes and Measures relating thereto and regulations made thereunder and from time to time in force[394].

A marriage celebrated according to the rites of the Church of England[395] must be registered by the clergyman by whom it is solemnised[396]. Immediately after the marriage[397] he must register in duplicate in two marriage register books[398]

---

[388] Unless already assigned to the Diocesan Board of Finance, the incumbent may assign his fee to the officiating minister. It seems that the officiating minister is entitled to request an additional non-statutory fee: *Legal Opinions concerning the Church of England* at pp. 174–175. The parties would be entitled to refuse to pay any additional fee unless given due warning.

[389] *Anglican Marriage in England and Wales* at para. 17.2. As this does not refer to custom according to the canon law, but according to the civil law, the custom must date back at least to 1189: *Bryant* v. *Foot* (1867) LR 2 QB 161, (1868) LR 3 QB 497.

[390] See the rubric after the Vows.

[391] This had to be a custom according to the common (civil) law: *Patten* v. *Castleman* (1753) 1 Lee 387; *Bryant* v. *Foot* (1867) LR 2 QB 161, (1868) LR 3 QB 497. See, too, **pp. 4, footnote 28, supra** and **223 et seq. infra**.

[392] The minister would not be entitled to insist upon the payment of the fee then and there before continuing with the service, as the fee may now be recovered as a debt: see the Ecclesiastical Fees Measure 1986, s. 7. For this reason, too, the time for payment cannot be a matter of Church order.

[393] Canon B 39, para. 1. See, too, **p. 196 et seq. infra**.   [394] Canon F 11, para. 2.

[395] Where the service is solemnised at the residence of a person who is house-bound or detained in accordance with the Marriage Act 1949, s. 26(1)(dd) the marriage must be registered in the marriage register book of any church or chapel which is in the same parish or extra-parochial place or, if there is no such church or chapel, in any adjoining parish: Marriage Act 1983, s. 1(7), Sch. 1, para. 17. See, too, **p. 176 et seq. supra**.

[396] Marriage Act 1949, s. 53(a). If the marriage is in a military chapel it must be registered by a clergyman specially appointed for that purpose: Marriage Act 1949, s. 69(4). When a marriage is solemnised in a licensed building or in the church or chapel of an adjoining parish or district in accordance with the Marriage Act 1949 s. 18, because of the repair or rebuilding of a church or chapel, the marriage must be registered in the marriage register books kept by the incumbent of the disused church or chapel: Marriage Act 1949, s. 18(3).

[397] The practice of beginning to make the entries prior to the marriage taking place is a dangerous one: see *Suggestions for the Guidance of the Clergy with reference to the Marriage and Registration Act, &c* at p. 4.

[398] Canon F 11, para. 1, states: 'In every parish church and chapel where . . . matrimony [is to be] solemnised there shall be provided register books of . . . marriage . . . '; they must be provided by the parochial church council: Canon F 14. They are furnished on application by the Registrar

particulars relating to the marriage[399] in the prescribed form[400]. Each entry must be signed by the minister, by the parties married[401] and by two witnesses[402].

No penalty is incurred if the clergyman discovers an error in the form or substance of the entry and within one calendar month after the discovery and in the presence of the parties married[403], who attest the same, he corrects the erroneous entry in the margin without alteration of the original entry[404].

N   Music and Flowers

When matrimony is to be celebrated in any church it belongs to the minister of the parish to decide what music is to be played, what hymns or anthems shall be sung or what furnishings or flowers should be placed in or about the church for the occasion[405]. The use of the organ is subject to the approval of the incumbent[406].

O   Civil Offences

By section 75 of the Marriage Act 1949[407]:

General for England and Wales. In rare cases, such as when the marriage is by special licence, there may be no marriage register books; in these circumstances the minister should make arrangement to use the register books of the parish church or, if these are not available, any others that can be obtained: *Anglican Marriage in England and Wales* at para. 16.2.

[399] The minister may ask the parties to the marriage the particulars required: Marriage Act 1949, s. 56. Anyone who knowingly and wilfully makes or causes to be made any false statement as to any of the particulars is guilty of an offence: Perjury Act 1911, s. 3(1)(b).

[400] Marriage Act 1949, s. 55(1). Where appropriate the particular type of licence should be specified: *Anglican Marriage in England and Wales* at para. 16.3. Care should be taken that the ink used is 'of a good black colour, and of permanent and indelible quality': *Suggestions for the Guidance of the Clergy with reference to the Marriage and Registration Act, &c* at p. 4.

[401] Phillimore, *Ecclesiastical Law* (2nd ed.), vol. I, at pp. 637–638 suggests that the wife should sign in the 'newly-acquired name of her husband' but it may also be argued that, as the signature is to identify the contracting parties, she should sign with her usual signature prior to her marriage. Particularly as many wives now retain their maiden names it is possible that the latter practice should now be preferred.   [402] Marriage Act 1949, s. 55(2). As to witnesses see **p. 184** *et seq. supra.*

[403] Or, if they are dead or absent, in the presence of the Superintendent Registrar and two other credible witnesses or in the presence of the churchwardens of the church or chapel in which the marriage was solemnised: Marriage Act 1949, s. 61(2), (5).

[404] Marriage Act 1949, s. 61(1). He must sign the marginal entry and add the date of the correction; it must be attested by those whose presence is required: Marriage Act 1949, s. 61(2). A similar entry must be made in the duplicate register book and the certified copy delivered to the Superintendent Registrar; if the latter has already been delivered, he must deliver to the Superintendent Registrar a separate certified copy of the erroneous entry and of the marginal correction: Marriage Act 1949, s. 61(3), (4).   [405] Canon B 35, para. 5. See, too, **p. 79** *et seq. supra.*

[406] *Legal Opinions concerning the Church of England* at pp. 190–191. The same applies to the use of the choir or bells: *Anglican Marriage in England and Wales* at para. 6.3.

[407] However, no prosecution can be commenced after the expiration of three years from the commission of the offence: Marriage Act 1949, s. 75(4).

(1)   Any person who knowingly and wilfully:

(a)   solemnises a marriage at any other time than between the hours of eight in the forenoon and six in the afternoon (not being a marriage by special licence . . .);

(b)   solemnises a marriage according to the rites of the Church of England without banns of marriage having been duly published (not being a marriage solemnised on the authority of a special licence, a common licence or a certificate of a superintendent registrar);

(c)   solemnises a marriage according to the said rites (not being a marriage by special licence or a marriage in pursuance of section 26(1)(dd) of this Act[408]) in any place other than a church or other building in which banns may be published;

(d)   solemnises a marriage according to the said rites falsely pretending to be in Holy Orders;

shall be guilty of an indictable offence and shall be liable to imprisonment for a term not exceeding fourteen years.

(2) Any person who knowingly and wilfully:

(a)   solemnises a marriage (not being a marriage by special licence . . .) in any place other than:

(i)   a church or other building in which marriages may be solemnised according to the rites of the Church of England;

. . .

(bb)   solemnises a marriage in pursuance of section 26(1)(dd) of this Act[409], otherwise than according to the rites of the Church of England . . . ;

(d)   solemnises a marriage on the authority of a certificate of a superintendent registrar . . . within twenty-one days after the day on which the notice of marriage was entered in the marriage notice book[410]; or

(e)   solemnises a marriage on the authority of a certificate of a superintendent registrar after the expiration of three months from the said day on which the notice of marriage was entered as aforesaid;

shall be guilty of an indictable offence and shall be liable to imprisonment for a term not exceeding five years.

In addition, section 76(1) of the 1949 Act creates offences in relation to the registration of marriages:

---

[408] See **p. 176** *supra*.   [409] See **p. 176** *supra*.

[410] A Superintendent Registrar cannot issue a licence dispensing with this requirement in relation to a marriage according to the rites of the Church of England, or in any church or chapel belonging to the Church of England or licensed for the celebration of divine worship according to the rites and ceremonies of the Church of England: Marriage Act 1949, s. 26(2) proviso; cp. *ibid*, s. 32.

Any person who refuses or without reasonable cause omits to register any marriage which he is required by this Act to register, and any person having the custody of a marriage register book or a certified copy of a marriage register book or part thereof who carelessly loses or injures the said book or copy or carelessly allows the said book or copy to be injured while in his keeping, shall be liable on summary conviction to a fine not exceeding fifty pounds ...

All these offences are in addition to any ecclesiastical offence that has been committed[411].

---

[411] See, too, **p. 97, p. 179, footnote 226,** and **p. 182** *supra*. In fact any offence under the 1949 Act is likely to be an ecclesiastical offence by reason of Canon B 35, para. 2, and Canon B 39, para. 1: see **p. 157** *et seq*.

8

FUNERALS

A Generally

It is the duty of every minister in all matters to observe the law from time to time in force in relation to the burial of the dead[1]. By reason of Canon B 38, para. 2:

> It shall be the duty of every minister to bury, according to the rites of the Church of England[2], the corpse or ashes of any person deceased within his cure[3] or of any parishioners or persons whose names are entered on the electoral roll of his parish[4] whether deceased within his cure or elsewhere that is brought to a church or burial ground or cemetery under his control in which the burial or interment of such corpse or ashes may lawfully be effected[5], due notice being given; except the person deceased have died unbaptised, or being of unsound mind have laid violent hands upon himself, or have been declared excommunicate for some grievous and notorious crime and no man to testify to his repentance; in which case and in any other case at the request of the relative, friend, or legal representative having charge of or being responsible for the burial[6] he shall use at the burial such service as may be prescribed or approved by the Ordinary[7], being a service neither contrary to, nor indicative of any departure from, the doctrine of the Church of England in any essential matter: Provided that, if a form of service available for the burial of suicides is approved by the General Synod under Canon B 2, that service shall be used where applicable instead of the aforesaid service prescribed or approved by the Ordinary, unless the person having charge or being responsible for the burial otherwise requests.

[1] Canon B 38, para. 1. Subject to this general duty the other paragraphs of Canon B 38 must also be obeyed: *ibid.*

[2] See, too, Canon B 1, para. 2, and **p. 3** *et seq. supra* and **Appendix 4** at **p. 280** *et seq. infra.* As to the rites themselves see **p. 207** *et seq. infra.*

[3] For the meaning of this phrase see **p. 134** *et seq. supra.* That there should be this wide meaning of the term is borne out by the rubrics at the commencement of The Order for the Burial of the Dead in the Book of Common Prayer. The exceptions set out in those rubrics, reflected as they are in Canon B 38, para. 2, show that the general duty must be correlative to the general right to burial: see **p. 201** *et seq. infra.*   [4] See 14 Halsbury's Laws of England (4th ed.) at para. 591 *et seq.*

[5] For example, such burial may be unlawful by reason of a closure order: see 10 Halsbury's Laws of England (4th ed.) at para. 1207 *et seq.*; see, too, **p. 202** *infra.* However, cremated remains may be buried in a closed churchyard under the authority of a faculty: *In re Kerr* [1894] P 284.

[6] In the ordinary course of events this does not mean the funeral director unless, of course, he is passing on the request of the relative, friend or legal representative.

[7] That is, the diocesan bishop: see **p. 218, footnote 28** *infra.*

If any doubts arise whether any deceased person may be buried according to the rites of the Church of England, the minister must refer the matter to the bishop and obey his order and direction[8].

B   Minister

Subject to what is said concerning the Burial Laws Amendment Act 1880[9], usually only an ordained person[10] may officiate at a funeral on consecrated ground[11]. However, the bishop[12] may authorise a deaconess[13], reader[14] or layworker[15], at the invitation of the minister of the parish[16] or extra-parochial place and with the goodwill[17] of the persons responsible[18], to bury the dead or read the burial service before, at or after a cremation[19].

If notice is given under the Burial Laws Amendment Act 1880[20], the burial

---

[8] Canon B 38, para. 6: 'If any doubts shall arise whether any person deceased may be buried according to the rites of the Church of England, the minister shall refer the matter to the bishop and obey his order and direction.' This provision is perhaps not felicitously worded, as it must be concerned with whether or not any of the exceptions apply rather than with the question whether an authorised service may be used; the infelicity probably arises by reason of the legislative changes made after the promulgation of Canon 68 of the 1603 Canons. The Canon refers to the diocesan bishop. Although there is no express saving in relation to the jurisdiction of the courts as there is in Canon B 5, para. 4, (see **p. 220, footnote 52 infra**), the courts must nevertheless remain the final arbiter because of Canon B 38, para. 1; see, too, *R* v. *Taylor*, cited in Phillimore, *Ecclesiastical Law* (2nd ed.), vol. I, at p. 653.

[9] See, too, the Local Authorities' Cemeteries Order 1977 (SI 1977 No. 204), art. 5(5).

[10] As to the ecumenical position see **p. 26 supra**.

[11] *Johnson* v. *Friend* (1860) 6 Jur. NS 280. This is so even where the consecrated ground is not in a churchyard but, for example, in a cemetery: *Wood* v. *Headingley-cum-Burley Burial Board* [1892] 1 QB 713 at p. 729 *per* Lord Coleridge CJ: 'No one can lawfully read a service over a corpse in a church yard, and for this purpose the consecrated portion of a cemetery is the same thing as a churchyard, unless he is the incumbent or some clergyman duly authorized by him.' As to the question of authorisation, however, see now Canon C 8, para. 2(d), and **p. 202 et seq. infra**.

[12] This must mean the diocesan bishop.   [13] Canon D 1, para. 4(c).

[14] Canon E 4, para. 2A.

[15] Canon E 7, para. 5(c). This provision does not apply to the Channel Islands: Canon E 7, para. 6.

[16] This clearly includes the incumbent (see *Wood* v. *Headingley-cum-Burley Burial Board* [1892] 1 QB 713 at p. 729 *per* Lord Coleridge CJ) but possibly also means anyone for the time being having the cure of souls: see **p. 134 et seq. supra**; cp. Church of England (Miscellaneous Provisions) Measure 1992, s. 2(6). When the cure is vacant the invitation may be given by the rural dean: Canon D 1, para. 4, Canon E 4, para. 2A, and Canon E 7, para. 5.

[17] This does not seem to require actual consent but permits the deaconess, reader or lay worker to proceed as long as there appears to be no opposition.

[18] This must refer to any relative, friend, or legal representative having responsibility for the burial or cremation rather than to the funeral director: cp. Canon B 38, para. 2.

[19] These Canons were promulgated in accordance with the Deaconesses and Lay Ministry Measure 1972. As to cremation see **p. 206 infra**.

[20] In relation to burials under this Act see 10 Halsbury's Laws of England (4th ed.) at para. 1141 *et seq.*; *Davies' Law of Burial, Cremation and Exhumation* (6th ed.) at p. 125 *et seq.*; see, also, *Legal Opinions concerning the Church of England* at p. 28. Save in so far as is expressly provided, nothing in the Act authorises or enables any minister who has not become a declared member of any church or denomination, or executed a deed of relinquishment under the Clerical Disabilities Act 1870, to

may be without a religious service or with such Christian and orderly religious service as those giving the notice think fit[21]. In this latter case any person or persons invited to do so by those having the charge of, or being responsible for, the burial may conduct the service[22] or take part in any religious act at the burial[23].

C   Right to Burial

Every parishioner[24] and inhabitant in a parish, as well as everyone dying in a parish[25], has the right[26] to be buried in the parish churchyard or burial ground[27],

do, or not to do, anything that he would not otherwise have been authorised or enabled to do: Burial Laws Amendment Act 1880, s. 14.

[21] Burial Laws Amendment Act 1880, s. 6. Everyone must be given free access to the churchyard or graveyard where it is taking place: *ibid.* The burial must be conducted in a decent and orderly manner: *ibid*, s. 7. As to the prevention of disorder see *ibid*, s. 8. In regard to cemeteries see the Local Authorities' Cemeteries Order 1977 (SI 1977 No. 204), art. 5(5).

[22] *Legal Opinions concerning the Church of England* at p. 28 suggests that the authority of the incumbent is required if an unordained person is to read the Church of England service. However, in spite of the generality of the *dictum* of Lord Coleridge CJ, in *Wood* v. *Headingley-cum-Burley Burial Board* [1892] 1 QB 713 at p. 729 (cited in **footnote 16 supra**), this view seems to run contrary to the express wording of the Act.

[23] 'Christian service' includes every religious service used by any church, denomination, or person professing to be a Christian: Burial Laws Amendment Act 1880, s. 6.

[24] Where by virtue of a pastoral scheme or otherwise a parish has more than one parish church and a building which was not the parish church immediately before the pastoral scheme is designated as the parish church, burial rights are not generally affected: Pastoral Measure 1983, s. 27(5)(c). On a union of parishes by such a scheme the persons residing within the limits of the parish thereby created have the rights and privileges (if any) of parishioners in respect of burials in that parish while it remains open for interments, provided that any parishioner, who before the union had burial rights in a churchyard within the limits of the new parish, continues to have those rights (rather than rights in any other churchyard) while that churchyard remains open for interments: *ibid* and Sch. 3, para. 15(1). On the creation otherwise than by union of a new parish by a pastoral scheme, the persons residing within the limits of the new parish continue to have the same rights and privileges in respect of burials which they enjoyed before but such rights cease when they obtain rights of burial as parishioners of the new parish: *ibid* and Sch. 3, para. 15(2). Where any persons by virtue of a pastoral scheme or order providing for the alteration of parish boundaries come to reside within a different parish, they have such rights and privileges in respect of burials as are possessed by parishioners of that different parish and not any others: *ibid* and Sch. 3, para. 15(3).

[25] *Ex parte Blackmore* (1830) 1 B. & Ad. 122 at p. 123 *per* Littledale J; *R* v. *Stewart* (1840) 12 Ad. & E. 773 at p. 778 *per* Lord Denman. This is so even if the deceased were the victim of an air or road accident and was, therefore, only a transient: *Legal Opinions concerning the Church of England* at p. 24; cp. *Cripps on Church and Clergy* (8th ed.) at p. 564. This does not prevent the personal representatives removing the body to the deceased's place of residence and demanding its burial there: *ibid.* The provisions relating to executed criminals have now been abolished: *Davies' Law of Burial, Cremation and Exhumation* (Shaw & Sons, 1993) (6th ed.) at pp. 130–131; see, too, 10 Halsbury's Laws of England (4th ed.) at para. 1118. Those executed for high treason, however, may not be admitted to Christian burial: see Phillimore, *Ecclesiastical Law*, vol. I, at pp. 667–668; see, further, *In re St Edmund's Churchyard, Gateshead* [1995] 3 WLR 253 at p. 259B–C.

[26] The right is enforceable in both the civil and ecclesiastical courts: 10 Halsbury's Laws of England (4th ed.) at para. 1118.

[27] See 10 Halsbury's Laws of England (4th ed.) at para. 1118. The right is only to burial in a usual manner: *Winstanley* v. *North Manchester Overseers* [1910] AC 7 at p. 16 *per* Lord Atkinson; see,

subject to any public health regulations[28]. A person who has such a right of burial in the churchyard or other burial ground of a parish has a similar right of burial therein of his cremated remains[29]; however, there is no such right where the churchyard or burial ground is closed, except in accordance with a faculty authorising the burial[30] or in an area which has been set aside by a faculty for the burial of cremated remains generally[31].

A person who has his name on the electoral roll of a parish at the date of his death has the same rights of burial as if he were a parishioner[32].

Those within the exception set out in Canon B 38, para. 2, have a right to burial, at least under the Burial Laws Amendment Act 1880[33].

D Authorisation and Duty to Bury

The minister of a parish[34] may perform a funeral service in any crematorium or cemetery situated in another parish if the deceased person dies in his parish

---

too, **p. 206 infra**. The selection of the particular grave is a matter for the discretion of the incumbent, although the right to a particular grave may be given by faculty: *In re Marks (deceased)*, (1994) 3 Ecc. LJ 352; 14 Halsbury's Laws of England (4th ed.) at para. 1315; Newsom & Newsom, *Faculty Jurisdiction of the Church of England* (2nd ed.) at p. 170; *Legal Opinions concerning the Church of England* at p. 25.

[28] See *Davies' Law of Burial, Cremation and Exhumation* (6th ed.) at pp. 47–49.

[29] Church of England (Miscellaneous Provisions) Measure 1992, s. 3(1). Section 11 of the Cremation Act 1902, which provided that an incumbent was not obliged to perform the burial service in certain circumstances, has now been repealed and has ceased to have effect: Church of England (Miscellaneous Provisions) Measure 1992, s. 2(5), s. 17(2), Sch. 4, Pt II.

[30] See *In re Kerr* [1894] P 284; Newsom and Newsom, *Faculty jurisdiction of the Church of England* (2nd ed.) at 154.

[31] Church of England (Miscellaneous Provisions) Measure 1992, s. 3(1) proviso.

[32] Church of England (Miscellaneous Provisions) Measure 1976, s. 6(1).

[33] It is unclear to what extent, if at all, the exception was part of the pre-Reformation canon law: see **p. 130, footnote 4 supra**. If in any particular case it was not, there was a right to burial until it was taken away by the statutory force of the rubric in the Book of Common Prayer; moreover, there could be no burial in consecrated ground without a form of service: see *Kemp* v. *Wickes* (1809) 3 Phillim. 264 at p. 295 (quoted at **pp. 207–326 infra**). Thereafter, the Burial Laws Amendment Act 1880, gave a right of burial in any case (on due notice according to the Act) without the rites of the Church of England: see, too, Interments (Felo de Se) Act 1882 (now repealed). Any Christian service might in such a case be used: see **p. 201 supra**. It may, of course, be argued that this was a new right and that, therefore, notice under the Act is still required. However, Canon B 38, para. 2, is in mandatory terms (note the words 'in which case . . . he shall use at the burial service'). On the one hand this may be interpreted as referring to the rite that must be used rather than as creating a duty to bury; if this view is correct, a minister may still himself refuse to bury persons falling within the exception, although he must not prevent their burial by others. On the other hand, Canon B 38, para. 2, may equally be interpreted as creating a duty to bury and, if so, a correlative right to burial has been created apart from the 1880 Act. If only for pastoral reasons, this latter interpretation may be preferred but, as there is doubt, until the question is elucidated by the courts a minister may not refuse burial in such circumstances without first referring the matter to the diocesan bishop; having done so he must obey his order and direction: Canon B 38, para. 6.

[34] In this context these words mean (a) the incumbent; (b) in a case where the benefice to which

or was resident[35] in his parish immediately before his death or his name was on the church electoral roll of his parish immediately before his death[36]. A person licensed for the time being under section 2 of the Extra-Parochial Ministry Measure 1967[37], to perform funeral services on premises forming part of, or belonging to, a university, college, school, hospital or public or charitable institution may perform a funeral service in any crematorium or cemetery if the deceased person was resident in any such premises or was employed by, or enrolled as a student at, the institution in question immediately before his death[38].

Where he is requested to do so, the minister of a parish[39] situated wholly or partly in an area which is chargeable with the expenses of the cemetery, or for the use of which a crematorium or cemetery has been designated by the bishop of the diocese concerned, is with respect to persons who are his own parishioners or who die in his parish or whose names are entered on the church electoral roll of his parish under the same obligation to perform or arrange the performance of funeral services in the crematorium or cemetery as he has in any churchyard of his parish[40].

In the above cases the performance of a funeral service does not require the consent, nor is it subject to the control, of the minister of the parish[41] in which it is performed[42]. It should be borne in mind, however, that any curate, deaconess, reader or lay worker would still require the relevant consent. In these and

---

the parish belongs is vacant (and (c) *infra* does not apply), the rural dean; (c) in a case where a suspension period applies to the benefice to which the parish belongs, the priest-in-charge (if any); and (d) in a case where a special cure of souls in respect of the parish has been assigned to a vicar in a team ministry by a scheme under the Pastoral Measure 1983 or by his licence from the bishop, that vicar: Church of England (Miscellaneous Provisions) Measure 1992, s. 2(6). 'Suspension period' has the same meaning as in the Pastoral Measure 1983: *ibid.*

[35] The term has its ordinary and natural meaning and is normally a matter of fact and degree. It usually embraces something more than a casual visit but the existence of a home is a highly significant factor, even though it may not have been visited for some time: see *Rayden and Jackson on Divorce and Family Matters* (16th ed.) at para. 5.2. 'The view of the Faculty Office is that the word "resides" for banns and [a Superintendent Registrar's Certificate] requires a physical presence and occupation of premises as a home. This need not be a permanent arrangement, but it must subsist at the relevant time': *Anglican Marriage in England and Wales* at para. 5.6; see, too, *Legal Opinions concerning the Church of England* at pp. 166–169.

[36] Church of England (Miscellaneous Provisions) Measure 1992, s. 2(2).

[37] See 14 Halsbury's Laws of England (4th ed.) at paras 690, 701 and 731.

[38] Church of England (Miscellaneous Provisions) Measure 1992, s. 2(3).

[39] See **p. 200, footnote 16** *supra*.

[40] Church of England (Miscellaneous Provisions) Measure 1992, s. 2(4). See, too, the Local Authorities Cemeteries' Order 1977 (SI 1977 No. 204), art. 17(1): 'The incumbent or priest in charge of an ecclesiastical parish situated wholly or partly in an area chargeable with the expenses of a cemetery shall, with respect to members of the Church of England who are his own parishioners or who die in his parish, where he is requested to do so, be under the same obligations to perform funeral services in the consecrated part, if any, of the cemetery as he has to perform funeral services in any churchyard of the ecclesiastical parish'.　　　　　　　　　[41] See **p. 200, footnote 16** *supra*.

[42] Church of England (Miscellaneous Provisions) Measure 1992, s. 2(1). It may also be performed without any further authority from the bishop of the diocese within which the parish is situated: Canon C 8, para. 2(d).

all other cases any such performance requires the consent of the incumbent[43] of the parish in which it is performed[44] and is therefore subject to his control.

The general duty to bury under Canon B 38, para. 2, has already been set out[45]. The breach of this duty is an ecclesiastical offence[46].

No person, other than a person having a right of burial in the churchyard or other burial ground of a parish, may be buried therein without the consent of the minister of the parish[47] but in deciding whether to give such consent he must have regard to any general guidance given by the parochial church council of the parish in respect to the matter[48].

E Notice[49]

Canon B 38, para. 2, requires that due notice is given[50] and without it there is no duty to perform the service[51]. In relation to baptisms 'due notice' is 'normally

[43] 'The incumbents are in each diocese the representatives of the bishop, who has been called the universal incumbent. No clergyman can lawfully take upon himself to intrude into a parish, for he cannot minister canonically without a licence from the bishop of the diocese to minister in a particular parish': *Wood* v. *Headingley-cum-Burley Burial Board* [1892] 1 QB 713 at p. 729 *per* Lord Coleridge CJ; see, further, Canon C 8. Presumably, therefore, the minister for the time being having the cure of souls may likewise give consent as he, too, represents the bishop: see **p. 133 *et seq. supra*.** In the absence of any such minister only the diocesan bishop can give such consent.

[44] *Johnson* v. *Friend* (1860) 6 Jur. NS 280. This is so even where the consecrated ground is not in a churchyard but, for example, in a cemetery. In *Wood* v. *Headingley-cum-Burley Burial Board* [1892] 1 QB 713 Lord Coleridge CJ, said at p. 729: 'No one can lawfully read a service over a corpse in a churchyard, and for this purpose the consecrated portion of a cemetery is the same thing as a churchyard, unless he is the incumbent or some clergyman duly authorized by him.'

[45] See **p. 199 *et seq. supra*.**

[46] Canon B 38, paras 1 and 2; 14 Halsbury's Laws of England (4th ed.) at para. 1357. A refusal may be an offence at common law: see 10 Halsbury's Laws of England (4th ed.) at para. 1135. It may possibly give rise to an action in damages: *ibid*.

[47] This means the incumbent of the benefice to which the parish belongs or, if the benefice is vacant, the minister acting as priest in charge of the parish or the curate licensed to the charge of the parish or, if there is no such minister or curate, the rural dean of the deanery in which the parish is: Church of England (Miscellaneous Provisions) Measure, 1976, s. 6(3). A refusal by an incumbent cannot be reviewed by the consistory court but, if such consent once given is acted upon and the non-parishioner would be prejudiced by its withdrawal, it cannot later be withdrawn: *In re St Nicholas, Baddesley Ensor* [1983] Fam 1 at p. 5G–H *per* Chancellor Anglionby.

[48] Church of England (Miscellaneous Provisions) Measure 1976, s. 6(2). The parochial church council is not entitled as of right to give guidance in relation to a particular case; moreover, the minister does not need to seek guidance if none has yet been given.

[49] As to notices under the Burial Laws Amendment Act 1880, see *ibid*, ss. 1 and 3; 10 Halsbury's Laws of England (4th ed.) at p. 1142; *Davies' Law of Burial, Cremation and Exhumation* (6th ed.) at pp. 127–128.

[50] The words imply that notice is given before the corpse or ashes are brought to be buried: *Titchmarsh* v. *Chapman* (1844) 3 Notes of Cases 370 at pp. 406–407 *per* Sir H Jenner Fust; 10 Halsbury's Laws of England (4th ed.) at para. 1136.

[51] *R* v. *Vicar of Bassingbourne* (1845) 9 JP Jo. 83; *Titchmarsh* v. *Chapman* (1844) 3 Notes of Cases 370; *Cooper* v. *Dodd* (1850) 2 Rob. Eccl. 270.

of at least a week'[52] but no such guidance is given concerning burials and different considerations seem to apply[53].

The convenience of the minister is clearly an important consideration[54] but all the circumstances must be taken into account[55]. For example, there will normally be a greater urgency in relation to the burial of a corpse than the burial of ashes. Sufficient time must, of course, be given in appropriate cases to allow the minister to enquire whether the deceased fell within any of the exceptions mentioned in Canon B 38, para. 2[56], and for the necessary preparations for a reverent interment to be made[57].

F Place and Mode of Burial

The selection of the particular grave is a matter for the discretion of the incumbent[58], although the right to a particular grave may be given by faculty[59]. A body may be buried in unconsecrated ground but the officiating minister must on coming to the grave first bless it[60].

---

[52] See Canon B 22, para. 1.

[53] This is perhaps borne out by the requirement of only 48 hours notice under section 1 of the Burial Laws Amendment Act 1880, although clearly a different length of notice is required when a minister is himself required to perform the service.

[54] See 10 Halsbury's Laws of England (4th ed.) at para. 1136. Canon 68 of the 1603 Canons spoke of 'convenient warning being given' to the minister and in relation to that Canon Sir H Jenner Fust said: 'A *warning* is not itself sufficient; it must be a *convenient* warning; that is, with reference to the circumstances of time, place and the occupations of the minister who might be so engaged in the performance of other services as to render a warning, under the circumstances, not a convenient warning': *Titchmarsh* v. *Chapman* (1844) 3 Notes of Cases 370 at p. 407. In spite of the difference in wording the same considerations seem to apply under the new Canon.

[55] See Phillimore, *Ecclesiastical Law*, (2nd ed.) vol. I at p. 672.

[56] And, if necessary, for the resolution of any doubt by the bishop: see Canon B 38, para. 6, and **p. 212** *et seq. infra*.

[57] See *Titchmarsh* v. *Chapman* (1844) 3 Notes of Cases 370 at p. 408 *per* Sir H Jenner Fust. It must be remembered, however, that the responsibility for digging the grave is not upon the incumbent but upon the persons responsible for the funeral arrangements: *Legal Opinions concerning the Church of England* at p. 25.

[58] *Fryer* v. *Johnson* (1755) 2 Wils. 28; *Ex parte Blackmore* (1830) 1 B. & Ad. 122. The incumbent's duty is merely to indicate the place at which the grave is to be dug, and its depth; he is not obliged to provide a grave digger and the responsibility for digging the grave is upon the persons responsible for the funeral arrangements: *Legal Opinions concerning the Church of England* at p. 25. Many churchyards have been buried over more than once but care must be taken not to disturb remains without a faculty: Newsom & Newsom, *Faculty Jurisdiction of the Church of England* (2nd ed.) at p. 153; 14 Halsbury's Laws of England (4th ed.) at para. 1325, note 7.

[59] *In re Marks (deceased)*, (1994) 3 Ecc. LJ 352; 14 Halsbury's Laws of England (4th ed.) at para. 1315; Newsom & Newsom, *Faculty Jurisdiction of the Church of England* (2nd ed.) at p. 170; *Legal Opinions concerning the Church of England* at p. 25.

[60] Canon B 38, para. 5. See, also, the Burial Laws Amendment Act 1880, s. 12: 'No minister in holy orders of the Church of England shall be subject to any censure or penalty for officiating with the service prescribed by law for the burial of the dead according to the rites of the said Church in any unconsecrated burial ground or cemetery or part of a burial ground or cemetery, or in any building thereon, in any case in which he might have lawfully used the same service, if such burial

The requirement in Canon B 38, para. 4(b), that the disposal of the ashes of a cremated body must be reverent is no more than a reflection of the general canon law[61]. Thus, although the mode of burial may be out of the ordinary[62], anything that creates irreverence[63] is illegal[64].

G Cremation

Cremation of a dead body is lawful in connection with Christian burial[65]. Where a body is to be cremated, the burial service may precede, accompany or follow[66] the cremation; it may be held either in the church or at the crematorium[67]. The ashes of a cremated body should be reverently disposed of[68] by a minister in a churchyard, or in some other burial ground consecrated by the bishop for the sole purpose of burying cremated remains[69], or on an area of land designated

ground or cemetery or part of a burial ground or cemetery had been consecrated. The relative, friend, or legal representative having charge of or being responsible for the burial of any deceased person who had a right of interment in any such unconsecrated ground vested in a burial board, or provided under any Act relating to the burial of the dead, shall be entitled, if he think fit, to have such burial performed therein according to the rites of the Church of England by any minister of the said Church who may perform the same.'

[61] See **p. 237** *et seq. infra* and Canon B 1, para. 2.

[62] For example, 'in an unusual manner, such as an iron coffin or in a vault, or with unusual accompaniments': *Winstanley* v. *North Manchester Overseers* [1910] AC 7 at p. 16 *per* Lord Atkinson. As to iron coffins see *R* v. *Coleridge* (1819) 2 B. & Ald. 806; *Gilbert* v. *Buzzard* (1821) 2 Hag. Con. 333.

[63] *Gilbert* v. *Buzzard* (1821) 2 Hag. Con. 333 at p. 344: 'That bodies should be carried in a state of naked exposure to the grave would be a real offence to the living, as well as an apparent indignity to the dead. Some involucra, or coverings, have been deemed necessary in all civilized and Christian countries; but chests and trunks containing the bodies, descending along with them into the grave, and remaining there till their own decay, cannot plead either the same necessity nor the same general use.' This, of course reflects an age when coffins were not the norm. The rubric before the prayers at the grave side in The Order for the Burial of the Dead in the Book of Common Prayer states: 'When they come to the Grave, while the corpse is made ready to be laid in the earth, the Priest shall say, or the Priest and Clerks shall sing . . . ' Stephens, *The Book of Common Prayer*, vol. II, at p. 1731 comments: 'When the body is stript of all but its grave attire, and is just being put into the ground, it is most likely to make the deepest impression upon us, and to strike us with the most serious apprehensions of our immortality. This happy opportunity the Church is unwilling to lose . . . ' In the present age when coffins are the norm, if not universally used, the rubric is best interpreted as referring to the readying of the coffin or urn for the committal.

[64] See **p. 237** *et seq. infra* and Canon B 1, para. 2. See, also, the Burial Laws Amendment Act 1880, s. 7.　　　　　　　　　　　　　　　　　　　　　　　　　　　　　[65] Canon B 38, para. 3.

[66] See *In re Dixon* [1892] P 386 at p. 394 *per* Dr Tristram; but cp. *In re St John, Hampstead* [1939] P 281 at p. 284 *per* Chancellor Errington.

[67] Canon B 38, para. 4(a). To this extent that which is said in *Legal Opinions concerning the Church of England* at p. 135 is misleading.

[68] ' . . . I cannot consider the placing of ashes in an urn, still less its contemplated storage, to be an interment': *In re St John, Hampstead* [1939] P 281 at p. 284 *per* Chancellor Errington (a case concerning disused burial grounds).

[69] See the Church of England (Miscellaneous Provisions) Measure 1992, s. 3(2).

by the bishop specifically for this purpose, or at sea[70]. A funeral service at a crematorium must be performed only in accordance with directions given by the bishop[71].

H   Still-Births

No-one who has control over, or who ordinarily buries bodies in, any burial ground may bury, or permit to be buried, any still-born child[72] before there is delivered to him a written certificate given by the registrar of Births, Deaths and Marriages or, if there has been an inquest, an order of the coroner[73].

The Alternative Service Book specifically provides prayers, and alternative psalms, that may be used at the burial or cremation of a still-born child[74]. It would seem to be permissible to include at least one or two of them in a service according to the Book of Common Prayer rite, although this would depend very much upon the pastoral situation[75].

I   Rites of Burial

(i)   Generally

Subject to the provisions of the Burial Laws Amendment Act 1880[76], one of the authorised burial services must be read if the burial is in consecrated ground. As Sir John Nicholl said in *Kemp* v. *Wickes*[77]:

> . . . the minister is to read the service; our Church knowing no such indecency as putting the body into the consecrated ground without the service being at the same time performed.

---

[70] Canon B 38, para. 4(b). It should be noted that the text does not follow the precise wording of the Canon.

[71] Canon B 38, para. 7. This must mean the diocesan bishop. He cannot, of course, give unlawful directions and therefore the directions cannot permit the use of rites not otherwise authorised. See, too, **p. 213** *infra*.

[72] That is, a child that has issued forth from its mother after the twenty-fourth week of pregnancy and which did not at any time after being completely expelled from its mother breathe or show any other sign of life: Births and Deaths Registration Act 1926, s. 12; Births and Deaths Registration Act 1953, s. 41; Still-Birth (Definition) Act 1992, s. 1.

[73] Births and Deaths Registration Act 1926, s. 5; Births and Deaths Registration Act 1953, s. 43(1), Sch. 1, para. 3. To do so is a criminal offence: Births and Deaths Registration Act 1926, s. 5 (as amended). [74] *Op. cit.* at pp. 322–333.

[75] See **p. 47** *et seq. supra*. The pastoral question is particularly emphasised in relation to funerals by Note 7 at p. 306 of the Alternative Service Book.

[76] See **p. 200** *et seq. supra*; see, too, the Local Authorities' Cemeteries Order 1977 (SI 1977 No. 204), art. 5(5). [77] (1809) 3 Phillim. 264 at p. 295.

If the burial is in unconsecrated ground the grave must be blessed on the minister's first coming to it, if the rites of the Church of England are to be used[78]. Indeed, no other rite may lawfully be used by a Church of England minister[79].

Especial care[80] should be taken to ensure that any variations made to any of the rites[81] pursuant to Canon B 5, para. 1, are merely minor and are not contrary to, nor indicative of any departure from, the doctrine of the Church of England in any essential matter[82]. This is exemplified by *Re Todd*[83] where the minister omitted the words 'As our hope is this our brother does' during the burial service because he erroneously believed that the deceased had died in a state of intoxication[84]. Although this case was decided before any flexibility was permitted in the performance of services, the same decision would certainly still be reached today. As the Bishop of Exeter said when delivering sentence[85]:

> It is plain and undeniable, that they were omitted, because the minister did not choose to give expression to the pious and charitable hope of the Church, that the deceased Christian brother resteth in Our Lord Jesus Christ, who is the Resurrection and the Life ... Even if the deceased had died in a state of intoxication, however his minister may have lamented it, however it may have impaired the hope of his being admitted to rest in Christ, yet it ought not, on just consideration of the terms of the Christian covenant, to have extinguished that hope, much less to have induced him to have proclaimed, or even to suggest, the extinction of it ... To hold the contrary – to assert for the priesthood a right to judge in every case of the final condition of the deceased – would be to claim a power of the Keys, above that to which Papal Rome ever dared to aspire, and which this reformed Church, while it maintains the just authority of its priest for edification, not for destruction, hath always most strongly repudiated.

---

[78] Canon B 38, para. 5. No minister can be compelled to perform any of the burial rites on unconsecrated ground: *Rugg* v. *Kingsmill* (1868) 5 Moo. PCCNS 79 at pp. 89–90. However, the relative, friend or legal representative having charge of, or being responsible for, the burial of any deceased person who had the right of burial in any unconsecrated ground is entitled, if he thinks fit, to have such burial performed therein according to the rites of the Church of England by any minister of that Church who is willing to perform the same: Burial Laws Amendment Act 1880, s. 12.

[79] Canon B 1, para. 2; see, however, **p. 26** *et seq. supra*. As to Canon B 38, para. 7, see **p. 207, footnote 71** *supra*.

[80] See, too, the Commentary by the Bishop of Winchester in the Funeral Service for a Child dying near the Time of Birth at p. 11 *et seq.*

[81] The Alternative Service Book itself provides for the use of additional material at the Committal and Interment of the Ashes '[i]f pastoral needs require': see Note 7 at p. 306.

[82] Canon B 5, para. 3.   [83] (1842) 3 Notes of Cases, Supp. li.

[84] The burial of those believed to have died in a state of intoxication seems to have been a particular problem: see, too, *Cooper* v. *Dodd* (1850) 2 Rob. Eccl. 270 at p. 272. This may have been partially connected with lesser excommunication and Canon 27 of the 1603 Canons: see **p. 239** *et seq. infra.*   [85] *Op. cit.* at pp. lii–liii.

(ii)   Prayers for the dead

It is legal to say prayers for the dead, unless those prayers embrace the Roman doctrine of purgatory[86].

(iii)   Before and after the funeral

The Alternative Service Book provides A Service which may be used before a Funeral[87]. This service is for use '[i]f the body is brought to church the day before the funeral'[88], although no doubt greater flexibility as to timing may also be used as the rubric seems to be merely directive rather than relating to Church order. Alternatively, the service may be said in the home before the body is taken to church[89]. The Alternative Service Book also provides Prayers after the Birth of a still-born Child or the Death of a newly-born Child; these may be used 'in church, in hospital, or in the home'[90].

An Order for the Burial of the Dead in Series 1 Burial Services[91] provides that the Service in Church may be used as a memorial service apart from the funeral[92].

(iv)   Location

In spite of the subsequent rubric in relation to the reading of the psalms[93] in the Order for the Burial of the Dead in the Book of Common Prayer, the rubrics at the commencement of the rite make it clear that the service might always be taken wholly at the grave side[94]. Indeed, the Alternative Service Book also states[95]:

The Service in Church the phrase 'in Church' does not preclude the possibility of the service being held elsewhere than in the parish church[96].

---

[86] 14 Halsbury's Laws of England (4th ed.) at para. 1044; see, too, **p. 55** *et seq. supra.*

[87] *Op. cit.* at p. 325 *et seq.*   [88] Note 46 at p. 325.

[89] See the rubric at the conclusion of the service: *op. cit.* at p. 327.

[90] Note 33 at p. 322.

[91] (Cambridge University Press, Oxford University Press, SPCK.) See, too, **p. 210** *et seq. infra.*

[92] See the rubric at the top of p. 21.

[93] 'After they are come into the Church ... ' Stephens, *The Book of Common Prayer*, vol. II, at p. 1719 says: 'But it is illegal to go into the church at the conclusion of the prayers at the grave, and there read the psalm and lesson.' However, that view was based on the then rigorist interpretation of the Book of Common Prayer. See, further, **p. 210, footnote 101** *infra.*

[94] 'The Priest and Clerks meeting the Corpse at the entrance of the Church-yard, and going before it, either into the Church, or towards the Grave ... ' The alternative was provided because of the possible state of the corpse and because of infectious diseases: Stephens, *The Book of Common Prayer*, vol. II, at p. 1719–1721. The 'clerks' referred to are the members of the choir: *ibid* at pp. 1712–1713.   [95] Note 2 at p. 306.

[96] This must be read subject to what is said below.

Moreover, as the Alternative Service Book also makes provision for the service to be said at sea[97], it is clear that this Note does not merely refer to other buildings. This being so, the Funeral Service for a Child Dying near the Time of Birth[98], and any of the other burial rites, may also be used outside.

Indeed, this is made clear by the Series 1 Burial Services which adopt the same introductory rubrics as in the Book of Common Prayer[99] but then state[100]:

The burial may precede the service in the church and the prayers.

The service in any rite may therefore be held partially inside and partially outside the church[101].

It is not lawful to take a funeral service in an undertaker's chapel[102].

(v)   Sermons and eulogies

Although the Book of Common Prayer makes no provision for a sermon, such provision is made in the Funeral Service in the Alternative Service Book[103]. The inclusion of a sermon in the rite according to The Book of Common Prayer would seem to be permitted either as being *de minimis* or by reason of Canon B 5, para. 1. If it has a Christian content, a 'sermon' also embraces a eulogy[104]. If the eulogy is a sermon, Canon B 18, para. 2, applies as to who may deliver it; if it is not, the delivery[105] of a eulogy probably also falls within Canon B 5, para. 1, or is *de minimis*. It must, of course, be reverent[106].

(vi)   Burial on land

In addition to the burial services[107] in the Book of Common Prayer and the Authorised Service Book, the General Synod has authorised the use of the Series

---

[97] Note 5 at p. 306.

[98] *Op. cit.*, p. 2, Note 2, states: 'The Service may take place in church, crematorium, hospital or home.' Presumably the reference to the service being taken at home is primarily in relation to when the burial or cremation has already taken place: see *ibid*, Note 3.

[99] See the rubrics, *op. cit.*, at pp. 5 and 6, 25 and 26.

[100] See the rubric, *op. cit.*, at p. 18; see, too, the first rubric at p. 29.

[101] Stephens, *The Book of Common Prayer*, vol. II, at p. 1719 says: 'But it is illegal to go into the church at the conclusion of the prayers at the grave, and there read the psalm and lesson.' However, that was based on the then rigorist interpretation of the Book of Common Prayer. This is also borne out by the question of separate committals in relation to cremation: see **p. 206 *supra***.

[102] *Legal Opinions concerning the Church of England* at pp. 134–136.

[103] See Note 6 at p. 313. Note 3 at p. 306 states: '**A Sermon** A sermon may be preached elsewhere than at section 6.' As these initial Notes deal with each of the various funeral services (see, for example, Note 4), this also permits the preaching of a sermon in the other Alternative Service Book funeral services. Even if this is incorrect, the inclusion of a sermon in those other services would seem to be *de minimis* or to fall within the ambit of Canon B 5, para. 1.

[104] See **p. 25 *supra***.   [105] Even by someone falling outside Canon B 18, para. 2.

[106] See **p. 237 *et seq. infra***.

[107] See, further, *Ministry at the Time of Death* and **p. 219 *infra***.

1 Burial Services[108]. The House of Bishops has also commended a Funeral Service for a Child Dying near the Time of Birth[109].

The Alternative Service Book provides for a Funeral Service with Holy Communion[110]. As the Order for the Burial of the Dead in Series 1 Burial Services also makes provision in relation to any celebration of Holy Communion on the day of the burial[111], there seems no reason why such a celebration should not be coupled with a burial service according to the Book of Common Prayer.

The Alternative Service Book also provides that in the case of a cremation the Committal may precede the church service[112]. Canon B 38, para. 4(a), also provides that:

> When a body is to be cremated, the burial service may precede, accompany, or follow the cremation; and may be held either in the church or at the crematorium

The same must also be true in relation to the rite according to the Book of Common Prayer[113]. The Order for the Burial of the Dead in the Series 1 Burial Services provides both for when the Order is used at the time of the cremation and when it is used at the burial of the ashes after cremation[114]. Indeed, the Funeral Service for a Child dying near the Time of Birth provides for the omission of the Committal altogether, if the burial or cremation has already taken place[115].

(vii)   Burial at sea

The Book of Common Prayer provides special words of committal for a service of burial at sea[116] and the Alternative Service Book provides particular variations in such circumstances[117].

---

[108] *Public Worship in the Church of England* (5th ed.) at p. 13.

[109] (Church House Publishing, 1991.) See **p. 212 *et seq. infra.***   [110] *Op. cit.* at p. 328.

[111] See *op. cit.* at p. 21.

[112] Note 6 at p. 306. *Ibid*, Note 4, envisages that the whole of the service may not take place at the crematorium.

[113] See *In re Dixon* [1892] P 386 at p. 394 *per* Dr Tristram; but cp. *In re St John, Hampstead* [1939] P 281 at p. 284 *per* Chancellor Errington.   [114] *Op. cit.* at p. 23.

[115] *Op. cit.* at p. 2, Note 3. It is therefore arguable that its omission from other rites in similar circumstances may be justified by reason of Canon B 5, para, 1. In these circumstances the Committal should still be used earlier, as Note 6 at p. 306 of the Alternative Service Book envisages. Indeed, this may be so even when the Funeral Service for a Child dying near the Time of Birth is used. The Alternative Service Book itself provides for the use of additional material at the Committal and Interment of the Ashes '[i]f pastoral needs require': see Note 7 at p. 306. A similar addition would be permissible in other rites under Canon B 5, para. 1, especially when the Committal or Interment takes place separately.

[116] Forms of Prayer to be used at Sea – At the Burial of their Dead at Sea.

[117] Note 5 at p. 306.

(viii) Burial of children

The Alternative Service Book provides a special service for the Funeral of a Child[118] and Series 1 Burial Services provide an Order for the Burial of a Child[119]. The Prayers after the Birth of a still-born Child or the Death of a newly-born Child in the Alternative Service Book may be used at the burial or cremation of such a child[120]. It would seem to be permissible to include at least one or two of these prayers in a service according to the Book of Common Prayer rite, although this would depend very much upon the pastoral situation[121].

The Funeral Service for a Child dying near the Time of Birth[122] specifically envisages that it may be used if the burial or cremation has already taken place[123].

The Alternative Service Book has provision for the combination of the Funeral of a Child with the Holy Communion service[124] and the Order for the Burial of the Dead provides for such occasions when an adult and child are buried together[125].

(ix) Exceptions

The exceptions set out in Canon B 38, para. 2, to the duty to read one of the normal burial rites reflect the rubric[126] at the commencement of the Order for the Burial of the Dead in the Book of Common Prayer:

> Here it is to be noted, that the Office ensuing is not to be used for any that die unbaptized, or excommunicate, or have laid violent hands upon themselves.

The reasoning behind this rubric was explained in *Kemp* v. *Wickes*[127]:

> ... [T]aking the context of the law, putting unbaptized persons in association with excommunicated persons and with suicides, both of whom are considered as no longer Christians, it leads to the same construction as the general import of the words; namely, that burial is refused to those who are not Christians at all, and not to those who are baptized according to the forms of any particular Church.

As has been seen[128], it is irrelevant by whom the baptism is administered as long as it is baptism with water in the name of the Trinity[129]. Moreover, the

---

[118] See *op. cit.* at p. 318 *et seq.*   [119] *Op. cit.* at p. 25 *et seq.*

[120] See Note 33 at p. 322.

[121] See **p. 47 *et seq. supra*.** The pastoral question is particularly emphasised in relation to funerals in Note 7 at p. 306 of the Alternative Service Book.   [122] (Church House Publishing, 1991.)

[123] Note 3 at *op. cit.*, p. 2.   [124] See *op. cit.* at p. 329 *et seq.*   [125] *Op. cit.* at p. 21.

[126] For the background to this rubric see **p. 130, footnote 4 *supra*.**

[127] (1809) 3 Phillim. 264 at p. 273.   [128] See **p. 131 *et seq. supra*.**

[129] *Kemp* v. *Wickes* (1809) 3 Phillim. 264; *Escott* v. *Mastin* (1842) 4 Moo. PCC 104; *Nurse* v. *Henslowe* (1844) 3 Notes of Cases 272; *Titchmarsh* v. *Chapman* (1844) 3 Notes of Cases 370; *R* v. *Vicar of Bassingbourne* (1845) 9 JP Jo. 83. In the case of the burial of a stranger his proper

exception in relation to those who are excommunicate applies only to greater excommunication[130] and, therefore, has extremely limited, if any, relevance to-day[131]. In so far as suicides are concerned, Canon B 38, para. 2, emphasises that the deceased was 'of sound mind'[132]; moreover, the minister's own opinion cannot prevail over a coroner's verdict[133].

When one of these exceptions applies[134], the minister must use at the burial such service as may be approved by the Ordinary[135], being a service neither contrary to, nor indicative of any departure from, the doctrine of the Church of England in any essential matter[136]. If a form of service for the burial of suicides is approved by the General Synod[137], that service must be used where applicable unless the person having charge of, or being responsible for, the burial requests the use of a service approved by the Ordinary[138]. A minister may not use or authorise any other form of service in spite of Canon B 5, para. 2[139].

(x) Cemeteries

In addition to the minister's duty only to use authorised rites[140], a funeral service at a crematorium or cemetery must be performed in accordance with directions given by the bishop[141].

baptism should be presumed: see *Cripps on Church and Clergy* (8th ed.) at p. 566. This accords with the legal maxim *omnia praesumuntur rite esse acta.*

[130] This is made clear by Canon 68 of the 1603 Canons upon which the present Canon is partially based: 'And if he shall refuse to ... bury ... (except the party deceased were denounced excommunicated *majori excommunicatione*, for some grievous and notorious crime, and no man able to testify of his repentance,) he shall be suspended ... ' As to testimony concerning repentance see Phillimore, *Ecclesiastical Law* (2nd ed.) vol. I, at pp. 669–670. As to greater excommunication see **p. 85, footnote 253** *supra*. [131] See **p. 25** *supra*.

[132] This was in any event the law: see Phillimore, *Ecclesiastical Law* (2nd ed.) vol. I, at p. 670. Indeed, the suicide must also have reached years of discretion: *Clift* v. *Schwabe* (1846) 3 CB 437 at pp. 472–476 *per* Pollock CB; *Dufaur* v. *Professional Life Assurance Co.* (1858) 25 Beav. 599 at p. 602. See, too, Briden & Hanson, *Moore's Introduction to English Canon Law* (3rd ed.) at pp. 82–82.

[133] *Cooper* v. *Dodd* (1850) 2 Rob. Eccl. 270; see, too, Phillimore, *Ecclesiastical Law* (2nd ed.) vol. I, at p. 671.

[134] Canon B 38, para. 6, states: 'If any doubts arise whether any person deceased may be buried according to the rites of the Church of England, the minister shall refer the matter to the bishop and obey his order and direction.' This provision is perhaps not felicitously worded as it must be concerned with whether or not any of the exceptions apply rather than with the question whether no authorised service may be used; the infelicity probably arises by reason of the legislative changes made after the promulgation of Canon 68 of the 1603 Canons. The Canon must refer to the diocesan bishop. Although there is no express saving in relation to the jurisdiction of the courts as there is in Canon B 5, para. 4, (see **p. 48** *et seq. supra*), the courts must nevertheless remain the final arbiter because of Canon B 38, para. 1; see, too, *R* v. *Taylor*, cited in Phillimore, *Ecclesiastical Law* (2nd ed.) vol. I, at p. 653. The minister would commit an ecclesiastical offence if he were to disobey such an order or direction; such a direction must be seen as obligatory, if only because of the change of wording so as to include 'direction' when the present Canon B 5, para. 4, was promulgated: see **pp. 31** *et seq.* and **48** *et seq. supra*. [135] That is, the diocesan bishop.

[136] Canon B 38, para. 2. See, further, **p. 218** *et seq. infra.*

[137] Under Canon B 2. It has not yet done so. [138] Canon B 38, para. 2.

[139] See **p. 220** *et seq. infra.* [140] Canon B 1, para. 2.

[141] Canon B 38, para. 7. This must mean the diocesan bishop. See, too, **p. 207, footnote 71** *supra*.

The Alternative Service Book provides for the omission of certain sections of the service when the whole service is said at the crematorium[142].

J   Fees

Fees may be charged in accordance with the current Parochial Fees Order[143].

K   Registers

(i)   Generally[144]

A minister[145] officiating at a burial according to the rites of the Church of England[146] must as soon as possible after the burial has taken place enter in the appropriate register book[147] of burials the particulars required; he must sign the register in the place provided[148].

Where such a burial takes place in an extra-parochial place, unless it takes place in the burial ground of a church or chapel for which a register book of burials has been provided[149], the minister officiating at the burial must as soon as possible after the burial has taken place send to the incumbent or priest in charge of such of the adjoining parishes as the bishop in whose diocese that place is may direct a certificate signed by him certifying when and where the burial took place and containing the required particulars[150].

On receiving such a certificate the incumbent or priest in charge must enter

---

[142] Note 4 at p. 306.

[143] Ecclesiastical Fees Measure 1986. Any such fee is recoverable as a debt: *ibid*, s. 7. During a vacancy in a benefice the fees which, but for the vacancy, would be paid to the incumbent must be paid to the diocesan board of finance or to such other person as the board, after consultation with the bishop, may direct: *ibid*, s. 3(1).

[144] For civil offences relating to burial registers and certificates see 10 Halsbury's Laws of England (4th ed.) at paras 1191–1195.

[145] For these purposes 'minister' means any person who is authorised to bury the dead according to the rites of the Church of England: Parochial Registers and Records Measure 1978, s. 3(5).

[146] This does not apply in relation to a burial which takes place in a cemetery to which an Act incorporating the Cemeteries Clauses Act 1847 applies or in a cemetery provided and maintained by a burial authority within the meaning of section 214 of the Local Government Act 1972: Parochial Registers and Records Measure 1978, s. 3(1), (4).

[147] A register book must be provided for every churchyard or burial ground belonging to a church or chapel used for burials: Canon F 11, para. 1; Canon F 14; Parochial Registers and Records Measure 1978, s. 1. Register books must be provided, maintained and kept in accordance with the Statutes and Measures relating thereto, and the rules and regulations made thereunder and from time to time in force: Canon F 11, para. 2.

[148] Parochial Registers and Records Measure 1978, s. 3(1). Canon B 39, para. 1, states: 'In all matters pertaining to the registers of baptisms, marriages, and burials every minister shall observe the law from time to time in force relating thereto.'

[149] By virtue of the 1978 Measure or any enactment repealed by it: Parochial Registers and Records Measure 1978, s. 3(2).   [150] *Ibid*.

particulars of the burial to which the certificate relates in the appropriate register book of burials[151].

A person required to register a burial who discovers an error in the form of substance of an entry is not liable to any penalty under the Forgery Act 1913[152], by reason only that within one month after the discovery of the error he corrects the erroneous entry[153] by an entry in the margin of the register book[154] but without altering the original entry[155].

(ii) Cathedrals, etc.

So far as is applicable and with necessary modifications the provisions concerning registers apply for any cathedral or collegiate church or any other church or chapel which does not belong to a parish[156].

---

[151] By virtue of the 1978 Measure or any enactment repealed by it: Parochial Registers and Records Measure 1978, s. 3(3). He must add the following words: 'According to the certificate of   received by me on the   day of   .'

[152] Now repealed but see the Forgery and Counterfeiting Act 1981, s. 30, Schedule, Pt I.

[153] In the presence of two persons who were present at the burial to which the entry relates or the churchwardens of the parish to which the register book belongs: Parochial Registers and Records Measure 1978, s. 4(1), (2)(b).

[154] The marginal entry must be signed by whomsoever the entry is made and must be attested by the persons in whose presence the entry is required to be made; the date of the entry must be added by the person by whom it is made: Parochial Registers and Records Measure 1978, s. 4(3).

[155] Parochial Registers and Records Measure 1978, s. 4.

[156] Parochial Registers and Records Measure 1978, s. 5.

9

OCCASIONAL SERVICES

A General

(i) Definition and choices

As has been seen[1], it is not entirely clear what services are known as the 'occasional offices'[2] but *The Oxford Dictionary of the Christian Church*[3] gives the following definition:

> **OCCASIONAL OFFICES**. In the [Book of Common Prayer], the services which in distinction from the constant offices of the Church (viz. Mattins and Evensong and the Holy Communion), are used only as occasion demand. They include Baptism, Confirmation, Matrimony, Visitation of the Sick, Communion of the Sick, Burial of the Dead, and the Commination.

As regards these services, other than the Order of Confirmation[4], the choice of which rite to use lies initially with the officiating minister[5].

(ii) Convocations

The Convocations of Canterbury and York may approve[6] within their respective provinces forms of service[7] for use in any cathedral, church or elsewhere on occasions for which no provision is made[8] in the Book of Common Prayer or by the General Synod under Canon B 2[9]. Such forms of service must in their opinion be reverent and seemly in both words and order[10]; they may not be

---

[1] See **p. 61** *et seq. supra*.

[2] See 14 Halsbury's Laws of England (4th ed.) at para. 936, Note 6.

[3] (2nd ed. 1974) at p. 989.   [4] See Canon B 3, para. 5; see, also, **p. 232** *infra*.

[5] Canon B 3, para. 4. See **p. 62** *supra*.

[6] Amendments may similarly be approved: Canon B 1, para. 1(e).

[7] These words have the same meaning as in Canon B 1: Canon B 4, para. 4; and see **p. 3, footnote 19** *supra*.   [8] See **p. 221** *et seq. infra*.

[9] Canon B 4, para. 1.

[10] In the unlikely event of any question arising as to whether the words and order are indeed reverent and seemly, a court would not be entitled to substitute its own views. On the other hand, if the reports of the proceedings of the Convocations did not disclose any consideration of this question, the court might then consider whether the form of service was *ultra vires* by reason of the lack of consideration of a necessary matter.

contrary to, nor indicative of any departure from, the doctrine of the Church of England[11] in any essential matter[12].

(iii) Archbishops

Similarly, the archbishops[13] may approve[14] forms of service[15] for use in any cathedral, church or elsewhere in the provinces of Canterbury and York on occasions for which no provision is made[16] in the Book of Common Prayer or by the General Synod under Canon B 2 or by the Convocations under Canon B 4[17]. Such forms of service must in their opinion be reverent and seemly in both words and order[18]; they may not be contrary to, nor indicative of any departure from, the doctrine of the Church of England[19] in any essential matter[20].

Any form of service made under Canon C 4A, para. 3, 'for deaconesses to be made deacon' should be seen as embraced within Canon B 4, para. 2, otherwise their use would still be illegal by reason of Canon B 1, para. 2[21].

Where a form of service[22] has been prepared with a view to its submission to the General Synod for approval by the Synod under Canon B 2, the archbishops[23] after consultation with the House of Bishops of the General Synod

[11] See Canon A 5. This is in accordance with the Church of England (Worship and Doctrine) Measure 1974, s. 5(1): 'References in this Measure to the doctrine of the Church of England shall be construed in accordance with the statement concerning that doctrine contained in the Canons of the Church of England, which statement is in the following terms: "The doctrine of the Church of England is grounded in the holy Scriptures, and in such teachings of the ancient Fathers and Councils of the Church as are agreeable to the said Scriptures. In particular such doctrine is to be found in the Thirty-nine Articles of Religion, the Book of Common Prayer, and the Ordinal."'

[12] This aspect is therefore subject to the general control of the courts. See, however, *R* v. *Ecclesiastical Committee of the Houses of Parliament, ex Parte The Church Society* [1994] COD 319, *The Times*, 4 November 1993; *Ex Parte Williamson, The Times*, 9 March 1994 (for full transcripts see Hill, *Ecclesiastical Law* at pp. 72 and 77 respectively).

[13] The wording of the Canon suggests that they may only act jointly. This would be confirmed by the use of the plural in Canon B 5, para. 2, if the plural were not also used in relation to the Convocations: see **footnote 23** *infra*. See also Canon C 4A, para. 4, and **p. 5, footnote 33** *supra*; see, further, the Church of England (Worship and Doctrine) Measure 1974, s. 7(2).

[14] The archbishops have approved the Service for Remembrance Sunday printed at pp. 84–90 of *The Promise of His Glory* for use in their respective provinces: see *op. cit.* at p. ix. Amendments may similarly be approved: Canon B 1, para. 1(e).

[15] These words have the same meaning as in Canon B 1: Canon B 4, para. 4; and see **p. 3, footnote 19** *supra*.   [16] See **p. 221** *et seq. infra*.

[17] Canon B 4, para. 2.

[18] In the unlikely event of any question arising as to whether the words and order are indeed reverent and seemly, a court would not be entitled to substitute its own views. On the other hand, any court would no doubt be extremely reluctant to conclude that the archbishops had failed to consider the question.   [19] See Canon A 5.

[20] This aspect is therefore subject to the general control of the courts. See, however, *R* v. *Ecclesiastical Committee of the Houses of Parliament, ex Parte The Church Society* [1994] COD 319, *The Times*, 4 November 1993; *Ex Parte Williamson, The Times*, 9 March 1994 (for full transcripts see Hill, *Ecclesiastical Law* at pp. 72 and 77 respectively).   [21] See, too, **p. 232** *et seq. infra*.

[22] These words have the same meaning as in Canon B 1: Canon B 5A, para. 3; and see **p. 3, footnote 19** *supra*.

[23] In comparison with Canon B 4, para. 2, and in the light of the necessity to consult the House of Bishops it would seem that the archbishops may only act jointly: see **footnote 13** *supra*.

may, prior to that submission, authorise its use for an experimental period[24] on such terms[25] and in such places[26] or parishes as they may designate[27].

(iv) Ordinaries

The diocesan bishop[28] may approve[29] forms of service[30] for use in any cathedral, church or elsewhere in the diocese[31] on occasions for which no provision is made[32] in the Book of Common Prayer or by the General Synod under Canon B 2[33] or by the Convocation or archbishops under Canon B 4[34]. Such forms of service must in his opinion be reverent and seemly in both words and order[35]; they may not be contrary to, nor indicative of any departure from, the doctrine of the Church of England[36] in any essential matter[37].

[24] The period must be specified by the archbishops: Canon B 5A, para. 1.

[25] The authorisation ought to specify the persons who may make up the congregation: Church of England (Worship and Doctrine) Measure 1974, s. 1(6). No doubt this specification may be in general terms.

[26] If the form of service has been authorised to be used in any church, the provisions of Canon B 3 (concerning the choice of the forms of service to be used) apply: Canon B 5A, para. 2; see **p. 60 *et seq. supra*.** The use of the words 'any church' is curious but would seem, in fact, to mean 'a church'.

[27] Church of England (Worship and Doctrine) Measure 1974, s. 1(6); Canon B 5A, para. 1.

[28] The Canon uses the word 'ordinary' but in this context that can only mean the diocesan bishop: see the Church of England (Worship and Doctrine) Measure 1974, s. 1(5)(a) and **p. 5, footnote 34** *supra*. This is in spite of the use of the word 'bishop' in Canon B 5, para. 4.

[29] Amendments may similarly be approved: Canon B 1, para. 1(e). Approval cannot be implied from a general commendation by the House of Bishops: see **p. 221 *infra*.**

[30] These words have the same meaning as in Canon B 1: Canon B 4, para. 4; and see **p. 3, footnote 19** *supra*.

[31] This would include authorisation in relation to a particular parish.

[32] See **p. 221 *et seq. infra*.**

[33] It is this provision which prevents a bishop approving a service, such as Series I Holy Communion, which is no longer authorised by the General Synod (other than perhaps for ecumenical joint worship), unless no provision has been made to replace the previous service: see **p. 228 *infra*.** On 26 January 1988, the House of Bishops considered 'customary variations' to the Book of Common Prayer which were not authorised for use but which had nevertheless been in customary use over many years. It thereupon passed a resolution: 'that the House of Bishops is agreed in regarding the continued use, where well established, of any form of service which has, at any time since 1965, been canonically authorised (notwithstanding the fact that such authorisation was not reviewed after it lapsed) as not being of "substantial importance", within the meaning of Canon B 5.4.' (The latter reference would now be to Canon B 5, para. 1; the previous Canon did not include the present definition of 'form of service'.) It may, of course, be that variations appearing within a particular service which is no longer authorised nonetheless fall within the provisions of Canon B 5, para. 1 (see, for example, **p. 52 *supra***). However, a complete service cannot as such fall within the ambit of para. 1 nor can the resolution circumvent the provisions of Canon B 5, para. 2. The resolution certainly cannot fetter a bishop's discretion under the Ecclesiastical Jurisdiction Measure 1963, s. 23: see 1(1) Halsbury's Laws of England (4th ed.) at para. 30.   [34] Canon B 4, para. 3.

[35] It seems, therefore, that it would not be open to a court to decide whether any such form of service is in fact reverent and seemly, other than in the extremely unlikely event that there was evidence to suggest that the bishop had not in fact considered the matter.   [36] See Canon A 5.

[37] This aspect is therefore subject to the general control of the courts. See, however, *R* v. *Ecclesiastical Committee of the Houses of Parliament, Ex Parte The Church Society* [1994] COD 319, *The Times*, 4 November 1993; *Ex Parte Williamson, The Times*, 9 March 1994 (for full transcripts see Hill, *Ecclesiastical Law* at pp. 72 and 77 respectively).

Diocesan bishops were first given statutory authority to prescribe or approve certain services in 1880. Section 13 of the Burial Laws Amendment Act 1880, provides that:

> ... it shall be lawful for any minister in holy orders of the Church of England authorised to perform the burial service, in any case where the burial of the dead according to the rites of the Church of England may not be used[38], and in any other case at the request of the relative, friend, or legal representative having the charge of the burial of the deceased, to use at the burial, such service, consisting of prayers taken from the Book of Common Prayer and portions of Holy Scripture, as may be prescribed or approved of by the ordinary[39], without being subject to any ecclesiastical or other censure or penalty.

By the Prayer Book (Further Provisions) Measure 1968[40], section 13 is now to have effect:

> ... as if reference to the [Office for the burial of the dead in the Book of Common Prayer] included a reference to any form of service available for the burial of suicides and authorised by Canon of the General Synod[41] or approved thereunder, and as if the words 'consisting of prayers taken from the Book of Common Prayer and portions of Holy Scripture' were omitted.

The wording of this provision might suggest that in cases (other than suicides) falling within section 13 the bishop may only approve a service consisting of prayers taken from the Book of Common Prayer and portions of Holy Scripture. However, although the General Synod is not mentioned in the 1880 Act, the 1968 Measure envisaged that it might use its powers in relation to suicides; thus its powers are not limited by the 1880 Act[42]. That being so, the bishop's powers

---

[38] That is in the circumstances set out in the rubric at the commencement of The Order for the Burial of the Dead in the Book of Common Prayer: namely, the burial of the unbaptised, certain suicides and excommunicates. For the ancient canon law on which the rubric is based see Gibson, *Codex Iuris Ecclesiastici Anglicani*, vol. I, at p. 450; see also *Ayliffes's Parergon Iuris Canonici* at pp. 132–133. Such persons have a (possibly limited) right of burial in consecrated ground (see, further, **p. 213, footnote 134** *supra*) but, if such a burial takes place, only an authorised form of service may be used. Although it may be argued that an excommunicate may never be buried in consecrated ground, the provision in any event only applies to greater excommunication (see Canon 68 of the 1603 Canons) and there is no present provision in the law for the passing of such a sentence: see, however, 14 Halsbury's Laws of England (4th ed.) at para. 1384. See, too, **p. 85, footnote 253** *supra*, Briden & Hanson, *Moore's Introduction to English Canon Law* (3rd ed.) at p. 85, footnote 9, and *Kemp* v. *Wickes* (1842) 3 Phillim. 264 at pp. 271–272 *per* Sir John Nicholl (although the latter does not consider the position of the Anglican Church abroad). See, further, **p. 199** *et seq. supra*.

[39] That is, the diocesan bishop: Fellows, *The Law of Burial* (Hadden, Best & Co., Ltd, 1940) at p. 42.

[40] Section 5, as amended by the Church of England (Worship and Doctrine) Measure 1974, s. 6(2), Sch. 1, para. 1.   [41] No such form of service has at present been authorised.

[42] Similarly, its powers under the Church of England (Worship and Doctrine) Measure 1974, are not limited in relation to burials: see s. 1(1)(a).

are not limited to cases relating to suicides either and he may exercise his powers under Canon B 4, para. 3, in all cases falling within section 13 of the Burial Laws Amendment Act 1880. Indeed, this is borne out by Canon B 38, para. 2[43].

(v) Minister

The minister having the cure of souls[44] may on occasions for which no provision is made[45] in the Book of Common Prayer or by the General Synod under Canon B 2 or by the Convocations[46], archbishops[47] or the diocesan bishop[48] under Canon B 4 use forms of service[49] considered suitable by him[50] for those occasions and may permit another minister to use that form of service[51]. All forms of service used must be reverent and seemly and neither contrary to, nor indicative of any departure from, the doctrine of the Church of England[52].

[43] See **p. 212** *et seq. supra.*

[44] The words 'minister having a cure of souls' is not defined but see **pp. 134** *et seq. supra* and **228** *et seq. infra.* He may permit another minister to use the same form of service. Although no other minister is entitled to decide what may be used, the diocesan bishop may give special authorisation in relation to a particular parish under Canon B 4, para. 3. (Note 2 to *Ministry at the Time of Death* at p. 3 states that only a deacon authorised by the bishop may use the rite but, unless the service has been authorised under Canon B 4, this can only be guidance to the minister having the cure of souls; it is probably best not to see this as a directive under Canon C 18, para. 4 (see **p. 31** *et seq. supra*) as a particular bishop may not have been party to the commendation.) Although the Canon might be read as only permitting another minister to use forms of service already used by the minister having the cure of souls, such an interpretation would seem to be unnecessarily restrictive; moreover, to use a form of service permitted by him, although not yet used by him, would almost certainly be *de minimis.* By Canon C 24, para. 2, every priest having a cure of souls must, except for some reasonable cause approved by the bishop of the diocese, 'diligently administer the sacraments and other rites of the Church'.

[45] See **pp. 9** and **26** *et seq. supra* and **221** *infra.* For examples relating to particular occasions see *Inaugural Services* (Grove Booklet on Ministry and Worship No. 32, 1974).

[46] As the plural imports the singular and the Convocations can only approve forms of service within their respective provinces, this must refer to the Convocation of the relevant province alone.

[47] That is, jointly: see **p. 217, footnote 13** *supra.*

[48] The Canon uses the word 'ordinary' but in this context that can only mean the diocesan bishop: see the Church of England (Worship and Doctrine) Measure 1974, s. 1(5)(a) and **p. 5, footnote 34** *supra.*

[49] These words have the same meaning as in Canon B 1: Canon B 5, para. 5; and see **p. 3, footnote 19** *supra.*

[50] This is a matter for the minister having the cure of souls and not for the court, unless the form of service were so unsuitable that no reasonable minister could reach that conclusion. The actual use, or permission to another minister to use, the form of service would in itself indicate that he regarded the occasion as suitable.

[51] Canon B 5, para. 2. Although the latter part of Canon B 5, para. 2, is narrower in its provisions than the Church of England (Worship and Doctrine) Measure 1974, s. 1(5)(b), the Canon is entirely lawful as the subsection is only an empowering provision. In effect ministers other than the minister having the cure of souls may use the form suggested or none at all. The officiating minister must then decide what alternatives within the service are to be used.

[52] See *In re St John the Evangelist, Chopwell* (1995) in **Appendix 6** at **pp. 287–288** *infra;* Canon B 5, para. 3; see, too, Canon A 5. If any question is raised concerning the observance of these provisions, it may be referred to the bishop in order that he may give such pastoral guidance, advice or directions as he may think fit but such reference is without prejudice to the matter in question being made the subject matter of proceedings under the Ecclesiastical Jurisdiction Measure 1963:

The use by ministers of such publications as *Lent, Holy Week, Easter*[53] and *The Promise of His Glory*[54] that have been commended by the House of Bishops[55] has been specifically catered for. In a note to the former it is stated:

These Services and Prayers have been commended by the House of Bishops of the General Synod and are published with the agreement of the House.

Under Canon B 4 it is open to each Bishop to authorize, if he sees fit, the form of service to be used within his diocese. He may specify that the services shall be those commended by the House, or that a diocesan form of them shall be used. If the Bishop gives no directions in this matter[56] the priest remains free, subject to the terms of Canon B 5[57], to make use of the Services as commended by the House[58].

Save for certain exceptions there stated, the note to the latter publication is to a like effect.

Nonetheless, this raises the question of the meaning of the words 'on occasions for which no provision is made'[59]. The prefaces to these services do not in themselves have any legal force, although they may be regarded as having persuasive effect in the absence of any other guidance. On their face the words may be taken to refer to occasions for which no form of service has otherwise been approved, such as Remembrance Sunday or Compline[60]. The prefaces, however, clearly go much further and make it clear that all the services there commended are considered to fall within the ambit of Canon B 5, para. 2. Thus, for example, a special form of the eucharist is provided in *Lent, Holy Week, Easter*[61] for Palm Sunday, although the Book of Common Prayer certainly makes provision for its usual rite to be used on that day. It therefore seems that the

---

Canon B 5, para. 4. The 'bishop' is the diocesan bishop: see **p. 48 *supra***. Care must be taken not to prejudge a service because of its provenance or because of any particular title; it is primarily the contents that require consideration: see *Bishop of Oxford* v. *Henly* [1909] P 319 at pp. 327–328.

[53] (Church House Publishing, Cambridge University Press and SPCK, 1986.)

[54] (Church House Publishing and Mowbrays, 1991) at p. ix. In spite of the exceptions there stated (see *ibid* at p. 369, Note) the Suggested Calendar and lectionaries may now be authorised pursuant to Canons B 4 and 5.

[55] See also *Patterns for Worship* (Church House Publishing) at p. x; *Ministry at the Time of Death* (Church House Publishing) at p. 2; *Services of Prayer and Dedication after Civil Marriage* (Church House Publishing) at p. 3.

[56] That is, pursuant to Canon B 5. The bishop's approval cannot be implied from the general commendation by the House of Bishops: see **pp. 5** and **58 *et seq. infra***. See, too, Canon B 4, para. 3, and Canon C 18, para. 4.

[57] This is a reference to Canon B 5, para. 3: see *supra*. The commendation does not guarantee the legality of its use.   [58] By reason of Canon B 5, para. 2.

[59] A service which has ceased to be authorised under Canon B 2 cannot thereafter be permitted under Canons B 4 or 5 unless no provision has been made to replace it. See, too, **pp. 8, 55, footnote 168**, and **97 *supra***.   [60] Called 'Night Prayer' in *Lent, Holy Week, Easter* at p. 58 *et seq.*

[61] *Op. cit.* at p. 76 *et seq.* This provision, however, seems to run contrary to what is said at *Patterns for Worship* at p. 239.

word 'special' or 'particular' should be inferred before the word 'occasions' both in Canon B 5, para. 2, and in Canon B 4[62].

Another problem that, fortunately, arises more rarely concerns section 13 of the Burial Laws Amendment Act 1880. As has been seen[63], the diocesan bishop's powers to approve services are not limited by that section or by section 5 of the Prayer Book (Further Provisions) Measure 1968[64]. However, Canon B 5, para. 2, must be read in the light of Canon B 38, para. 2[65], which clearly envisages that any such service requires the approval either of the General Synod or the Ordinary. That being so, in spite of the generality of Canon B 5, para. 2, no minister may himself use, or authorise, any other form of service[66].

An archidiaconal visitation service[67] cannot be authorised by the archdeacon[68]; if it has not been formally approved by the diocesan bishop under Canon B 4, para. 3[69], the legal responsibility for such a service depends upon the local minister having the cure of souls. The question of joint worship under Canon B 43, para. 9, is dealt with separately[70].

B Particular Services[71]

(i) Churching of Women and Thanksgiving for Children

The Service for the Thanksgiving of Women after Child-Birth in the Book of Common Prayer provides that the mother:

> at the usual time after her Delivery shall come into the Church[72] decently apparelled, and there shall kneel down in some convenient place, as hath been accustomed[73], or as the Ordinary shall direct[74].

---

[62] This is also borne out by the argument in relation to the Burial Laws Amendment Act 1880, s. 13, and the authority of the Ordinary to approve services: see **p. 218 *et seq. supra***. Save in rare cases it is unlikely that Canon B 5, para. 1, could otherwise be relied upon to justify the use of such forms of service, as too great a variation would amount to an amalgam of forms of service: see **p. 52 *supra***. However, the argument would not permit the use of services no longer authorised by the General Synod. See, too, *p. 218 supra*.　　　　　　　　　　　　[63] See **p. 219 *supra***.

[64] As amended by the Church of England (Worship and Doctrine) Measure 1974, s. 6(2), Sch. I, para. 1.　　　　　　　　　　　　　　　　　　　　　　　　　　[65] See **p. 199 *supra***.

[66] See, too, the *Legal Opinions concerning the Church of England* at p. 24.

[67] Note **p. 25, footnote 190 *supra***.

[68] Other than in a parish where he himself has the cure of souls.

[69] See **p. 218 *et seq. supra***.　　　　[70] See **p. 228 *et seq. infra***.

[71] This chapter only deals with such occasional services as do not fall more logically into chapters on specific services.

[72] However, Note 2 at p. 212 of the Alternative Service Book states in relation to the Thanksgivings for the Birth of a Child and after Adoption: '**The Place** These services should normally be used in church. Use in the home or in hospital is permitted at the discretion of the priest.' This being so it would seem that the use of the rite according to the Book of Common Prayer in the home or in hospital would be *de minimis*.

[73] The pre-Reformation custom was to kneel at the church door but this was not continued after the Reformation: see Stephens, *The Book of Common Prayer*, vol. III, at pp. 1755–1756; Phillimore, *Ecclesiastical Law* (2nd ed.) vol. I, at p. 645. The words are not, therefore, a reference to canonical custom but to local practice.　　　　　　　　[74] See the rubric at the commencement of the service.

Moore's Introduction to English Canon Law[75] suggests that there is an implication that the service of Churching of Women should be the first public service attended by the mother[76] but, if so, the implication fades in the light of the Alternative Service Book permitting the use of the equivalent Thanksgiving for the Birth of a Child[77] in the home or in hospital at the priest's discretion[78]. In fact, the words 'at the usual time after delivery' refer to the time usually then taken for the lying-in[79] and, therefore, the timing now depends upon the physical state of the woman concerned. Moreover, it would seem that the minister would not now commit an offence if the service used at home or hospital were to be that from the Book of Common Prayer[80]. The direction as to apparel is one dealing with good order and depends, therefore, upon current views of neatness and decency[81].

According to the Book of Common Prayer the woman must also 'offer accustomed Offerings'[82] but, in the light of modern stipends and the lack of any reference to offerings in the Alternative Service Book, it is likely that this duty is now abrogated[83].

The Churching of Women, like the services of Thanksgiving for the Birth of a Child[84] and after Adoption[85] in the Alternative Service Book, must be taken by a priest[86] or by a deaconess or lay worker[87].

[75] (3rd ed.) at pp. 81–82; see, too, Phillimore, *Ecclesiastical Law*, (2nd ed.) vol. I, at p. 647.

[76] Whether married or not: Phillimore, *Ecclesiastical Law*, (2nd ed.) vol. I, at pp. 646–647. The contrary argument based on the need for penance and the word 'fitting' in the rubric at the end of the service in the Book of Common Prayer could no longer be sustained, especially in the absence of public penance and the omission of the word 'fitting' in Note 4 in the Alternative Service Book at p. 212. [77] *Op. cit.* at p. 212.

[78] See Note 2 at p. 212. The service should, however, normally be used in church: *ibid.*

[79] Stephens, *The Book of Common Prayer*, vol. III, at p. 1752.

[80] The rubric is in this respect one of good Church order and the Alternative Service Book demonstrates that Church order has changed over the years: contrast Stephens, *The Book of Common Prayer*, vol. III, at pp. 1753–1754. Thus, even if not a variation 'in' a form of service within Canon B 5, para. 1, its use would nonetheless be *de minimis*.

[81] 'These words simply mean, neatly clothed. Thus, a poor woman in her working dress, or a lady dressed for a ball, would not satisfy the rubric': Stephens, *The Book of Common Prayer*, vol. III, at p. 1755. The example, however, seems to stray into realms of fashion and class distinction. Prior to 1662 a diocesan order that a woman should attend in a white veil was held to be enforceable on the basis that it was the common custom of the Church: *Shipden* v. *Redman* (1622) Palm 296; see, too, Phillimore, *Ecclesiastical Law* (2nd ed.) vol. I, at p. 645.

[82] Known as 'surplice fees': Cripps, *The Law relating to the Church and Clergy* at p. 502. These were for the maintenance of the priest: see Stephens, *The Book of Common Prayer*, vol. III, at pp. 1762–1763; Phillimore, *Ecclesiastical Law*, (2nd ed.) vol. I, at p. 646. See also *Naylor* v. *Scott* (1729) Ld Raymond 1558.

[83] In those parishes which were not bound by a standard table of fees under the Ecclesiastical Fees Measure, 1962, s. 2(4) (now repealed) it is arguable that the silence in the Alternative Service Book merely reflects the new position generally and that in such parishes the duty is not abrogated: see now the Ecclesiastical Fees Measure 1986, s. 11(3), Sch. 2, para. 1. In all other parishes the offering is now voluntary: 14 Halsbury's Laws of England (4th ed.) at para. 1045, note 3.

[84] See the Alternative Service Book at p. 213.

[85] See the Alternative Service Book at p. 218.

[86] See the rubric at the commencement of the service in the Book of Common Prayer and the reference in Note 2 in the Alternative Service Book at p. 212, although the rite in the Alternative service Book then uses the word 'minister'.

[87] If authorised by the diocesan bishop and at the invitation of the minister of the parish (or, when the cure is vacant, of the rural dean) or extra-parochial place: Deaconesses and Lay Ministry

At a service of Thanksgiving for the Birth of a Child or after Adoption[88], unless baptism is to follow immediately[89], the minister must explain to the parents that the service is not baptism, which is the sacrament instituted by Christ for those who wish to become members of his Church[90]. Whenever possible, in addition to both parents[91] or adoptive parents and the child, any other children of the family should be present[92].

(ii) Night Prayer

In *Lent, Holy Week, Easter* a form of service for the late evening was provided called Night Prayer[93] and based on the ancient office of compline. This was commended by the House of Bishops and may be used in accordance with the provisions of Canon B 5, para. 2. This was always intended to be susceptible to adaptation for other parts of the Church's year[94] and a separate edition has now been published[95], although it is unclear whether the adaptations suggested for other parts of the year[96] have been so commended[97].

Who is to act as minister is unspecified, although the notes to *Lent, Holy Week, Easter*[98] make it clear that its use at home is also envisaged. This being so, it would seem that anyone may act as minister; indeed, this is possibly[99] why the service ends with a prayer for a blessing[100] rather than with an actual blessing[101].

Measure 1972, s. 1(1)(a), (2), (3); Canon D 1, para. 4(b); Canon E 7, para. 5(b). This provision does not apply to the Channel Islands: Deaconesses and Lay Ministry Measure 1972, s. 2(2) and Canon D 1, para. 6, and Canon E 7, para. 6. No other Canon has yet been promulgated under section 1(1) of the Measure for any other person to take such a service but, even when one is, the wording of the subsection is such that it cannot embrace even a female deacon.

[88] The services may be used at Holy Communion either at the beginning or after the sermon; the Prayers of Intercession may then be omitted. They may also be used at Morning or Evening Prayer either at the beginning, after the second reading or after the sermon: see Note 4 at p. 212. If used on their own suitable hymns, set readings and a sermon may be added: see Note 5 at p. 212. Both services of thanksgiving provide for the presentation of 'a copy of one of the gospels' to the parents (see the rubrics at paragraphs 5 and 21 at pp. 215 and 220 respectively) but the presentation of the whole Bible or of the New Testament would, of course, be permissible.

[89] If baptism follows immediately, it is permissible to use only some of the sections in the services of thanksgiving: see Note 6 at p. 212.   [90] Note 1 at p. 212 of the Alternative Service Book.

[91] Although the Alternative Service Book provides for the possibility of there being more than one child born or adopted (see Notes 2 and 18 at pp. 213 and 218 respectively), it ignores the possibility that there may be only one parent present. Nevertheless, Note 3 at p. 212 makes it clear that the whole of the immediate family should be present 'whenever possible'; therefore, if the presence of both parents is not possible, the service may proceed with only one.

[92] Note 3 at p. 212 of the Alternative Service Book.   [93] *Op. cit.* at p. 58 *et seq.*

[94] *Op. cit.* at p. 58, Note.   [95] Jointly by Church House Publishing and Mowbrays.

[96] See pp. 10–13 and the lectionary at pp. 18–19 of the separate publication entitled *Night Prayer A Service for Late Evening.*

[97] The note within the front cover seems to suggest that they have not been so commended.

[98] *Op. cit.* at p. 58.

[99] Contrast, however, the prayer for a blessing in the service of Commination in the Book of Common Prayer. By reason of the first rubric and the rubric before the Miserere the service is clearly one to be taken by a priest.

[100] As it is in inclusive language, it is best seen as a prayer for a blessing.

[101] See, too, **p. 125 *et seq. supra.***

(iii) Ministry to the Sick

Apart from the Communion of the Sick[102] the Book of Common Prayer provides a service for the Visitation of the Sick; moreover, the General Synod has authorised the forms of service in *The Ministry to the Sick*[103]. The House of Bishops has also commended a form of service entitled *Ministry at the Time of Death*.

The rubric at the commencement of the Order for the Visitation of the Sick in the Book of Common Prayer envisages that the person taking the service is the 'minister of the parish'; indeed, in so doing it reflects the pre-Reformation canon law that imposed a duty on all rectors and vicars[104] to visit the sick[105]. Nonetheless, the rubric at the end of the Exhortation states that 'the Curate may end his exhortation in this place'. At first sight this reference to 'the Curate' might be thought to be a reference to the minister of the parish as he had the cure of souls[106] but this would be to ignore Canon 67 of the 1603 Canons which read:

When any person is dangereously sick in any parish, the Minister or Curate, having knowledge thereof, shall resort to him or her . . . to instruct and comfort them in their distress, according to the Book of Common Prayer . . .

This Canon was not being tautologous[107] but was imposing a similar duty on licensed curates. The Book of Common Prayer was therefore reflecting the Canon and the rubrics should not be so interpreted as to permit only those having cures of souls to take the service. On the other hand it is clear that the service must be taken by a priest[108]. The present Canon C 24 once again imposes a duty solely on those priests having a cure of souls but this seems to be concerned with visiting in general rather than with visting with the particular view of taking a service[109]; in no way, therefore, does it narrow the ambit of the Book of Common Prayer rubrics.

The service of Commendation at the Time of Death in *Ministry to the Sick* for the family and friends gathered at a death-bed underlines that it may be led 'by a priest or by any other Christian person'[110]. Even though a blessing is provided, it is only as an alternative and should only be given by a priest[111]. The service

---

[102] See **p. 117** *et seq. supra.*

[103] ASB 70. In addition to forms of service for sick communion (see **p. 117** *et seq. supra*) it includes a Commendation at the Time of Death and Prayers for use with the Sick.

[104] 'Rectores et Vicarii'.

[105] Lyndwood, *Provinciale Angliae* (Oxford, 1679) at pp. 63–64. See, too, Canon C 24, para. 6.

[106] Compare the words 'all Bishops and Curates' in the Prayer for the Church Militant in the Holy Communion Service according to the Book of Common Prayer.

[107] See also Canon 64 of the 1603 Canons the Latin text of which begins 'Rectores, vicarii et curati . . .'   [108] See the rubric before the Absolution.

[109] 'He shall be diligent in visiting his parishioners, particularly those who are sick and infirm . . .': Canon C 24, para. 6. See also Canon E 4, para. 2(a) (readers).

[110] See the Note at p. 37.   [111] See **p. 125** *et seq. supra.*

commended in *Ministry at the Time of Death* specifically provides alternatives[112] in the form of service whenever the minister is a deacon[113] or lay person[114]. In both services provision is made for the making of the sign of the Cross[115].

(iv)   Services of prayer and dedication after civil marriage[116]

Although this service need not be taken by a priest, only a priest should give a blessing; in all other cases the Grace should be used[117]. No such provision is spelt out in relation to the Absolution but, as it is printed with the word *'you'* in italics[118], the customary variation to 'us' is clearly envisaged when no priest is present[119].

(v)   Commination

This service from the Book of Common Prayer seems to have fallen into disuse. A number of the rubrics speak of its being taken by a priest, although he is also described as 'the minister'[120]. Particularly because the rubric before the Miserere distinguishes between the people on the one hand and 'the Priest and Clerks' on the other, it may be strongly argued that only a clerk in Holy Orders may take the service[121].

(vi)   Confession

The hearing of private (or auricular) confession is certainly legal in the Church of England[122] but only by a priest[123]. Indeed, Canon B 29, para. 4, provides that:

> No priest shall exercise the ministry of absolution in any place without the permission of the minister having the cure of souls thereof, unless he is by law authorised to exercise his ministry in that place without being subject to

[112] See Note 2 at p. 3. These alternatives are considered at **p. 126** *supra*.

[113] As to the effect of this Note under Canon B 5, para. 2, see **p. 220, footnote 51** *supra*.

[114] It is odd that a deacon, but not a lay person, should be authorised for this ministry by the bishop. See, too, **p. 48** *et seq. supra*.

[115] This is to recall the dying person's baptism into Christ: see the Note at p. 37 of *Ministry to the Sick*. When there is an anointing in the *Ministry at the Time of Death* Canon B 37, para. 3, provides for the use of pure olive oil 'consecrated by the bishop of the diocese or otherwise by the priest in accordance with [a] form of service [authorised by Canon B 1]'; this is in turn provided for in Note 4 of *Ministry at the Time of Death* at p. 4.   [116] See, too, **p. 192** *supra*.

[117] Note 7 at p. 4.   [118] See section 7 at p. 8.   [119] See, too, **p. 124** *et seq. supra*.

[120] No doubt this reflects the rubrics in Morning Prayer after which service the Commination should take place. See, too, **p. 123** *supra*.

[121] The clerks are the members of the choir: see **p. 206, footnote 63**, and **p. 209, footnote 94** *supra*.

[122] Canon B 29; *Rector and Churchwardens of Capel St Mary, Suffolk* v. *Packard* [1927] P 289, especially at p. 301 *per* the Dean of the Arches; 14 Halsbury's Laws of England (4th ed.) at para. 1047.

[123] See, too, Canon B 29, para. 1: 'and in the Absolution pronounced by the priest in the services of the Church' and **p. 124** *et seq. supra*. See, too, Canon C 24, para. 6.

the minister having the general cure of souls of the parish or district in which it is situated[124]: Provided always that, notwithstanding the foregoing provisions of the Canon, a priest may exercise the ministry of absolution anywhere in respect of any person who is in danger of death or if there is some urgent or weighty cause.

However, no specific form of service has been authorised[125] and in the meantime any such service falls within the ambit of Canon B 5, para. 2[126]. The Absolution ought to follow that in the Order for the Visitation of the Sick in the Book of Common Prayer[127]. It must always be borne in mind by the priest that the ecclesiastical law imposes a strict duty[128] upon him not to disclose any matter communicated to him during sacramental confession[129].

There is no place appointed where confession ought to take place, although confessional boxes are illegal in Anglican churches[130]. Nonetheless, it is obvious that in cases of urgency or danger of death a confession may be heard wherever is necessary; in other cases it is preferable that it is heard in open church[131].

---

[124] See the Extra-Parochial Ministry Measure 1967; 14 Halsbury's Laws of England (4th ed.) at paras 690 and 701.

[125] For general services of penitence see *Lent, Holy Week, Easter*, at p. 38 *et seq.*

[126] For a suggested form of service see the compilation by David Konstant, *A Shorter Prayer Book for Penitents* (Mayhew-McCrimmon Ltd, 1976).

[127] This is to ensure that Canon B 5, para. 3, is complied with. It was specifically so laid down in the 1622 Prayer Book: see Stephens, *The Book of Common Prayer*, vol. III at p. 1667.

[128] See *In re St Edmund's Chapel, Gateshead* [1995] 3 WLR 253 at pp. 258H–259B. It is not always understood in the common law courts or by writers of legal text books that this is not a claim to privilege but is a legal obligation imposed by the law of the realm on Anglican priests: 14 Halsbury's Laws of England (4th ed.) at para. 1047. Indeed, it is frequently mistaken for a similar, but differently based claim, made by priests of the Roman Catholic Church. Because the law imposes this duty on Anglican priests, the court is itself under a duty to ensure that the obligation is not broken. If a court were to attempt to force a priest to make disclosure, he should ask to be legally represented so that the situation may be fully argued; indeed, he would be entitled to such representation as he would be under threat of being in contempt of court.

[129] In this regard the proviso to Canon 113 of the 1603 Canons remains unrepealed: 'Provided always, that if any man confess his sins to the Minister, for the unburdening of his conscience, and to receive spiritual consolation and ease of mind from him; we do not any way bind the said Minister by this our Constitution, but do straitly charge and admonish him, that he do not at any time reveal and make known to any person whatsoever any crime or offence so committed to his trust and secrecy (except they be such crimes as by the laws of this realm his own life may be called into question for concealing the same), under pain of irregularity.' This proviso reflects the pre-Reformation canon law. The exception is likely only to refer to high treason: *In re St Edmund's Churchyard, Gateshead* [1995] 3 WLR 253 at pp. 258H–259B. See, too, 14 Halsbury's Laws of England (4th ed.) at para. 1047; Phillimore, *Ecclesiastical Law*, (2nd ed.), vol. I at pp. 538–547; Briden & Hanson, *Moore's Introduction to English Canon Law* at pp. 83–85; Bursell, *The Seal of the Confessional* (1990) 2 Ecc. LJ at pp. 84 *et seq.*; (1993) Journal of the Church Law Association of Canada, vol. I, at p. 152; cp. Elliott, *An Evidential Privilege for Priest-Penitent Communications* (1994) 3 Ecc LJ at p. 274. A sacramental confession is one where the penitent repents his sins and at the same time intends to reform; this is expressed in the rubric in the Order for the Visitation of the Sick in the Book of Common Prayer in the words 'humbly and heartily desires' absolution.

[130] *Davey* v. *Hinde* [1901] P 95; *Rector and Churchwardens of Capel St Mary, Suffolk* v. *Packard* [1927] P 289; see, also, *In re St Saviour's, Hampstead* [1932] P 134; *In re St Mary, Tyne Dock* [1954] P 369.

[131] See *Rector and Churchwardens of Capel St Mary, Suffolk* v. *Packard* [1927] P 289 at p. 301 *per* the Dean of Arches.

(vii)   Joint worship

Canon 43, para. 9, permits the incumbent[132] of a parish[133], with the approval of the parochial church council and the diocesan bishop, to invite members of certain other denominations[134] to take part in joint worship. Presumably this means other than attending as members of the congregation or carrying out any of the particular duties set out in Canon 43, para. 1[135]. However, 'joint worship' is nowhere defined, although it must clearly be some form of service[136]. Nonetheless, every Anglican minister is under a duty only to use forms of service authorised by Canon B 1 'except so far as he may exercise the discretion permitted by Canon B 5'[137]. That being so, and as no 'joint worship' has been approved under Canon B 2, the form of service must be one falling within Canon B 4 or Canon B 5, para. 2[138]. Unfortunately, Canon B 5 only gives 'the minister having the cure of souls' authority to use or permit such services and the definition of 'incumbent' in Canon B 43 is far wider[139]. It may therefore be argued that, in order to give Canon B 43 efficacy, the words 'minister having the cure of souls' in Canon B 5, para. 2, should be given a similar definition, at least when Canon 43, para. 9, applies.

Canon B 44 deals with local ecumenical projects. By subparagraph 4(1)(e) a bishop who has given his agreement to participation in such a project may make provision[140] for the holding in that area of 'joint services' with any other participating Church, including services of baptism and confirmation. Such joint services must, however, be such as are authorised under Canon B 1. Moreover, as a minister having the cure of souls[141] may only himself make, or permit, forms of service for use on occasions for which no provision is otherwise made[142], any joint service of baptism or confirmation must be those according to the Book of

---

[132] This is given a wide definition so as to include '(a) in a case where the benefice concerned is vacant (and paragraph (b) below does not apply), the rural dean, and (b) in a case where a suspension period (within the meaning of the Pastoral Measure 1983) applies to the benefice concerned, the priest-in-charge, and (c) in a case where a special cure of souls in respect of the parish has been assigned to a vicar in a team ministry by a scheme under the Pastoral Measure 1983 or by licence from the bishop, that vicar . . . ': see Canon B 43, para. 12(2), and **p. 26** *et seq. supra*.

[133] For a similar provision in relation to cathedrals, although without the need for an approval by any parochial church council, see Canon B 43, para. 10.   [134] See **p. 26** *supra*.

[135] See **p. 26** *et seq. supra*.

[136] It includes the blessing of a memorial in an Anglican churchyard by a Roman Catholic bishop in the presence of Anglicans: *In re St Edmund's Churchyard, Gateshead* [1995] 3 WLR 253 at p. 257D–F.

[137] See Canon B 1, para. 2, and **p. 3** *et seq. supra*. This includes any form of service approved under Canon B 2 or Canon B 4: Canon B 1, para. 1(d).

[138] That this is so is confirmed by the wording of the Church of England (Ecumenical Relations) Measure 1988, under which Canon B 43 is promulgated. Section 1 states: 'It shall be lawful for the General Synod to make provision by Canon – (a) for enabling a member of a Church to which this Measure applies to take part in public worship *in accordance with the forms of service* and practice of the Church of England . . . ' (emphasis supplied).   [139] See **footnote 132** *supra*.

[140] By an instrument in writing made after consultation with the parochial church council of each parish or part of a parish in the area of the project: *ibid*. For the meaning of consultation see **p. 122** *supra*.   [141] See the **previous paragraph** and **p. 134** *et seq. supra* in relation to these words.

[142] See **p. 221** *supra*.

Common Prayer or the Alternative Service Book until any special joint services are authorised[143]. These may nonetheless be approved by the archbishops or bishop[144] as Canon B 44, para. 4(2), states that:

A bishop shall not by any instrument made under this paragraph authorise any rite to be used in any service mentioned in subparagraph (1) . . . (e) . . . unless he is satisfied that the rite . . . to be used [is] not contrary to, nor indicative of any departure from, the doctrine of the Church of England in any essential matter'.

This provision would otherwise be unnecessary.

(viii)   Miscellaneous

A form of service is defined for the purposes of the Church of England (Worship and Doctrine) Measure 1974 as meaning[145]:

any order, service, prayer, rite or ceremony whatsoever, including the services for the ordination of priests and deacons and the consecration of bishops and the catechism or form of instruction before confirmation.

Indeed, it is not always easy to distinguish between suggested private prayers and what would normally be seen, ignoring this legal definition, as more formal services[146]. For example the Form of Prayer for the Anniversary of the day of Accession of the Reigning Sovereign includes readings and prayers for use in particular services but, in addition, there is a form of service that 'may be used on the same day at any convenient time'. It is unnecessary to consider each of these separately but it is clear that no prayer set out in an authorised prayer book, whether within a form of service loosely[147] so called or not, is 'contrary to, [or] indicative of any departure from, the doctrine of the Church of England in any essential matter'[148]. They may therefore be used as guidance in so far as Canons B 4 and 5 are concerned. Equally, the catechism may be similarly used[149].

---

[143] It may, however, be argued that greater varations under Canon B 5 may be made to services within an ecumenical context than might otherwise be the case. It is difficult to argue that ecumenical occasions are separate occasions from those covered by the present service books, especially because of the wording of section 1(a) of the Church of England (Ecumenical Relations) Measure 1988, and also the provisions of Canon B 44, para. 4(3)(b), concerning services of Holy Communion.

[144] The Church of England (Ecumenical Relations) Measure 1988, s. 1 states that 'It shall be lawful for the General Synod to make provision by Canon – (a) for enabling a member of a Church to which this Measure applies to take part in public worship *in accordance with the forms of service* and practice of the Church of England . . . ' (emphasis supplied). However, this should not be seen as restricting such forms of service to those existing when the Measure came into force. This being so, as Canon B 44, para. 4(2) makes plain, ecumenical forms of worship can be approved by the archbishops and bishops under Canon B 4, paras 2 and 3, respectively. It is probable that the Convocations have no such power as they are not mentioned in Canon B 44.

[145] Section 5(2). See, too, Canon B 1, para. 3.

[146] See the Forms of Prayer to be used at Sea in the Book of Common Prayer.

[147] That is, ignoring the strict legal definition under the 1974 Measure.

[148] See **p. 6** *supra*.

[149] See the Church of England (Worship and Doctrine) Measure 1974, s. 5(2) 'form of service'.

10

ORDINATION AND CONSECRATION

A Generally[1]

(i) Ordination

Ordination to the office of priest or deacon must take place on the Sunday immediately after the Ember Weeks; alternatively, it must take place on St Peter's Day, Michaelmas Day or St Thomas's Day, or upon a day within the week immediately following those days, or upon such other days, being a Sunday, a Holy Day[2] or one of the Ember Days, as the diocesan bishop on urgent occasion shall appoint[3].

The ordination must be in the cathedral church of the diocese or in another church or chapel[4] at the discretion of the bishop[5]. Any form of Holy Communion which is authorised by Canon B 1 may be used[6].

One of the archdeacons, or his deputy, or such other persons as by ancient custom[7] have the right so to do, must present each person who is to be ordained to the bishop[8]. Ordination must be by a bishop[9], although the priests taking part shall 'together with the bishop lay their hands upon the head of every person who receives the order of priesthood'[10].

---

[1] As to ecumenical services see **p. 45** *supra*.

[2] Holy Days are listed in the Table of Proper Lessons and Psalms in the Book of Common Prayer; a slightly different list appears in the Principal Holy Days and Festivals and Greater Holy Days in the Alternative Service Book at pp. 17–18. In addition the General Synod may approve Holy Days which may be observed generally or provincially, and also, subject to any directions of the Convocation of the province, the Ordinary may approve Holy Days which may be observed locally: Canon B 6, para. 5.   [3] Canon C 3, para. 1.

[4] This must be within his own diocese, unless the licence of the diocesan bishop of the diocese where the ordination is to take place is first obtained: see Phillimore *Ecclesiastical Law* (2nd ed.) vol. I, at p. 93.

[5] This almost certainly refers to the diocesan bishop, although the matter is unclear. The 'bishop of the diocese' is specifically referred to in Canon C 3, para. 1, and must be 'the bishop' referred to in para. 8; on the other hand 'the bishop' in paras 3 and 4 can only refer to the bishop taking the ordination.   [6] Canon C 3, para. 4A.

[7] Prima facie these words refer to a custom that predates the Reformation: see 14 Halsbury's Laws of England (4th ed.) at para. 306. Nonetheless, they were not originally contained in the rubric to the Book of Common Prayer but were added later. This being so it may well be that they only refer to long standing diocesan practice.

[8] Canon C 3, para. 3. This must refer to the bishop taking the service.

[9] See the Ordinal in both the Book of Common Prayer and in the Alternative Service Book.

[10] See, too, Canon C 3, para. 4.

(ii) Consecration

Consecration of a bishop must take place on a Sunday or Holy Day[11], unless the archbishop[12] for urgent and weighty cause appoints some other day[13]. There must be not less than three bishops 'present together and joining in the act of consecration', of whom one must be the archbishop of the province or a bishop appointed to act on his behalf[14].

(iii) Impediment

In the Book of Common Prayer provision is made in the rites of ordination to the diaconate and priesthood[15] for objection to be made to an ordination. The bishop must ask the people 'if there be any of you who knoweth any Impediment[16], or notable Crime'[17] and thereafter:

... if any great Crime or Impediment be objected, the Bishop shall surcease from Ordering that person, until such time as the party accused shall be found clear of that Crime[18].

However, the bishop should only stop the ordering of the particular ordinand to whom objection is taken and then only if the objection is based on an 'Impediment, or notable Crime' within the meaning of the rubric[19]. An objector who persists in interrupting the services once his objection is overruled is in danger of a prosecution under section 2 of the Ecclesiastical Courts Jurisdiction Act 1860[20].

[11] See **p. 230, footnote 2** *supra*.

[12] This must be a reference to the archbishop of the relevant province: cp. Canon C 2, para. 1.

[13] Canon C 2, para. 2.   [14] Canon C 2, para. 1.

[15] Objection to a bishop must be made at a stage prior to his confirmation: see 14 Halsbury's Laws of England (4th ed.) at para. 466 and Canon C 2.

[16] See Canon C 4 and *Brown* v. *Runcie*, *The Times*, 20 February 1991 (for a full transcript see Hill, *Ecclesiastical Law* at p. 68).

[17] For what amounts to such an impediment or crime see Phillimore, *Ecclesiastical Law* (2nd ed.) vol. I at pp. 93–95 and 14 Halsbury's Laws of England (4th ed.) at para. 658; see, too, Canon C 4 and the Archbishops' Directions set out in *The Canons of the Church of England* at pp. 184–186. In *Kensit* v. *The Dean and Chapter of St Paul's* [1905] 2 KB 249 Lord Alverston CJ said at pp. 256–257: 'The word "impediment" related originally to a number of matters, some of which can no longer be regarded as such – as, for instance, bastardy, and certain physical defects as the loss of a limb or eye – but included impediments which would still be considered as a bar to ordination, such as the fact that the candidate was an unbaptized person or was not of the requisite age for the orders to which he proposed to be ordained.' However, the view expressed *obiter* in the first part of this quotation must be treated with caution in the light of the subsequent passing of the Clergy (Ordination and Miscellaneous Provisions) Measure 1964, s. 8. See, too, *ibid*, ss. 2 and 9.

[18] *Scilicet*, or of the impediment.

[19] See *Kensit* v. *The Dean and Chapter of St Paul's* [1905] 2 KB 249. Clearly the best course may initially be to adjourn to the vestry with the objector while due consideration is given to the matter. Such a pause in the service could not in the particular circumstances itself amount to an offence.   [20] See **p. 247** *et seq. infra*.

In the Alternative Service Book, although the bishop still presents the candidates to the people with the question 'Is it therefore your will that they should be ordained?', no provision is made for any objection; indeed, the congregational response is set out as 'It is'[21]. Nonetheless, the question of impediments is clearly one of good order and the provisions in the Alternative Service Book cannot in these particular circumstances demonstrate that the reception of an objection is 'not of substantial importance' within the meaning of Canon B 5, para. 1[22]. Rather, just because it is itself a matter of good order, it would not be illegal for a member of the congregation to make an objection[23] within the rite according to the Alternative Service Book[24]; it would then be incumbent upon the bishop to proceed as directed in the Book of Common Prayer[25].

B Service

(i) Choice

The choice of which form of service is to be used must be made by the bishop or archbishop who is to conduct the service[26]. He must also determine who presides at the service 'in accordance with the rubrics of the service and having regard to tradition and local custom'[27].

In addition it is stressed in the Alternative Service Book that it is appropriate that the newly ordained should be invited by the bishop to exercise their ministry in the course of the service.[27A] As the rubric deals solely with appropriateness this cannot amount to a matter of Church order although what is appropriate in one rite must be appropriate in another.

(ii) Form

Ordination and consecration affect the legal status of the persons concerned[28]. It is for this reason that particular care must be taken to ensure that the form of

---

[21] See paragraph 12 at pp. 344, 356 and 370 and paragraph 15 at p. 371 respectively.

[22] This is confirmed by the fact that the bishop still has to direct the question to the congregation in the rite according to the Alternative Service Book.

[23] It is possible that he does so at his peril, if it is not based on an 'Impediment, or notable Crime'.

[24] *In re St Thomas, Pennywell* [1995] 2 WLR 154 at p. 169E–F.

[25] See, generally, *Williamson* v. *Dow* (1994) (unreported but referred to in Hill, *Ecclesiastical Law* at p. 219, footnote 12).

[26] Canon B 3, para. 5, and Note 4 at p. 338 of the Alternative Service Book.

[27] See Note 4 at p. 338 of the Alternative Service Book. In the light of Canon B 1, para. 2, the words regarding the rubrics add nothing, save perhaps to stress that there is no *ius liturgicum*: see **Appendix 3** at **p. 271** *et seq. infra*. The words as to 'tradition and local custom' refer to local practice: see **p. 4, footnote 28** *supra*.   [27A] See the *previous footnote*.

[28] See Canon C 1, para. 2, as to the indelibility of orders and Article XXXVI of the Articles of Religion. Relinquishment may, however, be made of the exercise of those orders: see 14 Halsbury's Laws of England (4th ed.) at para. 663. See, too, **p. 87** *supra*.

service used is a legally valid one[29], although Canon B 5, para. 1, nonetheless applies. Particular alterations are permitted to the Ordinal annexed to the Book of Common Prayer when women are being ordained[30].

The Ordinal annexed to the Book of Common Prayer provides that both ordination and consecration should take place 'after Morning Prayer is ended'[31]. This seems to envisage that the one should follow immediately after the other, rather than that they may not precede Morning Prayer. However, no such provision is made in the Alternative Service Book and, as it would not seem to be a matter of Church order, it may well be it is no longer necessary even when the Ordinal annexed to the Book of Common Prayer is used[32].

It is specifically laid down by Canon C 3, para. 4A, that any form of service of Holy Communion authorised by Canon B 1 may be used at an ordination. This Canon strictly only applies to the ordination of priests and deacons but the Alternative Service Book States[33]:

> Any form of service of Holy Communion which is authorized by Canon B 1 may be used at these Ordination Services (see Canon C 3.4A).

In spite of the specific reference to Canon C 3, para. 4A[34], this Note probably also makes lawful the use of any such Holy Communion service at a consecration according to the Alternative Service Book[35], as both service books speak of 'The Ordination' as well as 'the Consecration' of a Bishop[36]. The use of the Holy Communion service according to the Alternative Service Book with the consecration according to Ordinal annexed to the Book of Common Prayer can only be justified by reference to Canon B 5, para. 1[37]. Nonetheless, even if a rite were used that could not legally be justified, it would not invalidate the actual consecration itself.

---

[29] See 14 Halsbury's Laws of England (4th ed.) at para. 467. Canon C 4A, para. 4, permits the archbishops 'jointly [to] authorise forms of service for deaconesses to be ordained deacon, being forms of service which in both words and order are in their opinion reverent and seemly and are neither contrary to nor indicative from, the doctrine of the Church of England.' This should be seen as falling within their powers under Canon B 4, para. 2, otherwise the use of such forms of service would not be permitted by Canon B 1, para. 2.

[30] Canons C 4A, para. 3 and Schedule, and C 4B, para. 2; *Brown* v. *Runcie*, *The Times*, 20 February 1991 (for a full transcript see Hill, *Ecclesiastical Law* at p. 68).

[31] See the introductory rubrics.

[32] Because of the word 'after' in the rubric, it is more difficult here to argue that the two forms of service should be treated as one. Nevertheless, the introductory rubric itself relates to the actual form of the service of ordination or consecration and a failure to follows its provisions may therefore be seen as a variation 'in' the form of service. [33] Note 5 at p. 338.

[34] The difficulty is underlined by the legal maxim *expressio unius, excludio alterius.*

[35] Particularly in the light of Canon B 5, para. 1. The consecration and Holy Communion service are best seen in these circumstances as one form of service. Indeed, in the light of the meaning of 'service' in the Church of England (Worship and Doctrine) Measure 1974, s. 5(2), and of 'form of service' in Canons B 1–5 it is inevitable that one form of service may embrace a number of forms of service. [36] See *ibid* at p. 382.

[37] The consecration and Holy Communion service are best seen in these circumstances as one form of service but the matter is not beyond argument.

The introductory rubric in the Ordinal annexed to the Book of Common Prayer also provides that at an ordination the sermon or exhortation must declare the duty and office of those to be ordained. Once again there is no similar rubric in the Alternative Service Book and, as this is unlikely to be a matter of Church order[38], the subject for the sermon is at the discretion of the preacher. By reason of Canon B 5, para. 1, a preacher at an ordination following the Ordinal annexed to the Book of Common Prayer may also now legally preach on another subject.

The Alternative Service Book also specifically permits the presiding bishop to choose alternative Old or New Testament readings 'suitable to the occasion'[39]. It might have been argued that, because this provision was specifically made in relation to that particular rite, it underlined that the choice or readings in the Ordinal annexed to the Book of Common Prayer are of such importance that no change could be made under Canon B 5, para. 1. Nevertheless, such an argument, as well as ignoring the history of the law relating to changes to the lectionary, is difficult to advance in the light of the definition of 'form of service' now given in Canon B 5[40].

The antiphonal singing of the *Veni, Creator Spiritus* is specifically enjoined by the rubric in the Ordinal annexed to the Book of Common Prayer and similar antiphonal singing is now legal when using the Alternative Service Book[41]. The Ordering of Priests according to the Ordinal annexed to the Book of Common Prayer also provides for a period of silence immediately before the *Veni, Creator Spiritus*; a similar period of silence would also be legal during the Ordering of Deacons by reason of Canon B 5, para. 1, especially in the light of similar periods of silence enjoined by the Alternative Service Book[42].

(iii)   Vesture and symbols of office

The Alternative Service Book states[43] that:

Where it is agreed that those to be ordained are to be clothed in their customary[44] vesture, it is appropriate that this should take place after the Declaration.

This in practice refers to the vesture usually worn according to the tradition of churchmanship that each candidate represents. By reason of Canon B 5, para. 1, the same procedure may be adopted if the Ordinal annexed to the Book of Common Prayer is being used[45]. The same applies to the presentation of symbols of

---

[38] See, too, **p. 16** *supra.*
[39] See Note 6 at p. 338. See, too, Canon C 4A, para. 3, and Schedule.
[40] See **pp. 3, footnote 19**, and **127** *et seq. supra.*   [41] See **p. 79, footnote 201** *supra.*
[42] See Notes 15 at pp. 346, 359, 374 and 390; see, too, **p. 39, footnote 58** *supra.*
[43] Note 7 at p. 338.   [44] See **p. 4, footnote 28** *supra.*
[45] This is in spite of the second introductory rubric stating that, when the ordinands are presented to the bishop, they must be 'decently habited'. This is especially so as a bishop at his consecration must as a matter of good order also appear decently habited at the start of the service and the rubrics

office after the Giving of the Bible, namely, a chalice and paten to a priest or a pastoral staff to a bishop[46].

C Ordination

The Ordinal annexed to the Book of Common Prayer makes it clear that those who have been ordained must remain and receive Holy Communion[47]. No similar provision is made in the Alternative Service Book, although it is perhaps implied in Note 4[48] which states that:

... It is appropriate that the newly ordained should be invited by the bishop to exercise their new ministry in the course of the service.

In any event the provision in the Book of Common Prayer would seem to be a rubric dealing with Church order and therefore applicable to both rites[49].

In The Ordering of Priests in the Book of Common Prayer the rubric before the laying on of hands states that:

... the Bishop with the Priests present shall lay their hands severally[50] upon the head of everyone[51] that receiveth the Order of Priesthood.

Presumably this means every priest taking an active part in the service and not merely being in the congregation, in spite of the rubric before the *Veni, Creator Spiritus* speaking of 'the Priests, and others that are present'[52]. Fortunately a strict statutory interpretation is no longer necessary and the latter rubric only emphasises the participation of the whole congregation. That this is so is confirmed by the rubrics in the Alternative Service Book[53] which make it clear that the reference to those laying on hands is, in fact, to the priests who are assisting the bishop.

in the Ordinal annexed to the Book of Common Prayer thereafter provide for him to be 'vested with his Rochet' after the sermon and for him 'to put on the rest of the Episcopal habit' before the *Veni, Creator Spiritus*.

[46] See Note 8 at p. 338 of the Alternative Service Book and **p. 93** *et seq. supra*.

[47] See the rubric after the Gospel in The Ordering of Deacons and the rubric after the Giving of the Bible in the Ordering of Priests. [48] See *op. cit.* at p. 338.

[49] This is because it is concerned with the reception of Holy Communion rather than with the actual form of the service: see, too, *infra* and compare Canon B 12, para. 2.

[50] In practice this is taken to mean that the laying on of hands is to be on each ordinand severally and not that the priests one by one must lay their hands on each ordinand.

[51] This seems to be a rubric dealing with Church order and therefore also applicable when the Alternative Service Book is being used. However, the practice whereby not every priest lays his hand on each candidate may, perhaps, be justified by the necessity to ensure good order.

[52] See, too, **p. 18, footnote 120** *supra*.

[53] See paras 18 and 24 at pp. 362 and 378 respectively. See, too, Canon C 3, para. 4, and contrast the clearer wording of Canon C 2, para. 1: 'present together and joining in the act of consecration'.

The Alternative Service Book provides that, when presenting an ordinand, the archdeacon is to read 'the name of each person to be ordained . . . , and that of the place where he is to serve' as well as the ordinand's name[54]. By reason of Canon B 5, para. 1, the same procedure would now be legal when using the Ordinal annexed to the Book of Common Prayer.

D Consecration

The same arguments as to the reception of the sacrament[55], the laying on of hands by the 'Bishops present'[56] and silence[57] apply here as in the ordination of priests and deacons[58]. The reamining question concerns the readings. The Ordinal annexed to the Book of Common Prayer provides that the Epistle and Gospel are to be read by two different bishops[59] whereas the Alternative Service Book merely provides for 'the reader'[60]. Clearly in the latter rite bishops may still be the readers and, by reason of Canon B 5, para. 1, it seems that persons other than bishops may now legally be so even when the former rite is being used.

The Ordinal annexed to the Book of Common Prayer also provides that the archbishop is to sit 'in his chair near the holy Table' for the Presentation and for the prayer 'Brother, for as much as holy Scripture . . . ', whereas the Alternative Service Book makes no such provision. However, as posture is not a matter of importance in the Alternative Service Book[61], not only may the archbishop sit at similar parts of the service when using that particular rite but such a posture[62] need no longer be adopted when using the other rite[63].

[54] See para. 11 at pp. 344, 355, 370 and para. 14 at p. 371 respectively.

[55] See the rubric in the Ordinal annexed to the Book of Common Prayer after the reception of the Bible.

[56] See, too, **p. 18, footnote 120** *supra*. Cp. the rubric before the laying on of hands in the Ordinal annexed to the Book of Common Prayer and para.18 at p. 393 of the Alternative Service Book.

[57] See para. 15 at p. 390 of the Alternative Service Book.

[58] See **pp. 18, footnote 120** and **235** *supra*.   [59] See the rubrics before the two readings.

[60] See Notes 4, 6 and 8 at pp. 383, 384 and 385 respectively.

[61] See General Note 3 at p. 32.   [62] And position for the chair.

[63] See Canon B 5, para. 1.

11

GOOD ORDER

A Generally

As has already been seen[1], there is a general duty under the canon law to ensure that all divine worship is reverent and seemly[2]. More particularly, a minister must endeavour[3] in every service 'to ensure that the worship offered glorifies God.' Moreover, Canon B 20, para. 3, reflects the general canon law when it, too, states that it is the minister's duty 'to banish all irreverence' in the performance of any music[4].

In keeping good order in the church and, to a lesser extent, the churchyard the minister is given the assistance of certain members of the laity but he can never slough off his own responsibilities. For example, if he were to become aware that bawdy words were being sung to the tune of a hymn, or if drunken or rowdy behaviour were interrupting a service, the minister ought to stop the service until good order has been restored. Only in certain restricted circumstances[5] does the minister have the power physically to intervene to prevent disorder and these are, in fact, the same as for any other person. Nevertheless, the minister is under a positive duty to exercise those powers if no one else is restoring good order[6].

There is also a duty on other members of the congregation. According to Canon B 9:

1. All persons present in the time of divine service shall in the due places audibly with the minister say the General Confession, the Lord's Prayer, and the Creed, and make the answers appointed in the form of service.

2. They shall reverently kneel or stand when the prayers are read, and shall stand at the saying or singing of the Canticles and the Creed and at the reading of the holy Gospel, giving due reverence to the name of Jesus.

[1] See **p. 65** *et seq. supra*.
[2] See, also, Canon B 38, para. 4(b), Canons F 15 and 16, and the Burial Laws Amendment Act 1880, s. 7: see **p. 201, footnote 27** *supra* and **p. 258** *infra*. See, further, the rubric before The Communion of the Sick in the Book of Common Prayer and **p. 111** *supra*.
[3] Canon B 1, para. 2.
[4] Canon B 20, para. 3. See, also, the rubric at the commencement of the Churching of Women in the Book of Common Prayer as to the the woman being 'decently apparelled': see **pp. 222–223** *supra*.
[5] See *infra*.
[6] His primary duty is, of course, to take the service but that does not mean that 'occasions may not occur in which it may not be justifiable, and even unavoidable, for him to take part in suppressing any disorder or interruption in the church': *Cox* v. *Goodday* (1811) 2 Hag. Con. 138 at p. 141 *per* Sir William Scott.

B   Disorder by a Minister

In the unlikely case where the minister himself is the cause of disorder the proper course to follow depends on the actual circumstances. As Sir William Scott said in *Hutchins* v. *Denziloe and Loveland*[7]:

> ... if the minister introduces any irregularity into the service, [the church-wardens] have no authority to interfere, but they must complain to the ordinary of his conduct. I do not say there may not be cases where they may be bound to interpose; in such cases they may repress, and ought to repress, all indecent interruptions of the service by others, and are the most proper persons to repress them, and they desert their duty if they do not. And if a case could be imagined in which even a preacher himself was guilty of any act grossly offensive, either from natural infirmity or from disorderly habits, I will not say that the churchwardens, and even private persons, might not interpose to preserve the decorum of public worship. But that is a case of instant and overbearing necessity that supersedes all ordinary rules. In cases which fall short of such a singular pressure, and can await the remedy of a proper legal complaint[8], that is the only proper mode to be pursued by a churchwarden – if private and decent application to the minister himself shall have failed in preventing what he deems the repetition of an irregularity. At the same time, it is at his own peril if he makes a public complaint, or even a private complaint, in an offensive manner, of what is no irregularity at all, and is in truth nothing more than a misinterpretation of his own.

Clearly no one should act without first taking careful consideration; if someone were to act precipitously, he would be in grave danger himself of causing disruption or irreverence.

In addition, the provisions of section 2 of the Ecclesiastical Courts Jurisdiction Act 1860 apply equally to the clergy[9] as to the laity[10].

C   General Disorder

The general law of the land permits people themselves to intervene to prevent crime or to apprehend offenders in certain circumstances[11] and this applies equally

---

[7] (1792) 1 Hag. Con. 170 at pp. 173–174.

[8] See, for example, *Bishop of St Albans* v. *Fillingham* [1906] P 163 at p. 176 (a case where an incumbent purported to 'ordain' a layman 'to oppose certain ritual practices' (see *op. cit*, at p. 175) of a neighbouring incumbent.)   [9] *Vallancey* v. *Fletcher* [1897] 1 QB 265.

[10] See *infra*.

[11] As to the various powers set out in the text *supra*, see generally *Clerk & Lindsell on Torts* (Sweet & Maxwell Ltd, 1995) (17th ed.) at paras 12–33 *et seq.*; Smith and Hogan, *Criminal Law* (Butterworths, 1992) (7th ed.) at p. 253 *et seq.* and p. 435 *et seq.*

within the ecclesiastical context. It must, however, always be remembered that, if anyone acts outside the parameters within which the general law permits intervention, he will himself be breaking the law and may thereby become liable to criminal proceedings or an action in damages. Nevertheless, there is a common law right that permits anyone[12], whether a churchwarden[13] or not, to remove a person who is disturbing divine service[14].

(i) Lesser excommunication

Further, there is the duty on a minister in certain circumstances to refuse to administer Holy Communion to those who are 'notorious offenders'; this is otherwise known as lesser excommunication[15]. Nonetheless, it does not mean that the person so refused may not thereafter remain in church as long as he does not create any disturbance.

By the Sacrament Act 1547, section 8, it is laid down that at least one day before the celebration the 'priest who shall minister' the eucharist must:

... exhort all persons which shall be present likewise to resort and prepare themselves to receive the same. And when the day prefixed cometh, after a godly exhortation[16] by the minister made ... the said minister shall not without a lawful cause deny the same to any person who will devoutly and humbly desire it; any law, statute, ordinance, or custom contrary thereunto in any wise notwithstanding ...

This did not mean that those who were not confirmed could receive the sacrament[17]. Rather, it seems that the Church was entitled to determine who properly was a communicant[18] but was then restricted by the statute as to the grounds

[12] 'The duty of maintaining order and decorum in the church lies immediately upon the church-wardens, and if they are not present, or being present do not repress any indecency, they desert their proper duty. The officiating minister has other duties to perform, those of performing divine service. In saying this, I do not mean to say that occasions may not occur in which it may not be justifiable, and even unavoidable, for him to take a part in suppressing any disorder or interruption in the church': *Cox* v. *Goodday* (1811) 2 Hag. Con. 138 at 141 *per* Sir William Scott.

[13] The primary duty is that of the churchwarden: *Cox* v. *Goodday* (1811) 2 Hag. Con. 138 at 141 *per* Sir William Scott.

[14] *Glever* v. *Hynde* (1673) 1 Mod. Rep. 168; see, too, *Burton* v. *Henson* (1842) 10 M. & W. 105 at p. 108 *per* Alderson B (*obiter*) and *Williams* v. *Glenister* (1824) 2 B. & C. 699 at p. 702 *per* Abbot CJ.

[15] See **p. 85 *supra*** and Canon 68 of the 1603 Canons; see, too, *Thompson* v. *Dibdin* [1912] AC 533 at p. 539 *per* Lord Loreburn and, generally, *Banister* v. *Thompson* [1908] P 362 at p. 379 *et seq.*

[16] An exhortation in English was inserted in the Latin mass immediately before the administration; this was subsequently incorporated into the Book of Common Prayer, although nowadays it is invariably omitted: see 14 Halsbury's Statutes (4th ed.) at p. 735.

[17] Lyndwood, *Provinciale Angliae* at p. 40.

[18] See the rubric at the end of the Confirmation service: 'And there shall none be admitted to the holy Communion, until such time as he be confirmed, or be ready or desirous to be confirmed.' The

upon which such a communicant might thereafter be refused admission to the sacrament[19]. Indeed, prior to the statute a priest had to refuse the sacrament to non-parishioners (unless they were travellers[20]), other than in cases when the person was in danger of death[21].

Canon B 16, para. 1, states:

> If a minister be persuaded that anyone of his cure[22] who presents himself to be a partaker of the Holy Communion ought not to be admitted thereunto by reason of malicious and open contention with his neighbours, or other grave and open sin without repentance, he shall give an account of the same to the bishop of the diocese or other Ordinary of the place[23] and therein obey his order and direction, but so as not to refuse the sacrament to any until in accordance with such order and direction he shall have called him and advertised him that in any wise he presume not to come to the Lord's Table: Provided that in case of grave and immediate scandal to the congregation the minister shall not admit such person, but shall give an account of the same to the Ordinary within seven days after at the furthest and therein obey his order and direction. Provided also that before issuing his order and direction in relation to any such person the Ordinary shall afford to him[24] an opportunity for interview.

Nevertheless, Canon B 16 only applies to persons falling within Canon B 15A, para. 1(a)[25], namely:

> ... members of the Church of England who have been confirmed in accordance with the rites of the Church or are ready and desirous of being confirmed or who have been otherwise episcopally confirmed with unction or with the laying on of hands except as provided by the next following Canon.

The wording of Canon B 16, para. 1, follows that of the second rubric before the service of Holy Communion in the Book of Common Prayer, although it dif-

1549 Prayer Book read: ' ... As he be confirmed.' See, too, Stephens, *The Book of Common Prayer*, vol. III, at p. 1495. Canon B 15A, para. 1, has now expanded the category of those who must be admitted to the sacrament. By reason of the Sacrament Act 1547, these persons also may not be refused the sacrament, save in so far as Canon B 16 may apply: see *infra*.

[19] According to Lyndwood, *Provinciale Angliae* at p. 232, the sacrament should have been refused to those who had not been confessed.

[20] See, too, Ayliffe, *Parergon Iuris Canonici Anglicani* at p. 475.

[21] See Lyndwood, *Provinciale Angliae* at pp. 184 and 233.

[22] It seems, therefore, that only those having a cure of souls may instigate the matter. Nevertheless, once the Ordinary has given his directions, all ministers must abide by them: Canon B 15A, para. 1(a) proviso; Canon 14, C para. 3. As to cures of souls see **p. 134 *et seq. supra***.

[23] 'The references in this Canon to "the bishop of the diocese or other Ordinary of the place" and to "the Ordinary" include, in the case of the Ordinary being the bishop of the diocese and the see being vacant, the archbishop of the province or, in the case of the archbishopric being vacant or the vacant see being Canterbury or York, the archbishop of the other province': Canon B 16, para. 2.

[24] That is, the prospective communicant.

[25] As to others falling within Canon B 15A, para. 1, see **p. 242, footnote 34 *infra***.

fers from the wording of the original two rubrics[26]. Moreover, the present Canon is substantially different from its predecessors[27] and there is no equivalent rubric in the Alternative Service Book.

This latter omission is of particular importance as it raises in acute form the question of the extent to which, if at all, a rubric concerning good Church order in the Book of Common Prayer can govern behaviour in a service according to the Alternative Service Book[28]. It is, of course, true that Canon B 16, para. 1, is on the face of it applicable to both situations[29] but, although the canons bind the clergy in ecclesiastical matters, they do not of their own force bind the laity[30]. Moreover, as there is a duty on those who have been confirmed to receive the Holy Communion regularly, and especially at the festivals of Christmas, Easter and Whitsun[31], there must in any event be a corresponding right[32] to receive the

[26] The original rubrics read as follows: 'And if any of those be an open and notorious evil liver, or have done any wrong to his neighbours by word or deed, so that the Congregation be thereby offended; the Curate having knowledge thereof, shall call him and advertise him, that in any wise he presume not to come to the Lord's table, until he hath openly declared himself to have truly repented and amended his naughty life, that the Congregation may thereby be satisfied which before were offended; and that he hath recompensed the parties to whom he hath done wrong, or at least declared himself to be in full purpose so to do, as soon as he conveniently may. The same order shall the Curate use with those betwixt whom he perceiveth malice and hatred to reign; not suffering them to be partakers of the Lord's Table, until he know them to be reconciled. And if one of the parties so at variance be content to forgive from the bottom of his heart all that the other hath trespassed against him, and to make amends for that he himself hath offended; and the other party will not be persuaded to a godly unity, but still in his frowardness and malice; the Minister in that case ought to admit the penitent to the holy Communion, and not him that is obstinate. Provided that every Minister so repelling any as specified ... shall be obliged to give account of the same to the Ordinary within fourteen days after at the farthest. And the Ordinary shall proceed against the offending person according to the Canon.'

[27] Canon 26 of the 1603 Canons stated: 'No Minister shall in any wise admit to the receiving of the holy Communion, any of his cure or flock, which be openly known to live in sin notorious, without repentance; nor any who have maliciously and openly contended with their neighbours, until they shall be reconciled ... ' (Indeed, there was a rubric (now repealed) to a like effect as the latter part of the Canon.) By Canon 27 of the 1603 Canons no schismatics were to be admitted to Holy Communion. Moreover, by Canon 109 of the 1603 Canons 'notorious offenders' guilty of 'adultery, whoredom, incest, or drunkenness, or ... swearing, ribaldry, usury, [or] any other uncleanness and wickedness of life' were not to be admitted to Holy Communion 'till they be reformed'. It follows that great care must be taken in relation to the present law when considering cases decided under the old Canon. [28] See, generally, **p. 16** *et seq. supra.*

[29] 14 Halsbury's Laws of England (4th ed.) at para. 987 tacitly assumes that it does so apply.

[30] 14 Halsbury's Laws of England (4th ed.) at para. 308. [31] Canon B 15, para. 1.

[32] If the right were based solely on the canons it would be subject to Canon B 16, para. 1. However, according to *Jenkins* v. *Cook* (1876) 1 PD 80 at pp. 99–100: 'The prima facie right of a parishioner to partake of the Holy Communion might probably be maintained irrespective of any specific statutory enactment; but ... the right is distinctly declared by [the Sacrament Act 1547, s. 8] ... '; *R* v. *Dibdin* [1910] P 57 at p. 107 *per* Cozens-Hardy MR; *Thompson* v. *Dibdin* [1912] AC 533 at p. 539 *per* Lord Loreburn. An unlawful refusal is a breach of the ecclesiastical law: *Swayne* v. *Benson* (1889) 6 TLR 7 *per* Lord Penzance; see, too, *R* v. *Dibdin* [1910] P 57 at p. 137 *per* Farwell LJ. It is unclear whether this is a continuing offence or whether 'a refusal a second time is a fresh offence': see *Titchmarsh* v. *Chapman* (1844) 3 Notes of Cases 370 at p. 376 *per* Sir H Jenner Fust. Indeed, a refusal might found an action on the case: *Henley* v. *Burstow* (1666) 1 Keb. 947; *Harris* v. *Hicks* (1693) 2 Salk. 548; nowadays an unlawful refusal might, at the least, ground an action in defamation. In this respect it may be important to differentiate between those having a *right*

eucharist in those circumstances. Indeed, it seems likely[33] that the only circumstances in which the sacrament may be denied are those provided for by the Sacrament Act 1547. That Act imposes a statutory duty not to deny the sacrament 'without lawful cause . . . to any person[34] who would humbly and devoutly desire it . . . '. If the Canon correctly spells out what may be a 'lawful cause', then it applies equally to all rites[35]. In fact, not only is the present Canon similar in ambit[36] to the wording of the rubric[37] originally sanctioned by the Act of Uniformity 1662, but it follows the wording of the present rubric which was itself sanctioned by a Measure having statutory force[38]. The instances therein set out almost certainly, therefore, fall within what is a 'lawful cause'. It follows that in addition to the Sacrament Act 1547, both the rubric and Canon govern the situation under the Alternative Service Book.

A person may, therefore, be refused the sacrament if he does not qualify under

to receive the sacrament and those who *may* do so. See, too, *Taylor* v. *Timson* (1888) 20 QBD 671 at p. 683 *per* Stephen J: ' . . . [B]y imposing a general duty . . . the legislature confers a general right . . . '

[33] This argument was dismissed by the Dean of the Arches in *Jenkins* v. *Cook* (1873) LR 4 A & E 463 at p. 489 but was left open by the Privy Council on appeal ((1876) 1 PD 80 at p. 100): 'Neither is it necessary for their lordships to decide and they do not decide, that the Canons, which do not, as such, bind the laity, could of their own authority, prescribe "causes" which would be sufficient or "lawful" within the meaning of the [Sacrament Act 1547].' See, too, *Banister* v. *Thompson* [1908] P 362 at p. 385 *per* the Dean of the Arches; *R* v. *Dibdin* [1910] P 57 at pp. 110–111 *per* Cozens-Hardy MR, p. 120 *per* Fletcher Moulton LJ and at p. 138 *per* Farwell LJ.

[34] As to those others who fall into the category of those who may receive the sacrament: see Canon B 15A, para. 1, and the Admission to Holy Communion Measure 1972, pursuant to which the Canon was promulgated. In the light of the Sacrament Act 1547, and Canon B 15A, para. 1(a), proviso, these persons also may not be refused the sacrament: see, however, **p. 243, footnote 42 *supra***. See, too, *In re Perry Almshouses* [1898] 1 Ch 391 at pp. 399–400 *per* Stirling J, although based on the wording of the rubric alone. The problem raised at 14 Halsbury's Laws of England (4th ed.) at para. 561, note 7, seems to have been superseded by the new Canon.

By reason of Canon B 15A, para. 1, 'There shall be admitted to the Holy Communion: (a) members of the Church of England who have been confirmed in accordance with the rites of that Church or are ready and desirous to be so confirmed or who have been otherwise episcopally confirmed with unction or with the laying on of hands except as provided by [Canon B 16]; (b) baptised persons who are communicant members of other Churches which subscribe to the doctrine of the Holy Trinity, and who are in good standing in their own Church; (c) any other baptised person authorised to be admitted under regulations of the General synod; and (d) any baptised person in immediate danger of death.' Canon B 15A, para. 3, states: 'Where any minister is in doubt as to the application of this Canon, he shall refer the matter to the bishop of the diocese or other Ordinary and follow his guidance thereon.' Confirmation implies baptism: *In re Perry Almshouses* [1898] 1 Ch 391 at p. 400 *per* Stirling J.

[35] As to the original rubric it must be remembered that it was included at a time when members of the laity signified their intention to receive the sacrament to the minister 'at least some time the day before' (see the first rubric prior to the Holy Communion according to the Book of Common Prayer): see, further, **p. 103 *supra***. This practice has fallen into abeyance and there is no precise equivalent to Canon 22 of the 1603 Canons (now repealed): cp. Canon B 7. It would not, therefore, be lawful for a minister to refuse the sacrament on the grounds that such notice has not been given: see, too, *Stewart* v. *Crommelin* (1852), cited in *Clifton* v. *Ridsdale* (1876) 1 PD 331 at pp. 316 and 346–347.

[36] However, offence to the congregation may not now be necessary other than in relation to the proviso: see *infra*.   [37] See *supra*.

[38] See *R* v. *Ecclesiastical Committee of the Houses of Parliament, Ex parte The Church Society* [1994] COD 319, *The Times*, 4 November 1993; *Ex parte Williamson, The Times*, 9 March 1994 (for full transcripts see Hill, *Ecclesiastical Law* at pp. 68, 72 and 77 respectively).

Canon B 15A, para. 1. A person may similarly be refused if he does not 'humbly and devoutly desire it'[39]; presumably whether or not this is so is to be inferred from all the surrounding circumstances[40], although a failure to kneel to receive the sacrament should no longer by itself be taken as a lack of humility or devoutness[41].

Those occasions apart, therefore, the only occasion upon which the sacrament can lawfully be refused is when there is a 'lawful cause' under the 1547 Act. In this regard it has already been suggested that the situation must be governed (in part at least) by the rubric before the Communion service in the Book of Common Prayer and Canon B 16, para. 1. Although it remains possible[42] that it would also be a 'lawful cause' if the person attempting to receive the sacrament were an atheist, heretic or schismatic (as long as the provisions of Canon B 15A and Canons B 43 and 44 are always borne in mind[43]), it is unlikely[44].

Finally, of course, there are the provisions of the rubric and Canon themselves. Save where the proviso applies[45], no person may be refused[46] the sacrament[47] until the Ordinary has been consulted[48] and, in accordance with the order or direction of the Ordinary[49], the person has been told[50] that he should not come

---

[39] Sacrament Act 1547, s. 8. These words, if they stood alone, would be ambiguous as to whether the prospective communicant's subjective intentions are referred to (see, further, the Exhortation after the Prayer for the Church Militant in the Book of Common Prayer) or whether the reference is to the manner of his presenting himself viewed objectively. However, the complete wording is: 'any person *that will* devoutly and humbly desire it' (emphasis supplied). This suggests that it is the objective consideration that is paramount. Indeed, not only is this interpretation in accord with good Church order but it means that there is no overlap between a subjective intention and 'lawful cause'.

[40] For example, drunkenness at Christmas Midnight Mass.

[41] See **p. 50** *et seq. supra*. Similarly, to decline physically to 'exchange a sign of peace' in the rites of Holy Communion in the Alternative Service Book (see Notes 31 and 25 at pp. 129 and 189 respectively: 'All *may* exchange a sign of peace.' (emphasis supplied)) would by itself be insufficient, as a number of people find this devotionally distracting.

[42] In spite of the repeal of Canon 27 of the 1603 Canons which reflected the pre-Reformation canon law: see Lyndwood, *Provinciale Angliae* at p. 288 and Bullard, *Constitutions and Canons Ecclesiastical, 1604* at p. 174. Cp. *Jenkins* v. *Cook* (1876) 1 PD 80.

[43] It could clearly no longer be contended that occasionally to attend, for example, a Wesleyan place of worship makes a person a schismatic: see *Swayne* v. *Benson* (1889) 6 TLR 7. Clearly, too, the matter must also be approached by the minister with charity, giving the person concerned the benefit of any doubt: cp. *Re Todd* (1842) 3 Notes of Cases, Supp. li.

[44] If the Canons and rubrics do not delimitate what is a 'lawful cause' the Act would also apply to those falling within Canon B 15A, para. 1(b)–(d). Yet, if this were so it would make nonsense of the proviso to Canon B 15A, para. 1(a). [45] See *infra*.

[46] The words 'shall have him called and advertised' imports that a refusal will follow: *R* v. *Dibdin* [1909] P 57 at p. 85 *per* Bray J.

[47] It is for the minister to justify the refusal: *Swayne* v. *Benson* (1889) 6 TLR 7. Subject to what is said about a letter amounting to a refusal (*infra*), it should be noted that the rubric and Canon only come into effect when the person actually presents himself.

[48] The Ordinary must provide the alleged wrongdoer with an opportunity for an interview: see the final proviso to Canon B 16, para. 1. The final proviso governs the situation whether or not the other proviso applies. This is clear because the final proviso is contained in a separate sentence: thus the words 'any such person' must refer to either situation already referred to within the Canon.

[49] The warning should be given even if the Ordinary gives no directions concerning the notice.

[50] The person is entitled to be summoned to the minister and then informed of the situation. In practice the best course may be to write a letter in general terms explaining the situation and giving a time and place when the person concerned is invited to discuss the matter with the minister. A letter may amount to a refusal: *Banister* v. *Thompson* [1908] P 362 at p. 379.

to the altar in an attempt to receive the sacrament[51]. The rubric and Canon speak of a refusal in relation to 'anyone of his cure'[52], that is, one of the minister's parishioners; nonetheless, the 1547 Act is not so restricted and it seems likely that what would be a 'lawful cause' between an incumbent and parishioner would equally be a lawful cause whether or not a relationship of parish priest and parishioner exists.

The proviso apart, a refusal must be based upon any 'malicious and open contention with ... neighbours[53], or other grave and open sin without repentance'. Here the most important word is 'open'; if the contention or sin is not within general knowledge, no refusal ought to take place. Under the wording of the previous rubric it was necessary that 'the congregation be thereby offended' and it was, therefore, also necessary that the congregation was indeed offended thereby[54]. This was apparently because the minister was acting 'for the protection of the whole community'[55]. However, although it may be argued that it is no longer necessary for the congregation to be offended, other than in relation to the proviso[56] this requirement seems still to be implied by the use of the word 'open'[57]. If one of two contentious persons repents while the other does not, the repentant must no longer be refused the sacrament. The words 'malicious ... contention' and 'grave ... sin' must be given their natural meanings; they therefore relate to moral conduct[58]. In relation to the wording of the previous Canon[59] the Dean of the Arches said in *Banister* v. *Thompson*[60]:

[51] The refusal is to be judged at the time it takes place and cannot be justified by a subsequent referral to the Ordinary: see *Jenkins* v. *Cook* (1876) 1 PD 80 at pp. 105–106.

[52] This seems to reflect the old canon law which permitted a priest to refuse the sacrament to non-parishioners, save for travellers: see *supra*. The words would include those on the church electoral roll.

[53] Within the context of parishioners the word 'neighbours' presumably refers to any fellow parishioner or to anyone living within the immediate vicinity: a similar distinction seems to be drawn in the final rubric after The Communion of the Sick in the Book of Common Prayer: ' ... when none of the Parish or neighbours can be gotten to communicate with the sick in their houses ... ' Although it might be argued that the word should in any event be given its wider Christian connotation, it seems likely that a contention between persons in a wider context might well give rise to a 'lawful cause' under the 1547 Act. The word presumably also embraces the incumbent himself. This being so, the need for prior consultation with the Ordinary is of particular importance as it prevents the incumbent being judge in his own cause.

[54] *Banister* v. *Thompson* [1908] P 362 at p. 385 *per* the Dean of the Arches. At p. 387 the Dean said: 'Lastly, it must be such as to cause offence to the public conscience.'

[55] *Banister* v. *Thompson* [1908] P 362 at p. 385 *per* the Dean of the Arches.

[56] See *infra*. Because of the history of the wording of the present Canon (see the **present paragraph**), the words 'grave and immediate scandal *to the congregation*' (emphasis suplied) in the proviso probably do not include the minister himself.

[57] To the contrary it may be argued that it is the immediate scandal to the congregation that brings the proviso into play.

[58] See *Jenkins* v. *Cook* (1876) 1 PD 80 at p. 103; *Banister* v. *Thompson* [1908] P 362 at p. 385.

[59] Canon 26 of the 1603 Canons read: 'No Minister shall in any wise admit to the receiving of the holy Communion, any of his cure or flock, which be openly known to live in sin notorious, without repentance; nor any who have maliciously and openly contended with their neighbours, until they be reconciled ... ' Nonetheless, the Dean also took into consideration the wording of Canon 109 of the 1603 Canons: see *Banister* v. *Thompson* [1908] P 362 at p. 387.

[60] *Banister* v. *Thompson* [1908] P 362 at p. 385.

By an evil liver is intended a person whose course of life, as distinguished from some particular course of action, is in conflict with the moral code of Christendom.

In the result it was held in *Banister* v. *Thompson*[61] that the sacrament could not lawfully be refused to parties whose marriage was valid under the Deceased Wife's Sister's Marriage Act 1907. Although the wording is now different, the principles would seem to remain the same.

There is no reported case[62] upon whether the same is true in relation to a person divorced according to the civil law and remarried during the lifetime of the former spouse but the reasoning would seem to apply equally to both situations. Indeed, in *Thompson* v. *Dibdin*[63] Earl Loreburn said:

> It is inconceivable that any Court of law should allow as a lawful cause the cohabitation of two persons whose union is directly sanctioned by Act of Parliament and is as valid as any other marriage within this realm.

In relation to the proviso it is clear that the minister may only refuse the sacrament if there is both a 'grave' and 'immediate'[64] scandal to the congregation; in this regard offence to the congregation is certainly necessary[65]. In these circumstances an account must be given to the Ordinary within at least seven days and the minister must obey the Ordinary's order and directions[66].

(ii)   Arrest

According to the Police and Criminal Evidence Act 1984[67]:

Any person may arrest without warrant:

(a)   anyone who is in the act of committing an arrestable offence;
(b)   anyone who he has reasonable grounds for suspecting to be committing such an offence.

No ecclesiastical offence amounts to such an arrestable offence, as an arrestable offence is normally[68] one for which a person over twenty-one may be sentenced

---

[61] [1908] P 362. See, too, *R* v. *Dibdin* [1910] P 57; affd *sub nom. Thompson* v. *Dibdin* [1912] AC 533.

[62] In practice bishops have assumed a discretion in this matter: see 14 Halsbury's Laws of England (4th ed.) at para. 978, note 1.

[63] [1912] AC 533 at p. 540. Each judgment was to the same effect: *passim*.

[64] These words should be given their ordinary meanings: see *supra*.   [65] *Supra*.

[66] The Ordinary must provide the alleged wrongdoer an opportunity for an interview.

[67] Section 24(4).

[68] For the full definition of an arrestable offence, see the Police and Criminal Evidence Act 1984, s. 24. It includes an attempt to commit, or incitement, aiding and abetting, counselling or procuring any such offence: s. 24(3).

to a term of imprisonment for five years or more. Arrestable offences[69], however, include theft, criminal damage and all the serious offences against the person although not a mere assault or battery[70]. It must be noted, nonetheless, that the offence must actually be in the course of being committed. Once the offence has been committed, a person may arrest without warrant[71]:

> (a) any person who is guilty of the offence;
> (b) anyone who he has reasonable grounds for suspecting to be guilty of it.

This does not, however, protect an ordinary citizen[72] if, contrary to his belief, no offence has indeed been committed or if an offence is only about to be committed[73]. Section 3(1) of the Criminal Law Act 1967, further provides that:

> Any person may use such force as is reasonable . . . in effecting or assisting in the lawful arrest of offenders or suspected offenders . . .

However, this provision does not give powers of arrest additional to those already set out but specifies what force may be used in particular circumstances[74].

If an arrest is actually effected, it is the duty of the person who makes the arrest to ensure that the person arrested is taken before a magistrate or to a police station as quickly as is reasonably possible[75].

A churchwarden is given a specific power of arrest under section 3 of the Ecclesiastical Courts Jurisdiction Act 1860, and section 8 of the Burial Laws Amendment Act 1880[76].

---

[69] In addition, any person has a power of arrest where '(1) a breach of the peace has been committed in the presence of the person making the arrest or (2) the arrestor reasonably believes that such a breach will be committed in the immediate future by the person arrested although he has not yet committed any breach or (3) where a breach of the peace has been committed and it is reasonably believed that a renewal of it is threatened': *R* v. *Howell* [1982] 1 QB 416 at p. 426 *per* Watkins LJ; see, too, **p. 247, footnote 77 *infra*.**   [70] See the Criminal Justice Act 1988, s. 39.

[71] Police and Criminal Evidence Act 1984, s. 24(5).

[72] A policeman has wider powers: see *ibid*, s. 24(6), (7).

[73] For the position where an offence is about to be committed, see also *infra*.

[74] 'No doubt if a question arose [in relation to section 3 of the 1967 Act], the court, in considering what was reasonable force, would take into account all the circumstances, including in particular the nature and degree of force used, the seriousness of the evil to be prevented and the possibility of preventing it by other means . . . ': *per* Criminal Law Revision Committee (Cmnd 2659 at para. 23).

[75] *John Lewis & Co. Ltd* v. *Tims* [1952] AC 676 at p. 691; *Dallison* v. *Caffery* [1965] 1 QB 348. As the ecclesiastical law is part of the general law of England (*Edes* v. *Bishop of Oxford* (1667) Vaugh. 18 at p. 21; 14 Halsbury's Laws (4th ed.) at para. 304) and a minister has a duty to complete a service (see **p. 46 *supra***), it is arguable that he should first complete the service. This could only be so if there is no one else who could either lawfully finish the service or convey the arrested person. ' . . . [A]ll the circumstances of the case must be taken into consideration in deciding whether this requirement is complied with. A direct route and a rapid progress are no doubt matters for consideration, but these are not the only matters': *John Lewis & Co. Ltd* v. *Tims* [1952] AC 676 at p. 691 *per* Lord Porter.   [76] See *infra*.

(iii) Prevention

In addition section 3(1) of the Criminal Law Act 1967, provides that:

Any person may use such force as is reasonable in the circumstances in the prevention of crime . . .

These provisions embrace circumstances where a crime is being committed or is about to be committed[77]. Force which is reasonable in those particular circumstances may then be used, quite apart from any question of an arrest. However, it should be remembered that a breach of the ecclesiastical law is unlikely to amount to 'crime' within the meaning of this Act[78]. On the other hand, quite apart from the more usual criminal offences[79] to which the provisions apply, there are other common law offences, as well as specific statutory offences, which certainly fall within the definition.

These other common law[80] offences are those of preventing the decent burial of a dead body without lawful excuse[81], disturbing a Church of England clergyman in the performance of divine worship[82] and striking a person in a church or churchyard[83]. Indeed, it is also an offence at common law for anyone[84] to disturb divine service[85]. However, none of these are arrestable offences in so far as those who are not constables are concerned.

The Ecclesiastical Courts Jurisdiction Act 1860, section 2, provides:

Any person[86] who shall be guilty[87] of riotous, violent, or indecent behaviour in England in any cathedral church, parish or district church, or chapel of the

---

[77] In addition, any person may take reasonable steps to prevent a breach of the peace (whether occurring or threatening to occur), including in an appropriate case detaining the perpetrator against his will: *Lavin* v. *Albert* [1982] AC 546; see, too, **p. 245, footnote 69 supra**.

[78] This is because there is no provision for proceedings against the laity in the ecclesiastical courts (see 14 Halsbury's Laws of England (4th ed.) at para. 308). Whether it would include 'an offence against the laws ecclesiastical' by a clergyman (see the Ecclesiastical Jurisdiction Measure 1963, ss. 14(1), 17) is by no means clear. It applies to an offence under the Ecclesiastical Courts Jurisdiction Act 1860, s. 2.   [79] Including in this instance offences of assault or battery: cp. *supra*.

[80] The term is here used in contradistinction to the ecclesiastical *jus commune*: see 14 Halsbury's Laws of England (4th ed.) at para. 303.

[81] *R* v. *Hunter* [1974] 1 QB 95, especially at p. 98 *per* Cairns LJ.

[82] *R* v. *Parry* (1686) Trem PC 239, 15 Digest (Repl.) 801. It is unclear whether this would also include a lay person lawfully performing divine worship. However, in principle it is felt that it should, as the protection is aimed at the worship rather than at the person performing it. Compare the position under the Ecclesiastical Courts Jurisdiction Act 1860, s. 2: see *infra*.

[83] *Wilson* v. *Greaves* (1757) 1 Burr. 240 at p. 243 *per* Lord Mansfield.

[84] Including a clergyman, when preaching or otherwise: see Watson, *The Clergy-Man's Law* (Savoy, 1725) (3rd ed.) at p. 348.

[85] *Glever* v. *Hynde* (1673) 1 Mod. Rep. 168. Anyone present may remove the person causing the disturbance: *ibid*.

[86] This includes a clergyman: *Vallancy* v. *Fletcher* [1897] 1 QB 265; *Girt* v. *Fillingham* [1901] P 176. This seems also to reflect the position at the common law: see Watson, *The Clergy-Man's Law* at p. 348. See also **p. 238 et seq. supra**.

[87] The penalty is a fine on scale 1 or imprisonment not exceeding two months.

Church of England ... whether during the celebration of Divine service, or at any other time, or in any churchyard, or burial-ground, or who shall molest, let, disturb, vex, or trouble, or by any other unlawful means disquiet or misuse any preacher duly authorised to preach therein, or any clergyman in Holy Orders ministering or celebrating any sacrament or any Divine service, rite, or office in any cathedral, church or chapel, churchyard, or burial ground shall on conviction ... be liable to a penalty ...

The words 'divine service' are to be read in their widest sense and the words 'any divine service, rite, or office in any cathedral, church or chapel' are used[88]:

to cover all the services in the Church of England, including the celebration of the sacraments ...

Prior to the Church of England (Worship and Doctrine) Measure 1974, it was held[89] that to obstruct a priest from collecting the offertory during the Holy Communion service according to the Book of Common Prayer was not obstructing 'a clergyman in holy orders celebrating Divine service'[90] as the rubric before the Prayer for the Church Militant imposes that duty on 'the Deacons, Church-wardens, or other fit person appointed for that purpose'[91]. However, it is doubtful whether this is any longer good law. Not only might the decision well have been different if the information had charged an obstruction 'during the celebration of Divine service' by the other priest then present[92] but, as has been seen, a greater flexibility is now permitted concerning the rubrics. The relevant rubric is not such as to determine what must happen in services according to the Alternative Service Book[93] as it was recognised[94] that 'There is nothing improper in a priest ... making the collection.' Not only does the Alternative Service Book not lay down who should collect the offertory[95] but a priest might now rely upon Canon B 5 in relation to his collecting the offertory even within a Book of Common Prayer eucharist.

In *Matthews* v. *King*[96] the disturbance consisted mainly of the organised loud singing of hymns, other than those ordered for the day, throughout the whole service so as to make the officiating minister's voice inaudible[97]. As Lawrence J said[98]:

---

[88] *Matthews* v. *King* [1934] 1 KB 505 at p. 515 *per* Lawrence J.

[89] *Cope* v. *Barber* (1872) 7 CP 393. However, this case must now be read in the light of Canon B 5, para. 1.

[90] In *Cope* v. *Barber* (1872) LR 7 CP 393 at p. 403 *per* Willes J it was doubted whether the words protected a deacon whilst collecting the offertory.

[91] In *Cope* v. *Barber* (1872) LR 7 CP 393 it was held that the words 'other fit person' referred to a layman and assumed (at p. 403 *per* Willes J) that the appointment should be by the priest.

[92] That is, under the earlier part of section 2 of the Ecclesiastical Courts Jurisdiction Act 1860. As it was, the case hinged upon whether the priest collecting the offertory was himself celebrating at the relevant time.   [93] See **p. 48** *et seq. supra.*

[94] *Cope* v. *Barber* (1872) LR 7 CP 393 at p. 403 *per* Willes J.

[95] See Notes 34 and 27 at pp. 129 and 189 respectively.   [96] [1934] 1 KB 505.

[97] *Op. cit.* at p. 507.

[98] *Op. cit.* at p. 516. For a fascinating sidelight on this case see *Re St Hilary, Cornwall. King* v. *Roffe-Sylvester* [1938] 4 All ER 147 at p. 152F *et seq.*

The Act was designed to protect the clergyman from disturbance in the performance of his duties and to preserve order, decency and reverence in the
church in the performance of those duties; it has no reference to whether he
performs them properly . . .[99]

That being so, 'indecent behaviour' does not mean an action which tends to
corrupt or deprave but, rather, must be seen within the context of a service in
a sacred place; it therefore includes expressions of disapproval[100] or interference
with the proper and orderly conduct of the service[101]. Indeed, to raise a matter
against an ordinand not amounting in law to an impediment during the ordination service, when the congregation is asked if they know of any such impediment or crime, is also an offence[102]. A claim of right is no defence under the
statute[103].

Of course, merely because no words are actually being spoken, nor any action
expressly directed by the rubrics being carried out, it does not mean that divine
service is not still being celebrated. As was said in *Cope* v. *Barber*[104]:

[The priest] is entitled to the protection of the Act whilst ministering or celebrating any rite or office or making any movement towards, in, or after such
celebration.

Nowadays this would embrace both processions and periods of silence within
the service itself[105]. It should be noted that the earlier part of section 2 of the
Ecclesiastical Courts Jurisdiction Act 1860 applies whether or not the service is
actually being celebrated and, presumably, whether or not the minister is a
clergyman[106].

By Canon F 15, para. 2, churchwardens and their assistants[107] are under an
ecclesiastical duty:

[99] The case makes it clear that this means 'according to the law that applies to liturgy'. Thus the
precise nature of the service is immaterial: *Kensit* v. *Rose* (1898) 62 JP 489.
[100] Unless they are mere asides that do not interrupt the service: see *Jones* v. *Catterale* (1902) 18
TLR 367; *Abrahams* v. *Cavey* [1968] 1 QB 479 at p. 486.
[101] *Abrahams* v. *Cavey* [1968] 1 QB 479; *Girt* v. *Fillingham* [1901] P 176; *Jones* v. *Catterale*
(1902) 18 TLR 367.
[102] *Kensit* v. *Dean and Chapter of St Paul's* [1905] 2 KB 249. The particular problems arising
from the different wording of the Alternative Service Book are considered at **p. 233** *et seq. supra*.
[103] *Asher* v. *Calcraft* (1887) 18 QBD 607; *Kensit* v. *Dean and Chapter of St Paul's* [1905] 2 KB
249 at p. 257.
[104] (1872) LR 7 CP 393 at p. 402 *per* Willes J. Contrast, however, *Williams* v. *Glenister* (1824)
2 B & C 699 (notice read by a layman while clergyman walking from the communion table to the
vestry; this, however, depended upon a differently worded statute).
[105] See **pp. 65** *et seq.* and **75** *et seq. supra*.
[106] As was pointed out by Willes J in *Cope* v. *Barber* (1872) LR 7 CP 393 at p. 402, in certain
circumstances a lay person may perform a baptism. The Act was aimed at preventing the disturbance
of any divine service and, therefore, the first part of section 2 would seem to apply even though the
circumstances in which lay persons may take services (see **p. 17** *et seq. supra*) are now much wider.
This is in spite of the *obiter dictum* of Lawrence J in *Matthews* v. *King* [1934] 1 KB 505 at p. 516.
[107] Canon E 2, para. 3, states that: 'It shall be the duty of the sidesmen to . . . assist the churchwarden in the discharge of their duties in maintaining order and decency in the church and churchyard, especially during the time of divine service.' This refers to duly elected sidesmen (see Canon
E 2, para. 1) and does not include ushers at a wedding. As to Canon F 15, see **p. 257** *et seq. infra*.

... not to suffer any person so to behave in the church, church porch or church-yard during the time of divine service as to create a disturbance. They shall also take care that nothing be done therein contrary to the law of the Church[108] or of the Realm.

They are thus under a duty to intervene[109]. This does not prevent others from so intervening as long as they do so within the law.

Moreover, anyone committing an offence under the Act may[110]:

immediately and forthwith ... be apprehended and taken by any church-warden of the parish or place where the offence shall be committed, and taken before a justice of the peace of the county or place where the said offence shall be committed, to be dealt with according to law.

Not only, therefore, must the arrest occur there and then but only a church-warden may carry out the arrest[111]; moreover, it must be one of the church-wardens who actually takes the offender to the magistrate. This is in spite of Canon F 15, para. 3, which states that:

If any person be guilty of riotous, violent, or indecent behaviour in any church, chapel or churchyard, whether in any time of divine service or not, or of dis-turbing, vexing, troubling, or mis-using any minister officiating therein, the said churchwardens *or their assistants* shall take care to restrain the offender and if necessary proceed against him according to law (emphasis supplied).

In spite of its initial wording this Canon purports to reflect the general law and not section 2 of the 1860 Act[112], as that section makes no mention of church-wardens' assistants[113]. Moreover, the canons cannot give a general power not itself given by the statute[114]. It would, therefore, be foolhardy to attempt to rely on Canon F 15, para. 3, in the hope that it would assist a churchwardens' assistant in defending an action for wrongful arrest or false imprisonment. The words 'to restrain' must, therefore, be read as meaning no more than to stop the offender from so acting. That is not to say, however, that such an assistant

---

[108] In fact, the ecclesiastical law is itself part of the law of the Realm: 14 Halsbury's Laws of England (4th ed.) at para. 304.

[109] *Cox* v. *Goodday* (1811) 2 Hag. Con. 138 at p. 141 *per* Sir William Scott.

[110] Ecclesiastical Courts Jurisdiction Act 1860, s. 3.

[111] Contrast section 3(1) of the Criminal Law Act 1967, at **p. 246** *supra*.

[112] See **p. 257** *et seq. infra*.		[113] See **p. 258** *infra*.

[114] Canons do not of their own force bind the laity: see 14 Halsbury's Laws of England (4th ed.) at para. 308. Although they may do so if they reflect pre-Reformation canon law, it would be difficult to show that this is the case here (see *op. cit.* at para. 307), especially in the light of the specific wording of section 3. The ecclesiastical courts' jurisdiction to punish lay people for brawl-ing was abolished by the Ecclesiastical Courts Jurisdiction Act 1860, s. 1; although that section is now repealed, the jurisdiction does not revive.

should not bring criminal charges against the offender under section 2; it is only an arrest that would cause a problem[115].

By section 36 of the Offences Against the Persons Act 1861:

> Whoever shall, by threats or force, obstruct or prevent or indeavour to obstruct or prevent, any clergyman or other minister in or from celebrating Divine service or otherwise officiating in any church, chapel, meeting house, or other place of Divine worship, or in or from the performance of his duty in the lawful burial of the dead in any churchyard or other burial place, or who shall strike or offer any violence to, or shall, upon any civil process, or under pretext of serving any civil process, arrest any clergyman or other minister who is engaged in, or to the knowledge of the offender is about to engage in, any of the rites or duties in this section aforesaid, or who to the knowledge of the offender shall be going to perform the same or returning from the performance thereof, shall be guilty of [an offence][116].

The words 'or other minister' include a lay person acting as minister for the reasons already set out in relation to the Ecclesiastical Courts Jurisdiction Act 1860[117].

Finally, all burials performed under the Burial Laws Amendment Act 1880[118]:

> ... whether with or without a religious service, shall be conducted in a decent and orderly manner; and every person guilty of any riotous, violent or indecent behaviour at any burial under [the] Act, or wilfully obstructing such burial or any such service as aforesaid thereat, or who shall, in any such churchyard or graveyard as aforesaid, deliver any address, not being part of or incidental to

[115] Although the canons do bind the clergy (14 Halsbury's Laws of England (4th ed.) at para. 308), the Canon could not give a right to arrest a clergyman as that would be an interference with his rights at common law.

[116] This is not an arrestable offence in so far as a person not a constable is concerned.

[117] Indeed, the argument is even stronger in relation to this Act because of the words 'other minister', although no doubt they refer primarily to non-conformist ministers.

[118] Section 7. Such burials are those where it is intended that the burial should not be according to the burial rites of the Church of England or that it should not be in consecrated ground: see *Davies' Law of Burial, Cremation and Exhumation* (Shaw & Sons, 1993) (6th ed.) at pp. 127–128; 10 Halsbury's Laws of England (4th ed.) at para. 1141 *et seq.* By section 59 of the Cemeteries Clauses Act 1847: 'Every person who shall play at any game or sport, or discharge firearms, save at a military funeral, in the cemetery, or who shall wilfully and unlawfully disturb any persons assembled in the cemetery for the purposes of burying any body therein, or who shall commit any nuisance within the cemetery, shall forfeit ... for every such offence a sum [of money according to the magistrates' courts scale].' A cemetery for the purposes of the 1847 Act means the cemetery or burial ground, and the works connected with it, authorised to be constructed by that Act: s. 3; 10 Halsbury's Laws (4th ed.) at para. 1003, note 6. If the burial ground or other place for the interment of the dead is maintained by a burial authority, it is an offence wilfully to create any disturbance or any nuisance therein or wilfully to interfere with any burial taking place or with any grave, vault, tombstone or other memorial or any flowers or plants or any such matter or to play any game or sport therein: Local Authorities' Cemeteries Order 1977, (SI 1977 No. 204) art. 18(1); *Davies' Law of Burial, Cremation and Exhumation* at p. 117.

a religious service permitted by [the] Act, and not otherwise permitted by lawful authority, or who shall, under colour of any religious service or otherwise, in any such churchyard or graveyard, wilfully endeavour to bring into contempt or obloquy the Christain religion, or the belief or worship of any church or denomination of Christians, or other members or any minister of any such church or denomination, or any other person, shall be guilty of an offence[119].

Churchwardens have the same powers in relation to this section as under the Ecclesiastical Courts Jurisdiction Act 1860[120]. The words 'any riotous, violent or indecent behaviour' have the same meaning as under that Act.

(iv)   Trespass

(a)   Generally

In *Cole* v. *Police Constable 443A*[121] a man, who had been a professional guide to sightseers in Westminster Abbey, was excluded from the Abbey on the orders of the Dean when his special permit had lapsed; he refused to leave when requested to do so and was evicted without unnecessary violence. In spite of the fact that he was present during divine service, the eviction was held to be legal because he had become a trespasser.

Anyone who is on another person's land without proper authority is a trespasser; someone invited onto land or into premises, either expressly or by implication[122], becomes a trespasser if he fails to leave when requested to do so by someone having the proper authority. Similarly, there may be a trespass to moveable property. This being so:

Reasonable force may be used in defence of property, real or personal, so as to resist something in the nature of a trespass and in defence of actual possession . . . or the right of possession . . . [U]nreasonable force may not be used in resisting a trespass to property, and extreme violence will rarely be reasonable to such an end[123].

What is reasonable depends upon all the circumstances. For example, it might well be reasonable to use more force to protect a rare Elizabethan chalice than to protect a modern, mass produced one. Normally, a request to leave or to desist is necessary before force may be used but this is not so if there is no time to make such a request. The trespasser may be evicted or prevented by

---

[119]   Again, this is not an arrestable offence without warrant.
[120]   Burial Laws Amendment Act 1880, s. 8.   [121]   [1937] 1 KB 316.
[122]   In the ordinary course the mere fact of a church or churchyard being open would be sufficient invitation to enter in order to worship or view.
[123]   *Clerk & Lindsell on Torts* (Sweet & Maxwell, 1995) (17th ed.) at paras 29–05 and 29–08.

the possessor, his employee or agent[124]. However in the context of a church or churchyard the person using force must himself be careful not to create an unlawful disturbance. Unless the eviction is itself to prevent a disturbance, a person uses force at his peril[125]. In practical terms it is best, if possible, to leave matters to the churchwardens[126] or to redress before the ecclesiastical and civil courts.

(b) Cathedrals

Other than in relation to parish church cathedrals[127], cathedrals have no parishioners; nevertheless, a resident in the diocese has the right to attend divine service in his cathedral[128]. If asked to leave, others must do so even during divine service[129].

(c) Incumbent

Where a parish has no rector[130], the freehold of the church and churchyard[131] is normally in the incumbent[132]. Even when this is not so, the incumbent[133] has sufficient possession to found an action for trespass against wrongdoers[134]. This right, however, is subject to the rights of certain others. For example, the parochial church council and churchwardens have the right to enter the church and churchyard to fulfil their duties[135], although they are not entitled to break in to do so without further legal sanction[136].

---

[124] A churchwarden does not have the implied authority so to act upon the behalf of the incumbent: see *Taylor* v. *Timson* (1888) 20 QBD 671 at p. 673. An usher at a wedding would not have such authority unless it were expressly given to him. It could not be given other than by someone who has the primary right to remove the trespasser. It could not be given by an assistant curate or visiting minister.   [125] See *Asher* v. *Calcraft* (1887) 18 QBD 607; **p. 238 et seq. supra.**

[126] See **p. 257 et seq. infra.**

[127] That is, a cathedral in respect of which there is no corporate body known as the dean and chapter: Cathedrals Measure 1963, s. 53(1).

[128] *Anonymus*, Skinner 101; Gibson, *Codex Juris Ecclesiastici Anglicani* (2nd ed.) at p. 171; see, too, the recent opinion of the Legal Advisory Commission of the General Synod.

[129] See, further, **p. 252 et seq. supra.** As to seating see *Re the Pews of the Cathedral Church of St Columb, Londonderry* (1863) 8 LT 861 and **p. 256, footnote 163 infra.**

[130] Or the rector is the incumbent.

[131] Including any fixtures: see *Legal Opinions concerning the Church of England* at p. 145.

[132] *Jones* v. *Ellis* (1882) 2 Y. & J. 265 at p. 273; 14 Halsbury's Laws of England (4th ed.) at paras 581 and 1079.

[133] There is no decision as to the position of a minister in charge of a suspended benefice but, on balance, it is thought that he may have sufficient possession to found an action in trespass.

[134] *Jones* v. *Ellis* (1828) 2 Y. & J. 265 (perpetual curate). As to actions for trespass, see *Taylor* v. *Timson* (1888) 20 QBD 671 at pp. 680–681 *per* Stephen J (freeholder).

[135] See 14 Halsbury's Laws of England (4th ed.) at paras 553 and 581; *Legal Opinions concerning the Church of England* at p. 48. The diocesan bishop or the archdeacon is entitled to enter on his visitation: see 14 Halsbury's Laws of England (4th ed.) at paras 490 and 499. The diocesan bishop is also entitled to enter after issuing an express instruction as to his admission: see the recent opinion of the Legal Advisory Commission.

[136] *Lee* v. *Matthews* (1830) 3 Hag. Ecc. 169 at p. 173; *Jones* v. *Ellis* (1828) 2 Y. & J. 265; 14 Halsbury's Laws of England (4th ed.) at para. 581.

In addition a person resident[137] in the parish[138] has a right[139] of access to the church at the time of divine service[140], as well as a right to be married in the church and to buried in the churchyard[141]. The right exists as long as there is standing room[142], although if there is an available seat there is equally a right to use it[143]; the right can only exist, however, as long as no disturbance is being caused. Those who are not resident in the parish[144] have an implied leave or licence to enter[145] and remain in a church or churchyard that is open until requested to leave by someone having proper authority; they have no personal

[137] Whether or not he purports to be a member of the Church of England: *In re Perry Almshouses* [1898] 1 Ch 391 a pp. 399–400 *per* Stirling J; *In re Avenon's Charity, Attorney-General* v. *Pelly* [1913] 2 Ch 261 at p. 278 *per* Warrington J. The term has its ordinary and natural meaning and is normally a matter of fact and degree. 'Residence' usually embraces something more than a casual visit but the existence of a home is a highly significant factor, even though it may not have been visited for some time: see *Rayden and Jackson on Divorce and Family Matters* (16th ed.) at para. 5.2.

[138] See *The Case of the Parish of St Swithin in London* (1695) Holt KB 139 at p. 140: ' ... [I]f a person ceases to be a house-keeper, but continues still in the parish as a lodger, and goes to church, and is taken notice of as a parishioner, his interest which he had in the purchased pew continues.' (This implies that, if the person is not a householder, there must be a period of residence before he is recognised as a parishioner.); *Taylor* v. *Timson* (1888) 20 QBD 671 at p. 674. See, too, **p. 88** *supra*.

[139] When the church or churchyard is open other than for divine worship, they have an implied leave or licence to enter and may remain until requested to leave by someone having proper authority: see *infra*.

[140] *Jarrat* v. *Steele* (1820) 3 Phillim. 167 at p. 170 *per* Sir John Nicholl. Pace 14 Halsbury's Laws of England (4th ed.) at para. 562 the case is not authority for the proposition that the right is only to enter to *participate* in divine worship: see, too, Canon 90 of the 1603 Canons; Phillimore, *Ecclesiastical Law* (2nd ed.) vol. I at pp. 736–737; *Cole* v. *Police Constable 443A* [1937] 1 KB 316 (but see *ibid* at p. 333). It seems that anyone resident in the parish may remain as long as he does not disturb the service: see *Taylor* v. *Timson* (1888) 20 QBD 671 at p. 676 and **p. 239** *et seq. supra*. See, also, *Bishop of St David* v. *Baron de Rutzen* (1861) 7 Jur. NS 884 at p. 887 *per* Dr Lushington; **p. 239** *supra*. In *Cole* v. *Police Constable 443A* [1937] 1 KB 316 at p. 333 Goddard J stated: 'The church, by being dedicated to sacred uses, is being dedicated to the use of parishioners to be there for worship, and it seems to me, therefore, that the right of the parishioner to attend his church, which is indeed regarded by all writers upon the subject as clear, depends not upon the statute law but upon the older and wider common law.'

[141] 14 Halsbury's Laws of England (4th ed.) at para. 561.

[142] *Taylor* v. *Timson* (1888) 20 QBD 671 at p. 676 *per* Stephen J: 'Everybody knows cases in which for some reason or other a service is particularly popular. Suppose that more people attend such a service than can sit down, and that one of those present is willing to stand for the sake of listening to the sermon, or of honouring a particular festival, or even for the sake of hearing especially good singing, why should he not do so? I have heard of no authority which says a man behaving with particular propriety under such circumstances is liable to be forcibly removed by the churchwarden ... ' The judge left open the question of overcrowding (at p. 682) but, presumably, such a question would depend upon such factors as whether a danger were being caused (for example, in relation to fire regulations) or a disturbance of the service likely to result.

[143] *The Case of the Parish of St Swithin in London* (1695) Holt KB 139; *Groves and Wright* v. *Rector, etc. of Hornsey* (1793) 1 Hag. Con. 188 at p. 194 *per* Lord Stowell; *Walter* v. *Gunner* (1798) 1 Hag. Con. 314 at p. 317 *per* Sir W Scott.

[144] Even, it seems, if on the electoral role: see 14 Halsbury's Laws of England (4th ed.) at para. 591, note 3.

[145] *Cole* v. *Police Constable 443A* [1937] 1 KB 316 at p. 332 *per* Goddard J.

legal right to do so, however[146]. If they remain when properly requested to leave, they become trespassers[147] and reasonable force may be used to eject them[148].

(d) Churchwardens[149]

Churchwardens may have sufficient possession in the church to prevent persons entering without their permission and authority when it is not open for divine service[150]. The position, however, is not free from doubt[151].

The legal ownership of the plate, ornaments and other moveable goods[152] of the church is clearly vested in the churchwardens[153], although their care is in the parochial church council[154]. The powers of churchwardens are dealt with separately[155], although they also would be entitled to use reasonable force to prevent damage or wrongful removal of such moveables[156].

[146] *Cole* v. *Police Constable 443A* [1937] 1 KB 316 at pp. 330 and 332–336 *per* du Parq and Goddard JJ. The case was concerned with Westminster Abbey (a royal peculiar) and technically these views are *obiter dicta*. There seems little doubt, however, that they are a correct statement of the law. Du Parq J, however, went further and suggested (at p. 330) that there might be a right to worship at any other church, 'if he were prevented by reasonable cause from attending his own parish church and that other church were convenient for him to attend'; see, too, at p. 334 *per* Goddard J. Indeed, this would be consonant with the ancient law that 'Travellers are parishioners of every parish': see Phillimore, *Ecclesiastical Law*, (2nd ed.) vol. I at p. 521; and **p. 239 *et seq. supra*.** Canon 28 of the 1603 Canons did not permit 'strangers' to be admitted to Communion but this is no longer applicable.
[147] *Cole* v. *Police Constable 443A* [1937] 1 KB 316 at p. 332 *per* Goddard J.
[148] On the other hand nothing should be done in church which amounts to a disturbance, unless the ejection is itself to abate a disturbance: see **p. 247 *supra*.**
[149] Unless there is an existing pre-Reformation custom to the contrary there may usually be only two churchwardens: Churchwardens (Appointment and Resignation) Measure 1964, ss. 1, 12(2). Exeptions arise under the Pastoral Measure 1983, s. 27(5)(e), and *ibid*, Sch. 3, para. 4(2); see, too, the Church Representation Rules, r.16(1)(b),(4). See, further, 14 Halsbury's Laws of England (4th ed.) at paras 543 and 549. If the so-called deputies do not fall into these exceptions, they are no more than assistants: see **p. 257 *et seq. infra*.**
[150] *Jarrat* v. *Steele* (1820) 3 Phillim. 167 at pp. 169–170 *per* Sir John Nicholl. (In *Worth* v. *Terrington* (1845) 13 M. & W. 781 at p. 795 Parke B is reported as casting doubt on this authority but the report must be read subject to the note at *Cope* v. *Barber* (1872) LR 7 CP 393 at p. 404, note (1).) See, too, MacMorran, Garth Moore and Briden, *A Handbook for Churchwardens and Parochial Church Councillors* (Mowbray) (1989 ed.) at pp. 70–71, although no authorities are cited.
[151] In *Taylor* v. *Timson* (1888) 20 QBD 671 at pp. 680–681 (a case against a churchwarden) Stephen J said: 'If the boy was a trespasser, he was a trespasser on the freeholder, and the freeholder (the clergyman) must take his own view, whatever it may be, as regards bringing his action against somebody for trespassing in his church.'
[152] Canon E 1, para. 5. Except for the keys the right to the possession of which is, in the first instance, in the incumbent: *Lee* v. *Matthews* (1830) 3 Hag. Ecc. 169 at p. 173; *Daunt* v. *Crocker* (1867) LR 2 A & E 41. Fixtures, however, remain part of the freehold: see *infra*.
[153] Canon E 1, para. 5; *Attorney-General* v. *Ruper* (1722) 2 P. Wms 125. No one, not even a churchwarden, may remove such articles without a faculty (*Durst* v. *Masters* (1875) 1 PD 123 at pp. 126–127; on appeal (1876) 1 PD 373 at p. 383). Although a churchwarden could not be indicted for larceny of the moveables (see *Jackson* v. *Adams* (1835) 2 Bing. NC 402 at p. 408 – a case concerning bell ropes), it is possible that he could now be indicted for theft: see *Legal Opinions concerning the Church of England* (Church House Publishing, 1994) at p. 147. It is possible for others to have a lien on the goods, for example, by agreement: *Walker* v. *Clyde* (1861) 10 CBNS 381 (an organ).
[154] See 14 Halsbury's Laws of England (4th ed.) at paras 576 and 582.
[155] See **p. 257 *et seq. infra*.**   [156] Any removal without a faculty is unlawful.

(e) Memorials

A memorial in a church or churchyard remains private property[157]; armorial appurtenances, such as helmets, probably also remain in private ownership[158]. Such owners have a right to possession[159] and, therefore, may resist a trespass to their goods.

(f) Seating

A private person may have a right to the exclusive use of a specific pew during divine service and other religious observances at times when the church is open for worship[160]. Such a right may well give suffcient right to prevent a trespass but, particularly as the problem is likely to arise at the time of divine service, there is clearly a danger of a disturbance occurring[161] and the matter is best left to the churchwardens.

A person may also be allotted the right by the churchwardens to occupy the seat at all ordinary services; it must be claimed prior to the commencement of the service[162]. However, although such persons may[163] have a sufficient right to

---

[157] See 14 Halsbury's Laws of England (4th ed.) at para. 1085; Newsom & Newsom, *The Faculty Jurisdiction of the Church of England* (2nd ed.) at p. 145. An exclusive right of burial may also give rights of property over the surface of the plot: *Reed* v. *Madon* [1989] 1 Ch 408 (cemetery). However, in a churchyard this would have to be granted by faculty; moreover, burial in a churchyard does not give a right to erect any memorial: 14 Halsbury's Laws of England (4th ed.) at para.1315; Newsom & Newsom, *The Faculty Jurisdiction of the Church of England* (2nd ed.) at p. 170 *et seq*. No right to the exclusive use of any particular part of a churchyard, burial ground or other consecrated land for the purposes of sepulture (other than in a burial ground or cemetery under the Burial Acts 1852 to 1906 or the Public Health (Interments) Act 1879) can now be for more than 100 years: Faculty Jurisdiction Measure 1964, s. 8.

[158] *Re St Andrew's, Thornhaugh* [1976] Fam 230; cp. *Re St Mary's, Broadwater* [1976] Fam 222; and see Newsom & Newsom, *The Faculty Jurisdiction of the Church of England* (2nd ed.) at p. 145.

[159] Although subject to the faculty jurisdiction.

[160] See 14 Halsbury's Laws of England (4th ed.) at para. 1086; Newsom & Newsom, *The Faculty Jurisdiction of the Church of England* (2nd ed.) at pp. 119–120; *Re St Mary's, Banbury* [1986] Fam 24; on appeal [1987] Fam 136.   [161] See **p. 252** *et seq. supra*.

[162] *Vicar, etc. of Claverley* v. *Parishioners, etc. of Claverley* [1909] P 195; 14 Halsbury's Laws of England (4th ed.) at para. 1088.

[163] 'All a parishioner acquires by an allocation of a pew is, a right to sit in it . . . ; he has no right to exclude others from it, if he and his family do not occupy the entire of it. The churchwardens have a right to fill the pew, even though allocated to parishioners': *Re the Pews of the Cathedral Church of St Columb, Londonderry* (1863) 8 LT 861 *per* Dr Todd; *Horsfall* v. *Holland* (1859) 6 Jur. NS 278; *Brittle* v. *Umfreville* (1749) (unreported: Phillimore, *Ecclesiastical Law* (2nd ed.) vol. 2 at p. 1435, footnote (y)); *Kenrick* v. *Taylor* (1752) 1 Wils. 326; *Bunton* v. *Bateman* (1663) 1 Lev. 71; *Ashly* v. *Frecklton* (1682) 3 Lev. 73; *Vicar, etc. of Claverley* v. *Parishioners, etc. of Claverley* [1909] P 195 at p. 216 *per* Dr Tristram: 'Should a stranger be put into a seat prior to the commencement of the service and decline to leave it to enable the allottees to occupy it, he would be liable to an action at common law for disturbance of seat.' However, see *Stocks* v. *Booth* (1786) 1 Term Rep. 428 at p. 430 *per* Ashurst J: 'If bare possession were allowed to be sufficient title, it would be an encouragement to commit disorders in the church; for disputes would frequently arise respecting possession', and *ibid per* Buller J: 'This is an action on the case, and not an action for trespass. Trespass will not lie for entering into a pew, because the plaintiff has not exclusive possession . . . Therefore in an action on the case for disturbing the plaintiff in his pew, for which trespass will not lie, the plaintiff must prove a right either by prescription, or by faculty.'

possession[164] so as to permit them in law themselves to evict someone sitting in that particular part of the pew in which they normally sit, it would also be sensible for them to rely upon the assistance of the churchwardens.

D   Churchwardens

As has been seen[165], there is a common law right that permits anyone, whether a churchwarden or not, to remove a person who is disturbing divine service[166]. A churchwarden[167], particularly, has a right to use reasonable force to remove anyone causing such a disturbance[168]. Indeed, even before the service has begun, a churchwarden may remove someone whom he believes on reasonable grounds is likely to cause such a disturbance[169].

The churchwardens have a duty to maintain order and decency[170] both in the church and churchyard[171], especially at the time of divine service[172]; this may be fulfilled through the sidesmen, who are their assistants[173]. If the minister is causing a disturbance, however, they intervene at their peril and should therefore only do so in the clearest of cases[174].

[164] See *Dean* v. *Hogg* (1834) 10 Bing. 345 (hirer of a steamboat not having exclusive possession); *Holmes* v. *Bagg* (1853) 1 El & Bl 782 (cricket match).   [165] See **p. 238 *et seq. supra.***
[166] *Glever* v. *Hynde* (1673) 1 Mod. Rep. 168; see, too, *Burton* v. *Henson* (1842) 10 M. & W. 105 at p. 108 *per* Alderson B (*obiter*).   [167] As to deputies see **p. 255, footnote 149 *supra.***
[168] *Reynolds* v. *Monkton* (1841) 2 Mood. & R. 384.
[169] *Hartley* v. *Cook* (1833) 9 Bing. 728 at p. 735; *Burton* v. *Henson* (1842) 10 M. & W. 105.
[170] Canon E 1, para. 4; *Cox* v. *Goodday* (1811) 2 Hag. Con. 138 at 141 *per* Sir William Scott.
[171] In *Taylor* v. *Timson* (1888) 20 QBD 671 at p. 673 Stephen J stated that 'prima facie a churchwarden has no authority whatsoever outside the church'; in his view whatever authority they have in the churchyard is derived from statute. See, too, Cripps, *The Law relating to Church and Clergy* at p. 168. If this is indeed correct, it means that sidesmen have no authority in the churchyard, save over ecclesiastical persons; for example, they would have no authority to remove a person committing an act of indecency in a churchyard. This is because Canon E 2, para. 3, does not bind the laity unless it is merely a statement of already existing law. It is thought, however, in the light of the cases cited that the *obiter dictum* is incorrect. At the least it is likely that the churchwardens have authority in the churchyard in relation to services actually taking place there.
[172] 'In trespass the defendant justified as churchwarden, that he pull'd off the plaintiff's hat, he sitting covered in the church, in time of divine service, on which the plaintiff demurred, because the defendant pleads not guilty to all preter insultum, and as to that, that he put off his hat, and gave it him in his hand que est eadem, and per Curiam this is a good justification; and so to switch boys playing in the church-yard, or any disturbers of the peace in time of divine service . . . ': *Haw* v. *Planner* (1666) 2 Keb. 124. Of course, this must be read in the light of what would be proper discipline nowadays and in the light of modern manners. To impose physical punishment in any such circumstances would now be illegal; moreover, to remove someone's hat, unless it were actually disturbing the service in some way, would not nowadays be permissible. See, too, *Burton* v. *Henson* (1842) 10 M. & W. 105, especially at p. 108 *per* Alderson B. 'It is a duty of the churchwarden to proceed by legal and proper means, and no churchwarden can be punished for not enforcing what he considers the right of himself or of the parish, by means of what I must call violence, instead of referring the matter to the properly constituted tribunals': *Attorney-General* v. *Earl of Chesterfield* (1854) 18 Beav. 601 at pp. 606–607 *per* Sir John Romilly.
[173] Canon E 2, para. 3; *Palmer* v. *Tijou* (1824) 2 Add. 196 at pp. 200–201 *per* Sir John Nicholl.
[174] See *Hutchins* v. *Denziloe and Loveland* (1792) 1 Hag. Con. 170 at pp. 173–174 *per* Sir William Scott; *Attorney-General* v. *Earl of Chesterfield* (1854) 18 Beav. 596 at pp. 606–607 *per* Sir John Romilly; **p. 42 *et seq. supra.***

Canon F 15, para. 3 states:

> If any person be guilty of riotous, violent, or indecent behaviour in any church, chapel or churchyard, whether in any time of divine service or not, or of disturbing, vexing, troubling, or mis-using any minister officiating therein, the said churchwardens or their assistants shall take care to restrain the offender and if necessary proceed against him according to law.

As has been seen this is not so much a reflection of the Ecclesiastical Courts Jurisdiction Act 1860, section 2, as of the general law; it certainly cannot give powers of arrest apart from that statute, for example, to sidesmen[175]. In addition Canon F 15, para. 2 states that churchwardens and their assistants:

> . . . shall not suffer any person to behave in the church, church porch, churchyard[175A] during the time of divine service as to create disturbance. They shall also take care that nothing be done therein contrary to the law of the Church or of the Realm[176].

Moreover, by Canon F 15, para. 1, they must not:

> . . . suffer the church or chapel to be profaned by any meeting[177] therein for temporal objects inconsistent with the sanctity of the place, nor the bells to be rung at any time contrary to the direction of the minister.

Each of these Canons gives guidance as to what is not to be permitted. Care should be taken, however, to remember that ideas of behaviour alter from age to age. At one time it was thought that boys playing in the churchyard might be whipped[178]; however, forty-six years later such a course was being advised

---

[175] See **p. 245** *et seq. supra.*   [175A] Cp. **p. 257, footnote 171, supra.**

[176] In spite of the dichotomy expressed here, the law of the Church is part of the general law of the Realm: see 14 Halsbury's Laws of England (4th ed.) at para. 306.

[177] This would include a party in a hall that has been created within the church itself. Presumably, a wedding feast may be permitted as long as it does not become drunken or rowdy and as long as the speeches are not improper. Under Canon F 16, para. 1: 'When any church or chapel is to be used for a play, concert, or exhibition of films or pictures, the minister shall take care that the words, music, and pictures are such as befit the House of God, are consonant with sound doctrine, and make for the edifying of the people.' The minister must obey any general directions relating to such use of a church or chapel as are issued from time to time by the bishop or other Ordinary: *ibid,* para. 2. If any doubt arises as to the manner in which these provisions are to be observed, the minister must refer the matter to the bishop or other Ordinary, and obey his directions: *ibid,* para. 4. Canon F 16, para. 3, deals with fire precautions and similar matters.

[178] 'In trespass the defendant justified as churchwarden, that he pull'd off the plaintiff's hat, he sitting covered in the church, in time of divine service, on which the plaintiff demurred, because the defendant pleads not guilty to all preter insultum, and as to that, that he put off his hat, and gave it him in his hand que est eadem, and per Curiam this is a good justification; and so to switch boys playing in the church-yard, or any disturbers of the peace in time of divine service . . .': *Haw* v. *Planner* (1666) 2 Keb. 124. *Burton* v. *Henson* (1842) 10 M. & W. 105 at p. 108 *per* Alderson B. See, too, Watson, *The Clergy-man's Law* at p. 347.

against[179] and nowadays it would certainly be regarded as an excessive use of force. To remove a man's hat, even though men still do not usually wear hats indoors, would nowadays equally be likely to be illegal, unless the hat causes offence other than by the mere fact of its being worn. Not only may the hat be being worn out of respect[180] but it may perhaps be worn for medical reasons[181].

Similarly, although Canon B 9 sets out how the congregation ought to act and behave, it does not mean that a churchwarden or sidesmen may treat any failure[182] to comply with its provisions as 'indecent behaviour' or 'disturbance' within the meaning of Canon F 15. Canon B 9 states:

> 1. All persons present in the time of divine service shall audibly with the minister make the answers appointed and in due place join in such parts as are appointed to be said or sung.
> 2. They shall give reverent attention in the time of divine service, give due reverence to the name of Jesus and stand at the Creed and the reading of the Holy Gospel at the Holy Communion. When the prayers are read and Psalms and Canticles are said or sung, they shall have regard to rubrics of the service and locally established custom[183] in the manner of posture, whether standing, kneeling or sitting.

The proper test would seem to be whether the action or behaviour in question is reasonably causing distress or disturbance to others.

The right of the churchwarden to allocate seats in church[184] is also part and parcel of his duties of keeping order. Subject to private rights in pews[185]:

> ... the churchwardens may direct people where to sit, and where not to sit, and may do so beforehand or for a particular service or for an indefinite period ... This control of the seating accommodation belongs to the church-wardens in the interests of good order. They cannot exclude an orderly person on the ground that the church is full if he can stand in such part of the church as will not interfere with the conduct of the service. If a parishioner intrudes himself into a seat contrary to the directions of the churchwardens, they may remove him, provided that they do not use unnecessary force or cause a scandal by disturbing the worship of the church[186].

---

[179] *Taylor* v. *Timson* (1888) 20 QBD 671 at p. 679 *per* Stephen J.
[180] For example, by a Jew.   [181] See **p. 95** *supra*.
[182] For example, quietly to read a book.   [183] See **p. 4, footnote 28** *supra*.
[184] Tickets may be issued for a wedding but no parishioner may be refused admission on the grounds that he does not have one: *Legal Opinions concerning the Church of England* at p. 225.
[185] See 14 Halsbury's Laws of England (4th ed.) at para. 1086; **p. 256** *et seq. supra.*
[186] *Legal Opinions of the Church of England* (Church House Publishing, 1994) at p. 220; *Asher* v. *Calcraft* (1887) 18 QBD 607; see, too, 14 Halsbury's Laws of England (4th ed.) at paras 555 and 1088.

Indeed, as Grantham J said in *Asher* v. *Calcraft*[187]:

> I quite agree with what [the other judge] has said as to the right of the churchwarden in this particular place to separate a party of boys. Nothing is more likely to create a disturbance in church than a number of boys getting together.

No doubt many others would agree.

[187] (1887) 18 QBD 607 at pp. 613–614.

APPENDIX 1

CHURCH OF ENGLAND (WORSHIP AND DOCTRINE) MEASURE 1974

A Measure passed by the General Synod of the Church of England to enable provision to be made by Canon with respect to worship in the Church of England and other matters prescribed by the Book of Common Prayer, and with respect to the obligations and forms of assent or subscription to the doctrine of the Church of England; to repeal enactments relating to the matters aforesaid; and for purposes connected therewith.

1. Provision by Canon for worship in the Church of England

(1) It shall be lawful for the General Synod:

(a) to make provision by Canon with respect to worship in the Church of England, including provision for empowering the General Synod to approve, amend, continue or discontinue forms of service;

(b) to make provision by Canon or regulations made thereunder for any matter, except the publication of banns of matrimony, to which any of the rubrics contained in the Book of Common Prayer relate;

but the powers of the General Synod under this subsection shall be so expressed as to ensure the forms of service contained in the Book of Common Prayer continue to be available for use in the Church of England.

(2) Any Canons making any such provision as is mentioned in subsection (1) of this section, and any regulations made under any such Canon, shall have effect notwithstanding anything inconsistent therewith contained in any of the rubrics in the Book of Common Prayer.

(3) The General Synod shall provide by Canon:

(a) that decisions as to which of the forms of service authorised by or approved under Canon are to be used in any church in a parish or in any guild church shall be taken jointly by the incumbent and the parochial church council or, as the case may be, by the vicar of the guild church and the guild church council; and

(b) that in case of disagreement, and as long as the disagreement continues, the forms of service to be used in that church shall be those contained in the Book of Common Prayer unless other forms of service so approved were in regular use therein during at least two of the four years immediately preceding the date when the disagreement arose and the said council resolves that those other forms of service shall be used either to the exclusion of, or in addition to, the forms of service contained in the said Book.

This subsection shall not apply in relation to a cathedral which is a parish church nor to any part of a cathedral which is a parish church.

(4) Subsection (3) of this section shall not apply in relation to any of the services known as occasional services, but, in the case of those services, other than the Order of Confirmation, the General Synod shall provide by Canon that where more than one form of service is authorised by or approved under Canon for use on any occasion, the decision as to which form of service is to be used shall be made by the minister who is to conduct the service, but that if any of the persons concerned objects beforehand to the use of the service selected by the minister and he and the minister cannot agree as to which form is to be used, the matter shall be referred to the bishop of the diocese for his decision.

(5) Without prejudice to the generality of subsection (1) of this section, the General Synod may make provision by Canon:

(a) for empowering the Convocations, the archbishops and the bishops of the dioceses to approve forms of service for use on occasions for which no provision is made by forms of service contained in the Book of Common Prayer or approved by the General Synod or the Convocations under Canon;

(b) for empowering any minister to make and use minor variations in the forms of service contained in the said Book or approved by the General Synod, Convocation, archbishops or bishop under Canon and to use forms of service considered suitable by him on occasions for which no provision is made by any such form of service.

(6) The General Synod may provide by Canon that where a form of service is in course of preparation with a view to its submission to the General Synod for approval by the General Synod under Canon, the archbishops may authorise that service in draft form to be conducted by a minister in the presence of a congregation consisting of such persons only as the archbishop may designate.

(7) In the prayers for or referring to the Sovereign or other members of the Royal Family contained in any form of service authorised for use in the Church of England, the names may be altered, and any necessary alterations made, from time to time as the circumstances require by Royal Warrant, and those prayers as so altered shall be used thereafter.

2. Assent or subscription to doctrine

(1) It shall be lawful for the General Synod to make provision by Canon with respect to the obligation of the clergy, deaconesses and lay officers of the Church of England to assent or subscribe to the doctrine of that Church and the forms of that assent or subscription which may include an explanatory preface.

(2) In this section 'lay officers' means licensed lay workers, readers, lay judges of consistory or provincial courts, and lay holders of other offices admission to which is for the time being regulated by Canon.

3. Majorities required for final approval of Canons under section 1 and 2 and things done thereunder

No Canon making any such provision as is mentioned in section 1(1) or 2(1) of the Measure shall be submitted for Her Majesty's Licence and Assent unless it has been finally approved by the General Synod with a majority in each House thereof of not less than two-thirds of those present and voting; and no regulation under any Canon made under the said section 1(1) nor any approval, amendment, continuance or discontinuance of a form of service by the General Synod under any Canon shall have effect unless the regulation, the form of service or the amendment, continuance or discontinuance of a form of service, as the case may be, has been finally approved by the General Synod with such a majority as aforesaid in each House thereof.

4. Safeguarding of doctrine

(1) Every Canon or regulation making any such provision as is mentioned in section 1(1) of this Measure, every form of service or amendment thereof approved by the General Synod under any such Canon and every Canon making any such provision as is mentioned in section 2(1) of this Measure shall be such as in the opinion of the General Synod is neither contrary to, nor indicative of any departure from, the doctrine of the Church of England in any essential matter.

(2) The final approval by the General Synod of any such Canon or regulation or form of service or amendment thereof shall conclusively determine that the Synod is of such opinion as aforesaid with respect to the matter so approved.

(3) Where provision is made by Canon by virtue of section 1(5) of this Measure, the Canon shall provide for requiring the forms of service and variations approved, made or used thereunder to be neither contrary to, nor indicative of any departure from, the doctrine of the Church of England in any essential matter.

5. Interpretation

(1) References in this Measure to the doctrine of the Church of England shall be construed in accordance with the statement concerning that doctrine contained in the Canons of the Church of England, which statement is in the following terms: 'The doctrine of the Church of England is grounded in the holy Scriptures, and in such teachings of the ancient Fathers and Councils of the Church as are agreeable to the said Scriptures. In particular such doctrine is to be found in the Thirty-nine Articles of Religion, the Book of Common Prayer, and the Ordinal.'.

(2) In this Measure the following expressions have the meaning hereby assigned to them:

'the appointed day' means the day appointed under section 7(2) of this Measure;

'Book of Common Prayer' means the Book annexed to the Act of Uniformity 1662 and entitled 'The Book of Common Prayer and Administration of the Sacraments and other Rites and Ceremonies of the Church according to the use of the Church of England together with the Psalter of Psalms of David appointed as they are to be sung or said in Churches and the Form and Manner of Making, Ordaining and Consecrating Bishops, Priests and Deacons', as altered or amended by any Act or Measure or in accordance with section 1(7) of this Measure;

'church' includes any building or part of a building licensed by the bishop for public worship according to the rites and ceremonies of the Church of England;

'form of service' means any order, service, prayer, rite or ceremony whatsoever, including the services for the ordination of priests and deacons and the consecration of bishops and the catechism or form of instruction before confirmation;

'guild church' means a church in the City of London designated and established as a guild church under the City of London (Guild Churches) Acts 1952 and 1960; 'incumbent' includes:

(a)   a curate licensed to the charge of a parish or a minister acting as priest-in-charge of a parish in respect of which rights of presentation are suspended; and

(b)   a vicar in a team ministry to the extent that the duties of an incumbent are assigned to him by a scheme under the Pastoral Measure 1968 or his licence from the bishop;

'rubrics' of the Book of Common Prayer include all directions and instructions contained in the said Book, and all tables, prefaces, rules, calendars and other contents thereof.

6. Amendments, repeals, transitional provisions and savings

(1) Section 3 of the Submission of the Clergy Act 1533 (which provides that no Canons shall be contrary to the Royal Prerogative or the customs, laws or statutes of this realm) shall not apply to any rule of ecclesiastical law relating to any matter for which provision may be made by Canon in pursuance of this Measure.

(2) The enactments specified in Schedule 1 to this Measure shall have effect subject to the amendments set out in that Schedule, being amendments consequential upon the preceding provisions of this Measure.

(3) The Acts and Measures specified in Schedule 2 to this Measure are hereby repealed to the extent specified in column 3 thereof.

(4) Schedule 3 to this Measure, which contains transitional provisions and savings, shall have effect, but nothing in the said Schedule shall be taken as prejudicing section 38 of the Interpretation Act 1889 as applied by the Interpretation Measure 1925.

7. Short title, commencement and extent

(1) This Measure may be cited as the Church of England (Worship and Doctrine) Measure 1974.

(2) This Measure shall come into force on such day as the Archbishops of Canterbury and York may jointly appoint:

Provided that the powers to make Canons in pursuance of this Measure shall be exercisable before the appointed day, but no such Canon shall come into operation before the appointed day.

(3) This Measure shall extend to the whole of the provinces of Canterbury and York except the Channel Islands, but may be applied to the Channel Islands as defined in the Channel Islands (Church Legislation) Measures 1931 and 1957 or either of them in accordance with those Measures.

SCHEDULES

(Schedules 1 and 2 make amendments and repeals in accordance with section 6(2) and (3) of the Measure.)

Schedule 3

Section 6

TRANSITIONAL PROVISIONS AND SAVINGS

1. The repeal by this Measure of any provisions of the Prayer Book (Alternative and other Services) Measure 1965, the Prayer Book (Miscellaneous Provisions) Measure 1965 or the Prayer Book (Further Provisions) Measure 1968 shall not affect the validity of any approval, direction, consent, agreement or authorisation given, regulation made, or other thing done, under that provision before the appointed day, and any such approval, direction, consent, agreement, authorisation, regulation or other thing shall, if in force immediately before the appointed day, have effect as if it had been given, made or done under Canon.

2. Without prejudice to paragraph 1 of this Schedule, any business of the General Synod in the exercise of their functions under any provision of any Measures mentioned in that paragraph, being business which was pending immediately before the appointed day shall not abate by reason of the repeal of that provision but may be resumed by the General Synod in the exercise of their functions under any Canon corresponding (whether with or without modification) to that provision at the stage at which the business had reached immediately before the appointed day.

3. The shortened forms of service specified in the Schedule to the Act of Uniformity Amendment Act 1872 may be included in the services authorised by Canon notwithstanding the repeal of that Act by this Measure.

4. The repeal by this Measure of any provision of an Act or Measure shall not affect the validity of any Canon made under or by virtue of that provision, and no amendment or revocation of any of the rubrics contained in the Book of Common Prayer effected by any such provision shall be affected by the repeal of that provision by this Measure.

APPENDIX 2
CANONS B 1–5A AND C 8

B 1 OF CONFORMITY OF WORSHIP

1. The following forms of service shall be authorised for use in the Church of England:

(a) the forms of service contained in the Book of Common Prayer;

(b) the shortened forms of Morning and Evening Prayer which were set out in the Schedule to the Act of Uniformity Amendment Act 1872;

(c) the form of service authorised by Royal Warrant for use upon the anniversary of the day of accession of the reigning Sovereign;

(d) any form of service approved under Canon B 2 subject to any amendments so approved, to the extent permitted by such approval;

(e) any form of service approved under Canon B 4 subject to any amendments so approved, to the extent permitted by such approval;

(f) any form of service authorised by the archbishops under Canon B 5A, to the extent permitted by such authorisation.

2. Every minister shall use only the forms of service authorised by this Canon, except so far as he may exercise the discretion permitted by Canon B 5. It is the minister's responsibility to have a good understanding of the forms of service used and he shall endeavour to ensure that the worship offered glorifies God and edifies the people.

3. In this Canon the expression 'forms of service' shall be construed as including:

(i) the prayers known as Collects;

(ii) the lessons designated in any Table of Lessons;

(iii) any other matter to be used as part of a service;

(iv) any Table of rules for regulating a service;

(v) any Table of Holy Days which expression includes 'A Table of all the Feasts' in the Book of Common Prayer and such other Days as shall be included in any Table approved by the General Synod.

B 2 OF THE APPROVAL OF FORMS OF SERVICE

1. It shall be lawful for the General Synod:

(a) to approve forms of service for use in the Church of England and to amend any form of service approved by the General Synod under this Canon;

(b) to approve the use of any such form of service for a limited period, or without limit of period;

(c) to extend the period of use of any such form of service and to discontinue any such form of service;

and any form of service or amendment thereof approved by the General Synod under this Canon shall be such as in the opinion of the General Synod is neither contrary to, nor indicative of any departure from, the doctrine of the church of England in any essential matter.

2. Any approval, amendment, continuance or discontinuance of any form of service shall not have effect unless the form of service or the amendment, continuance or discontinuance thereof is finally approved by the General Synod with a majority in each House thereof of not less than two-thirds of those present and voting.

3. In this Canon the expression 'form of service' has the same meaning as in Canon B 1.

B 3 OF THE FORM OF SERVICE TO BE USED WHERE ALTERNATIVE FORMS ARE AUTHORISED

1. Decisions as to which of the forms of service authorised by Canon B 1, other than the services known as occasional services, are to be used in any church in a parish or in any guild church shall be taken jointly by the minister and the parochial church council or, as the case may be, by the vicar of the guild church and the guild church council. In this Canon 'church' includes any building or part of a building licensed by the bishop for public worship according to the rites and ceremonies of the Church of England.

2. If there is disagreement as to which of the said forms of service are to be used in any such church, then, so long as the disagreement continues the forms of service to be used shall be those contained in the Book of Common Prayer unless other forms of service authorised by Canon B 1 were in regular use therein during at least two of the four years immediately preceding the date when the disagreement arose and the parochial church council or guild church council, as the case may be, resolves that those other forms of service shall be used either to the exclusion of, or in addition to, the forms of service contained in the said Book.

3. The foregoing paragraphs of the Canon shall not apply in relation to a cathedral which is a parish church nor to any part of a cathedral which is a parish church.

4. Where more than one form of any of the services known as occasional offices, other than the Order of Confirmation, is authorised by Canon B 1 for use on any occasion the decision as to which form of service to be used shall be made by the minister who is to conduct the service, but if any of the persons objects beforehand to the use of the service selected by the minister and he and the minister cannot agree as to which form is to be used, the matter shall be referred to the bishop of the diocese for his decision.

5. Where more than one form of service of ordination of deacons or priests or of the ordination or consecration of a bishop is authorised by Canon B 1 for use, the decision as to which form of service is to be used shall be made by the bishop or archbishop, as the case may be, who is to conduct the service and, where more than one form of service of confirmation is so authorised, the decision as to which service is to be used shall be made by the bishop or archbishop, as the case may be, who is to conduct the service after consulting the minister of the church where the service is to be held.

6. In this Canon the expression "form of service" has the same meaning as in Canon B 1.

B 4 OF FORMS OF SERVICE APPROVED BY THE CONVOCATIONS, ARCH-BISHOPS OR ORDINARY FOR USE ON CERTAIN OCCASIONS

1. The Convocations of Canterbury and York may approve within their respective provinces forms of service for use in any cathedral or church or elsewhere on occasions for which no provision is made in the Book of Common Prayer or by the General Synod under Canon B 2, being forms of service which in both words and order are in their opinion reverent and seemly and neither contrary to, nor indicative of any departure from, the doctrine of the Church of England in any essential matter.

2. The archbishops may approve forms of service for use in any cathedral or church or elsewhere in the provinces of Canterbury and York on occasions for which no provision is made in the Book of Common Prayer or by the General Synod under Canon B 2 or by the Convocations under this Canon, being forms of service which in both words and order are in their opinion reverent and seemly and are neither contrary to, nor indicative of any departure from, the doctrine of the Church of England in any essential matter.

3. The Ordinary may approve forms of service for use in any cathedral or church or elsewhere in the diocese on occasion for which no provision is made in the Book of Common Prayer or by the General Synod under Canon B 2 or by the Convocation or archbishops under this Canon, being forms of service which in the opinion of the Ordinary in both words and order are reverent and seemly and are neither contrary to, nor indicative of any departure from, the doctrine of the Church of England in any essential matter.

4. In this Canon the expression 'form of service' has the same meaning as in Canon B 1.

B 5 OF THE DISCRETION OF MINISTERS IN CONDUCT OF PUBLIC PRAYER

1. The minister who is to conduct the service may in his discretion make and use variations which are not of substantial importance in any form of service authorised by Canon B 1 according to particular circumstances.

2. The minister having the cure of souls may on occasions for which no provision is made in the Book of Common Prayer or by the General Synod under Canon B 2 or by the Convocation, archbishops, or Ordinary under Canon B 4 use forms of service considered suitable by him for those occasions and may permit another minister to use the said forms of service.

3. All variations in forms of service and all forms of service used under this Canon shall be reverent and seemly and shall be neither contrary to, nor indicative of any departure from, the doctrine of the Church of England.

4. If any question is raised concerning the observance of the provisions of this Canon it may be referred to the bishop in order that he may give such pastoral guidance, advice or directions as he may think fit, but such reference shall be without prejudice to the matter in question being made the subject-matter of proceedings under the Ecclesiastical Jurisdiction Measure 1963.

5. In this Canon the expression 'form of service' has the same meaning as in Canon B 1.

B 5A OF AUTHORISATION OF FORMS OF SERVICE FOR EXPERIMENTAL PERIODS

1. Where a form of service has been prepared with a view to its submission to the General Synod for approval by the Synod under Canon B 2 the archbishops after consultation with the House of Bishops of the General Synod may, prior to that submission, authorise such form of service for experimental use for a period specified by them on such terms and in such places or parishes as they may designate.

2. Where any form of service has been authorised under paragraph 1 of the Canon for experimental use and it is proposed that it shall be used in any church the requirements of Canon B 3 shall apply.

3. In this Canon the expression 'form of service' has the same meaning as in Canon B 1.

C 8 OF MINISTERS EXERCISING THEIR MINISTRY

1. Every minister shall exercise his ministry in accordance with the provisions of this Canon.

2. A minister duly ordained priest or deacon, and, where it is required under paragraph 5 of this Canon, holding a licence or permission from the archbishop of the province, may officiate in any place after he has received authority to do so from the bishop of the diocese or other Ordinary of the place.

Save that:

(a) The minister having the cure of souls of a church or chapel or the sequestrator when the cure is vacant or the dean or provost and the canons residentiary of any cathedral or collegiate church may allow a minister, concerning whom they are satisfied either by actual personal knowledge or by good and sufficient evidence that he is of good life and standing and otherwise qualified under this Canon, to minister within their church or chapel for a period of not more than seven days within three months without reference to the bishop or other Ordinary, and a minister so allowed shall be required to sign the services register when he officiates: but nothing in this sub-paragraph authorises

(i) a minister or sequestrator in a parish to which a resolution in the form set out as Resolution A in Schedule 1 to the Priests (Ordination of Women) Measure 1993 applies, or

(ii) a dean or provost or the canons residentiary of a cathedral church to which a resolution in the form set out as Resolution A in Schedule 2 to the said Measure applies

to allow an act in contravention of that resolution to be committed.

(b) No member of the chapter of a cathedral church shall be debarred from performing the duties of his office in due course and exercising his ministry within the diocese merely by lack of authority from the bishop of the diocese within which the cathedral is situate.

(c) Any minister who has a licence to preach throughout the province from the archbishop or throughout England from the University of Oxford or of Cambridge, may preach the Word of God in any diocese within that province or throughout England, as the case may be, without any further authority from the bishop thereof.

(d) A funeral service which may, under section 2 of the Church of England (Miscellaneous Provisions) Measure 1992, be performed in a parish without the consent of the minister of the parish may be performed without any further authority from the bishop of the diocese within which the parish is situated.

3. The bishop of a diocese confers such authority on a minister either by instituting him to a benefice, or by admitting him to serve within his diocese by licence under his hand and seal, or by giving him written permission to officiate within the same.

4. No minister who has authority to exercise his ministry in any diocese shall do so therein in any place in which he has not the cure of souls without the permission of the minister having such cure, except at the homes of persons whose names are entered on the electoral roll of the parish which he serves and to the extent authorised by the Extra-Parochial Ministry Measure 1967, or in a university, college, school, hospital, or public or charitable institution in which he is licensed to officiate as provided by the said Measure and Canon B 41 or, in relation to funeral services, as provided by section 2 of the Church of England (Miscellaneous Provisions) Measure 1992.

5. A minister who has been ordained priest or deacon

(a) by an overseas bishop within the meaning of the Overseas and Other Clergy (Ministry and Ordination) Measure 1967;

(b) under section 5 of that Measure for ministry overseas;

(c) by a bishop in a Church not in communion with the Church of England, whose orders are recognised or accepted by the Church of England;

may not minister in the province in question without the permission of the archbishop of the province in question under the said Measure:

Provided that this paragraph shall not apply to any person ordained priest or deacon by any such bishop on the request and by the commission in writing of the bishop of a diocese in the province of Canterbury or York.

APPENDIX 3
JUS LITURGICUM

A constitution of Archbishop Chichele ordained that the feast of St John of Beverley should be perpetually kept throughout his province 'secundum usum Sarum Ecclesiae'[1]. In his great book on English canon law, *Provinciale Angliae*, Lyndwood commented[2] that this constitution was opposed to the general Western canon law as set out in Gratian's *Decretum*, which ordained that the divine office should be celebrated throughout a whole province 'secundum modum et usum Metropolitanae Ecclesiae'. However, he argued that the following of the Sarum usage was permitted because it arose 'ex longa consuetudine'. Indeed, such variations from the general law were permitted by the general law itself[3]. It follows, therefore, that other liturgical uses, such as those of Hereford and Lincoln, might equally have been legalised by local custom.

Gratian's *Decretum* was not compiled until *c*.1140 and Lyndwood stated the law as at *c*.1434[4]; in the meantime liturgical practice was also changing. Proctor and Frere in *A New History of the Book of Common Prayer*[5] describe the process in this way[6]:

> In England in early days it seems clear that [service] books differing considerably from one another were not only used but deliberately provided for use side by side in the same church. The inconvenience of this is obvious, but it was not apparently till the twelfth or thirteenth century that any serious attempt was made to remedy it. When the influential had reduced their own services to order, it was natural in the neighbourhood to follow them, and thus there grew up in the thirteenth century, under the guidance or with the sanction of the Bishop, the Diocesan Use, i.e. a species of service emanating from a cathedral, radiating widely throughout the diocese and even spreading into other dioceses[7].

Lyndwood was, of course, giving a legal explanation[8] for just this practice.

The force of custom depended in the first instance upon its existence for a long period of time[9] and it is therefore difficult to see what right there could be legally to authorise

---

[1] 'The Use of Sarum was so widely recognised as authoritative that the expression "It is done *secundum usum Sarum*" had become proverbial, and was employed outside ecclesiastical matters to signify "things done with exactness according to rule and precedent"': Daniel, *The Prayer-Book Its History, Language, and Contents* (20th ed.) (Wells, Gardner, Darton & Co., 1901) at p. 63.
[2] (Oxford, 1679) p. 104 gl. ad v. *Usum Sarum Ecclesiae*.
[3] 14 Halsbury's Laws of England (4th ed.) at para. 304.
[4] See J.H. Baker, 'William Lyndwood, LL.D.' (1992) 2 Ecc LJ 268.   [5] Macmillan, 1965.
[6] *Op. cit.* at pp. 13–14.
[7] See *Concerning the Service of the Church* in the Book of Common Prayer: 'And whereas heretofore there hath been great diversity in saying and singing in Churches within this Realm; some following *Salisbury* Use, some *Hereford* Use, and some of *Bangor*, some of *York*, some of *Lincoln* ... '; Stephens, *The Book of Common Prayer*, vol. I at p. 121.
[8] For a theological consideration see Gainer, *The Jus Liturgicum of the Bishop and the Church of Wales* in *Essays in CANON LAW* (University of Wales Press, 1992) at pp. 111 *et seq*.
[9] See (1989) 1 Ecc LJ (4) at p. 14.

any other liturgical use until the requisite time had expired. Nevertheless, the guidance or 'sanction' of the bishop (subject to such orders as were passed from time to time in the provincial synod and after consultation with his cathedral chapter) has been described as a *jus liturgicum* leaving a bishop free[10] to decree 'rites and ceremonies within his diocese'[11]. What is more, that it had the force of law is supported by the view of Sir Robert Phillimore[12]:

 ... the canon law unquestionably placed in the hands of the bishop the authority to govern all questions of ritual.

Nonetheless, even if there were such a *jus liturgicum* recognized in England, it is extremely doubtful whether it survived the Reformation. In order to have done so it must have been 'not ... repugnant contrariant or derogatory to the Laws or Statutes of the Realm' in 1543 when the ecclesiastical law was given statutory authority[13]. Although not on the face of it contrary to the common law nor to the statutes then in force, it would have been contrary to the Act of Uniformity 1548[14] once enacted[15]. This specifically recited that:

Where of long time there hath been had in this realm of England and in Wales divers forms of Common Prayer, commonly called the Service of the Church; that is to say, The Use of Sarum, of York, of Bangor, and of Lincoln; and besides the same now of late much more divers and sundry forms and fashions have been used in the cathedral and parish churches of England and Wales, as well concerning mattens or morning prayer and the evensong, as also concerning the holy communion, commonly called the Mass, with divers and sundry rites and ceremonies concerning the same, and in the administration of the sacraments of the church ... all and singular ministers in any cathedral or parish church, or other place within this realm ... shall ... be bounden to say and use the mattens, evensong, celebration of the Lord's Supper, commonly called the Mass, and administration of each of the sacraments, and all their common and open prayer, in such order and form as is mentioned in [The Book of the Common Prayer], and none other or otherwise.

[10] At least prior to the Prayer Book of 1548/9.
[11] Wordsworth and Littlehales, *The Old Service Books of the English Church* at p. 9, quoted by Vaisey J in *'Lawful Authority'*, *A Memorandum* appended to *The Canon Law of The Church of England* (SPCK, 1947) at p. 220.
[12] *Martin* v. *Mackonochie* (1868) LR 2 A. & E. 116 at p. 194 citing Van Espen. See, too, *Kemp* v. *Wickes* (1809) 3 Phillim. 264 at p. 268 *per* Sir John Nicholl. The claim put forward in *Read* v. *Bishop of Lincoln* (1889) 14 PD 148 at p. 149 to the effect that a bishop was not bound by the rubrics in the Book of Common Prayer was, it seems, in part based on such a claim.
[13] Canon Law Act 1543 s. 3. See 14 Halsbury's Laws of England (4th ed.) at para. 306.
[14] This statute was confirmed by the Act of Uniformity 1552 but repealed by the Repeal of Acts Act 1553. The latter Act was itself repealed by Act of Uniformity 1558. See, however, Garth Moore & Briden, *Moore's Introduction to English Canon Law* (2nd ed.) at p. 69; however, contrast the views of the present editors in Briden & Hanson *Moore's Introduction to English Canon Law* (3rd ed.) at p. 58 and see Stephens, *The Book of Common Prayer*, vol. I at p. 123.
[15] Unfortunately this is ignored by Gainer (see **p. 271, footnote 8** *supra*) at pp. 116–117.

A similar provision was also made in relation to the 1552 Prayer Book[16] which was annexed to the Act of Uniformity 1552. Indeed, both prayer books contained special provision for any ambiguities within them to be settled by the bishop, although the bishop's order might not be 'contrary to any thing contained in this Book'.

As Sir Robert Phillimore said in relation to the similar power in the 1662 Prayer Book[17],

> The authority which is to resolve these doubts and remove these difficulties, is that officer in whose hands, *previously to the statutory enactment of any prayer book*, the Church had placed a supreme command over all that relates to her ritual[18] (emphasis supplied).

The limited power to resolve ambiguities therefore replaced any previous *jus liturgicum*[19]. Indeed, the bishop could not depart from the prescribed services when himself the minister[20].

It is, therefore, not surprising that no mention seems to be made of a *jus liturgicum* in any reported case[21] until after the refusal of Parliament to sanction the 1928 Prayer

---

[16] Act of Uniformity 1552, s. 5.

[17] *Martin* v. *Mackonochie* (1868) LR 2 A. & E. 116 at p. 192. See, too, *Kemp* v. *Wickes* (1809) 3 Phillim. 264 at p. 283 where Sir John Nicholl stated that in 1573 the bishops 'certainly had not authority to alter the law; they had only authority to explain matters which were doubtful.'

[18] The words 'without prejudice nevertheless to any legal powers vested in the ordinary' in section 5 of the Act of Uniformity Amendment Act 1872 (see **p. 31** *et seq. supra*) seem to refer to the same power.

[19] *Attorney-General* v. *Wylde* (1947–1948) 48 SR 366 *per* Roper CJ at p. 386: 'Whether, before the Reformation, bishops in England had the power individually to prescribe the liturgy to be used in churches in their respective dioceses or not, it is, I think, clear that such a power did not exist after the first Act of Uniformity was passed. In particular . . . there could be no *jus liturgicum* vested in the bishops in England in face of the explicit provisions of the Act of Uniformity of 1662. Their powers as to liturgy were then restricted to the power to resolve doubts referred to in the Preface of the Prayer Book.' On appeal *sub. nom. Wylde* v. *Attorney-General for New South Wales, ex rel. Ashelford* (1948) 78 CLR 224 *per* Latham CJ at pp. 269–270: 'It was claimed on behalf of the defendant that bishops in olden times possessed, and still possess, a *jus liturgicum*, that is to say, a right of determining the liturgies to be used in the church. The evidence that ecclesiastical authorities believe that such a right exists to-day was very weak, but this is a question which depends upon evidence. The statutes to which reference has already been made prescribe a liturgy for the Church of England and the quotations which have been made from decisions of the Privy Council show that the bishops of the Church of England have not since the *Act of Uniformity* possessed any *jus liturgicum.*' See, too, *ibid per* Williams J at p. 303.

Gainer (see **p. 271 footnote 8,** *supra*) at p. 118 accepts that within the context of the Prayer Book services the *jus liturgicum* is confined within the ambit of these words. He nonetheless argues that 'The *jus liturgicum* could also be used to authorize services not provided for in the Prayer Book.' In so doing, however, he ignores the wording of the Acts of Uniformity and in particular s. 17 of the 1662 Act: ' . . . no form or order of common prayers, administration of sacraments, rites or ceremonies, shall be openly used . . . other than what is prescribed and appointed to be used in and by the same book . . . '.

[20] *Read* v. *Bishop of Lincoln* (1889) 14 PD 148 at p. 150 *per* the Archbishop of Canterbury.

[21] *Hutchins* v. *Denziloe and Loveland* (1792) 1 Hag. Con. 170 at p. 175 *per* Sir William Scott seems best to be regarded as a reference to the bishop's discretion given in the Prayer Book. The Act of Uniformity Amendment Act 1872, s. 5 (now repealed) was 'without prejudice nevertheless to any legal powers vested in the Ordinary'. This was probably a reference to the bishop's residual powers set out in the Book of Common Prayer, *Concerning the Service of the Church*: see **p. 31** *et seq. supra.*

Book. This refusal placed the bishops in a dilemma as the Convocations of both Canterbury and York had given their consent to such deviations from, and additions to, the 1662 Prayer Book as set out in the 1928 Prayer Book. In addition, the National Assembly of the Church of England had voted its approval. The bishops thereupon resolved[22]:

> That during the present emergency and until further order the bishops ... cannot regard as inconsistent with loyalty to the principles of the Church of England the use of such additions or deviations as fall within the limits of these proposals ... That accordingly the bishops, in the exercise of their legal[23] or administrative[24] discretion, will be guided by the proposals set forth in the Book of 1928, and will endeavour to secure that the practices which are consistent neither with the Book of 1662 nor with the Book of 1928 shall cease.

This, of course, raised a question of legality which ultimately came before the Court of the Arches in *In re Lapford (Devon) Parish Church*[25], a case concerning a proposed tabernacle for the reservation of the sacrament.

At first instance Chancellor Wigglesworth stated[26]:

> I know of no authority which compels me to hold that reservation is unlawful when it takes place with the sanction of the bishop. I do not consider that it is forbidden by article 28 or by the rubric at the end of the Communion service which was inserted for a wholly different reason, namely, for the prevention of the irreverent practices of Puritans. In my view, the prayer book neither forbids nor authorizes reservation; it makes no provision for it. Where the bishop considers that something not provided for is needed, it is for the bishop to make provision in the exercise of that authority which he has in his diocese. Where he considers reservation to be needed it is for him to sanction it, and where he sanctions it, this court can and should by faculty authorize such alterations or additions in the church as are necessary to secure that due provision is made for reservation.

---

[22] Cited in *In re Lapford (Devon) Parish Church* [1955] P 205 at p. 213.

[23] The only possible argument for a legal discretion (other than the *jus liturgicum* under discussion) is what was described by Williams J in *Wylde v. Attorney-General for New South Wales, ex rel. Ashelford* (1948) 78 CLR 224 at p. 306 as 'a negative *jus liturgicum*' arising from the right of the bishop to veto proceedings in the ecclesiastical courts under the Public Worship Regulation Act 1874. He, however, rejected such an interpretation of the Act within this very context (see at pp. 305–308). It was also rejected by Latham CJ at p. 266: 'The statute does not remove them from the category of offences, but provides a means of enabling the bishop lawfully to abstain from enforcing the law in cases in which he is of opinion that proceedings should not be taken. The statute therefore does not diminish the obligation to observe the Book of Common Prayer of 1662, but, on the contrary, assumes that that obligation exists.' See, too, at first instance *sub nom. Attorney-General v. Wylde* (1947–1948) 78 SR 366 *per* Roper CJ at pp. 386–387. That this view is correct is borne out by the fact that the 1874 Act only covered proceedings against incumbents (s.8) and therefore could not be seen as authorizing (even in a negative sense under section 9) liturgies celebrated by all ministers; it thus could not amount to a true *jus liturgicum*.

[24] These words in themselves underline that the bishops realised that they were on difficult ground.   [25] [1955] P 205.

[26] [1954] P 416 at p. 424.

However, it is difficult to see precisely what is being 'sanctioned'[27]. According to this ruling the rubric requiring the consumption of the elements at the end of the service was to be ignored; moreover, it was for the court alone to grant any necessary faculty relating to the building. In addition, no service is mentioned as connected with reservation, although presumably some prayers are to be made on the occasion of the reception of the sacrament. Perhaps the better view is that, having expressed the view that reservation was not forbidden by the rubric, the chancellor regarded the matter as falling to the bishop under his limited Prayer Book discretion; according to this view it would be necessary to decide what should happen to elements not consumed in order to prevent irreverent practices. Unfortunately this places a strained meaning on the word 'sanctioned'.

The rubric at the end of the Holy Communion service[28] orders that:

> If any remain of that which was consecrated it shall not be carried out of the church but the priest and any other of the communicants as he shall call unto him shall, immediately after the Blessing, reverently eat and drink the same.

On appeal[29] the Dean of the Arches stated[30] that:

> Whatever may have been the reason for the insertion of these words, I think that I am bound to take them as they stand, and they are inconsistent with any form of reservation.

He therefore expressly overruled Chancellor Wigglesworth in this regard. Unfortunately, however, the Dean's judgment is far from consistent. Having referred to various legal authorities against the legality of reservation, he continued[31]:

> So far the question of reservation by permission of the bishop had not come into prominence. But although the bishop has no doubt a large discretion in matters which are doubtful, or not fully provided by the rubrics, it does not enable him to legalize anything which is plainly illegal. Incidentally I should mention that an instance of the exercise of this discretion occurs in this case where the bishop has sanctioned the use

---

[27] Quoting this passage in *Rector and Churchwardens of Bishopwearmouth* v. *Adey* [1958] 3 All ER 441 at p. 445H Chancellor Garth Moore commented: 'In other words, where no other provision is made, the matter falls within the scope of the jus liturgicum . . .'. It seems unclear (see, too, *ibid*, at p. 447D–E) whether the Chancellor is referring to a power wider than the limited one conferred by the Prayer Book: see, moreover, Garth Moore & Briden, *Moore's Introduction to English Canon Law* (2nd ed.) at p. 69 and contrast Briden & Hanson, *Moore's Introduction to English Canon Law* (3rd ed.) at p. 58. However, in *In re Lapford* there is no mention of any *jus liturgicum*, a power which in any event could only relate to a matter of ritual or ceremony. Moreover, in neither case is there any consideration of its legal validity.

[28] In *St Luke's, Southport, The Times*, 1 October 1926, Chancellor Dowdall had already considered the force of this rubric. He stated that: 'The right of a Bishop to allow minor variations in the strict observance of the rubric was unchallenged.' However, he clearly misread the rubric itself (the priest does not *have* to have help in the consumption of the unused elements) and he may well mean only that the bishop's right was not disputed by the parties before him. In fact his decision seems to have been based on 'the discretion of a Bishop to dispense with the strict observance of a rubric' in particular circumstances of necessity such as when regular communicants are dangerously ill.

[29] [1955] P 205.   [30] At p. 210.   [31] At p. 211.

of the reserved Sacrament for the benefit of certain workers who by reason of their employment are unable to attend the ordinary services of Holy Communion. Clearly, any such extension should be carefully watched, but I regard it as a matter within the bishop's discretion.

These two quotations are clearly at variance one with the other[32] and, in fact, make no reference to any *jus liturgicum* beyond the limited discretion given by the Prayer Book itself. However, the Dean of the Arches then went on[33] to consider the bishops' resolution set out above:

Of course these resolutions could not alter the law in any respect[34]. But they did constitute a claim by the Church to do a number of illegal things within certain limits . . .

Thus the legality of the claim by the bishops to a 'legal or administrative discretion'[35] was expressly repudiated.

The first occasion (save once in passing[36]) when any express reference is made in an English case[37] to a *jus liturgicum* is in *Rector and Churchwardens of Bishopwearmouth* v. *Adey*[38] as an explanation of, and support for, what Chancellor Wigglesworth had said in *In re Lapford*. It seems unclear, however, whether Chancellor Garth Moore regarded this as a power wider than that given by the Prayer Book[39], as he did not go into any detail. Nor did he expressly consider the words of the Dean of the Arches just quoted, although he confessed that he did not 'wholly understand that judgment'[40].

The question was again considered in *In re St Nicholas, Plumstead*[41] where Chancellor Garth Moore adopted what he had said in the earlier case[42] and then spoke of 'reservation lawfully authorised by the exercise of the bishop's *jus liturgicum*'[43]. Again, however, he did not make clear the ambit of this power. This is important as in *Re St Peter and St Paul, Leckhampton*[44], although conceding that:

---

[32] The Dean of the Arches was apparently aware of the inconsistencies as at p. 214 he concluded 'That reservation of the Blessed Sacrament for any purpose is still, strictly speaking, illegal.' (In *Rector and Churchwardens of Bishopwearmouth* v. *Adey*, *supra*, at p. 446A–C Chancellor Garth Moore confessed that he did not wholly understand the Dean's judgment.)   [33] At p. 213.

[34] In Briden & Hanson, *Moore's Introduction to English Canon Law* (3rd ed.) at p. 58 it is pointed out, following the previous edition at p. 69, that 'there can be no legal validity in the purported exercise of an alleged episcopal discretion to allow the wholesale use of the deposited Prayer Book of 1928 . . .'. See, too, *Re St Peter and St Paul, Leckhampton* [1968] P 495 at p. 498A–B.

[35] Surely an oblique reference to the *jus liturgicum*, if it existed.

[36] See *Re St Mary's Tyne Dock* [1954] P 369 at p. 378.

[37] Unfortunately the Australian case of *Attorney-General* v. *Wylde* (1947–1948) 78 SR 366 (on appeal *sub nom. Wylde* v. *Attorney-General for New South Wales, ex rel. Ashelford* (1948) 78 CLR 224) has been previously ignored, although its authority is very persuasive; the court was applying the same law as in England and its decision as to the *jus liturgicum* (see **p. 273, footnote 19**, and **p. 274, footnote 23** *supra*) was part of the *ratio decidendi*.

[38] [1958] 3 All ER 441 at pp. 445H and 447D–E. See, further, *In re St Thomas, Pennywell* [1995] 2 WLR 154 at p. 162D–F.

[39] Garth Moore & Briden, *Moore's Introduction to English Canon Law* (2nd ed.) at p. 69 describes the *jus liturgicum* as finding 'a faint echo in that prefatory chapter to the Book of Common Prayer entitled "Concerning the Service of the Church" . . .'. See, too, the third edition at p. 57.

[40] At p. 446B.   [41] [1961] 1 All ER 298.   [42] At p. 229E–F.

[43] At p. 301A–B.   [44] [1968] P 495.

reservation ... was prima facie not legally permissible by reason of one rubric in the Book of Common Prayer ...

he nonetheless went on to restate his view that there was justification for his approach in the earlier cases[45]. Thus, although he also went on to speak of 'the last remaining *obstacle*'[46] being removed[47] by reason of the rubrics in the Alternative Services (second series), he did not concede that the exercise of any *jus liturgicum* meant the authorisation of anything illegal. Moreover, he continued in relation to those rubrics:

> ... significantly, no direction whatever is given as to the method of reservation. It is, therefore quite at large and, being quite at large, it must come within the *jus liturgicum* of the bishop and the discretion of the consistory court.

As has already been pointed out, in order to come within any *jus liturgicum*, there must be a direction relating to ritual or ceremonial. Indeed, the quotation suggests that the Chancellor expected some liturgical rite to accompany the physical acts of reservation; this is especially so as he had already spoken of reservation taking place 'during' the service[48]. Nevertheless, such directions (if ever given) are believed to be unusual. In practice:

> ... a bishop treats himself as entitled in his diocese to authorise reservation of the sacrament in a place of safety, for purposes which he defines[49].

On the other hand, although he does not say so, the Chancellor may have been assuming that the limited discretion given by the 1662 Prayer Book applies also to services authorised other than in that Book. If so, no question of a wider *jus liturgicum* arises[50].

In fact, it is necessary to turn to *Moore's Introduction to English Canon Law*[51] for a fuller statement of the Chancellor's views, although there is no discussion even there of any legal authorities. He says:

> Closely linked with the problem of lawful authority is the doctrine of the *jus liturgicum*, which is part of pre-Reformation canon law[52], and according to which, in some circumstances, it lies with the bishop to authorize what would otherwise be unlawful[53]. The doctrine finds a faint echo in that prefatory chapter to the Book of Common Prayer

---

[45] At pp. 498G–499A.

[46] At p. 499C–D (emphasis supplied). Perhaps a better word would have been 'objection'.

[47] '... at any rate in respect of reservation which takes place during (*sic*) a Communion Service as authorised by the Alternative Services (second series)': *ibid.*

[48] See the preceding footnote.

[49] Newsom & Newsom, *Faculty Jurisdiction of the Church of England* (2nd ed.) (Sweet and Maxwell, 1993) at p. 139.   [50] See the argument at **p. 33** *et seq. supra.*

[51] In the second edition at pp. 68–69.

[52] Nor is there any discussion of the problems created by the necessity for any pre-Reformation canon law, in order now to be recognized as binding, to be pleaded and proved to have been recognized, continued and acted upon in England since the Reformation: see 14 Halsbury's Laws of England (4th ed.) at para. 307; (1989) 1 Ecc LJ (4) at pp. 21–22.

[53] No authority is cited in support of this contention, which seems to ignore the views of Lyndwood: *supra.*

entitled 'Concerning the Service of the Church' ... It would seem that this reference to the bishop is limited to 'the manner how to understand, do, and execute, the things contained in the Book', whereas the *jus liturgicum*, while it might be taken to cover that ground, is concerned with a wider field than that which is contained in the Prayer Book.

It is submitted that there is no reason to suppose that the *jus liturgicum* has been abrogated by the Reformation settlement; but it has certainly been affected by it[54]. It clearly would not lie with the bishop to authorize anything forbidden by the Book of Common Prayer, for the Book has statutory authority. Nor, for the same reason, could he authorize the omission of anything enjoined in the Book. But, over that wide area for which no provision is made one way or the other, it is submitted that the *jus liturgicum* can still operate, and, indeed, that the exigencies of a situation may demand that it *should* operate in order to supply what would otherwise be grievously wanting.

It is difficult to see, however, how a discretion so emasculated can be regarded as still extant rather than entirely abrogated. The wording of the Act of Uniformity 1548 has already been mentioned, especially the words 'and all their common and open prayer, in such order and form as is mentioned in the ... book, *and none other or otherwise*'[55]. A similar provision was also made in the Act of Uniformity 1662, s. 17:

And be it further enacted ... that no form or order of common prayers, administration of sacraments[56], rites or ceremonies, shall be openly used in any church ... other than what is prescribed and appointed to be used in and by [the 1662 Prayer Book].

It is, therefore, difficult to envisage in what circumstances any *jus liturgicum* might thereafter apply[57]. This is the more so as the Church of England (Worship and Doctrine) Measure 1974 s. 1(5)(a) makes special provision by which:

... the General Synod may make provision by Canon ... for empowering the Convocations, the archbishops and the bishops of the dioceses to approve forms of service for use on occasions for which no provision is made by forms of service contained in

---

[54] In the third edition the first sentence of the second paragraph quoted has been altered so as to read (at pp. 57–58): 'It is suggested that the *jus liturgicum* has been seriously affected by the Reformation settlement in that there is no power in custom to override liturgical rites and ceremonies authorized by or under statute, Measure or canon.' The effect of Canon B 1, para. 2, is not there considered.   [55] Emphasis supplied.

[56] This would seem apt to embrace reservation in church, if any form of service is used; it would also seem to embrace the distribution of the reserved sacrament, if that takes place in the church. Indeed, there are difficulties in arguing that it permitted such distribution in private, at least to the sick, because of the provision made for the visitation of the sick in the 1662 Prayer Book.

[57] *In re St Thomas, Pennywell* [1995] 2 WLR 154 at p. 162D–F. See Briden & Hanson, *Moore's Introduction to English Canon Law* (3rd ed.) at p. 58. See, also, Gainer (see **p. 271, footnote 8, supra**) at pp 118 *et seq.*, although he unfortunately ignores the provisions of section 17 of the 1662 Act. Stephens, *The Book of Common Prayer*, vol. I, at p. 123 comments in relation to the bishop's power to resolve matters which are in doubt pursuant to *Concerning the Service of the Church* in the Book of Common Prayer: 'But the bishop is subordinate to the statute law, and where the rubrics are express, he has no authority to release any minister from obedience to them, or to determine anything "that is contrary to what is contained in the service book."'

the Book of Common Prayer or approved by the General Synod or the Convocations under canon . . .

Indeed, such provision has now been made by Canons B 2–4.

Finally, all canons bind the clergy in ecclesiastical matters[58] and Canon B 1 not only sets out what forms of service are presently authorised for use in the Church of England but Canon B 1, para. 2, states:

Every minister shall use only[59] the authorised services aforesaid[60], except so far as he may exercise the discretion allowed to him by Canon B 5.

It follows that, even in the most unlikely event of a broad *jus liturgicum* surviving until this century, it has clearly[61] now been abrogated[62].

---

[58] *Matthew* v. *Burdett* (1703) 2 Salk. 412; 14 Halsbury's Laws of England (4th ed.) at para. 308.

[59] See *In re St John the Evangelist, Chopwell* (1995) in **Appendix 6** at **p. 297** *infra*. See, too, Canon B 36, para. 1; see, further, **pp. 3** *et seq.* and **192** *et seq. supra*.

[60] See, too, Note 4 at p. 338 of the Alternative Service Book and **p. 232** *et seq. supra*.

[61] Cp. however, Hill, *Ecclesiastical Law* at p. 10, although no authority is cited.

[62] *In re St Thomas, Pennywell* [1995] 2 WLR 154 at p. 162D–F. It is not insignificant that the Guidelines issued jointly by the Archbishops of Canterbury and York on *Solemnisation of Marriage by Deacons* (see *Canons of the Church of England* (5th ed.) at p. 187) state in para. 3: 'The authorised services should be used without variation whether the officiating minister is bishop, priest or deacon.' This, however, is no doubt to ensure the validity of marriages: see, too, **p. 177** *et seq. supra*.

APPENDIX 4
LAWFUL AUTHORITY

By the Clerical Subscription Act 1865, a declaration of assent was to be made and subscribed before ordination[1], and before institution, collation or licensing[2]. The declaration was in the following form[3]:

> I, *A.B.*, do solemnly make the following declaration:
> I assent to ... the Book of Common Prayer and of the ordering of bishops, priests and deacons. I believe the doctrine of the ... Church of England ... as therein set forth, to be agreeable to the Word of God; and in public prayer and administration of the sacraments I will use the form in the said book prescribed, and none other, except so far as shall be ordered by lawful authority[4].

The final ten words, known as the 'exceptive words'[5], were new and were not defined. The new Canon 36[6] (passed to accord with the Act) was expressed to be 'for the avoiding of all ambiguities'; nevertheless, the exceptive words themselves were seen by some as incorporating doubt[7]. Indeed, according to Chancellor Vaisey writing in 1947,

> Attempts have been made to treat the word ['ordered'] as justifying the use of any rite of an 'ordered' character, and emanating from an authoritative source, as, for example, the Roman Mass[8].

---

[1] Section 4.   [2] Sections 5–8.

[3] Section 1. Canon 36 of the 1603 Canons was repealed and a new Canon substituted containing a declaration in the same terms as the statute: Phillimore, *Ecclesiastical Law* (2nd ed.), vol. 1, at p. 352.

[4] See *Archbishop of York on Reservation of Sacrament* (MacMillan & Co., 1900) at pp. 11–14.

[5] Vaisey, *'Lawful Authority'*, A Memorandum appended to *The Canon Law of the Church of England* (SPCK, 1947) at p. 216.   [6] See **footnote 3, *supra***.

[7] See Vaisey's article, *op. cit.* at pp. 218–219. The words 'according to the directions of lawful authority' appeared in section 25 of the Act of Uniformity 1662, when providing for the periodical alterations in the names of the sovereign and members of the royal family. In Stephens, *The Statutes relating to the Ecclesiastical and Eleemosynary Institutions* (London, 1845) at p. 577 a footnote states in relation to these words: '*i.e.* (according to practice) of the king or queen in council'. Vaisey accepted that this interpretation is correct and that the words in the 1865 Act had been adopted from the 1662 Act; he nevertheless concluded that the words did not mean the same in the later Act. His reasoning seems to be based on a section in the Edinburgh Corporation Act 1900, (as amended) relating to the sale of ice-cream and on the difficulty of Lord Davey in interpreting the words 'or any other day set apart for public worship by lawful authority': *Rossi* v. *Edinburgh Corporation* [1905] AC 21 at p. 29. However, not only was the Act passed a number of years after 1865 and the context of the words entirely different but Scotland is a different legal jurisdiction. In the result Vaisey's views (although described as 'the most workable explanation' in Briden & Hanson, *Moore's Introduction to English Canon Law* (3rd ed.) at p. 57) were by no means universally accepted: see, for example, 13 Halsbury's Laws of England (3rd ed.) at pp. 39 & 328; see, too, *Wylde* v. *Attorney-General for New South Wales ex rel. Ashelford* (1948) 78 CLR 224 at p. 260 *per* Latham CJ. See, too, **p. 36, footnote 33, *supra***.

[8] Vaisey (at **footnote 5, *supra***), at p. 218; see, too, **p. 113, footnote 134, *supra***. Vaisey further commented that 'Of such an interpretation the word is not, it is thought, susceptible'. This is a

Fortunately the matter is now governed by the Church of England (Worship and Doctrine) Measure 1974, and canons made under its provisions. Canon B 1 states:

1. The following forms of service shall be authorised for use in the Church of England:

    (a) the forms of service contained in the Book of Common Prayer;
    (b) the shortened forms of Morning and Evening Prayer which were set out in the Schedule to the Act of Uniformity Amendment Act 1872;
    (c) the form of service authorised by Royal Warrant[9] for use upon the anniversary of the day of the accession of the reigning Sovereign;
    (d) any form of service approved under Canon B 2 subject to any amendments so approved, to the extent permitted by such approval;
    (e) any form of service approved under Canon B 4 subject to any amendments so approved, to the extent permitted by such approval;
    (f) any form of service authorised by the Archbishops under Canon B 5A, to the extent permitted by such authorisation.

2. Every minister shall use only the forms of service authorised by this Canon[10], except so far as he may exercise the discretion permitted by Canon B 5 . . .

Moreover, by Canon C 15, para. 1(1)[11], in the declaration of assent a clergyman now affirms that:

> . . . in public prayer and administration of the sacraments, I will use only the forms of the services which are authorised or allowed by Canon.

Strangely, having set out *verbatim* the words of this declaration, *Moore's Introduction to English Canon Law*[12] still comments:

> It is . . . to be noted that the Prayer Book need not be followed if lawful authority decrees otherwise. The difficulty here, however, is that nobody knows what the term *jus liturgicum* comprises.

It then goes on to consider the old controversy as to the meaning of that term, whilst ignoring that the words 'lawful authority' are no longer used[13]. It also ignores that the

---

measured understatement, bearing in mind that any legal interpretation of the statute must have been against the background of the Act of Uniformity 1662.

[9] A Royal Warrant may also make any necessary alteration 'In the prayers for or referring to the Sovereign or other members of the Royal Family contained in any form of service authorised for use in the Church of England': Church of England (Worship and Doctrine) Measure 1974, s. 1(7).

[10] See, too, Canon B 43 and **p. 25** *et seq. supra*. See, further, Canon B 38, para. 2, and **p. 199** *et seq. supra*. [11] As substituted by Amending Canon No. 4.

[12] Briden & Hanson, *Moore's Introduction to English Canon Law*, (3rd ed.) at p. 57.

[13] Save that the words 'by authority' are used (i) in the rubric after the Creed in the Book of Common Prayer concerning the homilies; and (ii) in the prefatory words to the Forms of Prayer with Thanksgiving to Almighty God for use upon the anniversary of the sovereign's accession. However, the former must now be academic as no homilies have been published since 1571; moreover, the 1974 Measure has repealed both the Act of Uniformity 1662, and the relevant parts of the Clerical Subscription Act 1865: *ibid*, s. 6(3), Sch. 2. The latter is now covered by the Church of England (Worship and Doctrine) Measure 1974, s. 1(7). The words 'by lawful authority' still occur in the Burial Laws Amendment Act 1880, s. 7; this should now be taken as a reference to Canon B 1.

words had earlier been given a particular definition by the Prayer Book (Alternative and Other Services) Measure 1965, section 8[14] (now repealed).

As has been seen, the declaration of assent now only uses the words 'authorised or allowed by Canon'. Indeed, it cannot even be argued[15] that the words 'by Canon' govern only the word 'allowed', thereby leaving the word 'authorised' at large, as the Canon must be interpreted in the light of the other Canons[16]. Moreover, Canon B 1 is quite specific that the only authorised services are those there defined[17].

Thus the controversy as to 'lawful authority' is now a purely historical one[18]. The only way[19] in which deviation from the services authorised by Canon B 1 may now lawfully be made is pursuant to the Church of England (Worship and Doctrine) Measure 1974, or any canon made thereunder.

[14] Section 8 enacted: 'The forms of Service which are authorised by this Measure or which are authorised or enjoined by the exercise of the powers or authorities set out in section 10 of this Measure shall be the forms of Service which are ordered by lawful authority within the meaning of the Clerical Subscription Act 1865.' Section 10 embraced 'the use of any form of Service from time to time enjoined or authorised by Order in Council, Royal Warrant or Royal Proclamation'.

[15] Such an argument is not, in fact, advanced in Briden & Hanson, *Moore's Introduction to English Canon Law*. It is dealt with here *ex abundanti cautela*.

[16] The only contrary argument would arise if the use of any abridgement or adaptation of the services of Morning and Evening Prayer according to the Book of Common Prayer in certain university colleges is not to be seen as falling within Canon B 1, para. 1(a). However, such an argument destroys the validity of the word 'only' in Canon B 1, para. 2: see the Universities Tests Act 1871, as amended by the Church of England (Worship and Doctrine) Measure 1974, s. 6(3), Sch. 2; see, too, **p. 3, footnote 20**, and **p. 121** *supra*.

[17] See **p. 279** *supra*. See, too, *In re St John the Evangelist, Chopwell* (1995) in **Appendix 6** at **p. 297** *infra*.

[18] *In re St Thomas, Pennywell* [1995] 2 WLR 154 at p. 162F–G. 14 Halsbury's Laws of England (4th ed.) at para. 934, note 10.   [19] Unless and until any other Act or Measure is passed.

APPENDIX 5
TABLE OF KINDRED AND AFFINITY

PART I Prohibited degrees of relationship

A man may not marry his:
mother
adoptive mother
former adoptive mother
daughter
adoptive daughter
former adoptive daughter
father's mother
mother's mother
son's daughter
daughter's daughter
sister
wife's mother
wife's daughter
father's wife
son's wife
father's father's wife
mother's father's wife
wife's father's mother
wife's mother's mother
wife's daughter's daughter
wife's son's daughter
son's son's wife
daughter's son's wife
father's sister
mother's sister
brother's daughter
sister's daughter

A woman may not marry her:
father
adoptive father
former adoptive father
son
adoptive son
former adoptive son
father's father
mother's father
daughter's son
son's son
brother
husband's father
husband's son
mother's husband
daughter's husband
mother's mother's husband
father's mother's husband
husband's mother's father
husband's father's father
husband's son's son
husband's daughter's son
son's daughter's husband
daughter's daughter's husband
father's brother
mother's brother
brother's son
sister's son

PART II

Part II is concerned with marriages between a person in one column with a person in the other column:

Daughter of former wife
Former wife of father
Former wife of father's father

Son of former husband
Former husband of mother
Former husband of father's mother

Former wife of mother's father	Former husband of mother's mother
Daughter of son of former wife	Son of son of former husband
Daughter of daughter of former wife	Son of daughter of former husband

PART III

Part III is concerned with the marriage of a man with a person in the first column and with the marriage of a woman with a person in the second column:

Mother of former wife	Father of former husband
Former wife of son	Former husband of daughter

(i) The relationships marked with an asterisk do not appear in the Table in Canon B 31, para. 2. The relationships in italics were added by the Children Act 1975, s. 108(1), Sch. 3, para. 8. The relationships that have been underlined are those ceasing to have effect for the purposes of the civil law by reason of the Marriage (Prohibited Degrees of Relationship) Act 1986, Sch. 1, para. 8(a).

(ii) The terms 'brother' and 'sister' include a half-brother and half-sister respectively, whether legitimate or illegitimate: Canon B 31, para. 2; *Rayden and Jackson on Divorce and Family Matters* at p. 136.

APPENDIX 6

IN RE ST JOHN THE EVANGELIST, CHOPWELL[1]

Chancellor Bursell QC: The church of St John the Evangelist is a small church built by the local miners in the first part of this century on the hill above Chopwell. Although the mine is now closed and the building is therefore some distance from the hub of the community, the church is clearly much loved as well as being well cared for by the incumbent and congregation. It is not a listed building.

The present petition is brought by the incumbent, the Reverend Martin Wray, and the two churchwardens in respect of the installation of a nave altar platform and nave altar after the removal of eight pews. It has the unanimous support of the parochial church council. Indeed, on 29 October 1993, the archdeacon gave his written licence pursuant to rule 8 of the Faculty Jurisdiction Rules 1992, permitting the temporary re-ordering of the church so that experimentation might show the advisability of these proposals. This was clearly a success and the Diocesan Advisory Council recommend the proposals. As there are no objectors I have no hesitation in granting a faculty for these proposals. The pews that have been removed are to be sold and the proceeds used towards the general upkeep of the church.

The petition also requests a faculty for the introduction of a number of furnishings, namely:

(i)   a pair of altar standards;
(ii) two chairs, which are described as 'acolytes chairs';
(iii) two votive candle stands;
(iv) a thurible and stand;
(v)   a set of four chime sanctuary bells (otherwise known as a sanctus bell); and
(vi) a pair of seven branch candelabra.

In relation to each of these items the petition is unanimously supported by the parochial church council, the Diocesan Advisory Council is in favour and there is no objector. However, because of the case law in relation to items (ii), (iv) and (v), I requested the archdeacon formally to enter an objection so that the issue might be argued in open court. I did not feel that the same was necessary in relation to the two votive candle stands, or 'prickets'. For completeness' sake, however, I will also briefly outline the law in relation to all the other items.

In addition, during the hearing I gave leave for the petition to be amended without recitation so as to seek a confirmatory faculty in relation to two holy water stoups, a small one in the vestry and a larger one situated in the church porch. For the sake of convenience I will also return to this matter at the end of this judgment.

[1] [1995] Fam. 254.

For understandable pastoral reasons the Archdeacon of Durham felt that it would be inappropriate for him to act in this matter and the bishop therefore appointed a barrister, Mr James Patrick, to act in the archdeacon's place pursuant to section 16(3) of the Care of Churches and Ecclesiastical Jurisdiction Measure 1991. In effect Mr Patrick has acted as *amicus curiae* and once again I am indebted to him for all the assistance he has given.

(a)   *Altar standards and candlebra*: items (i) and (vi)

In so far as the altar standards are concerned they are, in effect, dummy candles 8½ inches high × 3½ inches wide in satin finish resting on brass stands, which in turn are 10 inches in diameter and 2 inches high. Into these stands are placed small wax candles or lights. These standards are therefore no more than a modern form of candlestick or holder and, as such, entirely legal: see *St Saviour's Church, Walthamstow* [1951] P 147. Indeed, in that case the Dean of the Arches said at p. 152:

> ... I have come to the conclusion that, although the use of two altar lights must be regarded as the traditional and recognized use of the Church of England, I cannot hold that the use of more than two is necessarily illegal. The two lights are there 'for the signification that Christ is the very true Light of the World'; and I have not been able to discover that the use of more than two lights on or behind the Holy Table has any other significance. They are lit on the more important occasions to give greater dignity to the service.

In these circumstances it seems to me immaterial whether those lights are held by separate candlesticks, or by a pair of seven branch candelabra standing in the sanctuary, and the faculty will therefore include these items also.

(b)   *Acolytes' chairs*: item (ii)

On the other hand, portable (as opposed to free standing) candlesticks have in the past been held to be illegal. The description in the petition of two 'acolytes chairs' therefore led Mr Patrick to enquire into their intended use when Father Wray gave evidence. It transpired that what already occurs is that at the commencement of the service a procession is formed from the vestry to the nave altar. This procession comprises a thurifer, a crucifer, acolytes (carrying candles and the altar book) and, of course, the priest. During this procession the candles are lit but, as they tend to drop wax, they are then snuffed out before being relit for the gospel procession. During much of the rest of the service the acolytes sit on chairs.

Chairs are not, of course, in themselves illegal but, if their purpose is in relation to illegal activities, no faculty can be granted in relation to them. As Lord Cairns said in *Martin* v. *Mackonochie* (1868) LR 2 PC 365 at p. 387:

> There is a clear and obvious distinction between the presence in Church of things inert and unused, and the active use of the same things as a part of the administration of a sacrament or of a ceremony.

I therefore need to turn to the legality of two related matters, namely, processions and the carrying of lighted candles.

In the light of the frequency of processions in cathedrals and churches throughout the land, it may come as a surprise to many that processions have in the past been declared illegal. Thus, in *Elphinstone* v. *Purchas* (1870) LR 3 A & E 66 at pp. 96–97 Sir Robert Phillimore declared as illegal processions that are 'so conducted as to constitute a further rite or ceremony . . . in addition to those prescribed by the rubrics'. Indeed, although that case was concerned with processions 'in connection with the morning and evening services', the same legal reasoning of necessity applied to all such processions by reason of the then prevailing rigorist interpretation of the Book of Common Prayer: see *In re St Thomas, Pennywell* [1995] 2 WLR 154 at pp. 166G–167H. Indeed, it mattered not whether there were crucifers, thurifers, or acolytes with or without lighted candles or gospel book: any procession not provided for by the rubrics was necessarily illegal. For this reason in *Enraghts' Case* (1881) 6 QBD 376 (affmd *Sub. nom. Enraght v. Lord Penzance* at (1882) 7 App Cas 240) an inhibition was issued in relation to ceremonial processions; see, too, *Sumner v. Wix* (1870) LR 3 A & E 58 at pp. 64–65. Again, in *Rector and Churchwardens of Capel St Mary, Suffolk v. Packard* [1927] P 289 at p. 304 and *In re St Mary, Tyne Dock* [1954] P 369 at p. 379 faculties were refused for candle holders that had been, or were to be, used ceremonially.

However, as was decided in *In re St Thomas, Pennywell* [1995] 2 WLR 154 at pp. 167H–168E, the previous rigorist interpretation of the Book of Common Prayer has now been swept aside. Indeed, as I said at p. 169G–H:

> The effect of all this may be demonstrated by reference to candles. The ceremonial use of candles has in the past been regarded as illegal because there was no provision for such ceremony within the Book of Common Prayer: see, for example, *Sumner v. Wix* (1870) LR 3 A & E 58 and *Martin v. Mackonochie* (1868) LR 2 PC 365, 387–392. For this reason a paschal candle-holder was only permitted to be retained as long as it was not ceremoniously used: *In re St Mary, Tyne Dock* [1954] P 369, 379 *per* Hylton-Foster Ch. Now, however, not only is the ceremonial use of candles permitted by the baptism service in the Alternative Service Book (see p. 248) but it is also provided (see note 4, at p. 241) that: 'A lighted candle, which may be a paschal candle, may be ready so that other candles may be lighted from it.' Once the rigorist interpretation of the Book of Common Prayer disappeared, the use of candles ceremonially in either rite must be regarded as legal.

Those words were not, of course, strictly necessary to that decision but I adopt them now as part of the *ratio decidendi* in the present case.

Indeed, matters go further. The Alternative Service Book is authorised by the General Synod pursuant to Canon B 2, para. 1. However, the well known service books *Lent, Holy Week, Easter* and *The Promise of His Glory* (unless authorised by a diocesan bishop for use in his diocese pursuant to Canon B 4) are only commended for use by the House of Bishops of the General Synod 'subject to the terms of Canon B 5'. The House of Bishops is primarily composed of diocesan bishops (see 14 Halsbury's Laws of England (4th ed.) at para. 416) and Canon C 18, para. 1, provides in relation to a diocesan bishop that 'it appertains to his office to teach and uphold sound and wholesome doctrine'. The relevant parts of Canon B 5 state:

1.   The minister who is to conduct the service may in his discretion make and use variations which are not of substantial importance in any form of service authorised by Canon B 1 according to particular circumstances.
2.   The minister having the cure of souls may on occasions for which no provision is made in the Book of Common Prayer or by the General Synod under Canon B 2 or

by the Convocations, archbishops, or Ordinary under Canon B 4 use forms of service considered suitable by him for those occasions and may permit another minister to use the said forms of service.

3. All variations in forms of service and all forms of service used under this Canon shall be reverent and seemly and shall be neither contrary to, nor indicative of any departure from, the doctrine of the Church of England in any essential matter.

4. If any question is raised concerning the observance of the provisions of this Canon it may be referred to the bishop and he may give such pastoral guidance, advice or directions as he may think fit, but such reference shall be without prejudice to the matter in question being made the subject-matter of proceedings under the Ecclesiastical Jurisdiction Measure, 1963.

The reference to 'the bishop' in Canon B 5, para. 4, must be to the diocesan bishop but, as is clear, the final arbiter of the legality of any such variation or service used pursuant to Canon B 5, paras 1 and 2, is the ecclesiastical court. Nevertheless, because of the commendation of the above service books by the House of Bishops, it is extremely unlikely that any ceremony enjoined within them will be contrary to, or indicative of any departure from, the doctrine of the Church of England in any essential matter. It is therefore prima facie permissible for me to consider these services which are commended for use by the House of Bishops.

In *Lent, Holy Week, Easter* the Easter Liturgy provides for a procession with lighted candles and even suggests that the light for the Easter Candle may be taken from a bonfire outside the church (see notes 4 and 5 at pp. 226–227 and notes 10–15 at pp. 229–230). In addition *The Promise of His Glory* provides for a Candlemas procession with lighted candles (see notes 1, 32 and appendix at pp. 272, 280 and 283 respectively). In the latter, too, processions are envisaged in both *The Eucharist of Christmas Night* and *A Service for the Feast of the Baptism of Our Lord* (see notes 1 and 4 at pp. 171 and 210 respectively).

In all these circumstances I am satisfied that processions, with or without lighted candles, are prima facie doctrinally acceptable within the Church of England; therefore, there may be such processions, even if ceremonial in character, in services used pursuant to Canon B 5, para. 2. Moreover, as the previous rigorist interpretation of rites and rubrics no longer applies to any service book (see *In re St Thomas, Pennywell* [1995] 2 WLR 154 at p. 168D), the incorporation of such processions into other services authorised under Canons B 2 to 4 are equally legal by reason of Canon B 5, para. 1, as long as the requisite variations are not 'of substantial importance . . . according to particular circumstances'. In either event any procession must always be both 'reverent and seemly' and part of worship that 'glorifies God and edifies the people': see Canon B 5, para. 3, and Canon B 1, para. 2.

Each case involving an appeal to Canon B 5, para. 1, must be looked at in the particular circumstances of the case but, having considered the evidence of Father Wray, I am satisfied that the processions described by him fall within the ambit of Canon B 5, para. 1. In the event, therefore, the acolytes' chairs may also be authorised by faculty.

(c)   *Votive candle stands*: item (iii)

I now turn to the matter of the votive candle stands, or prickets. I am aware that such stands have been introduced into a number of cathedrals, including the cathedrals of Durham and St Albans; nevertheless, such an introduction does not prove their legality.

Such items are equally legal or illegal whether introduced into a cathedral, church or chapel. Nevertheless, I am unaware of any reported case dealing with such legality save *St Edward, Castle Donnington* (1994) 3 Ecc LJ 349. The report of that case, however, is unfortunately short although the relevant part reads as follows:

> A votive candle stand could be seen in many Church of England cathedrals and parish churches and the fact there might be none in a particular geographical area was not a reason for not allowing the introduction of one such into one of the churches in that area. Traditions within a particular church change as congregations and their attitudes change and provided there was sufficient support for such a change after consultation, the introduction of the votive stand, which a majority of the worshipping congregation supported, and which the DAC approved, was to be allowed.

Chancellor Seed's more detailed reasoning is unfortunately not reported.

It is therefore necessary to look at the votive candle stands in the light of other authority. On the one hand, to adopt the words of the Judicial Committee of the Privy Council in *Westerton* v. *Lidell* (1857) Moore's Special Report 1 at p. 156, such stands would not be 'used in the performance of the rites and services of the church'. On the other hand, neither would they be 'subsidiary to the services' and, for that reason, legally permissible: see *Martin* v. *Mackonochie* (1868) LR 2 PC 365 at p. 390. Indeed, they are not even 'articles the use of which is required in the services and ministrations of the Church': *Westerton* v. *Lidell* (1857) Moore's Special Report 132 at p. 156; *In re St Thomas, Pennywell* [1995] 2 WLR 154 at p. 171E–G.

However, as Father Wray tells me in relation to the present case, such stands are used solely to aid private devotion and, save in relation to the one matter to which I will advert at the end of this paragraph, the ecclesiastical law does not seek to limit, or impinge upon, the private devotions of its members: see *Read* v. *Bishop of Lincoln* [1891] P 9 at p. 89. Indeed, to adopt the words of Sir Robert Phillimore in *Martin* v. *Mackonochie* (1868) LR 2 A & E 116 at p. 133 such matters are 'wisely left to every man's discretion'. (See, too, the comment of the Dean of the Arches in *Rector and Churchwardens of Capel St Mary, Suffolk* v. *Packard* [1927] P 289 at p. 298 where he stated *in arguendo*: 'It is repellant to me to be asked to inquire into the private devotions of the Rector.') Items that assist private devotions may in my view, therefore, be admitted into a church as long as they do not detract from the devotions of others nor, more particularly, from the actual services and ministrations within the church itself. The votive candle stands will, therefore, be permitted by faculty, although only 'until further order' so that the court may retain control in the unlikely event that they become used for what are called in the old cases 'superstitious uses': see Newsom & Newsom, *Faculty Jurisdiction of the Church of England* 2nd ed. (1993) at pp. 125–126.

(d) *Thurible and stand*: item (iv)

I now turn to the thurible and stand. In *Martin* v. *Mackonochie* (1868) LR 2 A & E 116 at p. 215 Sir Robert Phillimore stated:

> To bring in incense at the beginning or during the celebration, and remove it at the close of the celebration of the eucharist, appears to me to be a distinct ceremony, additional and not even indirectly incident to the ceremonies ordered by the Book of Common Prayer.

Moreover, as the Archbishops of Canterbury and York said in their opinion *On the Lawfulness of the Liturgical Use of Incense and the Carrying of Lights in Procession* (Macmillan & Co's Official Reports, 1899) at p. 13:

> The very meaning of an ornament is that it is a thing to be used for the fitting performance of a ceremony, and if no ceremony be prescribed the so-called ornament has no place.

The ceremonial use of incense is nowhere required in the rites of the Book of Common Prayer and, therefore, in the light of the then pertaining rigorist interpretation of that service book it was necessarily an illegal ceremony. For this reason the use of incense within a service was illegal (see also *Sumner* v. *Wix* (1870) LR 3 A & E 58 at p. 66; *Gore-Booth* v. *Bishop of Manchester* [1920] 2 KB 412) and faculties for censers required for such illegal ceremonies were refused: see *Rector and Churchwardens of Capel St Mary, Suffolk* v. *Packard* [1927] P 289 at p. 305. There was nonetheless no legal impediment to the use of incense for merely fumigatory purposes as long as it was not done as part of a ceremony: *In re St Mary, Tyne Dock* [1954] P 369 at p. 380 *per* Chancellor Hylton-Foster: ' . . . the thurible and the incense boat are susceptible of lawful use . . . '. Indeed in their opinion *On the Lawfulness of the Liturgical Use of Incense and the Carrying of Lights in Procession* at p. 14 the Archbishops pointed out that:

> If used at all, [incense] must be used (in George Herbert's language) to sweeten the Church, and outside the worship altogether.

In his evidence Father Wray made it plain that his use of incense was not merely fumigatory but, rather, that it was carried in procession so that it might be used during the eucharist to cense the altar, the gospel book and (at the offertory) the bread and wine. What then is the present legal position? In their opinion cited above the Archbishops pointed out at pp. 12–13:

> Yet it is right to observe that even now the liturgical use of incense is not by law permanently excluded from the Church's Ritual. The Section in Elizabeth's Act which allows the Crown, with the consent of the Archbishop of Canterbury, to order new ceremonies does not forbid the inclusion of the use of incense in such new ceremonies if such are ordered . . . Many things might become probable when our toleration of one another had risen to a higher level, which are not probable at present.

The ceremonial use of incense is not, therefore, in itself contrary to Anglican doctrine.

It is true that such new ceremonies as have been authorised or commended do not include the use of incense, although (as Mr Patrick points out) *The Promise of His Glory* in the *Sentences and Prayers for Use from the Epiphany to Candlemas* adverts to the symbolic purpose of incense in the prayer at the offering of incense (see note 4 at p. 224). However, as I have already noted, the rigorist interpretation of service books upon which the previous law was based no longer applies. Moreover, as the preface to the Alternative Service Book (although not itself part of what is actually authorised: see p. 8, 'Authorisation') acknowledges:

Rapid social and intellectual changes . . . together with a worldwide reawakening of interest in liturgy, have made it desirable that new understandings of worship should find expression in new forms and styles. Christians have become readier to accept that, even within a single church, unity need no longer be seen to entail strict uniformity of practice.

Thus, although particular liturgical practices remain understandably dear to particular congregations, there is indeed now a greater toleration of the liturgical practices of others. This being so (and subject to what I say later in relation to the ornaments rubric), I am satisfied that the liturgical use of incense described by Father Wray (and already widely followed in other parishes) is a variation not of substantial importance. Therefore, a minister may now in his discretion permit the use of incense in an authorised service pursuant to Canon B 5, para. 1. I again emphasize that any such variation depends upon the particular circumstances of the case and must always be carried out in a 'reverent and seemly' manner. Here, having met Father Wray, I am sure it will be so carried out. This being so, I readily grant a faculty both for the thurible and its stand.

(e) *Sanctuary bells*: item (v)

What then of the set of four chime sanctuary bells? Father Wray tells me that he wishes to use this sanctus bell at the time of the invocation of the Holy Spirit and at the elevation of the host and chalice so as to concentrate the minds of the congregation and to gain their attention; he also wishes its use at the time when the celebrant receives communion as a signal for the congregation themselves to approach in order to receive the holy sacrament.

There is no doubt that the ringing of a sanctus bell as part of the eucharist was an illegal ceremony whilst the rigorist interpretation of the Book of Common Prayer prevailed: see *Elphinstone* v. *Purchas* (1870) LR 3 A & E 66 at pp. 98–99, on appeal *Hebbert* v. *Purchas* (1872) LR 4 PC 301 at p. 307. Indeed, in *Rector and Churchwardens of Capel St Mary, Suffolk* v. *Packard* [1927] P 289 at p. 305 it was also pointed out by the Dean of the Arches that:

> . . . the sacring bell or gong, which is sounded at Holy Communion during the consecration . . . is an illegal ornament, not being included in the ornaments of the Church mentioned in the First Prayer Book of Edward VI, and its use has been more than once prohibited as unlawful.

So strong was this feeling that in *Vicar and Churchwardens of St John the Evangelist, Clevedon* v. *All Having Interest* [1909] P 6, where leave was sought to make structural alterations to enable a bell in the tower to be rung 'from the interior of the church at certain moments in the Communion Service' (see at p. 14), Chancellor Chadwyck-Healey said at p. 14:

> The bell is tolled, or has been tolled, during the consecration prayer in the Communion Service, that is to say, at the moment of the elevation of each of the sacred elements. I am quite aware that the ringing of a bell at the time of the celebration of the Holy Communion is a matter of comfort to many people who cannot, either by reason of sickness or other causes, be present at church. I am also of course aware that the ringing of the sanctus or sacring bell was enjoined by early constitutions of our Church . . . But

the use of the sanctus bell has been expressly decided to be unlawful . . . in *Elphinstone* v. *Purchas*, and that decision is binding on this Court. It is true that the bell the subject of that suit was a hand bell rung in the church, but I am unable to trace any distinction between such a bell sounded at the Altar and the use of one of the bells in the tower, rung at the like moments and for the like purposes.

With respect to the learned Chancellor it is unclear to me, unless there was evidence before him that is not mentioned in his judgment, how the bell at St John the Evangelist, Clevedon, was rung 'for the like purposes' as the hand bell in the case of *Elphinstone* v. *Purchas*. However, that does not alter the strength of the other decisions to which I have referred. The only possibly contrary decision of which I am aware is that of *Re St Mary's, West Fordington* (1956) reported briefly in *Opinions of the Legal Advisory Commission* (6th ed.) at p. 143 where the installation of a church bell was permitted 'although its ringing on occasions at Holy Communion might strictly be a breach of good order'. Even if this were 'strictly a breach of good order' in the particular case, it seems to have been treated by the Chancellor as a matter that was *de minimis* (a principle now given statutory recognition in ecclesiastical cases by the Care of Churches and Ecclesiastical Jurisdiction Measure 1991, s. 11(8)).

In spite of these cases in *Lent, Holy Week, Easter* it is suggested that bells may be rung as part of the Easter Liturgy: see *op. cit.*, note 8 at p. 227. Although this may be read as a reference to bells situated in the belfry, it seems more appropriately to be seen as a reference to bells within the congregational part of the church; this is because of the suggestion that they may be rung both 'at section 19' (that is, at the time of the singing of the Gloria or an appropriate hymn) and at the end of the service. Yet, even if my understanding of this note is incorrect, there seems to be no doctrinal reason why a bell should not be rung for the purposes set out by Father Wray.

The only outstanding question in relation to such sanctus bells (as indeed in relation to a thurible and stand when used within an actual service) is the ornaments rubric referred to by the Dean of the Arches in *Rector and Churchwardens of Capel St Mary, Suffolk* v. *Packard* [1927] P 289 at p. 305 (see *supra*). However, for the reasons I set out in *In re St Thomas, Pennywell* [1995] 2 WLR 154 at pp. 170F–171F that is no longer an obstacle. For all of these reasons, therefore, I have reached the conclusion that such a use of a sanctus bell now falls within the ambit of Canon B 5, para. 1, and is legal. A faculty may therefore issue in relation to the four chime sanctuary bells.

(f)   Elevation of the Host

I should, however, add a further rider to what I have said in relation to sanctus bells in the light of Father Wray's evidence that this bell would *inter alia* be rung at the elevation of the host and chalice, although he was never asked to amplify what form this 'elevation' takes.

The Book of Common Prayer provides specific manual acts in relation to the elements in the Prayer of Consecration in the service of Holy Communion; indeed, in reliance upon these acts it was held in *Martin* v. *Mackonochie* (1868) LR 2 A & E 116 at pp. 202–203; (1869) LR 3 PC 52 at pp. 62–64 that to elevate the chalice was illegal. The reasons for this were twofold: first, that the elevation of the sacrament so that it might be adored is contrary to the tenets of the Church of England and, second, that the physical act went further than the rubric required. As the Privy Council stated in relation to the original charge (see (1869) LR 3 PC 52 at p. 62):

That would have been . . . a charge which would have raised a distinct and definite issue, whether the elevation of the Paten or the elevation of the Cup were or were not a *bona fide* raising it so far only as is necessary for anything to be raised, that is, to be taken from the table, or whether or not there was some ulterior purpose, that is to say, an act of elevation wholly distinct from, and going beyond what is necessary, for the mere purpose of taking the Paten and Cup into the hands of the officiating Minister.

Although the 'traditional manual acts' may be still be used in the eucharistic rites of the Alternative Service Book (see note 16 at p. 117), save for the minister's taking the bread and cup into his hands before the Prayer of Thanksgiving and replacing them on the holy table, Rite A does not provide for the use of any manual acts, except in relation to the Fraction (see note 43 at p. 142). Rite B follows the rubrics in the Book of Common Prayer in the First Thanksgiving (see p. 191), except that the Fraction may be postponed until later in the service (see note 34 at p. 195); the Second Thanksgiving has more limited manual acts (see p. 194), followed by a separate Fraction.

In so far as the Alternative Service Book is concerned it seems that the manual acts may not be of substantial importance and that by reason of Canon B 5, para. 1, they may therefore be omitted, or varied within the ambit of the rubrics, in either Rite. On the other hand, in so far as the Book of Common Prayer is concerned their omission or variation may be far more difficult to justify because of the history of that particular rite. However, now that the rigorist interpretation of the Book of Common Prayer is past, the lifting of the sacrament higher than strictly necessary in order to raise them from the table, for example, in a dramatic gesture would seem now to be legal in any Rite unless by so doing the minister were intending to convey, or promote, a doctrine contrary to the tenets of the Church of England: see Canon B 5, para. 3. In this regard I, of course, remind myself that the earlier judgments may still be binding in so far as matters of doctrine are there decided: see *In re St Thomas, Pennywell* [1995] 2 WLR 154 at pp. 168C and 172F.

(g) *Holy water stoups*

I turn now to the question of the confirmatory faculty for the two holy water stoups. The small stoup came to my attention on entering the vestry that had kindly been set aside for my use as a retiring room during the hearing. The larger holy water stoup in the porch was drawn to my attention by Mr Patrick. Also in the vestry was a laminated sheet on one side of which are the following words:

HOLY WATER
Christ the Living Water,
Whenever we sign ourselves
with holy water
in the name of the Father, and of the Son
and of the Holy Spirit,
we remind ourselves of God's gift of Baptism
and
we renew our Baptism promises

In addition, between the first two lines there is a depiction of the crucified Lord.

This sheet emphasizes, as the positions of the water stoups in any event require, that the use of holy water from the stoup is used for private devotion; its presence also indicates that Father Wray is rightly concerned to teach his flock the significance of the symbolism concerned. It was for this reason that I requested a copy of that sheet to be sent to me so that I might refer to it in this judgment. On its receipt, however, I found that on its other side there was a form of service entitled *A Rite of Blessing and Sprinkling Holy Water* quite separate from the signing with holy water already referred to. It may, therefore, be convenient if I deal with that aspect also, although always bearing in mind that I do so without the benefit of argument and that my conclusions are necessarily *obiter dicta* as they are not necessary for the matters that I must otherwise decide. I will do so at the end of this judgment where a copy of the rite is also set out in an appendix.

Returning to the question of the water stoups, their first mention in a reported case is in *Elphinstone* v. *Purchas* (1870) LR 3 A & E 66 at p. 108. The charge against the Reverend Mr Purchas was:

> That [he] . . . caused holy water, or water previously blessed or consecrated, to be poured into divers receptacles for the same in and about the said church, in order that the same might be used by persons of the congregation before and during the time of Divine service, by way of ceremonial application thereof; and [he] used the same, or caused or permitted the same to be used.

In the event Sir Robert Phillimore found that:

> There is no evidence to sustain the averments that Mr Purchas caused holy water or water previously blessed or consecrated to be poured into divers receptacles in and about the church, or that he blessed or consecrated any water, or that he used it himself, or that he caused it to be used by others; there is evidence that there was water in the church, and that some of the congregation crossed themselves with it.

The charges were therefore not made out, although it may be noted that no word of censure was expressed as to the use of water as a private devotion. Indeed, on appeal under the name of *Hebbert* v. *Purchas* (1871) LR 3 PC 605 at p. 651 the Judicial Committee of the Privy Council reached a similar conclusion:

> As to the Holy or consecrated water in the Church, the evidence does not go to the full extent of the charge. There is no proof whatever, that the Water placed in the Church was consecrated at all, nor that it was put there by the Respondent, with the purpose of its being used as the Congregation seem to have used it. This is a penal proceeding, and each charge must be strictly proved as alleged.

This wording may, of course, by inference raise questions as to the legality of what had taken place but it may also be queried whether even viewed at its highest there could even under the rigorist interpretation of the Book of Common Prayer have been a breach of the law, other than if the water were used 'by way of ceremonial application' during divine service.

In *Davey* v. *Hinde* [1901] P 95 two water stoups had been placed in the church near an entrance. They were, however, introduced without a faculty and were therefore ordered to be removed. Dr Tristram stated (at pp. 120–121) that:

... according to Mr Hammond's evidence, [they] are used by one in ten of the congregation on entering and going out of the church in the same manner as is usual in Roman Catholic churches. An order will be made for the removal of these water stoups as illegal erections in the church.

Unfortunately, because of procedural irregularities, the case had to be reheard and on this occasion, without setting out any argument and more particularly without reference to *Elphinstone* v. *Purchas* or *Hebbert* v. *Purchas*, Dr Tristram stated (at p. 237) that they were also to be removed 'as having been introduced into the church without a faculty, and as inappropriate ornaments for an English church'.

Until legalised by a faculty the introduction of any item into a church is illegal and the decision in *Davey* v. *Hinde* is at the very least technically correct. Nevertheless, in so far as it seems to state that the water stoups were illegal, it fails to elucidate upon its reasoning. Be that as it may, being a decision of the Consistory Court of Chichester, the decision is in any event not binding upon me.

A holy water stoup was next considered in *Rector and Churchwardens of Capel St Mary, Suffolk* v. *Packard* [1927] P 289. Here the stoup was in the porch and the rector taught the children to use holy water from the stoup by making the Sign of the Cross with the water on entering and leaving the church. However, the Dean of the Arches had stated *in arguendo* (at p. 293) that, other than in a disciplinary case, the teaching of a clergyman is of the smallest possible relevance except to 'throw light on the user or intended user of particular ornaments and furniture'. He, however, ordered its removal because 'it is an illegal ornament, and its use has been more than once condemned: *Hebbert* v. *Purchas; Davey* v. *Hinde.*'. This case, again, does not technically bind me as it is a decision of the appellate court of the other province; nevertheless, subject to what I say below, I would in practice have felt myself bound to follow it unless the law has subsequently changed. This is in spite of the fact that it seems to have been treated thereafter with some reserve.

In *In re St Mary, Tyne Dock* [1954] P 339, where the stoup was 'very small and inconspicuously situated' in the vestry and only kept 'in case a visiting clergyman should wish to use it', Chancellor Hylton-Foster permitted its retention and applied the principle of *de minimis*. However, I note in passing that by so doing the Chancellor tacitly accepted that the use of a holy water stoup cannot be doctrinally unacceptable within the Church of England.

Finally, I am told by Mr Patrick (and, of course, entirely accept) that he has seen a faculty for a holy water stoup at the Church of the Holy Nativity, Knowle, granted by the present Chancellor of Bristol.

The cases of *Elphinstone* v. *Purchas, Davey* v. *Hinde* and *Rector and Churchwardens of Capel St Mary, Suffolk* v. *Packard* were, of course, all decided when the only legal rites were those set out in the Book of Common Prayer. Moreover, at that time no liturgical ceremonies other than those contained in that service book could lawfully be carried out because of the rigorist interpretation that then pertained. However, this is no longer the law and the case of *Rector and Churchwardens of Capel St Mary, Suffolk* v. *Packard* is no longer binding: see *In re St Thomas, Pennywell* [1995] 2 WLR 154 at pp. 165G–168C.

In fact, the liturgy of the Church of England has moved on in various ways since those earlier decisions. In particular, the service book *The Promise of His Glory* has been commended by the House of Bishops for use in accordance with Canon B 5, para. 2. That service book provides *A Service for the Feast of the Baptism of Our Lord* (see p. 210 *et seq.*) in which water is sanctified or blessed (see paragraphs 21 and 22). At the end of the service rubric 30 then states (at p. 221):

> The water may be sprinkled over the people, or placed in vessels by the door for them to make the Sign of the Cross as they leave, or poured out over the threshold.

Such a vessel, of course, even if temporary fulfils precisely the function of a holy water stoup. (However, it should be noted in passing that, in spite of the wording of rubrics 17 and 20, the water should not be poured into the bowl of the font because of Canon F 1, para. 3: 'The font bowl shall be used for the water at the administration of Holy baptism and for no other purpose whatsoever.'.)

Moreover, as has been seen, because of the commendation for the above service by the House of Bishops, it is most unlikely that a ceremony enjoined within it will be seen as contrary to, or indicative of any departure from, the doctrine of the Church of England in any essential matter: see Canon B 5, para. 3 (*supra*). More particularly, and in spite of the earlier decisions as to holy water stoups, it follows that such an item can no longer be regarded as an 'illegal ornament' or 'an ornament inappropriate for an English church', especially when the holy water is used as an aid to private devotion.

Therefore, even if the small stoup in the vestry were a matter falling within the principle of *de minimis* (which I would otherwise decide), both it and the larger stoup in the porch are items for which faculties may properly be granted. This is especially so when they are used, as here, to facilitate matters of private devotion. I, therefore, grant a confirmatory faculty in relation to each of them.

(h)   *A Rite of Blessing and Sprinkling Holy Water*

(α) The rite

I now turn to *A Rite of Blessing and Sprinkling Holy Water*, always bearing in mind that it is not one of those services specifically authorised under Canons B 2–4 nor is it one commended by the House of Bishops.

I do not know in what circumstances this rite is actually used, if at all, at St John the Evangelist, Chopwell. If it is, the initial rubric declares:

> When this rite is celebrated it takes the place of the penitential rite at the beginning of Mass. The Kyrie is omitted.

If, contrary to this rubric, the rite is in fact used as a separate service, Canon B 5, para. 2, provides:

> The minister having the cure of souls may on occasions for which no provision is made in the Book of Common Prayer or by the General Synod under Canon B 2 or by Convocations, archbishops, or Ordinary under Canon B 4 use forms of service considered suitable by him for those occasions and may permit another minister to use the said form of service.

Indeed, subject to my conclusions below, as no such provision has been made there is no reason why the rite should not be used as a separate form of service, although the reference in the last prayer to the eucharist is likely then to be omitted.

Nevertheless, different considerations apply if the rite were to be used in accordance with its opening rubric. Within an Anglican church the only mass that can legally be celebrated is one authorised by Canon B 1. Moreover, as the Kyrie is not included in the Holy Communion service according to the Book of Common Prayer, in law the rubric must within an Anglican setting refer to Rites A and B in the Alternative Service Book or to the similar rites commended by the House of Bishops in *Lent, Holy Week, Easter* and *The Promise of His Glory*.

Canon B 5, para. 1, permits the minister who is to conduct the service:

in his discretion [to] make and use variations which are not of substantial importance in any form of service authorised by Canon B 1 according to particular circumstances.

Rites A and B are, of course, so authorised and the question therefore arises whether the alterations suggested by the opening rubric would, if adhered to, be 'of substantial importance' in the particular circumstances.

In this regard the Kyrie is optional in both Rites A and B (see the Alternative Service Book at pp. 121 and 179) and its omission within the rite under consideration must, therefore, be equally permissible. However, the rite itself provides 'confessions' (choice B is more particularly an actual confession) and an absolution different from those in Rites A and B. If I had to consider the use of such a different confession and absolution *in vacuo*, I would have little difficulty – at least in relation to choice B – in deciding that it did not amount to a variation which was 'of substantial importance'. In fact, in *A Service of the Word and Affirmations of Faith*, being a service authorised pursuant to Canon B 2, variations from the set confession and absolution are permitted 'on particular occasions' both in Morning Service or Evening Prayer and in a Service of the Word with Holy Communion Rite A; yet only authorised forms of confession and absolution thereafter set out are then allowed: *op. cit.* at p. 11.

Nevertheless, the question does not end there. When dealing with *Affirmations of Faith*, the same publication provides 'adaptions of the historic creeds and other affirmations of Faith', although these may 'only be used in non-statutory services or in an authorized Service of the Word': *op. cit.* at p. 23. Bearing in mind the repeal of the majority of the Act of Uniformity 1662, and what I said in *In re St Thomas, Pennywell* [1995] 2 WLR 154 at pp. 167H–168C, the meaning of the words 'non-statutory services' is by no means clear, although I presume that they mean any form of service authorised under Canon B 1, para. 1, pursuant to the Church of England (Worship and Doctrine) Measure, 1974. (I appreciate that difficulty is caused to such an interpretation by reason of section 1(5)(b) of the 1974 Measure but it does at least give some meaning to the words adopted.) Thus there are wider restrictions on variations to historic affirmations of faith (as one might expect) than there are in relation to confessions and absolutions. It therefore follows that *A Service of the Word and Affirmations of Faith* draws its own particular distinctions as to when its set variations may be made; moreover, its restrictions in relation to confessions and absolutions are not expressed to apply beyond Morning Service or Evening Prayer or a Service of the Word with Holy Communion Rite A. In any case, it does not seek to ensure that all variations from those set confessions and absolutions are necessarily 'of substantial importance'.

In the result (subject to the two matters that I am about to turn to and with some hesitation in relation to the variation from the set confession and absolution if the rite is used as part of Rites A or B), I have come to the conclusion in all the circumstances that the use of this rite according to its introductory rubric on appropriate occasions would indeed be a variation permitted by Canon B 1, para. 1; in doing so, I especially bear in mind the emphasis in this particular rite upon baptism and the washing away of sins. I emphasize again, however, that this conclusion is not necessary to the other matters that I have to decide and is thus only an *obiter dictum*.

(β) *Sign of the Cross*

It will be seen from the appendix that the rite envisages the priest's making the Sign of the Cross (note the symbol †) at the blessing of both the water and the salt. In *Read* v. *Bishop of Lincoln* [1891] P 9 at pp. 88–94 the Court of the Archbishop of Canterbury held that the making of the Sign of the Cross in the absolution and the benediction were both illegal ceremonies in the rites according to the Book of Common Prayer: see, further, *Elphinstone* v. *Purchas* (1870) LR 3 A & E 66 at pp. 108–109. Nevertheless, the making of the Sign of the Cross as part of a service cannot be doctrinally unacceptable as it is, of course, enjoined (although on the the candidate's forehead) in all Anglican rites of Baptism. What rendered it illegal was only the rigorist interpretation then required of the forms of service.

In these circumstances I am entirely satisfied that the manual blessing of the water and salt in this particular rite would not be illegal by reason of Canon B 5, para. 4. Indeed, the making of the Sign of the Cross over the congregation at either the absolution or the blessing in any form of service would now seem to be entirely legal by reason of Canon B 5, para. 1.

(γ) *Aspergill*

There is one further matter that arises in relation to this rite. The penultimate rubric makes provision for the sprinkling of the clergy and congregation with holy water from a 'sprinkler', or aspergill. There is no doubt that such a ceremony would have been illegal under the rigorist interpretation of the Book of Common Prayer and, indeed, a ceremony of Asperges was one of the causes of the disturbance in *Matthews* v. *King* [1934] 1 KB 505. Now, however, it is clear that a similar ceremony is envisaged in *A Service for the Feast of the Baptism of Our Lord* in *The Promise of His Glory*: see rubric 30 at p. 221 (supra). It follows, for the same reasons as I have outlined in relation to holy water stoups, that such a ceremony can no longer be seen as contrary to Anglican doctrine or illegal.

In conclusion, therefore, a faculty will issue in relation to each of the matters prayed in the amended petition. There will be no order as to costs.

APPENDIX

A RITE of BLESSING and SPRINKLING HOLY WATER

When this rite is celebrated it takes the place of the penitential rite at the beginning of Mass.

The Kyrie is omitted.

After greeting the people the priest remains standing at his chair. A vessel containing the water to be blessed is placed before him. Facing the people he invites them to pray, using these or similar words.

Dear friends
this water will be used

to remind us of our baptism.
Let us ask God to bless it
and to keep us faithful
to the Spirit he has given us.
After a brief silence, he joins hands and continues, using one of the following:

A God our Father,
    your gift of water brings life
    and freshness to the earth;
    it washes away our sins
    and brings us to eternal life.

    We ask you now to bless † this water,
    and to give us your protection
    on this day which you have made your own.
    Renew the living spirit of your life within us
    and protect us in spirit and body,
    that we may be free from sin
    and come into your presence
    to receive your gift of salvation.
    We ask this through Christ our Lord.
    Amen.

B Lord God almighty,
    creator of all life, of body and soul,
    we ask you to bless † this water:
    as we use it in faith forgive our sins
    and save us from all illness and the power of evil.

    Lord,
    in your mercy give us living water,
    always springing up as a fountain of salvation:
    free us, body and soul, from every danger,
    and admit us to your presence in purity of heart.

    Grant this through Christ our Lord.
    Amen.

Or during the Easter Season:

C Lord God almighty,
    hear the prayers of your people:
    we celebrate our creation and redemption.
    Hear our prayers and bless † this water
    which gives fruitfulness to the fields,
    and refreshment and cleansing to man.
    You chose water to show your goodness when
    you led your people to freedom through the Red
    Sea and satisfied their thirst in the desert with

water from the rock.
Water was the symbol used by the prophets to
foretell your new covenant with man.
You made the water of baptism holy by Christ's
baptism in the Jordan;
by it you give us a new birth and renew us in
holiness.
May this water remind us of our baptism,
and let us share the joy of all who have been
baptised at Easter.

We ask this through Christ our Lord.
Amen.

*Where it is customary, salt may be mixed with the holy water. The priest blesses the salt
saying:*
Almighty God, we ask you to bless † this salt as
once you blessed the salt scattered over the
water by the prophet Elisha.
Wherever this salt and water are sprinkled,
drive away the power of evil, and protect us
always by the presence of your Holy Spirit.

Grant this through Christ our Lord.
Then he pours the salt into the water in silence.

*Taking the sprinkler, the priest sprinkles himself and his ministers, then the rest of the
clergy and people. He may move through the church for the sprinkling of the people.
Meanwhile, an antiphon or another appropriate song is sung. When he returns to his
place and the song is finished, the priest faces the people and with hands joined, says:*
May almighty God cleanse us of our sins,
and through the eucharist we celebrate
make us worthy to sit at his table
in his heavenly kingdom.
Amen.
When it is prescribed, the Gloria is then sung or said.

INDEX